IFIP Advances in Information and Communication Technology 678

Editor-in-Chief

Kai Rannenberg, Goethe University Frankfurt, Germany

Editorial Board Members

IFIP Advances in Information and Communication Technology

The IFIP AICT series publishes state-of-the-art results in the sciences and technologies of information and communication. The scope of the series includes: foundations of computer science; software theory and practice; education; computer applications in technology; communication systems; systems modeling and optimization; information systems; ICT and society; computer systems technology; security and protection in information processing systems; artificial intelligence; and human-computer interaction.

Edited volumes and proceedings of refereed international conferences in computer science and interdisciplinary fields are featured. These results often precede journal publication and represent the most current research.

The principal aim of the IFIP AICT series is to encourage education and the dissemination and exchange of information about all aspects of computing.

More information about this series at https://link.springer.com/bookseries/6102

Luis M. Camarinha-Matos ·
Filipa Ferrada
Editors

Technological Innovation for Connected Cyber Physical Spaces

14th IFIP WG 5.5/SOCOLNET
Doctoral Conference on Computing,
Electrical and Industrial Systems, DoCEIS 2023
Caparica, Portugal, July 5–7, 2023
Proceedings

Springer

Editors
Luis M. Camarinha-Matos (iD)
School of Science and Technology
NOVA University of Lisbon
Monte Caparica, Portugal

Filipa Ferrada (iD)
School of Science and Technology
NOVA University of Lisbon
Monte Caparica, Portugal

ISSN 1868-4238   ISSN 1868-422X (electronic)
IFIP Advances in Information and Communication Technology
ISBN 978-3-031-36009-1   ISBN 978-3-031-36007-7 (eBook)
https://doi.org/10.1007/978-3-031-36007-7

This Springer imprint is published by the registered company Springer Nature Switzerland AG
The registered company address is: Gewerbestrasse 11, 6330 Cham, Switzerland

Preface

These proceedings focus on the research and development of technological innovation in connected cyber-physical spaces, gathering selected results from engineering doctoral programs. Digital technologies have been boosting the integration and intertwining of these spaces with a profound impact on all sectors of society including industry, energy, healthcare, services, etc. These include a large variety of technologies, e.g., Internet of Things, Cyber-Physical Systems, Sensing, Data Analytics and Machine Learning, Human-Machine Interfaces, Energy Harvesting, and Smart Communications, among others. As systems become smarter, with increasing levels of cognition and autonomy there is a growing need to properly design and govern innovative collaborative environments populated by heterogeneous intelligent systems oriented to tackle societal challenges from a human-centric perspective.

The 14th Advanced Doctoral Conferences on Computing, Electrical and Industrial Systems (DoCEIS 2023) aimed to serve as a platform for doctoral researchers to share and discuss their ideas and findings in various inter-related areas of engineering. It sought to foster a strong multidisciplinary dialogue and create collaborative opportunities for young researchers, while also providing a supportive environment for valuable feedback from colleagues. As such, participants were challenged to look beyond the specific technical aspects of their research question and explore how their work could contribute to technological innovation in digitalization and virtualization, which was the central theme of the event. It is worth noting that current trends in strategic research programs underscore the importance of multidisciplinary and interdisciplinary approaches in driving innovation. Funding agencies increasingly require researchers to incorporate these approaches into their research agendas. In this context, the challenge proposed by DoCEIS is a contribution to the process of acquiring such skills, which are mandatory in the profession of a PhD [1].

DoCEIS 2023, which was sponsored by SOCOLNET, IFIP, and IEEE IES, attracted 47 paper submissions from a good number of PhD students and their supervisors from 15 countries. This book comprises 22 works selected by the International Program Committee for inclusion in the main program and covers a good spectrum of application domains. As such, research results and ongoing work are presented, illustrated, and discussed in areas such as:

- Energy Communities
- Smart Energy and Power Systems
- Intelligent Manufacturing
- Health and Biomedical Information Systems
- Intelligent Computational Systems
- Electronics and Communications

We anticipate that this compilation of papers will offer readers an inspiring array of fresh ideas and thought-provoking challenges within a multidisciplinary framework.

The diverse nature of these results is intended to ignite and stimulate further research and development endeavours, fostering a broader exploration of new directions.

We express our sincere gratitude to all the authors for their valuable contributions to this publication. Additionally, we extend our appreciation to the dedicated members of the DoCEIS International Program Committee. Their assistance in the article selection process and their insightful comments have greatly contributed to enhancing the overall quality of the papers.

May 2023   Luis M. Camarinha-Matos
                                                                         Filipa Ferrada

Reference

1. L.M. Camarinha-Matos, J. Goes, L. Gomes, P. Pereira (2020). Soft and Transferable Skills Acquisition through Organizing a Doctoral Conference. *Education Sciences* 10(9), 235. https://doi.org/10.3390/educsci10090235

Organization

14th IFIP/SOCOLNET Advanced Doctoral
Conference on COMPUTING, ELECTRICAL AND
INDUSTRIAL SYSTEMS
Monte Caparica, Portugal, 5–7 July 2023

Conference and Program Chair

Luis M. Camarinha-Matos   NOVA University of Lisbon, Portugal

Organizing Committee Co-chairs

Luis Gomes   NOVA University of Lisbon, Portugal
João Goes   NOVA University of Lisbon, Portugal
Pedro Pereira   NOVA University of Lisbon, Portugal
Filipa Ferrada   NOVA University of Lisbon, Portugal

International Program Committee

Antonio Abreu	Polytechnic Institute of Lisbon, Portugal
Vanja Ambrozic	University of Ljubljana, Slovenia
Bachir Benhala	Sidi Mohamed Ben Abdellah University, Morocco
Luis Bernardo	NOVA University of Lisbon, Portugal
Frede Blaabjerg	Aalborg University, Denmark
Xavier Boucher	École Nationale Supérieure des Mines de Saint-Étienne, France
Luis Brito Palma	NOVA University of Lisbon, Portugal
Giuseppe Buja	University of Padova, Italy
Ana Cabrera Tobar	Universitat Politècnica de Catalunya, Spain
Luis M. Camarinha-Matos	NOVA University of Lisbon, Portugal
Wojciech Cellary	WSB University in Poznan, Poland
Noelia Correia	University of Algarve, Portugal
Filipa Ferrada	NOVA University of Lisbon, Portugal
Florin G. Filip	Romanian Academy of Sciences, Romania
Maria Helena Fino	NOVA University of Lisbon, Portugal
Adrian Florea	'Lucian Blaga' University of Sibiu, Romania

José M. Fonseca	NOVA University of Lisbon, Portugal
João Goes	NOVA University of Lisbon, Portugal
Luis Gomes	NOVA University of Lisbon, Portugal
Juanqiong Gou	Beijing Jiaotong University, China
Paul Grefen	Eindhoven University of Technology, The Netherlands
Tomasz Janowski	UNU Unit on Policy-Driven Electronic Governance, Poland
Robert Karam	University of South Florida, USA
Vladimir Katic	University of Novi Sad, Serbia
Srinivas Katkoori	University of South Florida, USA
Arianit Kurti	Linnaeus University, Sweden
Matthieu Lauras	IMT Mines Albi, France
Marin Lujak	University Rey Juan Carlos, Spain
João Martins	NOVA University of Lisbon, Portugal
Rui Melicio	University of Évora, Portugal
Paulo Miyagi	University of São Paulo, Brazil
Saraju Mohanty	University of North Texas, USA
Eric Monmasson	Université de Cergy-Pontoise, France
Filipe Moutinho	NOVA University of Lisbon, Portugal
Vincent Naessens	KU Leuven, Belgium
Ana Inês Oliveira	NOVA University of Lisbon, Portugal
Luis Oliveira	NOVA University of Lisbon, Portugal
Rodolfo Oliveira	NOVA University of Lisbon, Portugal
Angel Ortiz	Universitat Politècnica de València, Spain
Nuno Paulino	NOVA University of Lisbon, Portugal
Pedro Pereira	NOVA University of Lisbon, Portugal
Dirk Pesch	University College Cork, Ireland
Paulo Pinto	NOVA University of Lisbon, Portugal
Armando Pires	Polytechnic Institute of Setubal, Portugal
Graziano Pravadelli	Università degli Studi di Verona, Italy
Ricardo J. Rabelo	Federal University of Santa Catarina, Brazil
Laavanya Rachakonda	University of North Carolina Wilmington, USA
Luis Ribeiro	Linköping University, Sweden
Enrique Romero-Cadaval	University of Extremadura, Spain
Carlos Roncero	University of Extremadura, Spain
Thilo Sauter	Danube University Krems, Austria
Catarina Silva	Polytechnic Institute of Leiria, Portugal
Krassen Stefanov	Sofia University "St. Kl. Ohridski", Bulgaria
Thomas Strasser	Austrian Institute of Technology, Austria
Zoltán Ádám Tamus	Budapest Univ. of Technology & Economics, Hungary
Kleanthis Thramboulidis	University of Patras, Greece
Damien Trentesaux	University of Valenciennes, France
Zita Vale	Polytechnic Institute of Porto, Portugal

Oleksandr Veligorskyi Chernigiv National University of Technology, Ukraine
Manuela Vieira Polytechnic Institute of Lisbon, Portugal
Ramon Vilanova Universitat Autònoma de Barcelona, Spain
Lai Xu Bournemouth University, UK
Alois Zoitl Johannes Kepler University Linz, Austria

Local Organizing Committee (PhD Students)

André Grilo, Portugal
Branislav Couceiro, Angola/Portugal
Bruno Rêga, Portugal
Caterina Serafinelli, Italy/Portugal
Diogo Dias, Portugal
Francisco Neves, Portugal
João Xavier, Portugal
Leonardo Miúdo, Angola/Portugal
Mohammad Khodamoradi, Iran/Portugal
Nelson Freitas, Portugal
Paulo Pina, Portugal
Shiva Maiidzadeh, Iran/Portugal
Zahra Afkhami, Iran/Portugal

Technical Sponsors

 Society of Collaborative Networks

 IFIP WG 5.5 COVE
Co-Operation infrastructure for Virtual Enterprises
and electronic business

Organizational Sponsors

Organized by:

PhD Program in Electrical and Computer Engineering

Contents

Health and Biomedical Information Systems

Intelligent Computational Systems

Electronics and Communications

Energy Communities

A Critical Review of District Heating and District Cooling Socioeconomic and Environmental Benefits

S. M. Masum Ahmed[✉], Edoardo Croci, and Annamaria Bagaini

Centre for Research on Geography, Resources, Environment, Energy and Networks (GREEN), Bocconi University, Via Guglielmo Roentgen, 1, 20136 Milan, Italy
masum.ahmed@unibocconi.it

Abstract. Heating energy demand accounts for almost 50% of global final energy consumption. The cooling demand is also rising, accounting for 16% of the building sector's final electricity consumption. District heating and cooling (DH-DC) can significantly reduce overall energy consumption and CO_2 emissions considering the use of green sources and new technologies. Identifying and assessing the benefits generated by DH-DC is crucial for supporting policymakers and driving sustainable financing. This paper aims to identify and categorise DH-DC benefits through a literature review focusing on methods to assess them. In this review, 35 research works have been considered and analysed. Benefits identified in the literature broke down into four categories: benefits for the energy system, end-users, environment, and society. Benefits are well recognised in the literature; however, most studies focused on qualitative analysis with a low impact on DH-DC project assessment. Results will be used to design a new integrated assessment framework.

Keywords: District Energy System · Benefits Assessment · Energy Turn · Policy Recommendation

1 Introduction

Energy demand is escalating driven by increasing global populations and fast-growing economies. According to the Energy Information Administration (EIA) of the United States (US), global energy demand will increase by 47% over the next 30 years [1]. Buildings are responsible for about a third of global energy consumption and a quarter of CO_2 emissions [2]. Almost half of the energy demand for buildings is used for space and water heating and less in cooking [1]. Cooling demand is also growing, accounting for 16% of the building sector's final electricity consumption [3]. District heating and cooling (DH-DC) is considered one of the viable options to reduce overall energy consumption and CO_2 emissions of buildings and meet the Paris Agreement goals [4–6].

A district heating (DH) system is comprised of a pipeline network that connects several buildings and provides heat using centralized heat generation facilities [7]. "District cooling is the cooling equivalent of district heating" [8], by transporting cooled water to

© IFIP International Federation for Information Processing 2023
Published by Springer Nature Switzerland AG 2023
L. M. Camarinha-Matos and F. Ferrada (Eds.): DoCEIS 2023, IFIP AICT 678, pp. 3–18, 2023.
https://doi.org/10.1007/978-3-031-36007-7_1

buildings. DH-DC system provides several energy services, including space heating, air conditioning, and domestic hot water (DHW) [7, 8]. China, Russia, and Europe cover almost 90% of the world's DH energy production [9]. An estimation of the total length of distribution pipelines is 600,000 km around the globe and 200,000 km in the European Union [10]. While the biggest DH network is located in China [9]. Globally, there are around 6,000 active DH networks and only 115 DC systems located in Europe [11].

DH-DC systems evolved through the years, increasing their performance and their efficiency. Looking at DH systems, in the first generation (1GDH) heat was supplied from a central station and delivered to consumers utilizing a network of pipes. The first commercially available DH was established in the US in the 1880s, using steam as a heat carrier [12]. Afterwards, the second-generation DH (2GDH) was established massively in Europe in the 1930s, using superheated water as a heat carrier [12]. A crucial development of DH happened in Scandinavian countries, which is considered as third generation DH (3GDH) in the 1980s. It worked by reducing the temperature of the heat carrier to lower than 100 °C [12]. Key features of 3GDH are having various heat sources and a network of pre-insulated pipes into the ground. In fourth generation DH (4GDH) in the 2020s, the supply temperature was reduced compared to 3GDH, at a 60–70 °C range. Additionally, heat pumps and CHP units of 4GDH have great efficiencies than 3GDH at these lower temperature levels [12]. The fifth generation DH (5GDH) concept is built with a thermal network which delivers and extracts heat at very low temperatures. In 5GDH, heat pumps operated bidirectionally to meet both the heating and cooling demands of end-users. Key features of 5GDH are thermal storage (using the ground as storage), reduced thermal losses (negligible at very low temperatures), and the possibility of using uninsulated pipelines [12].

Looking at DC systems evolution, the first generation DC (1GDC) pipeline refrigeration systems were unveiled in the US in the 1890s [13]. 1GDC consisted of centralised condensers and decentralised evaporators (decentralised evaporators and centralised evaporators using refrigerant and brine, respectively, as a carrier) [13]. Sequentially, a major shift occurred as the second generation DC (2GDC), where old distributing fluid substitutes to water in the US in the 1960s [13]. The third generation district cooling (3GDC) was launched in France and Sweden in the 1990s, where several cooling sources were available, including cold from absorption chillers and natural cold sources [13]. Alternatively, fourth generation district cooling (4GDC) emerged first in Denmark in the 2020s. 4GDC comprises various energy (electricity and heating) sectors by employing centralised and decentralised technologies, including electric heat pumps, absorption heat pumps, natural sources, and cold storage facilities to satisfy buildings cooling demands [13]. 5GDC heat operated bidirectionally to meet the cooling demands of end-users. 5GDC operating temperature range is between −5 to 20 °C. There are several crucial features of 5GDH, e.g. very low temperature network, thermal storage, and enhancing network performance by reducing thermal losses [12].

The source of the DH-DC system, including geothermal, solar thermal, biomass, petroleum products, natural gas, coal, surface or groundwater, etc., and the technology used (internal combustion, steam cycles, gas turbines, combined cycles, chillers, etc.) mainly depend on the resources available on-site. Furthermore, one of the most remarkable aspects of this technology is its ability to recover and exploit heat/cold produced by third-party sources on site; if not converted into the distribution network, it should be dispersed [14]. Considering that fossil fuels still supply more than 60% of the energy needed in buildings by using autonomous heating/cooling systems, the replacement of those with DH-DC can increase energy saving and efficiency and reduce the overall CO_2 emissions [1–4]. Indeed, a DH-DC system allows energy production with greater efficiency compared to autonomous heating/cooling systems using the same resource. Moreover, a DH-DC system can lead to significant environmental benefits, allowing a reduction of both local harmful pollutants (e.g., nitrogen oxides, sulphur oxides, particulates, etc.) and GHG emissions. Besides, when DH-DC systems are integrated with other technologies, it can generate additional benefits [15].

Emerging technologies such as IoT, digital twin, cloud computing and cyber physical system (CPS) can indeed be exploited, especially in the new generations (5GDH and 4GDC) of DH-DC systems, to reduce energy consumption, increase smart energy management, integrate renewables and distributed energy sources [16]. Among them, CPS can play a decisive role in this sector [16]. There are several benefits that could be generated by CPS in the DH-DC systems, such as improving energy efficiency, facilitating the decarbonisation process and reducing costs of network maintenance and energy bills for users [17], however, this is an untapped research sector.

Although benefits generated by DH-DC systems are well recognised by the literature [18–25], considering economic, social, and environmental benefits, those are not performed by all projects to the same extent. Understanding which project generated higher benefits is crucial for driving sustainable financing as stated and encouraged by the EU taxonomy (EU taxonomy is a classification method that produces an environmentally sustainable economic practices [26]). The main objective of this work is to identify and categorise DH-DC system benefits by looking at the literature with a focus on approaches and methods applied to measure them. In this work, the relationship between CPS and DH-DC systems is also analysed. We found that benefits are clearly recognised but a significant research gap exists in terms of benefits assessment. The novelty of this work is understanding how DH-DC benefits recognised in the literature are measured to develop a new integrated assessment framework that can be used to evaluate the socioeconomic and environmental sustainability of DH-DC projects.

The paper is organised into five different sections. Section 2 is devoted to the relationship between District Energy System and Cyber Physical System. Section 3 describes the methodology of the work. In Sect. 4, the results are analysed and discussed. Finally, Sect. 5 concludes the paper.

2 Relationship Between District Energy System and Cyber Physical System

A cyber-physical system (CPS) is an interconnection between a computer and a physical system. The "cyber-physical systems" concept was introduced for the first time in 2006 by Helen Gill of the National Science Foundation in the US [27]. There are several applications of CPS, including DH-DC systems, automotive systems, industrial automation, home automation, smart grid, HVAC systems, security system, water treatment plants, and traffic control systems [28].

Considering the application of CPS in the DH-DC systems, it can help to enhance the overall DH-DC performance by improving energy efficiency and efficient maintenance management [29]. Thermal energy storage facilities can be exploited as much as possible with CPS, which also improves the stability of the system during the scarcity of renewables. Furthermore, CPS can be utilized to find problems without human intervention for finding faults in the DH-DC system, which reduces a lot of effort and money. Basically, the cost of maintenance will be reduced with consequent benefits for the energy supplier and the final users in terms of reduced bills. The integration of CPS in DH-DC can also improve the reliability and cybersecurity of DH-DC systems with derived benefits in terms of energy generation and supply, energy efficiency, the safety of occupants and CO_2 reduction.

In the long run, CPS can potentially give more benefits than the traditional DH-DC system [16]. However, in literature, such benefits were considered only partially with few scientific works considering this integration. The literature is limited regarding the benefits of CPS in DH-DC. Results show that some benefits emerge and there is a need to increase the knowledge about the integration of CPS in DH-DC and also in terms of measuring and evaluating those benefits. We will develop an assessment framework for evaluating DH-DC projects defining suitable and consistent methodologies to measure them. This is an open topic that needs to be enlarged. The poor literature existing in this regard is an opportunity to increase knowledge and open a new research line. This work will contribute to understanding the existing gaps in recognising the relevance of integrating "DH-DC system" and "cyber-physical systems".

3 Methodology

In order to identify the most recurring DH-DC benefits, we perform a literature review. DH and DC produce similar benefits and are treated at the same level. Moreover, benefits generated by DC systems alone are less explored in literature since heating is usually more energy-consuming. For those reasons, we concentrate the analysis only on DH system. At first, we conducted a literature search with the aim to discover studies investigating and assessing DH benefits from different points of view. We used the Scopus database by exploring a set of keywords, also considering CPS integration. The search was conducted on existing literature using four keywords: "district heating", "district heating" and "benefit", "district heating" and "benefit" and "economics", "district heating" and "benefit" and "Cyber physical". Only the last 16 years of research (2007–2022) are considered for this literature review. A total of 35 research works have been considered, including scientific papers, conference papers and reports. Through the literature review, we identified the most recurring DH benefits that emerged in the selected research works. Benefits have been categorised according to their features based on the European Network of Transmission System Operators for Electricity (ENTSO-E) district heating benefit framework [30], namely benefits for the energy system, benefits for the environment, benefits for the user and benefits for society. Finally, we evaluated benefits identified according to the method adopted to quantify/measure them, namely "qualitative method (I)", "quantitative method (Q)", and "monetisation method (M)".

4 Results and Discussion

4.1 "DH Benefits" Literature Analysis

An analysis was conducted on scientific studies regarding DH and their capacity to generate benefits by using the Scopus database. It can be observed in Fig. 1. That DH research started growing in the 1980s, and then after 2005, the research work increased drastically. After 2005 more research papers were found considering and analysing benefits generated by those systems, with a strong increase after 2015 following the Paris Agreement and the increased concerns regarding heating and cooling system energy consumption and related CO_2 emissions.

Looking at papers focused on DH benefit economic assessment, a very low number of papers emerged in the literature. Finally, the integration of DH benefits and Cyber-physical systems seem less considered in the literature, with only 5 papers conducting research on it, starting in 2015 (Fig. 1).

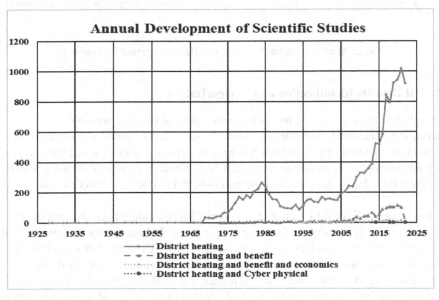

Fig. 1. Annual evolution of the scientific literature concerning DH [Data processed by Scopus].

Figure 2 illustrates scientific studies by research fields. The highest portion of the research conducted was related to energy and engineering research fields, followed by "Environmental science". In "Economic, Econometrics and Finance" and "Social science", papers are quite limited to less than 2% of the total sample. Other research fields, e.g. "Business, Management and Accounting" and "Decision Sciences", were also barely considered in the literature.

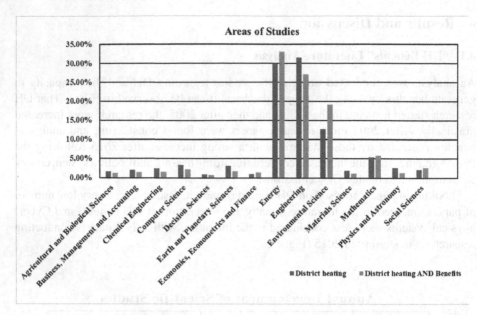

Fig. 2. Scientific studies by study area [Data processed by Scopus].

4.2   DH Benefits Identification and Categorization

Through the literature review, we could identify several benefits generated by DH, considering environmental, social and economic benefits. DH benefits are well described in the literature that mainly comes from Asian and European countries where those systems are well developed, in particular: Austria, China, Croatia, Denmark, Estonia, Finland, Germany, Italy, Japan, South Korea, Netherlands, Poland, Russia, Sweden, UK, and the US.

Based on the ENTSO-E benefit framework [30], we categorised the benefits into 4 categories, namely 1) benefits for the energy system, 2) benefits for the environment, 3) benefits for the user and 4) benefits for society. Since the aim of this paper is understanding also the methods/approaches to measure and evaluate them, in the following part, each category is described, and each benefit is analysed in terms of frequency of appearance in the literature and the method adopted to quantify and measure it, according to 3 method types, i.e. "qualitative method (I)", "quantitative method (Q)", and "monetisation method (M)".

Benefits for the Energy System. DH systems can be very important for the energy system to gain several benefits. After analysing the current literature, several benefits are identified for the energy system, including energy efficiency, flexibility (not depending on one specific source), RES integration, scaling of peaks in demand - reduction of energy demand, reduction of power consumption primary sources, security supplies, electric security system, stabilization system (heat storage), and storage possibilities. Those benefits are found in 23 scientific works among the selected resources. Energy efficiency was considered as a key benefit in 11 research however, only 2 works developed a method to monetise and quantify it, while in 9 works, this benefit was identified but not further analysed. The flexibility of energy sources was identified as a benefit in 3 sources, yet one developed a method to monetise it. Besides, RES integration was found as a benefit in 6 research. In 4 studies, this benefit was only identified, not monetised or quantified. Similarly, "scaling of peaks in demand - reduction of energy demand" was noticed as a benefit in 2 works, without implementing any method to qualify or monetise it. The "reduction of power consumption primary sources" was found as a benefit in 15 works, where 2 studies developed a method for benefit monetization by adopting the avoided cost method, and 6 quantified benefits. "Security supplies" is monetised only by one research among 5 papers that mentioned it as a key benefit. "Electric security systems" was found in 5 studies, whereas two of them developed a method to monetise it. The benefit "stabilization system (heat storage)" was quantified, and "storage possibilities resources" was only identified without any further analyses. Further analysis of DH system benefits for the energy system is summarized in Table 1.

Table 1. DH system benefits for the energy system according to coherent literature.

DH Benefit	Assessment approach	References	Methodology	Geographic area
Energy efficiency	I	[14, 20, 31–37]	–	Europe, UK, Sweden, Croatia, General, China
	M	[21]	Report case studies	US
	Q	[38]	–	Estonia
Flexibility (not depending on one specific source)	Q	[36]	–	Italy
	I	[39]	–	Europe
	M	[40]	–	Germany
RES integration	I	[37, 39, 41, 42]	–	Italy, China, Europe
	Q	[31]	–	Italy, China, Europe
	M	[40]	–	Germany
Scaling of peaks in demand - Reduction of energy demand	I	[20, 32]	–	UK, Europe

(continued)

Table 1. (*continued*)

DH Benefit	Assessment approach	References	Methodology	Geographic area
Reduction of power consumption primary sources	I	[14, 20, 37, 39, 40, 43, 44]	–	Sweden, Croatia, General, Europe, Austria, China
	Q	[36, 41, 43, 45–47]	–	Italy, Europe, Sweden
	M	[18]	Avoided cost	EU
		[22]	Avoided cost	South Korea
Security supplies	I	[14, 20, 21, 40]	–	Croatia, US, Europe, Austria
	M	[48]	Report case studies	EU
Electric security system	M	[21]	Avoided cost	US
		[48]	–	EU
	I	[19, 32, 38]	–	UK, Estonia
Stabilization system (heat storage)	Q	[49]	–	EU
Storage possibilities	I	[21]	–	US

Benefits for the End User. DH systems can be very significant for the end user to acquire several benefits. Total 9 scientific works identified benefits for the end users among selected resources. Those benefits are comfort, average risk avoided in the house, more relationship between consumer and producer, lower maintenance cost, reduction of pollutants associated with health issues, space saving (engaged by technologies for heat production), vibration reduction, heat supply security, and decreased system cost. "Comfort" was found as a benefit in 3 works where 2 works developed 2 methods to monetise by adopting "willingness to pay (WAP)" and "hedonic pricing", respectively. Besides, "average risk avoided in the house" is monetised in one research by adopting the WAP method. However, 3 benefits "more relationship between consumer and producer", "lower maintenance cost", and "reduction of pollutants associated with health issues" were only identified, not monetised or quantified further. "Heat supply security" was identified as a benefit in 3 works; however not further quantified. In addition, 3 resources identified "space saving (engaged by technologies for heat production)", where 2 works monetised the benefit. "Decreasing the system cost" is another crucial benefit for the

Table 2. DH system benefits for the end user according to coherent literature.

DH Benefit	Assessment approach	References	Methodology	Geographic area
Comfort	I	[14]	–	Croatia
	M	[50]	WAP	South Korea
		[18]	Hedonic pricing	Europe
Average risk avoided in the house	I	[39]	–	Europe
	M	[51]	WAP	South Korea
More relationship between consumer and producer	I	[39]	–	Europe
Lower maintenance cost	I	[39, 41]	–	Italy, Europe
Reduction of pollutants associated with health issues	I	[21]	–	US
Space saving (engaged by technologies for heat production), vibration reduction	M	[51]	WAP	South Korea
		[21]	Report case studies	US
	I	[39]	–	Europe
Heat supply security	I	[38, 39, 41]	–	Italy, Estonia, Europe
Decreases the system cost	M	[23]	–	Denmark

end user, and it is monetised only once. More analysis of DH system benefits for the end user is performed in Table 2.

Benefits of Environment. DH systems can be very important for the environment to obtain several benefits. We found environmental benefits in 27 resources, those benefits are environmental and health damage avoided, resource recovery from waste, CO_2 reduction, CO_2 reduction equivalent, reduced consumption of water resources, and reduction of pollutants (no CO_2). Among them, 2 benefits "CO_2 reduction equivalent" and "reducing consumption of water resources" were quantified the benefits but not monetised. 21 sources identified "CO_2 reduction" as the highest among environmental benefits for DH; however, 11 works quantified the benefits and 3 works monetised by utilizing avoided cost, shadow price and ICR methods, respectively. In addition, avoided cost was applied to monetise the benefit "environment and health damage avoided" in one research work. The benefits "resource recovery from waste", and "reduction of pollutants (no CO_2)" were quantified in 2 studies. Besides, the "reduction of pollutants (no CO_2)" was also

Table 3. DH system benefits of environment according to coherent literature.

DH Benefit	Assessment approach	References	Methodology	Geographic area
Environmental and health damage avoided	M	[48]	Avoided cost (damage factor)	EU
Resource recovery from waste	I	[31, 39];	–	Europe
CO_2 reduction	I	[10, 20, 32, 39, 42, 52, 53]	–	UK, General, Italy, Denmark, Europe
	Q	[14, 22, 33, 36, 38, 41, 43, 45, 46, 49, 54]	–	Croatia, Sweden, Italy, South Korea, Estonia, Europe
	M	[18]	Avoided cost, shadow price	Europe
		[37]	ICR	China
		[47]	Tool (EnergyPLAN)	Europe
CO_2 reduction equivalent	Q	[24, 34, 36, 54]	–	Sweden; Europe
Reducing consumption of water resources	Q	[37]	–	China
Reduction of pollutants (no CO_2)	I	[39, 44, 52]	–	Denmark, General
	Q	[14, 37]	–	Croatia, China
	M	[25]	Avoided cost, Pollution tax, Tool (Crystal Ball)	China

monetised with avoided cost and pollution tax methods. Table 3 provides an overview of further investigation of environmental benefits of DH system.

Benefits for the Society. Different benefits can be obtained by utilizing DH systems. Overall, 7 scientific works considered numerous benefits of DH for the society such as health damage avoided, impacts on macroeconomics / local economy recovery (GDP, growth and employment derived from investments and energy efficiency), exploitation of local resources, and reduction of energy poverty. After analysing selected works, 2 benefits, "Reduction of energy poverty" and "Exploitation of local resources" were identified and not further quantified or monetised. The "impacts macroeconomics/local economy recovery" is regarded as an essential benefit, and it's monetized in 2 research by employing the "input-output model" and software (MOVE2social). Table 4 describes the analysis of DH system benefits for the society.

Table 4. DH system benefits for the society according to coherent literature.

DH Benefit	Assessment approach	References	Methodology	Geographic area
Health damage avoided	M	[48]	Avoided cost (damage factor)	EU
Impacts on macroeconomics/local economy recovery (GDP, growth and employment derived from investments and energy efficiency)	I	[21, 32, 38]	–	US, UK, Estonia
	M	[48]	Input-output model	EU
	M	[19]	Tool (MOVE2social)	Austria
	Q	[11]	–	Denmark
Exploitation of local resources	I	[39]	–	Europe
Reduction of energy poverty	I	[32]	–	UK

Following the analysis of the scientific and grey literature, it is possible to state that the most assessed benefits – i.e. with methods that quantify and monetise them – are the benefits for the energy system: improvements in energy efficiency and primary energy consumption. The environmental benefits that are measured and monetised refer to the "reduction of emissions" (CO_2 reduction taken into consideration) and the "reduction of pollutants". Among the methodologies for monetisation, the major methods are the avoided cost (savings obtained by applying DH-DC instead of another technology) and WAP (willingness to pay for DH as an alternative to other technology).

In general, the number of studies monetising the benefit generated by DH systems was significantly less than studies evaluating benefits in a qualitative way. Moreveor, Tables 1, 2, 3 and 4 are significantly related to one another and can be utilized to better recognize the advantages of DH systems while assessing a DH project's benefits. According to our results, it is necessary to develop a compressive assessment framework to monetise and quantify benefits, in order to help policymakers and stakeholders in decision-making and in driving finance towards sustainable DH projects. This can guide municipalities, generation companies, service providers, and users in undertaking better decision-making by looking at the effective impacts.

4.3 Categorising Benefits of Using the District Energy System and Cyber Physical System Together

Cyber physical system definition is well defined in the literature, but analysis of benefits in DH-DC systems is quite limited. Through the literature review we found that several benefits of the DH-DC system can be acquired with the help of CPS for stakeholders, planners and users. Various benefits could be generated by CPS in the DH-DC systems, such as enhancing energy efficiency, facilitating the decarbonisation process and decreasing energy bills for users. In this work, benefits generated by the integration of DH-DC systems and CPS are categorised into four different categories (i) benefits for the energy system: energy management, storage possibilities, system stabilization, RES integration and flexibility, (ii) benefits for end users: enhance safety awareness, security alert system, energy efficiency (reducing energy cost), thermal comfort and low maintenance cost, (iii) environmental benefits: CO_2 reduction, and reduction of pollutants excluding CO_2, and (iv) benefits for society: maintenance management, safety measurement, employability, damage avoided for the environment and health (multiple pollutants), investment opportunities, reduction of energy poverty and exploitation of local resources. These benefits can be acquired by integrating CPS with DH-DC system in the future. As limited research work is conducted in this sector, in future, we can integrate CPS with DH-DC and conduct more research to grasp the possibilities of technologies in this sector to quantify the benefits of DH-DC.

5   Conclusions and Further Work

This study aims to identify and categorize the benefits of DH-DC systems. A review of scientific literature has been conducted by utilizing the Scopus database and using 4 keywords: "district heating", "district heating" and "benefit", "district heating" and "benefit" and "economics", and "district heating" and "benefit" and "Cyber physical". Overall, 35 research works are included in this review. We also analysed scientific studies by research field and found that energy, engineering, and environmental science had the highest portion of papers, while the economic research field rarely considers this topic. Benefits identified were categorised into four categories using the ENTSO-E benefit assessment framework, namely benefits for the energy system, end-users, environment, and society. Benefits for the energy system include: increased energy efficiency; increased security supplies; increased the safety of the electrical system; waste heat recovery. Environmental benefits include: reduction of CO_2 emissions; reduction of local pollutants; environmental and health damage avoided. Benefits for the user include: increased thermal comfort; lower maintenance cost; heat supply security; space savings. Benefits for society include: impacts macroeconomics; exploitation of local resources; reduction of energy poverty.

Moreover, benefits were analysed by looking at the methods adopted to quantify and monetise them, namely: qualitative method (I), quantitative method (Q), or monetisation method (M). After analysing the literature, we observed only a few works quantified or monetised the benefits of DH-DC; more papers were conducted using a qualitative approach to analyse them. Results will be used to develop an innovative assessment framework to quantify benefits, which will provide operational support for analysing the benefits generated by DH-DC system as it can support stakeholders in decision-making, and investors in driving financing towards sustainable projects. Moreover, the untapped potential of CPS in DH-DC systems could be integrated as well in future to improve energy planning, energy management, maintenance check and many more applications. Furthermore, new opportunities can be obtained from DH-DC system; for example, new business models can be introduced by utilizing 5GDH and/or 4GDC technology and CPS. As a result, more businesses and job opportunities will be created for society.

Acknowledgments. This project has received funding from SmartGYsum project which is the European Union's Horizon 2020 research and innovation programme under the Marie Skłodowska-Curie grant agreement no. 955614.

References

1. Global energy demand to grow 47% by 2050, with oil still top source: US EIA I S&P Global Commodity Insights. https://www.spglobal.com/commodityinsights/en/market-insights/latest-news/oil/100621-global-energy-demand-to-grow-47-by-2050-with-oil-still-top-source-us-eia. Accessed 13 Feb 2023
2. Heating - Fuels & Technologies – IEA. https://www.iea.org/fuels-and-technologies/heating. Accessed 15 Feb 2023
3. Cooling - Fuels & Technologies – IEA. https://www.iea.org/fuels-and-technologies/cooling. Accessed 13 Feb 2023
4. Global CO_2 emissions rebounded to their highest level in history in 2021 - News – IEA. https://www.iea.org/news/global-co2-emissions-rebounded-to-their-highest-level-in-history-in-2021. Accessed 17 Feb 2023
5. Rezaie, B., Rosen, M.A.: District heating and cooling: review of technology and potential enhancements. Appl. Energy **93**, 2 (2012). https://doi.org/10.1016/j.apenergy.2011.04.020
6. The Paris Agreement I UNFCCC. https://unfccc.int/process-and-meetings/the-paris-agreement. Accessed 20 Feb 2023
7. Toffanin, R., Curti, V., Barbato, M.C.: Impact of Legionella regulation on a 4th generation district heating substation energy use and cost: the case of a Swiss single-family household. Energy **228**, 120473 (2021). https://doi.org/10.1016/j.energy.2021.120473
8. District heating and cooling I Climate Technology Centre & Network I Tue (2017). https://www.ctc-n.org/technologies/district-heating-and-cooling. Accessed 23 Feb 2023
9. District Heating – Analysis – IEA. https://www.iea.org/reports/district-heating. Accessed 23 Feb 2023
10. Werner, S.: International review of district heating and cooling. Energy **137**, 617–631 (2017). https://doi.org/10.1016/j.energy.2017.04.045
11. Buffa, S., Cozzini, M., D'Antoni, M., Baratieri, M., Fedrizzi, R.: 5th generation district heating and cooling systems: a review of existing cases in Europe (2019). https://doi.org/10.1016/j.rser.2018.12.059
12. Lund, H., et al.: Perspectives on fourth and fifth generation district heating. Energy **227**, 120520 (2021). https://doi.org/10.1016/j.energy.2021.120520
13. Østergaard, P.A., et al.: The four generations of district cooling - A categorization of the development in district cooling from origin to future prospect. Energy **253**, 124098 (2022). https://doi.org/10.1016/j.energy.2022.124098

14. Doračić, B., Novosel, T., Pukšec, T., Duić, N.: Evaluation of excess heat utilization in district heating systems by implementing levelized cost of excess heat. Energies (Basel) **11**, 575 (2018). https://doi.org/10.3390/en11030575
15. Gusmeroli, S.: Immagine in copertina: panorama di CityLife_Milano. (2018)
16. Inderwildi, O., Zhang, C., Wang, X., Kraft, M.: The impact of intelligent cyber-physical systems on the decarbonization of energy. Energy Environ Sci. **13**, 744–771 (2020). https://doi.org/10.1039/C9EE01919G
17. Inderwildi, O., Zhang, C., Kraft, M.: Cyber-Physical Systems in Decarbonisation. Presented at the (2022). https://doi.org/10.1007/978-3-030-86215-2_2
18. Davide, S.: Guide to cost-benefit analysis of investment projects : economic appraisal tool for cohesion policy 2014–2020. European Commission, Directorate-General for Regional and Urban policy (2015)
19. Moser, S., Mayrhofer, J., Schmidt, R.-R., Tichler, R.: Socioeconomic cost-benefit-analysis of seasonal heat storages in district heating systems with industrial waste heat integration. Energy **160**, 868–874 (2018). https://doi.org/10.1016/j.energy.2018.07.057
20. Werner, S.: Benefits with more District Heating and Cooling in Europe. Rome (2007)
21. US Department of Energy: Energy Efficiency and Energy Security Benefits of District Energy (2019)
22. Kim, H.-W., Dong, L., Choi, A.E.S., Fujii, M., Fujita, T., Park, H.-S.: Co-benefit potential of industrial and urban symbiosis using waste heat from industrial park in Ulsan Korea. Resour. Conserv. Recycl. **135**, 225–234 (2018). https://doi.org/10.1016/j.resconrec.2017.09.027
23. Sorknæs, P., Nielsen, S., Lund, H., Mathiesen, B.V., Moreno, D., Thellufsen, J.Z.: The benefits of 4th generation district heating and energy efficient datacentres. Energy **260**, 125215 (2022). https://doi.org/10.1016/j.energy.2022.125215
24. Djuric Ilic, D., Trygg, L.: Economic and environmental benefits of converting industrial processes to district heating. Energy Convers. Manag. **87**, 305–317 (2014). https://doi.org/10.1016/j.enconman.2014.07.025
25. Yan, Q., Qin, C.: Environmental and economic benefit analysis of an integrated heating system with geothermal energy—a case study in Xi'an China. Energies (Basel) **10**, 2090 (2017). https://doi.org/10.3390/en10122090
26. EU taxonomy for sustainable activities. https://finance.ec.europa.eu/sustainable-finance/tools-and-standards/eu-taxonomy-sustainable-activities_en. Accessed 27 Feb 2023
27. Krämer, B.J.: Evolution of cyber-physical systems: a brief review. In: Suh, S., Tanik, U., Carbone, J., Eroglu, A. (eds.) Applied Cyber-Physical Systems. pp. 1–3. Springer New York, New York, NY (2014). https://doi.org/10.1007/978-1-4614-7336-7_1
28. Lee, E.: The past, present and future of cyber-physical systems: a focus on models. Sensors **15**, 4837–4869 (2015). https://doi.org/10.3390/s150304837
29. Matsunaga, F., Zytkowski, V., Valle, P., Deschamps, F.: Optimization of energy efficiency in smart manufacturing through the application of cyber–physical systems and industry 4.0 technologies. J Energy Resour. Technol. **144**, (2022). https://doi.org/10.1115/1.4053868
30. ENTSO-E Guideline for Cost Benefit Analysis of Grid Development Projects (2015)
31. Connolly, D., et al.: Heat Roadmap Europe: combining district heating with heat savings to decarbonise the EU energy system. Energy Policy **65**, 475–489 (2014). https://doi.org/10.1016/j.enpol.2013.10.035
32. Kelly, S., Pollitt, M.: An assessment of the present and future opportunities for combined heat and power with district heating (CHP-DH) in the United Kingdom. Energy Policy **38**, 6936–6945 (2010). https://doi.org/10.1016/j.enpol.2010.07.010
33. Weinberger, G., Amiri, S., Moshfegh, B.: On the benefit of integration of a district heating system with industrial excess heat: an economic and environmental analysis. Appl. Energy **191**, 454–468 (2017). https://doi.org/10.1016/j.apenergy.2017.01.093

34. Olsson, L., Wetterlund, E., Söderström, M.: Assessing the climate impact of district heating systems with combined heat and power production and industrial excess heat. Resour. Conserv. Recycl. **96**, 31–39 (2015). https://doi.org/10.1016/j.resconrec.2015.01.006

35. Allan, G., Eromenko, I., Gilmartin, M., Kockar, I., McGregor, P.: The economics of distributed energy generation: a literature review. Renew. Sustain. Energy Rev. **42**, 543–556 (2015). https://doi.org/10.1016/j.rser.2014.07.064

36. Comodi, G., Lorenzetti, M., Salvi, D., Arteconi, A.: Criticalities of district heating in Southern Europe: lesson learned from a CHP-DH in Central Italy. Appl. Therm. Eng. **112**, 649–659 (2017). https://doi.org/10.1016/j.applthermaleng.2016.09.149

37. Fang, H., Xia, J., Zhu, K., Su, Y., Jiang, Y.: Industrial waste heat utilization for low temperature district heating. Energy Policy **62**, 236–246 (2013). https://doi.org/10.1016/j.enpol.2013.06.104

38. Volkova, A., Mashatin, V., Hlebnikov, A., Siirde, A.: Methodology for the improvement of large district heating networks. Environ. Climate Technol. **10**, 39–45 (2012). https://doi.org/10.2478/v10145-012-0009-7

39. Euroheat & Power. https://www.euroheat.org/. Accessed 17 Feb 2023

40. Schwaeppe, H., et al.: Analyzing intersectoral benefits of district heating in an integrated generation and transmission expansion planning model. Energies (Basel) **15**, 2314 (2022). https://doi.org/10.3390/en15072314

41. Noussan, M.: Performance indicators of District Heating Systems in Italy – Insights from a data analysis. Appl. Therm. Eng. **134**, 194–202 (2018). https://doi.org/10.1016/j.applthermaleng.2018.01.125

42. Famiglietti, J., et al.: Environmental Life Cycle Assessment scenarios for a district heating network. An Italian case study. Energy Reports **7**, 368–379 (2021). https://doi.org/10.1016/j.egyr.2021.08.094

43. Broberg Viklund, S., Johansson, M.T.: Technologies for utilization of industrial excess heat: potentials for energy recovery and CO2 emission reduction. Energy Convers Manag. **77**, 369–379 (2014). https://doi.org/10.1016/j.enconman.2013.09.052

44. Rosada, J.: Characteristics of district heating - advantages and disadvantages. Energy Build. **12**, 163–171 (1988). https://doi.org/10.1016/0378-7788(88)90061-8

45. Ilaria, B.: Teleriscaldamento e sistemi energetici integrati: metodologia di valutazione dei benefici energetici ed ambientali e strumenti di incentivazione. Enea (2009)

46. Calise, F., D'Accadia, M., Barletta, C., Battaglia, V., Pfeifer, A., Duic, N.: Detailed modelling of the deep decarbonisation scenarios with demand response technologies in the heating and cooling sector: a case study for Italy. Energies (Basel) **10**, 1535 (2017). https://doi.org/10.3390/en10101535

47. Lund, H., et al.: The status of 4th generation district heating: research and results. Energy **164**, 147–159 (2018). https://doi.org/10.1016/j.energy.2018.08.206

48. Jakubcionis, M., et al.: Best practices and informal guidance on how to implement the Comprehensive Assessment at Member State level. Publications Office of the European Union, Luxembourg (Luxembourg) (2015). https://doi.org/10.2790/79453

49. Connolly, D., Lund, H., Mathiesen, B.V.: Smart Energy Europe: The technical and economic impact of one potential 100% renewable energy scenario for the European Union. Renew. Sustain. Energy Rev. **60**, 1634–1653 (2016). https://doi.org/10.1016/j.rser.2016.02.025

50. Yoon, T., Ma, Y., Rhodes, C.: Individual Heating systems vs. District Heating systems: what will consumers pay for convenience? Energy Policy **86**, 73–81 (2015). https://doi.org/10.1016/j.enpol.2015.06.024

51. Kim, H.-J., Lim, S.-Y., Yoo, S.-H.: The convenience benefits of the district heating system over individual heating systems in korean households. Sustainability **9**, 1348 (2017). https://doi.org/10.3390/su9081348

52. Danish Energy Agency: District Heating Assessment Tool. (2016)
53. Werner, S.: Ecoheatcool WP4–Possibilities with more District Heating in Europe. www.eco heatcool.org. Accessed 28 Feb 2023
54. Broberg Viklund, S., Karlsson, M.: Industrial excess heat use: systems analysis and CO2 emissions reduction. Appl. Energy. **152**, 189–197 (2015). https://doi.org/10.1016/j.apenergy. 2014.12.023

A Collaborative Dimension for Renewable Energy Communities

Kankam O. Adu-Kankam[1,2(✉)] and Luis M. Camarinha-Matos[1]

[1] School of Science and Technology, UNINOVA – CTS and LASI, Nova University of Lisbon, Campus de Caparica, 2829-516 Monte de Caparica, Portugal
k.adu@campus.fct.unl.pt, cam@uninova.pt
[2] School of Engineering, University of Energy and Natural Resources (UENR), P. O. Box 214, Sunyani, Ghana

Abstract. Renewable Energy Communities (RECs) are collective entities whose membership is based on free and voluntary participation. RECs may involve groups of citizens, social entrepreneurs, public authorities, and community organizations that participate either directly or indirectly in the energy transition by exchanging energy-related goods and services either "for-profit" or "non-profit" within a community or ecosystem. REC members can jointly produce their own energy, which can be used locally, stored, sold, or shared with others in the ecosystem. Despite several pilot implementations of RECs, several challenges remain in terms of organization, governance and creation of incentives for participation, etc. To address these challenges, we propose the exploitation of a collaborative dimension. Thus, the concept of Collaborative Renewable Energy Community (CREC) is introduced as a type of REC that adopts collaborative principles and mechanisms to facilitate the production, sale, and sharing of renewable energy within an ecosystem. Just like many emerging concepts, the dominant literature in energy communities loosely points to this idea of CRECs but in a sparse, sometimes incoherent, disjointed, and disorganized manner, which creates a sense of ambiguity and confusion, making it difficult to comprehend the importance of the concept. In this work, we attempt to clarify the CREC concept, shed some light on their organizational structure, introduce their governance systems, and identify the types of collaborative mechanisms that can be adopted. Simulation was used as a preliminary validation of the proposed approach and models. The article further discusses some potential applications of CRECs.

Keywords: Collaborative Networks · Energy Ecosystems · Collaborative Renewable Energy Community · Collaborative Digital Twins · Renewable Energy Communities

1 Introduction

In recent years, the growth of Renewable Energy Communities (RECs) around the world has been huge. The primary reason for this rapid development is the benefits that RECs are claimed to bring to the ongoing energy transition. The dominant literature in the field

© IFIP International Federation for Information Processing 2023
Published by Springer Nature Switzerland AG 2023
L. M. Camarinha-Matos and F. Ferrada (Eds.): DoCEIS 2023, IFIP AICT 678, pp. 19–37, 2023.
https://doi.org/10.1007/978-3-031-36007-7_2

suggests that RECs can become a channel for a democratic, transformative, and equity-enhancing means towards a just energy transition [1]. These claims are highlighted in several studies. For instance, in [2], RECs are understood to play social roles such as energy poverty alleviation. Similarly, RECs are suggested to promote sustainable energy production and consumption in [3], enhance gender parity and equity for energy access [4], and finally, promote citizen participation in renewable energy projects [5]. According to [6], RECs are collective entities that are based on voluntary and open participation. REC members are constituted of stakeholders, who are principally natural persons, local authorities, including municipalities, or small enterprises. Their union is often motivated by a common objective, such as environmental, economic, or social (community benefits). Members of RECs collectively engage in the generation of energy, particularly from renewable sources. Other activities include energy sharing, consumption, aggregation, storage, energy efficiency services, or charging services for electric vehicles. By sharing the costs and benefits of renewable energy systems, these communities can make renewable energy more accessible and affordable to a wider range of people, both within and outside the community. RECs can take many different forms, from small-scale neighbourhood projects [7] to larger initiatives that involve multiple communities and organizations [8]. They can be initiated by individuals [9], local governments [10], non-profit organizations [11], or private companies [12], and can involve various types of renewable energy technologies. The concept of REC is based on the idea of energy democracy, implying that everyone should have a say in how their energy is produced and consumed [13]. By working together, members of RECs can create a more equitable and sustainable energy system that benefits everyone.

In this work, we attempt to clarify some emerging concepts within the domain of RECs. The article is based on the fact that various variants of RECs are emerging within the renewable energy space that need to be clearly identified, explored and exploited. More specifically, the notion of Collaborative Renewable Energy Communities (CREC) has begun to emerge within this space and the need to identify and distinguish such communities from the general notion of RECs motivates this work. As such, the following questions are addressed.

Q1: What are RECs?

a. What are the motivations for RECs?
b. What are some of the existing cases of RECs?
c. What are the obstacles / barriers to the advancement of RECs?
d. What role can collaborative networks play to help overcome (some of) the mentioned barriers?

Q2: What are Collaborative Renewable Energy Communities (CRECs)? What are the main aspects of CRECS? (Namely in terms of structure and organization, governance, involving mechanisms of collaboration etc.

Q3: What are some potential use cases of the CREC concept?

2 Relationship with Connected Cyber-Physical Spaces

A CREC can be perceived as a type of REC that adopts collaborative mechanisms and principles to manage aspects of energy generation and consumption within a community or energy ecosystem. The physical component of the REC may include groups of individuals, organizations, and businesses that own renewable energy resources and are motivated by a common goal; therefore, they come together to form the community. Furthermore, it is suggested that the cyber layer may be constituted of (a) a digital twin layer and (b) a virtual organization layer. Embedded in the digital twin layer is the notion of cognitive intelligence, which enables the digital twins to make rational decisions on behalf of their physical counterparts. These rational decisions facilitate the way energy is sustainably generated, stored, consumed and distributed in the ecosystem [14]. This can be achieved through shared ownership of renewable energy resources and engaging in collective decision-making, actions, and endeavours [15]. This, therefore, suggests a connection that can fascinate the exchange of information between the cyber component and the physical component, creating the notion of a cyber-physical system.

The relationship between CRECs and connected cyber-physical spaces is a symbiotic one. The integration of renewable energy technologies with connected cyber-physical spaces can enable better energy management, distribution, and consumption. For instance, these communities can integrate sensors, actuators, and smart devices to collect real-time data about energy generation and consumption within the ecosystem. These sets of data can be used by a CREC to make decisions that can help optimize the way energy is generated, stored, consumed and distributed in the community.

Furthermore, CRECs can benefit from the integration of connected cyber-physical spaces, which can facilitate the creation of virtual entities such as virtual power plants (VPPs) [14]. These VPPs can aggregate the energy generated from multiple renewable sources and distribute it to the grid, helping to create a more stable and reliable energy supply. The integration of renewable energy technologies with connected cyber-physical spaces can enable more efficient, sustainable, and resilient energy systems, benefiting both the communities and the society.

3 What Are RECs?

A REC is a collective entity that is autonomous, operates in line with the applicable national laws, is based on open and voluntary participation, and is effectively governed by shareholders or members who are situated close to the renewable energy project. The establishment and operation of RECs are supported by legal frameworks such as the European Union Directive 2018/2001 [4]. This directive mandates member states of the European Union to ensure that final customers, especially household customers, are allowed to participate in a REC while upholding their rights and obligations as final customers and without being subjected to unjustified or discriminatory conditions or procedures that would prevent their participation, provided that their participation does not constitute their primary commercial or profit motive.

RECs can contribute to the alleviation of fossil fuel dominance in the current grid in several ways. For example, they can contribute to energy justice by promoting more equitable access to renewable energy resources and reducing the disproportionate impacts of energy production and consumption on marginalized communities [16]. One of the main avenues for RECs to promote energy justice is to make renewable energy more accessible and affordable to more people. By pooling resources and sharing the costs and benefits of renewable energy systems, communities can make it possible for more people to access clean and sustainable energy sources. RECs can also help to address the unequal impacts of energy production and consumption on marginalized communities and genders. For example, many low-income and minority communities are disproportionately impacted by pollution and other negative effects of fossil fuel energy production [17]. By supporting the transition to renewable energy sources, communities can reduce these impacts and create a more just and sustainable energy system. In addition, renewable energy communities can promote energy democracy by giving people a greater say in how their energy is produced and consumed. By working together, community members can create a more participatory and democratic energy system that benefits everyone, not just a few powerful stakeholders but also to include marginalized genders such as women. Overall, renewable energy communities can play an important role in promoting energy justice by making renewable energy more accessible, reducing the negative impacts of energy production and consumption on marginalized communities, and promoting greater democratic participation in the energy system. Renewable energy communities can contribute to increasing citizens' participation in renewable energy as well.

3.1   What Are the Motivations for RECs?

The current literature in this field provides several motivations for RECs. Among them we can mention:

(a) Sustainability: By promoting renewable energy sources like solar, wind, and hydro power, communities can reduce their dependence on fossil fuels and contribute to the fight against climate change [18].
(b) Energy independence: By generating their own energy, communities can become less reliant on external energy sources and become more self-sufficient [19].
(c) Cost savings: This is achieved by pooling resources and sharing the costs of renewable energy systems. In doing so, communities can make it more affordable for everyone to access clean and sustainable energy sources [20].

Other motivations may include:

(d) Community building: By working together on renewable energy projects, communities can build social connections/cohesion, and foster a sense of shared purpose and accomplishment [21].
(e) Environmental justice: By transitioning to renewable energy sources, communities can reduce the negative environmental impacts of energy production and consumption on marginalized communities and create a more just environment and equitable energy system [22].
(f) Health and well-being: RECs can be motivated by a desire to improve public health and well-being by reducing air pollution and other negative health impacts associated with fossil fuel energy production [23].

(g) Economic Development: Finally, RECs can be motivated by a desire to promote local economic development. By investing in renewable energy projects, communities can create jobs and stimulate economic growth, while also promoting environmental sustainability and energy independence [24].

3.2 What Are Some Existing Cases of RECs?

Currently, there are many existing RECs cases that are spread around the world. For instance, in Germany, France, the Netherlands and Denmark a huge number of community projects are thriving and contributing to the strong growth of renewables in these countries [25]. In the European Union alone, there are over 7700 RECs involving over two million people [26]. The United Kingdom also has over 5000 RECs [26]. In Table 1, a few successful cases are shown. These cases were selected from a case study that was conducted in [27].

Table 1. Some selected cases of successful RECs

Case	Name	Description of the community
1	Feldheim, Germany	In Germany's Brandenburg region, the village of Feldheim receives all of its electricity from renewable sources. Own wind and photovoltaic power plants provide heat and electricity to households and businesses. Biogas plants connected to the local grid provides the community with power and heat
2	Wildpoldsried, Germany	Wildpoldsried is a small farming community that has been able to invest in new municipal infrastructure without going into debt, Wildpoldsried produces 321 percent more electricity than it needs and is bringing in $5.7 million annually
3	Westmill Solar Co-operative	More than 20,000 polycrystalline PV panels spread across 30 acres at the location generate 4.8 GWhr/year, which is about comparable to the yearly electricity consumption of 1,600 typical houses and to avert 2,000 tonnes of carbon dioxide emissions. It is believed to be the first and biggest community-owned, cooperatively controlled solar farm in the UK
4	Bristol Energy Cooperative	The UK's largest community-owned solar rooftop, with over 2000 solar panels. It is thought to be the largest rooftop solar project to date in the UK. There is a sizable 1 MW solar array on the brand-new Bottle Yard Film Studios

As seen in Table 1, RECs can have different composition, different objectives, different capacities, varying sizes with different power outputs.

3.3   What Are the Obstacles and Barriers to the Advancement of RECs?

There are several obstacles and barriers that can limit the chances of RECs to thrive. In a recent report published by "friends of the earth, Europe" [25] the following key barriers were highlighted.

(a) Access to the grid: RECs must have access to the energy grid in order to successfully sell its energy. However, this access is frequently barred. This is due to the fact that grid operators, who are not compelled to connect projects owned by the local community and do not perceive it as being in their best interest, are the ones who operate the grid for profit.
(b) Lack of access to funds/capital: Due to limited access to capital to invest, vulnerable communities in low-income areas are most severely impacted by this. The fact is that banks and other lending institutions frequently have a poor understanding of what a community energy project is and what kind of business model is acceptable, plays a key component of the financial challenge. Only a small number of nations have enough successful and running projects to provide banks the confidence to lend.
(c) Policy and regulatory barriers: In some areas, regulations may limit the ability of communities to install renewable energy systems or may favour fossil fuel energy sources over renewable sources.
(d) NIMBYism: Meaning "not in my backyard," can also be a barrier to RECs. Some residents may oppose to renewable energy projects in their communities due to concerns about noise, visual impacts, or property values.
(e) These mentioned obstacles and barriers can make it difficult for renewable energy communities to thrive.

However, in the same report [25] the following recommendation were provided.

A) The grid should be managed for the benefit of the general public, considered as a common asset, and held in public ownership. Cities' local governments are in a good position to manage their local grids and make sure they are ready for a locally controlled, decentralized energy system.
B) Governments must establish a supportive legislative environment that encourages and enables the growth of RECs in their respective national contexts.
C) A single national government contact point where community energy projects can go for guidance and assistance is required. They may get all the information they require from this administrative point of contact, who can also walk them through the procedure.

3.4   What Role Can Collaborative Networks Play to Help Overcome (Some of) These Barriers?

Collaborative Networks (CN) can play an important role in overcoming some of the obstacles and barriers facing RECs, leading to the notion of CREC. Here are a few ways in which collaborative networks can help:

(a) CREC Virtual Power Plant (CREC-VPP): Through collaboration, small-scale distributed generation that is found within these CREC environments can be aggregated into the equivalent of a power plant with adequate capacity, which can enable the CREC to enter into negotiations, competition, and trading with traditional power plants in the energy market [27].

(b) CREC Grid Management: Through collaboration, resources within the community can be aggregated and be used to provide ancillary services such grid management and demand response services to the grids. In Sect. 4.4, Scenario 2 of this work, these ideas are partially demonstrated.

(c) Resilience and increased survivability in turbulent times: By working together, each member in the ecosystem compliments the other. The inadequacy of one member is complimented by the adequacy of the other. This helps to build a resilient ecosystem. By working together, communities can have a stronger voice and can push for changes at the local, regional, and national levels. This capacity can also be used to negotiate for better trading terms on the energy market [28].

4 Introduction to Collaborative Renewable Energy Communities

In this section, we describe 3 key facets of a CREC, namely: (a) how CRECs are organized, (b) how they are governed, and (c) the various collaborative mechanism that they can engage in. The succeeding paragraphs explain each facet in detail.

4.1 Organization of CRECs

In terms of organization, the following main elements can be introduced:

CREC Manager: This entity is responsible for the administration, organization, and management of the ecosystem. The manager shall also act as an opportunity broker who finds collaborative opportunities for the ecosystem. For instance, the manager could coordinate with external entities such as the distribution service operator to determine windows of opportunity when the ecosystem could be used to render ancillary services to the grid. The manager could also be responsible for conflict resolution, incentivization, and the promotion of sustainable behaviours within the ecosystem.

Virtual Organizations Breeding Environment (VBE): A VBE can be perceived as a **business ecosystem** where members have some form of binding agreement to work together. VBEs have been studied extensively in the domain of Collaborative Networks [29]. In such a business arrangement, it is always vital for members to be prepared and willing to join in the collaboration process since there may be critical situations where the window of opportunity is limited and calls for a prompt reaction, particularly when the timeframe for joint reaction is constrained. "Being ready" entails building a foundation of mutual trust between the participants, compatible operating methods, and collaboration agreements. A VBE can be seen as a long-term association of entities that are ready to cooperate anytime an opportunity comes in order to meet these needs. This strategy can be used to ensure preparedness and speed up the development of collaborative networks. In a similar manner, the grid is a very sensitive infrastructure that requires a quick response time in order to avoid catoptric failure like a system collapse. In this sense, CRECs can be organized in the form of VBEs so that the associated members will be better equipped and prepared to take advantage of any grid-related opportunities that may arise. Examples of such opportunities may include (a) grid management services like demand response, (b) vending energy to the grid, and (c) disaster management services.

Virtual Organization (VO) Formation: A VO is a temporary organization that can be formed out of a VBE to take advantage of a business opportunity. VOs are a class of collaborative network that have received a lot of attention and raised expectations across a range of application areas [14]. One method to stay adaptable and survive market volatility is to be able to swiftly form VOs in response to business opportunities and have them tailored to the needs of each particular opportunity. This notion is not just useful in the business world, but also in non-business settings such as incident management and disaster management processes, where multiple entities need to work together in a swift, decisive and efficient manner. Agility is best exemplified by the notion of groups of organizations quickly transforming into a collaborative form focused on a mission or objective. Similarly, CREC VOs can be formed in the context of CRECs VBE in order to strategically take advantage of business opportunities like selling renewable energy to the grid or utilizing the strength of collective actions by aggregating resources found in the CREC ecosystem, like deferrable loads, and using them to swiftly respond to demands on the grid. In Fig. 1 we illustrate a scenario of three CREC Vos, namely VO1, VO2 and VO3, which are formed from a CREC VBE to take advantage of grid opportunities 1, 2 and 3.

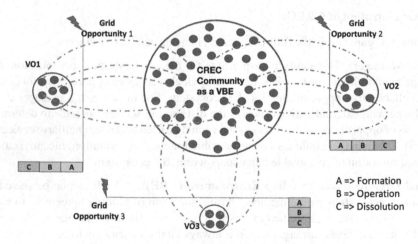

Fig. 1. A CREC as a VBE where multiple dynamic VOs can be created.

Digital Twin Approach to Organizing CRECs: Another key aspect of the CRECs is the potential to adopt or harness the benefits of the ongoing digital transformation agenda to transform the way these ecosystems are established and function. For instance, members within these ecosystems can be represented as digital twins or software agents within the cyber-physical space. This is because digital twins can be assigned with some basic decision-making capabilities that may appear laborious and daunting for human to undertake. For instance, the idea of deferring the use of certain appliances for the purposes of controlling consumption can better be carried out by digital twins than humans. In this sense, sensors from the physical energy assets in the ecosystem can be used to collect operational data at the appliances level and be used to update the digital twin counterparts, making them "living models" [30] of the physical assets, meaning that a digital twin should constantly be updated with new data coming in from the operational environment of the physical asset in order to monitor its current condition for efficient decision-making and prediction of future behaviours. The living models of the physical asset can also be endowed with cognitive intelligence to facilitate their autonomy and collective decision-making capabilities. Figure 2 illustrates how the CREC notion relates to the concepts of digital twins and virtual organizations. Referring to Fig. 2, two key layers of the CREC ecosystem can be observed:

(a) The physical layer: This is the lowest layer of the ecosystem. It is composed of all the physical entities that come together to form the CREC ecosystem. All the energy assets, sensors, actuators, and communication channels/media are located in this layer.

(b) The cyber layer. As the name suggests, this layer is located in the cyberspace. It is comprised of two sub-layers. These are:

  A) The digital twin layer: This is the middle layer, and it is composed of the digital-twins or digital replicas of all the energy assets that are located in the physical layer. The CREC manager is also located in this layer. This is a decision-making layer, and usually, cognitive intelligence and collaborative algorithms can be exhibited by each digital twin from here.

  B) The virtual organization: This is the uppermost layer of the ecosystem. This layer is temporal and dynamic. It can be described as an ad-hoc layer. This is because it is usually formed when the need for a collaborative venture occurs. This is where all the collaborations occur.

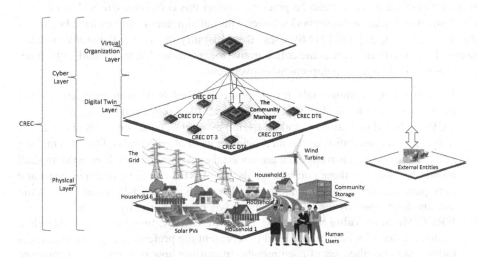

Fig. 2. The notion of a CREC Ecosystem

4.2 Governance of CRECs

Governance is "a set of coordinating and monitoring activities" that enables the survival of the collaborative partnership or institution [31]. Governance in a collaborative network is broadly about the processes and structures of public policy, decision making, and management that engage people constructively across the boundaries of public agencies, levels of government, and/or the public, private and civic spheres in order to carry out a common purpose that could not otherwise be accomplished. Collaborative networks are structures of interdependence that involve multiple actors in order to solve problems or achieve collective goals that cannot be achieved by a single actor. As a result, they represent circumstances in which political or administrative actors must interact with others in order to obtain resources, forge political alliances, and address issues that are larger than the scope of a single actor. In this sense we propose a polycentric and decentralized governance method with a CREC manager who plays a coordinating role and promotes collaborative behaviours. According to [32] the term "polycentric governance" refers to many "formally independent" centres of decision-making that happens in a coherent manner with consistent and predictable patterns of interacting behaviours, to the extent that they take each other into account in competitive relationships, enter into various contractual and cooperative undertakings, or use central mechanisms to resolve conflicts. In this case they may be referred to as operating as a "system". The CREC manager will be responsible for the general administration, decision making regarding collaborative opportunities, resources sharing, value co-creation, incentivization, sharing of risks and rewards and confect resolution etc.

4.3 Various Collaborative Mechanisms of CRECs

Collaboration plays a crucial role in the CREC concept. Collaborative behaviours, techniques and mechanism that can be practiced within this ecosystem are borrowed from the domain of Collaborate Networks. Several partial simulation studies have been conducted in [15, 28, 33] and [34] to assess the feasibility of these collaborative mechanisms. Discussed below are some collaborative mechanisms that these works illustrate, now positioned in a more comprehensive overview.

(a) **Community/Common Goals**: It is proposed that the CREC as an ecosystem should be driven by the notion of common goals. It is further suggested that membership to a CREC should be voluntary and motivated by a set of common goals which could range from sustainability, economic, social, or technological goals. Decision making and collaborative endeavours that are undertaken within the CREC ecosystem shall mostly be based on these common goals. The CREC can have multiple goals and may pursue multiple goals concurrently. The goals of the CRECs can be dynamic and are determined by the CREC manager when an opportunity is found.

(b) **CREC Member Value Systems**: Members of a CREC may have their individual "values systems" which can be used to represent the preferences, priorities, expectations and contributions of each member regarding how they intend to contribute to the mentioned community goals. Members of CRECs can have multiple value systems and this can be ranked in order of priority. The notion of value system can empower members of CRECs to contribute flexibly to community goals.

(c) **Goal Compatibility**: Goal compatibility is a decision-making process where members of a CREC compare their value system(s) with the proposed community goals to ascertain if there is a match or compatibility between their value system(s) and the community goal. Members of a CREC accept invitations to participate in community goals on the grounds that one or more of their values is compatible with the proposed community goal. In the instance of incompatibility between the members value system and the community goals, the invitation is declined.

(d) **Resource Sharing:** Resource sharing is a collaborative attribute that places emphases on sharing or access to underutilized goods and services, which prioritizes efficient utilization and accessibility over ownership. Resource sharing is also an attribute of the sharing economy which promotes sustainability [35]. The fundamental resources that can be shared in the CREC ecosystem may include both physical and virtual energy asset and services. These resources can be shared on a peer-to-peer basis or in a centralised architecture. Sharing resources in the CRECs can enhance cost savings and reduce the waste of resources that is associated with underutilization due to personal ownership.

(e) **Formation of Virtual Organizations (VOs):** In the context of CRECs, the manager identifies a business opportunity on the grid, sends invitations to members of the ecosystem. Members whose value systems are compatible with the goal will accept the invitation. A VO constituting of members with accepted invitations can be formed by the manager to pursue the opportunity. In reality, compatibility of value systems should not be a sufficient condition. It would be also necessary to consider the current context/current preferences of the member. But this was left for later developments.

(f) **Incentives:** Incentive is another attribute of collaboration that is relevant to materializing the CREC concept. An incentive is a crucial component of any collaborative endeavour. It has the ability to persuade a passive member of a community to become an active participant or collaborator based on a promise of some form of reward or acknowledgment. In a CREC ecosystem, participation in collaborative endeavours is rewarded. This is because value is co-created in the ecosystem and the created value is equitably shared amongst the collaborators. The use of incentives in CRECs is intended to increase the willingness of members and motivate them to participate in collaborative endeavours.

(g) **Delegation:** By representing the households within the CRECs with their respective cognitive digital twins, it is possible to delegate on these digital twins the responsibility to act or make some kind of rational or basic decision on behalf of the physical households. Delegation refers to the permission or authority that is given to the digital twin to act on behalf of the physical household. Due to the cognitive intelligence of CREC's digital twins, they can have cognisance of (a) whether they are delegated or not, thus, whether they are permitted to participate in collaborative endeavours or not, (b) the value system of the physical household and, (c) the proposed community goal(s).

(h) **Delegated Autonomy:** This refers to the degree or level of permission that is given to each CREC's digital twin. It constitutes the specific instruction that a household owner may assign to it digital twin to be followed in carrying out its preferences and contribution towards community goals and collaborative endeavours.

(i) **Collective Decision-making:** Collective decision is a situation in which people decide among the options that are available to them. In such cases, the final decision can no longer be attributed to any particular person in the group. This is so that every person can contribute to the final result. In collective decision-making, individual choices and group decisions are in alignment. Collaborative decision-making is one of the most effective processes for gaining support from other stakeholders, establishing consensus, and fostering creativity. In the CREC ecosystem, decisions are made on a collective basis. This enables each member to contribute in one way or another towards the community's goals and objectives.

4.4 Some Selected Simulation Outcomes in Support of the CREC Concept

In this section we briefly discuss some partial outcomes from simulation studies that were conducted in line with the proposed CREC concept. Detail of these works can be found in [15, 28, 33] and [34]. In this section the outcome of two scenario is shown.

Simulation Conditions: The conditions for modelling the considered scenarios are as follow: A CREC population of 100 members, comprising 50% prosumers, and 50% consumers. The simulation is run for seven simulation days. The considered appliances are (a) washing machine, (b) dish washer, and (c) clothes dryer. These appliances are referred to as deferrable loads because their use can be deferred to a later time without affecting the quality of service to the user. A multi-method simulation approach that integrated three simulation techniques (system dynamics, agent base, and discrete event) is adopted. The Anylogic simulation environment was used.

Scenario 1: Resource sharing: In Case 1 (Fig. 3a), resource sharing was disabled. In Case 2 (Fig. 3b), sharing was enabled. For the sharing enabled case, surplus energy from the prosumers is shared with a centralized community storage. Comparing Figs. 3a and 3b, it can be observed that in the case where sharing was disabled, consumption from the grid was about 54% and there was no consumption from the community storage. However, when sharing was enabled, consumption from the grid dropped from 54% to 47%, and consumption from community storage appreciated from 0% to 10%. This shows that without resource sharing, dependence on the grid could be higher within the CREC. This observed outcome is a result of collaborative efforts by the CREC digital twins.

Scenario 2: Here we explore delegation i.e., the permission or authority that is given to a CREC digital twin to act on behalf of the physical household. In Case 1 (Fig. 4a), all the digital twins (100%) are delegated to defer the use of their deferrable loads between the window of opportunity (T1 and T2). The window of opportunity in this case represents an opportunity to contribute to grid management by reducing consumption from the grid during the peak period between T1 and T2. In Case 1, it can be observed that there is absolutely no consumption within the window. Figure 4b represents case 2. In this case, 80% of the population is delegated, 20% are undelegated. It can be observed that there was some consumption within the window. This consumption is a result of the 20% undelegated digital twins.

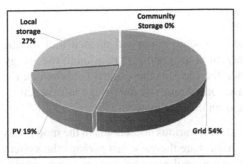
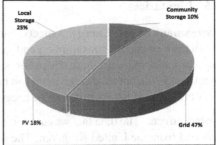

Fig. 3a. Case 1: Sharing disabled   **Fig. 3b.** Case 2: Sharing

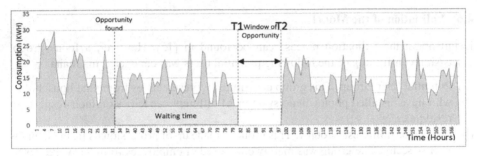

Fig. 4a. Case 1: 100% delegation

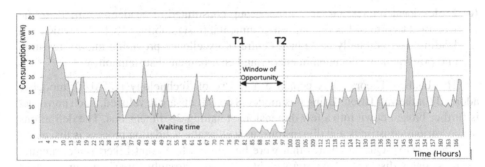

Fig. 4b. Case 2: 80% delegation

This therefore suggests that collaboration between CREC members can have some considerable effect on the power grid and can be considered for grid management services such as demand response.

4.5 Limitations

Assessment of the Energy Aspects: Since Anylogic is not a dedicated tool for the simulation of energy consumption and generation, the results, in relation to the energy aspects may not be accurate. However, since the focus of the work is to show that the mentioned collaborative behaviours can have some impact on the energy infrastructure, the obtained results can however be accepted on these grounds.

Data Source: The data that was used to model the various households in the model was sourced from the United Kingdom. The authors share the view that perhaps the system should also be verified using other data sources since the use-behaviours of households in Ghana for instance may be different from that of the UK.

4.6 Validation of the Model

Detail about the validation process can be found in [15]. However, a focus group discussion constituting of the following potential users was conducted in Ghana.

(a) Potential User Group. This group constituted representatives from nine households who have installed photovoltaic systems of different capacities on their respective residences.
(b) Professional Interest Group 1. This group is made up of professionals from Ghana's energy sector. The group was mainly composed of employees from the Volta River Authority of Ghana (VRA) the Electricity Company of Ghana (ECG), and the Bui Power Authority
(c) Professional Interest Group 2. This group constituted of academic staff from the Regional Centre of Energy and Environmental Sustainability (RCEES), which is a leading internationally accredited centre of excellence providing quality research and postgraduate education in energy and environmental sustainability.

The Unified Theory of Acceptance and Use of Technology (UTAUT) model is adopted for the validation. Using this model, 8 constructs are developed. Each construct is further broken down into a few dimensions, totalling 28 dimensions. The definitions of the various constructs and dimensions, as well as the validation process is discussed in detail in [15]. Questionnaires that were based on a five-point Likert scale, ranging from "strongly disagree", having a weight of "1" to "strongly agree" having a weight of "5" is administered. Data from 31 respondents is collected and used for the analysis. The outcome of the validation process is show in Table 2.

The general conclusion from this validation is that the respondents agreed to all the 8 construct and 28 dimensions of the Model. This can be interpreted as a unanimous acceptance to the fact that the developed model, that was demonstrated to them is fit for its intended purpose, despite the identified limitations.

Table 2. Results of the validation process

Construct	Dimensions	Average score (Based on 31 respondents)	Concluding Remarks (Based on the Likert scale)
PE:	PE1	4.55	Strongly agree
	PE2	4.48	Agree
	PE3	4.45	Agree
	PE4	4.26	Agree
EE:	EE1	4.29	Agree
	EE2	4.32	Agree
	EE3	4.39	Agree
	EE4	4.26	Agree
SI	SI1	4.03	Agree
	SI2	3.97	Agree
	SI3	4.16	Agree
FC	FC1	4.48	Agree
	FC2	4.10	Agree
	FC3	4.58	Strongly Agree
	FC4	4.13	Agree
	FC5	4.39	Agree
UI:	UI1	4.58	Strongly Agree
	UI2	4.55	Strongly Agree
	UI3	4.48	Agree
GA:	GA1	4.52	Strongly Agree
	GA2	4.32	Agree
	GA3	4.16	Agree
Co:	Co1	4.23	Agree
	Co2	4.35	Agree
	Co3	4.26	Agree
DG:	Dg1	4.23	Agree
	Dg2	4.35	Agree
	Dg3	4.35	Agree

5 Potential Use Cases of CRECs

Grid Management - Demand Response. In this context the CREC manager can aggre-gate resources within the community to be used in support of grid management activi-ties. For instance, deferrable loads can be utilized to achieve this purpose. In the CREC ecosystem, the manager could ensure a collective deferral of these loads to ensure that consumption within the ecosystem is significantly minimized. By adopting the concept of CRECs, several grid management techniques as shown in Sect. 4 can be achieved. For instance, a grid management VO can be formed to provide ancillary services, such as helping to shift loads from peak periods to off-peak periods using the concepts of "delegated autonomy" and "value system" compatibility. Similarly, a VO can be formed with the objective of minimizing consumption from the grid by ensuring that deferrable loads are delegated to make maximum use of renewable energy sources when available. Additionally, the ecosystem could use the VO formation techniques to aggregate and export surplus energy from within the community to the grid, particularly when the ecosystem generates surplus renewable energy. This could be accomplished through a collaboration effort between the CVPP-E manager, a distribution service operator, the energy market, and the CREC digital twin themselves.

Disaster Response Management. For example, if a disruptive event or catastrophic failure occurs anywhere inside or outside of the ecosystem, several potential Emergency Virtual Organizations (EVO) can be formed to assist emergency response teams in planning and carrying out the necessary disaster response/recovery operations. In such circumstances, the CREC digital twins can collect valuable data regarding the extent to which the different physical households have been impacted by the disaster. Such data from CREC digital twins can be used to assess the general impact of the disruptive event on the entire community. From the collected data, the response team can develop the most effective rescue plan. Similarly, an ad-hoc EVO can also be formed in such circumstances to aggregate energy that can be used to support critical infrastructures or parts of the community that are in dire or critical need of energy. Additionally, with their cognitive intelligence and decision-making capabilities, CREC digital twins can take autonomous decisions, such as isolating the physical household that are considered to be vulnerable or susceptible to cascading failures from the grid to avoid further damage or catastrophe.

Real World Implementations. In the current stage of the work, only simulation-based developments were performed. For a real-world implementation, the following strategy is devised:

(a) Identification and Selection of Suitable Sensors and Actuators: Although the market is saturated with many of these devices, some preliminary studies need to be conducted to identify the most suitable and compatible units. Additionally, smart appliances will also be explored to determine how their integrated smart capabilities can be utilized in this sense.

(b) Digital Twin Service Provider: The service of a suitable "digital twin as a service provider" needs to be identified, assessed, and procured. This provider may be expected to provide the digital twin environment (DTE) to host the digital twins. Further assessment needs to be carried out to determine if the implementation of intelligent and collaborative algorithms can be supported in their DTEs. Some service providers that have already been identified include: Ansis Twin Builder, Bosch IoT suit, IBMs Digital Twin Builder, and Azure Digital Twins.

(c) Other smart home portals that are currently available may also be explored to determine if they could provide DTE services. Some portals that have already been identified include: openHAB, Home Assist, ioBroker, Ago Control, OpenMotics, and Domoticz.

(d) After completing the first 3 milestones, thus steps (a), (b), and (c) a prototype CREC constituting a few households will be developed. This prototype will be used for further studies to advance these ideas.

After the prototype implementation, other collaborative scenarios, such as disaster management, as well as other collaborative behaviours like value co-creation and the sharing of rewards, would be further explored. Furthermore, it would be relevant to consider the development of a governance framework as well as the detailed architecture of the CREC ecosystem.

6 Conclusion

The objective of this article is three-fold: (a) to provide a brief description of RECs, (b) introduce the CREC concept as an emerging case of RECs, and (c) describe some possible use cases of the CREC concept. The key highlight of the paper is the introduction of the CREC concept, and the partial demonstration of the feasibility of the concept. Although the authors acknowledge that these ideas are still in the developmental stage and that several studies are needed to advance the concepts, we share the opinion that these concepts are feasible and may have the potential to improve the way RECs are organized and how they function. The CREC idea can also introduce efficiency into the management of RECs and the grid, as human interference and decision making can be reduced. It is foreseen that through the technique of "delegation" certain daily and mundane tasks can be delegated to CREC digital twins to be performed on behalf of their users. Such unexciting activities may involve daily decisions, preferences, and changes in consumer behaviour towards sustainable energy use. Furthermore, the notion of value system can enable consumer to flexible contribute to sustainability endeavours without affecting their expected quality of service.

Acknowledgments. The authors acknowledge the Portuguese FCT program UIDB/00066/2020 and UIDP/00066/2020 for providing financial support for this work. The University of Energy and Natural Resources and UNINOVA-CTS are hereby acknowledged for supporting this work with their research facilities and resources.

References

1. Hanke, F., Guyet, R., Feenstra, M.: Do renewable energy communities deliver energy justice? Exploring insights from 71 European cases. Energy Res. Soc. Sci. **80**, no. August, 102244 (2021). https://doi.org/10.1016/j.erss.2021.102244
2. Interreg Europe: Empowering Citizens for Energy Communities: A Policy Brief from the Policy Learning Platform on Low Carbon Economy, no. November, pp. 1–24 (2022)

3. Tarpani, E., et al.: Energy communities implementation in the european union: case studies from pioneer and laggard countries. Sustainability **14**(19), 12528 (2022). https://doi.org/10.3390/su141912528
4. The European Union: Directive (EU) 2018/2001 of the European Parliament and of the Council of 11 December 2018 on the promotion of the use of energy from renewable Sources. Off. J. Eur. Union **82**(L 328), 82–209 (2018)
5. Lennon, B., Velasco-Herrejón, P., Dunphy, N.P.: Operationalizing participation: Key obstacles and drivers to citizen energy community formation in Europe's energy transition. Sci. Talks **5**(Nov 2022), 100104 (2023). https://doi.org/10.1016/j.sctalk.2022.100104
6. REScoop.EU. Q&A: What are 'citizen' and 'renewable' energy communities? (2019). https://www.rescoop.eu/uploads/rescoop/downloads/QA-What-are-citizens-energy-communities-renewable-energy-communities-in-the-CEP.pdf. Accessed 03 Apr 2023
7. Boles, S., Cornwell, J., Rob Del Mar, Reichers, J., Schultz, A.: Study on small- scale and community-based renewable. Oregon Dep. Energy 1–48 (2022)
8. Eitan, A., Fischhendler, I.: The architecture of inter-community partnerships in renewable energy: the role of climate intermediaries. Policy Stud. 1–17 (2022). https://doi.org/10.1080/01442872.2022.2138307
9. Jackson County Green Energy Park. Jackson County Green Energy Park – Renewable Energy From Landfill Methane Gas – Dillsboro NC. https://www.jcgep.org/. Accessed 06 Mar 2023
10. Bringault, A., Eisermann, M., Lacassagne, S., Fauchadour, N.: Cities heading towards 100% renewable energy by controlling their consumption Food for thought and action, France (2016). https://energy-cities.eu/wp-content/uploads/2018/11/publi_100pourcent_final-web_en.pdf. Accessed 03 Apr 2023
11. Empowerment, G.: Green Empowerment | Village Solutions for Global Change (2022). https://greenempowerment.org/. Accessed 06 Mar 2023
12. Ta'u, A.S.: American Samoa Island Community Microgrid - Clean Energy Group (2022). https://www.cleanegroup.org/ceg-projects/resilient-power-project/featured-installations/american-samoa-microgrid/. Accessed 06 Mar 2023
13. Judson, E., Fitch-Roy, O., Soutar, I.: Energy democracy: a digital future? Energy Res. Soc. Sci. **91**(February), 102732 (2022). https://doi.org/10.1016/j.erss.2022.102732
14. Adu-Kankam, K.O., Camarinha-Matos, L.M.: Towards collaborative Virtual Power Plants: trends and convergence. Sustain. Energy, Grids Networks **16**, 217–230 (2018). https://doi.org/10.1016/j.segan.2018.08.003
15. Adu-Kankam, K.O., Camarinha-Matos, L.M.: Modeling collaborative behaviors in energy ecosystems. Computers **12**(2), 39 (2023). https://doi.org/10.3390/computers12020039
16. Sovacool, B.K., Burke, M., Baker, L., Kotikalapudi, C.K., Wlokas, H.: New frontiers and conceptual frameworks for energy justice. Energy Policy **105**, 677–691 (2017). https://doi.org/10.1016/j.enpol.2017.03.005
17. Donaghy, T., Jiang, C.: Fossil fuel racism: how phasing out oil, gas, and coal can protect communities. Greenpeace, pp. 1–46 (2021)
18. Chaichana, C., Wongsapai, W., Damrongsak, D., Ishihara, K.N., Luangchosiri, N.: Promoting community renewable energy as a tool for sustainable development in rural areas of Thailand. Energy Procedia **141**, 114–118 (2017). https://doi.org/10.1016/j.egypro.2017.11.022
19. In focus: Energy communities to transform the EU's energy system. https://energy.ec.europa.eu/news/focus-energy-communities-transform-eus-energy-system-2022-12-13_en. Accessed 20 Mar 2023
20. Roberts, M.B., Sharma, A., MacGill, I.: Efficient, effective and fair allocation of costs and benefits in residential energy communities deploying shared photovoltaics. Appl. Energy **305**, 117935 (2022). https://doi.org/10.1016/j.apenergy.2021.117935

21. IRENA. Community-ownership Models. Innovation landscape brief 2020, Innovation Landscape Brief. Abu Dhabi. https://www.irena.org//media/Files/IRENA/Agency/Publication/2020/Jul/IRENA_Community_ownership. Accessed 03 Apr 2023
22. van Bommel, N., Höffken, J.I.: Energy justice within, between and beyond European community energy initiatives: a review. Energy Res. Soc. Sci. **79**(2020), 102157 (2021). https://doi.org/10.1016/j.erss.2021.102157
23. Mayer, A., Smith, E.K.: Exploring the link between energy security and subjective well-being: a study of 22 nations. Energy Sustain. Soc. **9**(1), 1–13 (2019). https://doi.org/10.1186/s13705-019-0216-1
24. Interreg Europe, "Renewable Energy Communities, A Policy Brief from the Policy Learning Platform on Low-carbon economy (2018). https://www.interregeurope.eu/sites/default/files/inline/20180830_Policy_brief_Renewable_Energy_Communities_PB_TO4_final.pdf. Accessed 03 Apr 2023
25. Friends of the Earth-Europe, Barriers and Threats to the People-Owned Energy Revolution Barriers to Community Ownership Covered Below (2021). https://friendsoftheearth.eu/wpcontent/uploads/2021/05/FOEE_barriers_and_threats.pdf. Accessed 03 Apr 2023
26. European Commission: State of the Energy Union 2021 – Contributing to the European Green Deal and the Union's recovery, no. COM (2021) 950 final. European Commission, Brussels. https://www.ffms.pt/sites/default/files/2022-07/state_of_the_energy_union_report_2021.pdf. Accessed 03 Apr 2023
27. Adu-Kankam, K.O., Camarinha-Matos, L.M.: Emerging community energy ecosystems: analysis of organizational and governance structures of selected representative cases. In: Camarinha-Matos, L.M., Almeida, R., Oliveira, J. (eds.) DoCEIS 2019. IAICT, vol. 553, pp. 24–40. Springer, Cham (2019). https://doi.org/10.1007/978-3-030-17771-3_3
28. Adu-Kankam, K.O., Camarinha-Matos, L.M.: Modelling 'Delegated Autonomy' in cognitive household digital twins. In: 2022 11th International Conference on Renewable Energy Research and Application (ICRERA), pp. 192–199 (2022). https://doi.org/10.1109/ICRERA55966.2022.9922673
29. Camarinha-Matos, L.M., Afsarmanesh, H.: Classes of collaborative networks. In: Putnik, G.D., Cunha, M.M. (eds.) Encyclopedia of Networked and Virtual Organizations, vol. 1, pp. 106–111. IGI Global (2008)
30. Melesse, T.Y., Di Pasquale, V., Riemma, S.: Digital Twin models in industrial operations: state-of-the-art and future research directions. IET Collab. Intell. Manuf. **3**(1), 37–47 (2021). https://doi.org/10.1049/cim2.12010
31. Bryson, J.M., Crosby, B.C., Stone, M.M.: Designing and implementing cross-sector collaborations: needed and challenging. Public Adm. Rev. **75**, 647–663 (2015). https://doi.org/10.1111/puar.12432.Designing
32. Ostrom, E.: Beyond markets and states: polycentric governance of complex economic systems. Am. Econ. Assoc. **100**(3), 641–672 (2010)
33. Adu-Kankam, K.O., Camarinha-matos, L.: Delegating autonomy on digital twins in energy ecosystems. Int. J. SMART GRID **6**(4) (2022). https://doi.org/10.20508/ijsmartgrid.v6i4.257.g253
34. Adu-Kankam, K.O., Camarinha-Matos, L.M.: Modelling "Cognitive Households Digital Twins" in an energy community. In: Bendaoud, M., Wolfgang, B., Chikh, K. (eds.) ICESA 2021, pp. 67–79. Springer, Singapore (2022). https://doi.org/10.1007/978-981-19-0039-6_6
35. Stanoevska-Slabeva, K., Lenz-Kesekamp, V., Suter, V.: Platforms and the Sharing Economy: An Analysis. Report from the EU H2020 Research Project Ps2Share: Participation, Privacy, and Power in the Sharing Economy (2017). https://www.bi.edu/globalassets/forskning/h2020/ps2share_platform-analysis-paper_final.pdf. Accessed 11 Feb 2022

Storage System for Energy Communities

Adriana Mar[(✉)], Pedro Pereira, and João Martins

NOVA School of Science and Technology, Center of Technology and Systems (UNINOVA-CTS)
and Associated Lab of Intelligent Systems (LASI), NOVA University Lisbon, Caparica, Portugal
`am.jesus@campus.fct.unl.pt`

Abstract. Energy communities play a critical role as stakeholders in modern
power grids. However, operating such communities can be challenging due to the
complexities, uncertainties, and conflicting objectives involved. The purpose of
this paper is to showcase how the integration of a storage system into an energy
community can contribute to maintaining the well-being of each community member during grid faults. The study models two distinct energy communities, taking
into account non-controllable and controllable devices in each home as sources of
consumption and power supply sources such as PV systems installed in community
homes, as well as power from the main grid or storage system.

Keywords: Energy Community · Storage Systems · Genetic Algorithms ·
Energy Efficiency

1 Introduction

This paper aims to study the energy storage systems applied to the Energy Community
concept in order to make this reality more reliable together with the use of renewable
energy production, in this case, Photovoltaic systems.

Also, thinking in nearly Zero Energy Buildings (nZEB) or Net Zero Energy Buildings
(NZEB), one of the possibilities to use the produced energy that it is not used at the
moment is to store it and use it later. Considering this, it is important the study of this
type of systems to know which one is better for each case, either to apply on a building
or to use on an Energy Community.

1.1 Energy Community

Energy Communities (EnC), mostly microgrid based, are considered to be a key stake-
holder of modern electrical power grids. Operating a microgrid based EnC is a challenging topic due to the involved uncertainties, complexities and often conflicting objectives.
Furthermore, as any other grid, they are also subject to operating faults. In order to
improve their resilience, EnC flexibility can provide enhance support to the community
as a whole.

© IFIP International Federation for Information Processing 2023
Published by Springer Nature Switzerland AG 2023
L. M. Camarinha-Matos and F. Ferrada (Eds.): DoCEIS 2023, IFIP AICT 678, pp. 38–51, 2023.
https://doi.org/10.1007/978-3-031-36007-7_3

The European Commission defines EnC as groups consisting of citizens, Individuals and entities, including social entrepreneurs, public authorities, and community organizations, who play an active role in the generation, trade, distribution, and consumption of sustainable energy [1, 2]. Moreover, with the advancement and wider accessibility of renewable energy, citizens have emerged as significant contributors to the energy system, known as prosumers. Typically, a community comprises individuals who share something in common and can actively participate in energy production or consumption as users. As renewable energy issues have become more widespread and accessible, citizens are now recognized as active players in the system and are referred to as prosumers. Essentially, a community is a social group that shares something in common, with a group of users who can actively participate in either energy consumption or production [3, 4].

EnCs are created by integrating energy conversion, transmission, and consumption at a community level. Within the energy context, EnCs can address various relevant issues, such as balancing energy flow, decreasing peak load during high-demand periods, implementing territorial energy planning, connecting different energy sources, and mitigating environmental impacts. [5]. On the other hand, when a fault occurs in an Electrical Power Grid (EPG), a power decrease or a power outage can occur, EnC can be a solution not only to maintain the power supply inside the community as well as to improve the resilience of EPG as an all. This can be achieved considering the energy flexibility of each house as well as of the entire community. The concept of energy flexibility consists on the energy management of appliances of each house inside the EnC in order to change their working time to balance the power, due to a decrease of power.

In this work, the term Energy Community refers to a group of users interconnected by the Low Voltage (LV) grid, as it is possible to observe in Fig. 1. On an EnC, besides the possibility of storage devices, each house can have renewable energy production as well as electrical devices that are possible to control. Instead of using the production for their own consumption, the user can storage and share it with the EnC in order to be used when it's necessary. On the other hand, considering some consumption devices' energy flexibility, it is possible to manage the community's energy to improve the LV grid resilience when a change occurs in the main grid.

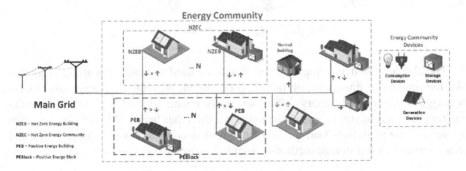

Fig. 1. Energy community scheme.

The literature identifies various types of energy communities. Some include Net Zero Energy Buildings (NZEBs) [6]; Positive Energy Buildings (PEBs) [7]; individual homes equipped with controllable devices and renewable energy production capabilities, which are grouped together within a community to leverage their collective flexibility. [8]; prosumers; or even plain consumers [9].

As technology and solutions for NZEBs continue to evolve, the concept has progressed to Positive Energy Buildings (PEBs). A building is deemed a PEB if its exported energy during a defined period (usually a year) is greater than its imported energy [10]. Additionally, as shown in Fig. 1 a group of buildings that actively manage their energy consumption and flow, maintain a positive annual energy balance, and interact with the larger energy system are known as Positive Energy Blocks (PEBlocks) or Positive Energy Districts (PEDs) [11–14].

1.2 Energy Storage Systems

Energy storage consists on a process of converting electrical energy into different forms of energy that can be stored for converting again into electrical energy when necessary. There are many different storage technologies which can be catalogue in different ways, such as the type of storage (mechanical, electromechanical, electrical, chemical or thermal), the storage duration (short-term or long-term storage), capital cost, capacity, efficiency or environmental impact [15]. In this paper, following the literature review, the technologies will be categorized into storage types, as shown in Fig. 2.

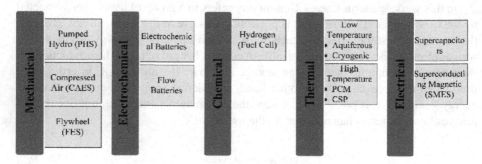

Fig. 2. Energy storage technologies

The choice of which storage method should be used depends on a group of factors like the amount of energy or the power to be stored, the time of storage (short-term or long-term), portability, energy efficiency, costs among others. Flywheels or supercapacitors are used in short-term applications, on the other hand CAES or flux batteries are suitable for peak-hour load leveling when high energy storage is required. Different characteristics of the storage methods presented above are compered in Table 1.

Table 1. Comparison of technical characteristics of energy storage systems.

		Efficiency	Response Time	Power Capacity	Lifetime	Discharge time	Capital Cost
Mechanical Batteries	PHS [16–22]	65–85%	<1 min	100–10000 MW	30–60 years	Hours - days	500–4600 $/kW
	CAES [23–25]	70–80%	Sec - min	100–300 MW	~40 years	Hours - days	400–800 $/kW
	FES [22, 26–30]	90–95%	Very fast (<ms)	<250 kW	15–20 years	seconds	100–350 €/kW
Electrochemical Batteries	Lead Acid	60–78%	<5 ms	0–20 MW	3–15 years	Seconds - hours	300–600 $/kW
	Lithium ion	85–97%	<5 ms	0.1–50 MW	5–15 years	Minutes - hours	1200–4000 $/kW
	Sodium-based	75 – 90%	<5 ms	0.05–10 MW	10–15 years	Seconds - hours	1000–3000 $/ kW
	Nickel-based	60–70%	<5 ms	0–40 MW	10–20 years	Seconds - hours	500–1500 $/kW
Flow Batteries	Redox Flow	75–85%	<5 ms	0.3–15 MW	5–20 years	Seconds – 10 h	600–1500 $/kW
	Hybrid Flow	60–80%	<5 ms	0.05–10 MW	5–20 years	Seconds – 10 h	400–2500 $/kW
Chemical Batteries Hydrogen Fuel Cell		20–50%	<5ms	0.001–50 MW	5–20 years	Minutes - hours	500–10k $/kW

1.3 Community Energy Storage Systems

Storage devices are suitable to absorb surplus generation to periods where demand is higher than the available power. Community energy storage (CES) systems are getting more attention as a suitable solution of innovation for sustainable energy transition. For Parra et. al, a CES is located on the consumption level, given a positive impact to end users and network operator [31]. More focused on community engagement, Van der Stelt, mentioned CES as a system located on the consumption level but with the capability to perform multiple applications in order to manage demand and supply, having positive impacts for both, consumers and DSOs [32]. Also, for Van Oost Koirala, CES is defined as *" an energy storage system with community ownership and governance for generating collective socio-economic benefits such as higher penetration and self-consumption of renewables"* [33]. Koirala also refers that CES systems will reduce dependence on fossil fuels, energy bills and increase local economy. Moreover, Barbour and Parra concluded that CES is a more effective system than residential energy storage and presents benefits from the economic point of view, reducing the life-cycle cost of energy storage by 37%

when compared the use of CES with individual household application [34, 35]. Koirala, [33], presented different CES configurations that are described below:

- **Shared residential energy storage (SRES)**: In this configuration each user can have his own energy storage, up to 20kWh, in their own premises and the energy can be shared among the community users, using the local physical grid.
- **Shared local energy storage (SLES)**: The local configuration energy storage as a capacity of tens to hundreds of kWh and it is installed in the local neighborhood, is shared by physical grid and has community ownership. This type of CES configuration provides multiple benefits namely higher flexibility and energy security.
- **Shared virtual energy storage (SVES)**: this type of community is different from the other two mentioned since this is a virtual community, i.e., the energy storage is installed at different locations, inside or outside of EnC, and have independent ownership and governance. The energy storage is aggregated and virtually shared through the main grid considering the market design and regulations.

1.4 Storage Systems for Energy Community Connected with Cyber Physical Spaces

A connected cyber-physical space refers to a network of devices, systems, and spaces that are interconnected and can communicate with each other. These spaces can include buildings, transportation systems, and energy systems. By connecting these spaces, we can create an intelligent and responsive energy ecosystem that optimizes energy usage and reduces waste.

A storage system for an energy community is an important component of this ecosystem. It can help to balance the supply and demand of energy within the community by storing excess energy during times of low demand and releasing it during times of high demand. This can help to reduce the need for energy from external sources, which can be expensive and environmentally harmful.

When integrated with connected cyber-physical spaces, a storage system can become even more effective. For example, sensors within buildings can communicate with the storage system to determine when energy demand is highest and when it is lowest. The storage system can then release energy during times of high demand to help reduce strain on the grid and save energy costs. Additionally, electric vehicles can be charged using energy from the storage system, which can help to further reduce demand from external sources.

2   Storage System for Energy Community

This chapter presents the introduction of a storage system on an Energy community as well as the use of Genetic Algorithm to improve the usage of renewable energy during the day.

2.1   Energy Community Description

For the sake of simplicity, in Fig. 1 Energy community scheme.a general Energy Community (EnC) is depicted, comprising **N** dwellings that are equipped with controllable household electrical devices. Among these dwellings, **n** have renewable energy supply equipment in the form of PV systems, while **y** has storage systems. The EnC modeling framework can be divided into three layers: the physical layer, the modeling layer, and the device layer. The physical layer provides a comprehensive description of the community, including the number of houses and occupants, as well as the equipment (i.e., appliances), storage, and supply infrastructure for each home.

The modeling layer is responsible for parameterizing all data collected from the physical layer and modeling the renewable energy sources, storage devices, and household appliances. Finally, the device layer controls the EnC system and its flexibility. The demand, storage, and supply of each residence, as well as the entire EnC, are managed through the device layer. These three layers are illustrated in Fig. 3.

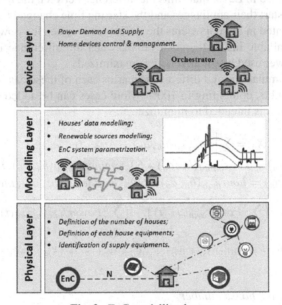

Fig. 3. EnC modelling layers.

The framework of this EnC takes into account a 24-h active power chart that includes both demand and generation, as described by Eqs. (1) and (2) respectively. In these equations, (d) represents demand power and (g) represents generated power.

$$d^N \equiv \left[d^N(1) \cdots d^N(t) \right], t \in [0 - 24] \tag{1}$$

$$g^N \equiv \left[g^N(1) \cdots g^N(t) \right], t \in [0 - 24] \tag{2}$$

N denotes the number of the considered EnC houses and t the time.

The community's total demand (T_d) and PV total generation (T_g) are given by Eqs. (3) and (4), respectively.

$$T_d = \sum_{i=1}^{N}(d(i)) \tag{3}$$

$$T_g = \sum_{i=1}^{N} (g(i)) \tag{4}$$

In the device layer, the supply and demand load of each house within the community, as well as the overall EnC, will be managed, taking into account their flexibility.

2.2 Genetic Algorithms Applied to Energy Community Flexibility

The cost function, presented in Eq. 7 will minimize a combination of n considerations. In this specific case will minimize the combination between two cases:

$1 - X_A$, formulated in Eq. 5, that sums the difference between the initial time chosen by house users to start their appliances and the starting time changed by the algorithm.

$2 - X_B$, formulated in Eq. 6, presents the difference between the power consumption and the power available inside the solar curve, when the difference is minimized, it means that the power used by photovoltaic is maximized.

For different simulations and different scenarios each of these cases, X_A and X_B will have different weights, combining in 100%. More cases can be added to cost function depending on what it is intended to minimize.

$$\left\{ \begin{array}{l} X_A = \sum \left| Ap_{initial}(h_n, a_n) - Ap_{final}(h_n, a_n) \right| \\ Ap_{initial}(h_n, a_n) = hour_{initial}(h_n, a_n) * 60 + minute_{initial}(h_n, a_n), in\, minutes \\ Ap_{final}(h_n, a_n) = hour_{final}(h_n, a_n) * 60 + minute_{final}(h_n, a_n), in\, minutes \end{array} \right. \tag{5}$$

$$X_B = \left| \left(\sum Power_{available}(t) \right) - \left(\sum Power_{consumption}(t) \right) \right| \tag{6}$$

$$f_{cost} = \min((X_A * w_a) + (X_B * w_b) \cdots + (X_n * w_n)) \tag{7}$$

Considering:

h_n – represents the house number

a_n – represents appliance number

t – represents solar window, $t \in$ [10 am;6pm]

$w_a, w_b, \ldots, w_n$ represents the weight of each category (%)

For the simulation of this work two combinations of weights were considered:

$$f_{cost1} = \min((X_A * 80\%) + (X_B * 20\%))$$

$$f_{cost2} = \min((X_A * 30\%) + (X_B * 70\%))$$

This will allow to understand different behaviors on the energy community regarding the energy flexibility and the use of photovoltaic system considering the wellbeing of the users.

3 Simulation

For this work, was considered one energy community for simulation with thirteen houses, consumption devices, PV system with the characteristics presented in Table 2 and storage system inside the community.

Taking into account the system, to test different possibilities for the community level, is considered two scenarios with two distinct weights:

Scenario I a) – in this scenario the PV generation is the only available power inside the community as well as the storage energy and is considered f_{cost1}.

Scenario I b) – in this scenario the PV generation is the only available power inside the community as well as the storage energy and is considered f_{cost2}.

Table 2. PV model & Inverter parameters used for the reference system with 4kWp.

	Parameters	Value	Unit
PV	A	1,60	m^2
	P_{MPPT}	285	W_p
	$T_{c,NOCT}$	46	°C
	G_{NOCT}	800	Wm^{-2}
	α	−0.003	$°C^{-1}$
	$T_{a,NOCT}$	20	°C
	$T_{c,STC}$	25	°C
	P_p	4000	W
Sunny Tripower 4.0 Inverter	η_{inv}	97.1	%
	P_{AC}	4000	W

Initially, the algorithm characterizes the load and production balance of each house and the EnC by utilizing the available information. This includes considering the type of fault scenario that may occur and incorporating user input regarding power consumption, along with the available power production. After that, the genetic algorithm runs in order to find the best solution taking into consideration the population size among other definitions of the algorithm.

To support the simulations presented in this work, ambient temperature data (T_amb) and solar radiation (G) data were acquired from the photovoltaic geographical information system (PVGIS). The data was collected with a 15-min resolution and the location point used was the NOVA School of Science and Technology (38o 39′ 36″ N/9o 12′ 11″ W). Regarding household devices, the noncontrollable devices' load is based on Richardson's model [36], that considers if it is a week or weekend day and the number of people living in the dwelling. Since noncontrollable devices are used, the load for each house is considered static. Meanwhile, only event-based controllable devices were used for this study, and their characteristics are presented in Table 3. For simplicity, a maximum of three appliances were assumed to be operational per day, specifically a washing machine, dryer machine, and dishwasher. Users can select the starting time (hour:minute) and indicate if the house has a functioning PV panel using a dedicated application interface.

Table 3. Electrical appliance considered for this work.

Appliance	Cycle duration [min]	Mean cycle power [W]	Standby power [W]	Controllable
Lights	Usage Dependent	Usage Dependent	0	No
Washing Machine [House 1; House 2; House 3]	137	401	1	Yes
Dryer Machine [House 1; House 2; House 3]	59	[1900; 2333; 2000]	1	Yes
Dishwasher [House 1; House 2; House 3]	59	[2000; 1859; 2150]	0	Yes

3.1   Scenario I – Total Cutoff from Main Grid, Community 1

This energy community consists of thirteen houses, seven of which have PV system. The community also has an energy storage system with a maximum power of 3kW. For this scenario, the initial working hours considered for simulation are presented on Fig. 4 as well as the houses with and without PV system.

On Fig. 4 it is possible to analyze the total house load consumption for community taking into account appliances initial working hours, as well as the total PV load for this community. Regardless the appliances considered, the consumption load also contains lights load during all day that is on or off and it is not considered for the GA optimization.

Considering Fig. 4, it is possible to understand that a considerable quantity of solar energy is wasted since the appliances are working out of the solar hours. On Fig. 5, genetic algorithm is used for optimization considering f_{cost1}.

Analysing Fig. 5 and Table 4 it is possible to understand that all of the appliances were moved to a starting hour inside of the solar hours window and only the lights remained turned on night hours. It is also possible to discuss that an anergy storage with 3kW it is not enough for a thirteen houses energy community since at 6pm it is possible to see that battery is fully charged and it is not capable to maintain lights on for the entire period.

Considering Fig. 6, together with Table 4, it is possible to understand that considering f_{cost2}, the appliances were all moved in for working times inside solar window time as in scenario I a) of community, but as expected the total difference of minutes from the initial time working for the appliances is bigger than in scenario I a) since the X_A factor have a lower weight on cost function.

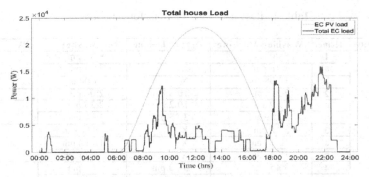

Fig. 4. Total house load for energy community.

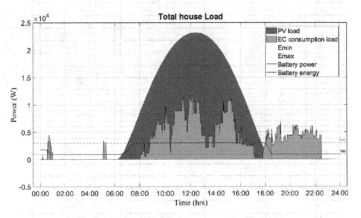

Fig. 5. Total house load after Genetic Algorithm, scenario I a).

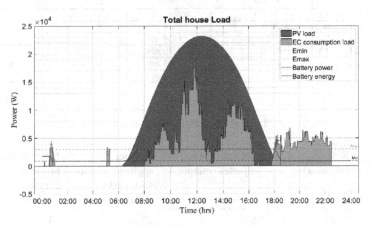

Fig. 6. Total house load after Genetic Algorithm, scenario I b).

Table 4. Resume of GA solutions for community.

Community	Home	Washing Machine	Dryer Machine	Dishwasher	PV
1	1	8:00 am	X	9:30 pm	
	a)	1:48 pm	X	4:03 pm	√
	b)	10:08 am	X	11:04 am	
	2	8:30 am	10:30 am	2:00 pm	√
	a)	9:39 am	10:28 am	2:36 pm	
	b)	10:39 am	3:25 pm	3:14 pm	
	3	3:15 pm	X	10:00 pm	
	a)	10:19 am	X	12:12 pm	√
	b)	10:37 am	X	11:44 am	
	4	3:45 pm	5:30 pm	6:00 pm	
	a)	1:47 pm	10:43 am	11:41 am	X
	b)	2:09 pm	11:24 am	11:10 am	
	5	6:00 pm	8:00 pm	9:30 pm	
	a)	3:39 pm	11:53 am	11:44 am	√
	b)	12:08 am	10:19 am	1:35 pm	
	6	7:00 am	X	9:30 pm	
	a)	9:53 am	X	10:33 am	X
	b)	2:31 pm	X	10:52 am	
	7	6:30 am	X	2:30 pm	
	a)	2:08 pm	X	1:28 pm	√
	b)	10:36 am	X	10:57 am	
	8	7:00 pm	X	X	
	a)	11:41 am	X	X	X
	b)	1:39 pm	X	X	
	9	9:00 am	X	9:00 pm	
	a)	2:10 pm	X	2:27 pm	√
	b)	11:37 am	X	2:31 pm	
	10	6:00 pm	X	1:30 pm	
	a)	9: 52 am	X	11:19 am	X
	b)	1:10 pm	X	2:11 pm	
	11	10:00 am	12:00 pm	8:30 pm	
	a)	1:17 pm	2:32 pm	2:38 pm	√
	b)	1:55 pm	3:08 pm	2:38 pm	
	12	7:00 pm	9:00 pm	X	
	a)	3:26 pm	12:28 pm	X	√
	b)	12:37 pm	11:24 am	X	
	13	9:00 am	11:30 am	X	
	a)	2:49 pm	10:43 am	X	X
	b)	11:51 am	2:20 pm	X	

Table 5. Simulations' summary

Scenario		Simulation Time (minutes)	Total difference of minutes (minutes)	Number of appliances inside solar curve (10 am – 6 pm)	Number of Houses inside the community
I	a)	182	8718	29/29	13
	b)	383	9247	29/29	

4 Conclusions

Regarding the results obtained and showed on Sect. 4, it is concluded that for the use of an energy community completely disconnected from the main grid, an energy storage system is needed since some of the appliances can be moved and optimized for the solar time window but others cannot so it is important to have an appropriate ESS for the community not only to storage the unused energy produced by PV system but also to maintain the EnC working during night time.

For this specific study, it is possible to conclude that ESS was not enough to fulfill the necessities of the community since from community 1 a lot of produced energy was wasted. Also, on community 2 in spite of being a smaller one, the ESS it is not enough to fulfill the necessities from 8pm onwards.

To analyze the different scenarios, 3 metrics were considered, and are presented on Table 5:

- Simulation Time;
- Total difference of minutes (in minutes) from the initial working time for the final working time changed by the GA;
- Number of appliances inside solar curve.

Considering both factors, X_A and X_B, it is possible to affirm that both scenarios meet the metrics. For scenario I a) where the weight was higher for the minimization of total difference time from the initial working time of the appliances for the final working time. As it is possible to analyze on Table 5, for scenario I a) of community 1 the time was 8718 min versus 92447 min for scenario I b) of community 1. Regarding the number of appliances working inside of solar time window both scenarios presented the total number of appliances, 29, working on the solar time window.

With these simulations was possible to understand that houses energy flexibility can be used not only to maintain the users' wellbeing when a fault occurs or it is necessary to change the energy flow, but also to consider better energy price markets, to improve the resilience of the grid, or even to consider the connection of electrical vehicles to community's grid.

Acknowledgments. This research was funded by the Portuguese FCT program, Center of Technology and Systems (CTS) UIDB/00066/2020 / UIDP/00066/2020.

References

1. Azarova, V., Cohen, J., Friedl, C., Reichl, J.: Designing local renewable energy communities to increase social acceptance: evidence from a choice experiment in Austria, Germany, Italy, and Switzerland. Energy Policy **132**, 1176–1183 (2019). https://doi.org/10.1016/J.ENPOL.2019.06.067
2. Cohen, J., Moeltner, K., Reichl, A., Schmidthaler, M.: An empirical analysis of local opposition to new transmission lines across the EU-27. Energy J. **37**, 59–82 (2016). https://doi.org/10.5547/01956574.37.3.jcoh

3. Huang, Z., Yu, H., Peng, Z., Feng, Y.: Planning community energy system in the industry 4.0 era: Achievements, challenges and a potential solution. https://www.sciencedirect.com/science/article/pii/S1364032117304768 (2017). https://doi.org/10.1016/j.rser.2017.04.004

4. IEC Technical Committee 1 (Terminology): IEC 60050 - International Electrotechnical Vocabulary – Welcome. http://www.electropedia.org/. Accessed 10 Feb 2020

5. Ceglia, F., Esposito, P., Maurizio, S.: Smart energy community and collective awareness: a systematic scientific and normative review. In: Business Management Theories and Practices in a Dynamic Competitive Environment, pp. 139–149. EuroMed Press (2019)

6. Visa, I., Duta, A. (eds.): CSE 2017. SPE, Springer, Cham (2018). https://doi.org/10.1007/978-3-319-63215-5

7. Paci, S., Bertoldi, D.: Enabling Positive Energy Districts across Europe : energy efficiency couples renewable energy (2020). https://doi.org/10.2760/452028

8. Pontes Luz, G., Amaro E Silva, R.: Modeling Energy Communities with Collective Photovoltaic Self-Consumption: Synergies between a Small City and a Winery in Portugal (2021). https://doi.org/10.3390/en14020323

9. Sarfarazi, S., Deissenroth-Uhrig, M., Bertsch, V.: Aggregation of households in community energy systems: an analysis from actors⇔ and market perspectives. Energies **13** (2020). https://doi.org/10.3390/en13195154

10. Rehman, H.,, Reda, F., Paiho, S., Hasan, A.: Towards positive energy communities at high latitudes. Energy Convers. Manag. **196**, 175–195 (2019). https://doi.org/10.1016/j.enconman.2019.06.005

11. Ala-Juusela, M., Crosbie, T., Hukkalainen, M.: Defining and operationalising the concept of an energy positive neighbourhood. Energy Convers. Manag. **125**, 133–140 (2016). https://doi.org/10.1016/j.enconman.2016.05.052

12. Walker, S., Labeodan, T., Maassen, W., Zeiler, W.: A review study of the current research on energy hub for energy positive neighborhoods. In: Energy Procedia, pp. 727–732. Elsevier, Amsterdam, the Netherlands (2017). https://doi.org/10.1016/j.egypro.2017.07.387

13. Bartholmes, J.: Smart cities and communities. https://ec.europa.eu/inea/sites/inea/files/4._smart_cities_and_communities_j.bartholmes_k.maniatis.pdf (2017)

14. Bartholmes, J.: Smart Cities and Communities SCC1 - 2018. 24 (2017)

15. Argyrou, M.C., Christodoulides, P., Kalogirou, S.A.: Energy storage for electricity generation and related processes: technologies appraisal and grid scale applications (2018). https://doi.org/10.1016/j.rser.2018.06.044

16. Kousksou, T., Bruel, P., Jamil, A., El Rhafiki, T., Zeraouli, Y.: Energy storage: applications and challenges (2014). https://doi.org/10.1016/j.solmat.2013.08.015

17. Poullikkas, A.: Optimization analysis for pumped energy storage systems in small isolated power systems. Open Access J. J. Power Technol. **93**, 78–89 (2013)

18. Hadjipaschalis, I., Poullikkas, A., Efthimiou, V.: Overview of current and future energy storage technologies for electric power applications (2009). https://doi.org/10.1016/j.rser.2008.09.028

19. Denholm, P., Kulcinski, G.L.: Life cycle energy requirements and greenhouse gas emissions from large scale energy storage systems. Energy Convers. Manag. **45**, 2153–2172 (2004). https://doi.org/10.1016/j.enconman.2003.10.014

20. Kaldellis, J.K., Zafirakis, D.: Optimum energy storage techniques for the improvement of renewable energy sources-based electricity generation economic efficiency. Energy **32**, 2295–2305 (2007). https://doi.org/10.1016/j.energy.2007.07.009

21. Denholm, P., Holloway, T.: Improved accounting of emissions from utility energy storage system operation (2005). https://pubs.acs.org/sharingguidelines. https://doi.org/10.1021/es0505898

22. Mahlia, T.M.I., Saktisahdan, T.J., Jannifar, A., Hasan, M.H., Matseelar, H.S.C.: A review of available methods and development on energy storage. Technol. Update (2014). https://doi.org/10.1016/j.rser.2014.01.068
23. Chen, H., Cong, T.N., Yang, W., Tan, C., Li, Y., Ding, Y.: Progress in electrical energy storage system: a critical review (2009). https://doi.org/10.1016/j.pnsc.2008.07.014
24. Denholm, P., Ela, E., Kirby, B., Milligan, M.: The role of energy storage with renewable electricity generation. In: Energy Storage: Issues and Applications, pp. 1–58 (2011)
25. Bilgili, M., Ozbek, A., Sahin, B., Kahraman, A.: An overview of renewable electric power capacity and progress in new technologies in the world (2015). https://doi.org/10.1016/j.rser.2015.04.148
26. Mousavi G, S.M., Faraji, F., Majazi, A., Al-Haddad, K.: A comprehensive review of Flywheel Energy Storage System technology (2017). https://doi.org/10.1016/j.rser.2016.09.060
27. Sebastián, R., Peña Alzola, R.: Flywheel energy storage systems: Review and simulation for an isolated wind power system (2012). https://doi.org/10.1016/j.rser.2012.08.008
28. Bolund, B., Bernhoff, H., Leijon, M.: Flywheel energy and power storage systems (2007). https://doi.org/10.1016/j.rser.2005.01.004
29. Liu, H., Jiang, J.: Flywheel energy storage-an upswing technology for energy sustainability. Energy Build. 39, 599–604 (2007). https://doi.org/10.1016/j.enbuild.2006.10.001
30. Evans, A., Strezov, V., Evans, T.J.: Assessment of utility energy storage options for increased renewable energy penetration (2012). https://doi.org/10.1016/j.rser.2012.03.048
31. Parra, D., Norman, S.A., Walker, G.S., Gillott, M.: Optimum community energy storage system for demand load shifting. Appl. Energy. 174, 130–143 (2016). https://doi.org/10.1016/j.apenergy.2016.04.082
32. van der Stelt, S., AlSkaif, T., van Sark, W.: Techno-economic analysis of household and community energy storage for residential prosumers with smart appliances. Appl. Energy. 209, 266–276 (2018). https://doi.org/10.1016/j.apenergy.2017.10.096
33. Koirala, B.P., van Oost, E., van der Windt, H.: Community energy storage: A responsible innovation towards a sustainable energy system? Appl. Energy. 231, 570–585 (2018). https://doi.org/10.1016/j.apenergy.2018.09.163
34. Parra, D., Gillott, M., Norman, S.A., Walker, G.S.: Optimum community energy storage system for PV energy time-shift. Appl. Energy. 137, 576–587 (2015). https://doi.org/10.1016/j.apenergy.2014.08.060
35. Barbour, E., Parra, D., Awwad, Z., González, M.C.: Community energy storage: A smart choice for the smart grid? Appl. Energy. 212, 489–497 (2018). https://doi.org/10.1016/j.apenergy.2017.12.056
36. Richardson, I., Thomson, M., Infield, D.: A high-resolution domestic building occupancy model for energy demand simulations. Energy Build. 40, 1560–1566 (2008). https://doi.org/10.1016/j.enbuild.2008.02.006

Renewable Energy Communities in Africa:
A Case Study of Five Selected Countries

Mathew Anabadongo Atinsia[3,4], Kankam O. Adu-Kankam[1,2(✉)],
and Felix Amankwah Diawuo[3,4]

[1] School of Science and Technology, UNINOVA – CTS and LASI, Nova University of Lisbon,
Campus de Caparica, 2829-516 Monte de Caparica, Portugal
`k.adu@campus.fct.unl.pt`
[2] School of Engineering, University of Energy and Natural Resources (UENR), P. O. Box 214,
Sunyani, Ghana
[3] Regional Centre for Energy and Environmental Sustainability (RCEES), UENR, Sunyani,
Ghana
`mathew.atinsia@uenr.edu.gh`
[4] School of Energy, Department of Renewable Energy Engineering, UENR, Sunyani, Ghana

Abstract. It is claimed that the success of Renewable Energy Communities
(RECs) depends on sound policies that provide security to community investments and investors, as well as reliable sources of funding, good community
organization, and how the community is governed. These elements facilitate the
participation of the citizen and are key to the growth and survivability of any
REC. It is further claimed that sound policies can drive novel and viable business
models, innovative financing and remuneration schemes, the adoption of smart
technologies, social acceptance, and, most importantly, increase in citizen participation. In Africa today, RECs are in their infancy stages of development and
require immense attention. To better understand and characterize how RECs in
Africa are developing, a systematic literature review is carried out on five selected
cases located in South Africa, Malawi, Cameroun, Togo, and the Ivory Coast. The
study aims to analyze how governmental policies, organizational structures, types
of governance, ownership schemes, sources of funding, the composition of the
communities, and types of renewable energy resources (RER), are facilitating the
development of these RECs in Africa. How value is created and shared amongst
members of the community is also considered. The findings of this study show that
RECs in Africa are faced with the challenges, of inadequate governmental policy
frameworks, unsustainable financial models, and low community ownership, and
the dominant RERs are solar and biogas. Other findings include low levels of
citizen engagement, participation, and knowledge about RECs.

Keywords: Renewable Energy Communities · Policy Framework · Financial
Model · Resource Ownership · Community Organization · Sources of Funding

© IFIP International Federation for Information Processing 2023
Published by Springer Nature Switzerland AG 2023
L. M. Camarinha-Matos and F. Ferrada (Eds.): DoCEIS 2023, IFIP AICT 678, pp. 52–64, 2023.
https://doi.org/10.1007/978-3-031-36007-7_4

1 Introduction

Electrical energy is claimed to play a crucial role in the everyday lives of humans in contemporary society [1]. This has resulted in a heavy reliance on energy across many sectors of today's society [2]. However, the bulk of the electricity that is used to satisfy these surmounting needs of society is fundamentally generated from fossil fuel sources, which have been declared environmentally unfriendly, and unsustainable and contribute to an increase in temperature and the emission of greenhouse gases [3]. Data from the dominant literature in this area indicate that the presence of carbon dioxide in the atmosphere today is 40% higher than it was in the nineteenth century [4]. Furthermore, the rate at which the earth's natural resources are being depleted to meet the insatiable needs of man, in this case, electrical energy, is very alarming [5]. Due to the problematic nature of fossil fuel sources, experts have recommended the transition to renewable energy sources (RES) as a viable alternative [6].

Transitioning from fossil fuels to RES is a step towards a more sustainable and cleaner energy system [5]. The integration of RES could help to promote energy democracy, energy decentralization, and energy justice [7]. This means allowing people to make their own decisions in terms of their energy generation and use [8]. Again, considering the ongoing changes in the organization of energy systems (the energy transition) in the direction of increased penetration of RES in the energy systems, it is observed that RECs are gradually becoming a key component of the power grid [9]. However, the success of RECs depends on many other things, including sound government policies, reliable funding sources, good governance, and good organization [9, 10]. For instance, considering best practices around the world, particularly in Europe, legal frameworks/policies such as the Renewable Energy Directive (REDII) offer protection to citizens and communities across Europe by providing the appropriate environment, that facilitates local investments in renewable energy projects [11].

Firstly, the REDII provides a dedicated definition for RECs as legal entities, for citizens and small to medium-sized enterprises to set up renewable energy (RE) projects and engage in energy-related activities, organized democratically to provide benefits to the local community [11].

Secondly, the REDII includes enforceable rights to protect participants investing in renewables, such as producing, selling, sharing, storing, and self-consumption of RE, without unfair charges or procedures, and accessing energy markets directly or through a third party. In addition to this member states are obliged to also create enabling frameworks that provide access to finance and technical expertise, build capacity for local authorities, and remove unjustified barriers to community projects [11]. Considering this, it can therefore be argued that the existence of this directive has helped RECs to flourish very well in Europe. Currently, there are over 7,700 RECs in Europe and still counting [12]. Similar policies have facilitated the growth of RECs in other countries such as Great Britain, with RECs numbering over 420. The same is the case in Australia with over 100 cases [13].

However, in Africa, the idea of RECs is new and emerging. Its growth is slow and needs attention on several fronts [14]. A report by IRENA and AfDB [15] points out that less than 3% of global renewable energy jobs are in Africa. Also, Africa has a low rate of access to clean cooking and electrification technologies, with only 46% having access in 2019 representing 906 million people [15]. Therefore, it is envisaged that the idea of RECs could expedite access to electricity and decrease energy poverty and injustice in Africa. However, to better understand the prospect of RECs as a panacea to energy poverty and injustice in Africa, it is relevant to understand how these communities are being formed, financed, and governed, the types of RES that are available and the level of involvement of the local indigenes. For these reasons and more, this work uses systematic literature reviews to analyze 5 selected REC cases located in South Africa, Malawi, Cameroun, Togo, and the Ivory Coast. The justification for the selection of a case was based on geographic location. Some attempt was made to identify and select a case from all the geographical/geopolitical regions of Africa namely west, south, east central and north of Africa. This was to ensure that there was an even spread and fair representation. However, there were some challenges finding cases that were located in northern part of Africa. To help address these problems, the following research questions are defined,

RQ1: What governmental policies are currently in place to support the development and sustainability of the selected REC cases?

RQ 2: How are these RECs organized?

- What system of governance is adopted to govern these RECs?
- Who are the owners and what resources do they own in these RECs?
- What are the sources of funding for these RECs?
- What are the compositions of these RECs?
- How is value created and how does it benefit the local community?
- What RER are mostly found in these RECs?

1.1 Related Work

This section focuses on related works that will form part of a broader work in future works. In [14], a systematic review is conducted on 46 RECs in Sub-Saharan Africa (SSA). The finding of the research indicates most of the communities in SSA are not sufficiently empowered to institute and manage their energy projects. This calls for further research to be made on how SSA countries can create innovative and supportive regulatory environments and develop models that can help them to institute and manage their projects. In [16] a comprehensive study was conducted on the barriers and opportunities with RE development in Africa. This research found that the development of RE is hampered by groups of factors such as poor institutional framework and infrastructure, high initial capital costs, weak dissemination strategies, lack of skilled manpower, poor baseline information, and weak maintenance service. A similar study that examined the challenges and opportunities for RE deployment in sub-SSA was carried out [17]. Some of the challenges that were realized from the study are inadequate technical, financial, and human resources, weak institutional and regulatory frameworks, and socio-political barriers. The study recommended that there is a need to strengthen the institutional and regulatory framework that will support the development of community energy projects. The author further recommended that there is a need for capacity building, harmonization of financial resources, and enhancement of energy security. A study was conducted on four renewable energy projects located in four different communities in Ethiopia. The outcome shows that the use of decentralized renewable energy systems have improved livelihood concerning income; productive use, health, and education affected men and women differently [18]. The findings further suggest that there is a need for procedural justice measures, such as community consultation and participation, to create a sense of community ownership. This, in turn, can lead to the long-term sustainability of these projects. Another study in [19] highlighted the importance of a decentralized renewable energy system in achieving UN energy access goals. It confirms that added value approach in mini-grid planning is capable of ensuring sustainability and promoting the development of energy access projects. Another study which is aimed at producing a strategic framework for the development of smart cities by transforming urban communities into smart-energy systems through a gradual process. This study proposed a strategic framework for the development of smart cities by gradually transforming urban communities into smart-energy systems. The developed framework considers social, technological, and economic aspects and also uses a bottom-up approach for decision-making. The proposed decision constructs provide feasible practical solutions for smart transformations to enhance the sustainability, livability, and revitalization of a community [20].

2 Contribution to Connected Cyber-Physical Spaces

A cyber-physical space environment is a network of interconnected digital and physical systems that work together to enable seamless data exchange and decision-making [21]. This environment includes a range of technologies such as the Internet of Things (IoT), sensors, actuators, automation systems, cloud computing, and data analytics [22]. In a cyber-physical space environment, physical systems are connected to digital systems, creating a "smart" system that can monitor, analyze, and respond to changes in the environment in real-time [22]. This environment can be used in various applications, such as smart cities [26], intelligent transportation systems [23], and smart grids [24]. The goal of a cyber-physical space environment is to enhance efficiency, reduce costs, and improve the quality of life for individuals and communities. RECs have the potential to significantly contribute to a connected cyber-physical space in Africa. According to a report by the United Nations Economic Commission for Africa (UNECA) on the potential of RE in Africa, it was found that RE can lead to the creation of smart grids that optimize energy use and reduce waste, as well as decentralized energy systems to power local communities [25]. These systems can also be integrated into smart grids to create a more resilient and reliable energy infrastructure. Additionally, the energy data generated by local communities can be collected, analyzed, and used to improve energy efficiency and reduce costs, as noted in a report by the International Renewable Energy Agency (IRENA) [15] and Africa development bank (AfDB) [15] on the RE Market Analysis which also covers the role of RE in African development [15]. RECs can therefore contribute to the development of e-mobility infrastructure by providing charging stations for electric vehicles, reducing reliance on fossil fuels, and promoting sustainable transportation. Overall, the development of RECs in Africa can help create connected cyber-physical spaces that promote sustainable energy use and reduce the carbon footprint of African communities.

3 Methodology

A systematic literature review method [26–28] was used to provide an unbiased and comprehensive selection of cases. The selection followed a rigorous and transparent process of searching and analyzing academic and non-academic literature related to RECs in Africa. The process was in four stages. The first stage comprised the case selection which was guided by the combination of key words from columns 1,2 and 3 of Table 1. Each keyword in column 1 was used t in combination with the keywords in columns 2 and 3. The search engines that were consulted included Scopus, Google Scholar, Google Search, Science Direct and others from books and YouTube. Cases that met the initial criteria were forty-eight. Out of this number thirty-eight were taken out because they were constituted of publications that mentioned RECs in Africa. For most of these cases, the sources of information were shared information online. The second stage was the case screening stage where the cases that were out of the study scope were excluded. The criteria for case inclusion was that (a) the case must be geographically located in Africa, (b) the case must be active, (c) the sources of energy must be of renewable source, (d) the case must be a community based and provide evidence of the social, economic, and environmental benefits to the community. The criteria for a case to be excluded was that the case falls outside the inclusion criteria. At this stage, three cases were excluded. The third stage was the eligibility stage. This entailed cases that fit in the scope of the study. At this stage, seven cases were considered. Further screening was done to see if they met the inclusion and exclusion criteria. Two cases were taken out because they did not meet the inclusion criteria. The final stage is the case inclusion stage were the five cases that met the inclusion criteria were retained for analysis.

Table 1. Keywords combination for the selection of cases.

Column 1.	Column 2	Column 3
Renewable energy	Community	Africa
Decentralized energy		
Green energy		
Local energy		
Distributed energy		

4 Results and Discussion

4.1 Governmental Policies

The purpose of RQ1 is to find out what governmental policies are supporting the development of RECs in Africa. To help answer this question, we reviewed available information on energy policies in the five selected countries. The outcome is shown in Table 2. According to the table, these countries have government policies that support the general development and deployment of RE. However, specific policies that are in support of

RECs were not found. This is a major concern as the absence of such policies may imply there is no legal protection or security for investors and the local communities, should they decide to invest in RECs locally. The development and implementation of policies and legal frameworks can be a good enabler for the stability and growth of RECs. Other benefits may include increased investor confidence, increased numbers of REC projects and subsequent access to clean energy, reduced reliance on fossil fuels, and improved energy security. It is however recommended that policymakers in Africa may have to consider the development of some regulatory frameworks to protect RECs in Africa.

Table 2. Renewable Energy Policies

Country	General Governmental Policies in Support of Renewable Energy	Specific Governmental Policies that support RECs
South Africa	Renewable Energy Independent Power Producer Procurement Program (REIPPPP). [29]	None found
	Integrated Resource Plan (IRP). [30].	
Malawi	Nationals Energy Policy [31]	None found
	Renewable Energy Feed in Tariffs (REFITS) [32]	
Togo	Rural Electrification Program [33]	None found
Cameroon	National Policy, Strategy, and Action Plan for Energy Efficiency. [34]	None found
Ivory Coast	National Energy Efficiency Action Plan (PANEE). [35]	None found

RECs in Europe are guided by the REDII which mandates every member state to give priority to these communities [11]. The RED II provides the necessary legal backing to set up these projects and engage in energy-related activities to provide benefits to the local community [11]. Furthermore, REDII provides the capacity to invest in renewables, such as producing, selling, sharing, storing, and self-consuming RE, without unfair charges or procedures, and accessing energy markets directly or through a third party.

4.2 Organization

Using REDII as a reference, RECs are supposed to be legal entities that operate autonomously without any interference from government authorities or encounter any bureaucratic governmental process. Such communities are considered best practices because they are fully autonomous. RQ2 aimed to investigate the organizational structure of RECs in Africa. The organization was classified under 5 key headings. These include (a) how the community is governed, (b) who owns what, (c) how they are funded, (d) their composition and (e) how value is created and how it benefits the local community. The outcome of the analysis is shown in Table 3 and are discusses in the following chapters.

Table 3. The organisation of RECs in the selected cases.

Name of REC	System of governance	Owners of the project/resources	Sources of funding	Composition of the REC	How are Values created and benefits
Cookhouse Wind farm [36]	Not mentioned	African Infrastructure Investment Managers (AIIM) and the Local Community Trust. Old Mutual	African Infrastructure Investment Managers (AIIM) and the Local Community Trust	African Infrastructure Investment Managers (AIIM) and the Local Community Trust	Not mentioned
Sitolo Community solar grid [37]	Not mentioned	Malawi Government UNDP & GEF	Malawi Government UNDP & GEF	Malawi Government UNDP & GEF	Not mentioned
Solar Microgrid Avétonou [37]	Not mentioned	Togo Rural Electrification and Renewable Energy Agency (AT2ER)	Togo Rural Electrification and Renewable Energy Agency (AT2ER)	Togo Rural Electrification and Renewable Energy Agency (AT2ER)	Not mentioned
Togolese Smart Solar Kiosk [38]	Not mentioned	EkoEnergy	EkoEnergy	EkoEnergy	Not mentioned
Mezam division domestic biogas [39]	Not mentioned	UNDP	UNDP	UNDP	Not mentioned

4.2.1   System of Governance

From Table 3, it can be seen that all the REC cases did not mention any specific governance system that is being used unlike the cases found in the European Union. The absence of a clearly defined system of governance for these REC cases is concerning. This may raise issues of transparency regarding how well the local community is represented in decision-making processes. Again, the absence of well-defined governance structures can lead to confusion and misunderstandings about the roles and responsibilities of different actors involved in the RECs. There is therefore a need to investigate further to ascertain if this is the case for the majority of RECs in Africa.

4.2.2 Who Owns What?

Table 3 shows that the owners of all the energy resources (the entire project) in these cases are the financiers of the project, which is normally the case. However, the observed financiers in these cases are not from the local communities. This means the local communities do not own anything in these projects and therefore they may have limited control over the projects. The absence of community ownership in these RECs is concerning as it can restrict the benefits to the local community, and this can lead to a sense of disempowerment, alienation and disenfranchisement.

4.2.3 Sources of Funding

From Table 3, it can be seen that the selected cases are principally funded by NGOs, governmental agencies, and charitable organizations. There is no indication that the funds are generated locally, or that the local communities have some stake or shares in these projects. This is likely to affect ownership and the buy-in of the local communities since the sense of ownership may not be strong, even if it is present. Moreover, relying solely on external sources of funding is risky and may be unsustainable, as these projects may be stalled or cease to operate if the source of funding is curtailed. Furthermore, the fund owners may have their priorities and objectives, which may not always align with those of the local communities or the region as a whole. This, therefore, suggests the need to consider alternate financing schemes like "build, operate, and transfer" that can enable ownership of the project to be transferred to the local communities after a certain agreed period, or the project could be loaned to the community to be paid-off over a certain defined period so that the communities can take ownership and manage these projects in the best interest of their community.

4.2.4 Composition

From Table 3 it can be seen that these RECs lack diversity in their composition. In these communities, you don't find diversity in the composition of the community. In all these cases, the community is composed of one or two entities who are usually the financiers and who also double as owners of the projects. For instance, comparing the case with similar RECs like Wildpoldsried in Germany, [39], it is observed that the community is comprised of (a) Project financiers, (b) a grid management company, (c) research partners, (d) smart grid markets solutions provider, (e) research and grid technology partner, and (f) consumers. It appears that the financiers of the projects in the studied cases play a monotonous role in these communities. The observed composition might affect the resilience of the community. For instance, when only project funding agencies are involved in RECs, the focus may primarily be on funding and project implementation, rather than addressing the broader social economic, and environmental issues in the community. Moreover, the absence of local representation in these communities can affect the acceptance of these projects in the local communities. Local communities often have unique insights and knowledge about local challenges and opportunities, which can be crucial in shaping effective local development strategies.

4.2.5 Value Creation and Its Benefit to the Local Community

In other cases, across Europe, like [41, 42] it can be observed that value is created in the form of electrical energy and related services. In the observed cases, value is also created in the same way. For instance, the energy generated by the cookhouse wind farm is sold to Escom Holdings SOC. However, it is not clear how the local community benefits from the value that is created from the sale of electrical energy. Since there is limited involvement of the local communities in these RECs, likely, they may not benefit adequately. The concern here is that this can lead to exploitation and may subject the project to opposition and NIMBYism. There is therefore a need for RECs to prioritize the creation of other values in the form of job creation and community investment. In this case, there is a win-win situation for both and community and the project which can lead to success.

4.2.6 Types of Renewable Energy Resources Available

The final aspect of the study is about the types of RE resources that are available in these REC cases. The outcome is shown in Table 4.

Table 4. RECs and their respective Energy Resources

REC	Energy Resources
Cookhouse Wind Farm [36]	Wind
Sitolo Community Solar Grid [37]	Solar
Solar Microgrid Avétonou [37]	Solar
Togolese Smart Solar Kiosk [38]	Solar
Mezam Division Domestic Biogas [39]	Biogas

From Table 4 it can be seen that the renewable energy resources utilized in these communities are wind, solar, and biogas, indicating limited exploits for more renewable energy sources. However, it should be noted that other green energy technologies like storage, biomass, and hydro, have not been widely utilized in these communities and could be further explored to enhance the operations of renewable energy communities (RECs) in Africa. Also, other types of solutions can be looked at like smart cities, smart grids and microgrids.

Limitations

This review was limited by (1) Not many cases of REC in Africa. (2) Difficulty of finding cases in North Africa and (3) Insufficient online information on the internet. Hence these limitations may affect the generalizability of the findings and the feasibility of the proposed recommendations. Nonetheless, this study serves as a foundation for future research on RECs in Africa.

5   Conclusion and Future Works

The objective of the study is to analyze how governmental policies and organizational structures are helping RECs. Concerning governmental policies, the outcome shows that there are general policies to support renewable energy and energy efficiency in the related countries. However, regarding RECs, there seem to be no such policies in place, With the. Organisational structures it is also found that the studied cases are funded and owned by NGOs, charity organizations, and government agencies. This defeats the democratic dimension of RECs. Again, the system of governance is not clearly defined and the value that is generated is not known to benefit the local communities.

Considering the outcome of the study, it might be a good idea to consider emulating the successful cases or best practices that occur around the world, so that RECs in Africa can be well developed to provide the expected benefits to their local communities. The need for a comprehensive framework that encompasses the legal, governance, funding and composition of RECs in Africa is urgent. This will create a friendly environment for RECs to operate smoothly without challenges. Moreover, African governments need to have regional strategies that give RECs more priorities.

This initiative can begin at the regional level of the African continent. Currently, there are 8 regional economic blocks in Africa. These include (a) the Arab Maghreb Union (AMU), (b) the Community of Sahel-Saharan States (CEN-SAD), (c) the Common Market for Eastern and Southern Africa (COMESA), (d) the East African Community (EAC), (e) Economic Community of Central African States (ECCAS), (f) Economic Community of West African States (ECOWAS), (g) Intergovernmental Authority on Development (IGAD), and (h) the Southern African Development Community (SADC). Each block is responsible for the development of a sustainable and economic environment for member countries.

It is recommended that perhaps it is time to initiate dialogues at these levels of decision-making, regarding the development of RECs in Africa, taking into consideration the context of community in the African sense. It is also recommended that proper financial models could be developed to support the growth and development of RECs in Africa.

In future works, we aim to expand this study by (a) increasing the number of cases, (b) organizing focus group discussions (physically or virtually) with owners/actors or members of these communities to solicit their views and input towards the development and proposition of a comprehensive framework and policy guidelines for the establishment and operation of RECs in Africa. This work and the proposed future works form part of the preliminary ongoing PhD work which is planned to focus on renewable energy communities in Africa. At this preliminary stage of the work, the interest of the researcher is to gain understanding of the current situation of RECs in Africa.

Acknowledgement. The authors acknowledge the contributions of the University of Energy and Natural Resources, and the UNINOVA CTS (FCT program UIDB/00066/2020 and UIDP/00066/2020) for supporting this work with their research facilities and resources.

References

1. Liu, L., Guo, X., Lee, C.: Promoting smart cities into the 5G era with multi-field Internet of Things (IoT) applications powered with advanced mechanical energy harvesters. Nano Energy **88**, 106304 (2021). https://doi.org/10.1016/j.nanoen.2021.106304
2. Kober, T., Schiffer, H.-W., Densing, M., Panos, E.: Global energy perspectives to 2060 – WEC's World Energy Scenarios 2019. Energy Strateg. Rev. **31**, 100523 (2020). https://doi.org/10.1016/j.esr.2020.100523
3. Our World In Data. Our World In Data. Primary energy consumption by world region. Oxford Martin School (2021). https://ourworldindata.org/grapher/primary-energy-consumption-by-region?time=1965..2021
4. Ritchie, H., Roser, M., Rosado, P.: CO_2 and Greenhouse Gas Emissions. Our World Data (2020). https://ourworldindata.org/greenhouse-gas-emissions
5. Gyamfi, Samuel, Derkyi, Nana S.A.., Asuamah, Emmanuel Y., Aduako, Israel J.A..: Renewable Energy and Sustainable Development. In: Sustainable Hydropower in West Africa, pp. 75–94. Elsevier (2018). https://doi.org/10.1016/B978-0-12-813016-2.00006-X
6. Amin, N., Song, H., Shabbir, M.S.: What factors contribute to environmental degradation in G11 economies? Emphasizing the importance of renewable and non-renewable energy sources. Int. J. Sustain. Dev. World Ecol. **29**(5), 472–482 (2022). https://doi.org/10.1080/13504509.2022.2059720
7. Jenkins, K.E.H.: Energy justice, energy democracy, and sustainability: normative approaches to the consumer ownership of renewables. In: Lowitzsch, J. (ed.) Energy Transition, pp. 79–97. Springer, Cham (2019). https://doi.org/10.1007/978-3-319-93518-8_4
8. Koirala, B., Hakvoort, R.: Integrated community-based energy systems: aligning technology, incentives, and regulations. In: Innovation and Disruption at the Grid's Edge: How Distributed Energy Resources are Disrupting the Utility Business Model, pp. 363–387 (2017). https://doi.org/10.1016/B978-0-12-811758-3.00018-8
9. Sakah, M., Diawuo, F.A., Katzenbach, R., Gyamfi, S.: Towards a sustainable electrification in Ghana: a review of renewable energy deployment policies. Renew. Sustain. Energy Rev. **79**, 544–557 (2017). https://doi.org/10.1016/j.rser.2017.05.090
10. Shem, C., Simsek, Y., Hutfilter, U.F., Urmee, T.: Potentials and opportunities for low carbon energy transition in Vietnam: a policy analysis. Energy Policy **134**, 110818 (2019). https://doi.org/10.1016/j.enpol.2019.06.026
11. EU. Directive (EU) 2018/2001 of the European Parliament and of the Council of 11 December 2018 on the promotion of the use of energy from renewable sources (recast). Off. J. Eur. Union **2018**(L 328), 82–209 (2018)
12. S. of the E. U. European Commission. Contributing to the European Green Deal and the Union's Recovery, No. COM(2021) 950 final. European Commission, pp. 1–31. Brussels (2021). https://eur-lex.europa.eu/resource.html?uri=cellar:67d54e0f-363d-11ec-bd8e-01aa75ed71a1.0001.02/DOC_1&format=PDF
13. Enel Green Power. Renewable energy communities in Italy and in Europe (2023). https://www.enelgreenpower.com/countries/europe/Italy/renewable-energy-communities/renewable-energy-communities-italy-europe
14. Ambole, A., Koranteng, K., Njoroge, P., Luhangala, D.L.: A review of energy communities in sub-saharan africa as a transition pathway to energy democracy. Sustain. **13**(4), 1–19 (2021). https://doi.org/10.3390/su13042128
15. IRENA and AfDB. Renewable Energy Market Analysis: Africa and Its Regions. Abu Dhabi and Abidjan (2022)
16. Ouedraogo, N.S.: Opportunities, barriers and issues with renewable energy development in Africa: a comprehensible review. Current Sustain./Renew. Energy Reports **6**(2), 52–60 (2019). https://doi.org/10.1007/s40518-019-00130-7

17. Bishoge, O., Kombe, G., Mvile, B.: Renewable energy for sustainable development in sub-Saharan African countries: challenges and way forward. J. Renew. Sustain. Energy **12** (2020). https://doi.org/10.1063/5.0009297
18. Wiese, K.: Energy 4 all? Investigating gendered energy justice implications of community-based micro-hydropower cooperatives in Ethiopia. Innov. Eur. J. Soc. Sci. Res. **33**(2), 194–217 (2020). https://doi.org/10.1080/13511610.2020.1745059
19. Stritzke, S., Jain, P.: The sustainability of decentralised renewable energy projects in developing countries: learning lessons from Zambia. Energies **14**(13), 3757 (2021). https://doi.org/10.3390/en14133757
20. Zaidan, E., Ghofrani, A., Abulibdeh, A., Jafari, M.: Accelerating the change to smart societies-a strategic knowledge-based framework for smart energy transition of urban communities. Front. Energy Res. **10** (2022). https://doi.org/10.3389/fenrg.2022.852092
21. Wang, B., Zhou, H., Yang, G., Li, X., Yang, H.: Human Digital Twin (HDT) driven human-cyber-physical systems: key technologies and applications. Chinese J. Mech. Eng. **35**(1), 11 (2022). https://doi.org/10.1186/s10033-022-00680-w
22. Tyagi, A.K., Sreenath, N.: Cyber Physical Systems: analyses, challenges and possible solutions. Internet Things Cyber-Physical Syst. **1**, 22–33 (2021). https://doi.org/10.1016/j.iotcps.2021.12.002
23. Cassandras, C.G.: Smart cities as cyber-physical social systems. Engineering **2**(2), 156–158 (2016). https://doi.org/10.1016/J.ENG.2016.02.012
24. Adu, K., Camarinha-Matos, L.: Delegating Autonomy on Digital Twins in Energy Ecosystems (2022). https://doi.org/10.20508/ijsmartgrid.v6i4.257.g215
25. Ejigu, M.: Sustainable development indicators framework for Africa and initial compendium of indicators (2011)
26. Snyder, H.: Literature review as a research methodology: an overview and guidelines. J. Bus. Res. **104**, 333–339 (2019). https://doi.org/10.1016/j.jbusres.2019.07.039
27. Petrosino, A., Lavenberg, J.: Systematic reviews and meta-analyses: Best evidence on 'what works' for criminal justice decision makers. West. Crim. Rev. **8**(1), 1–15 (2007). https://www.scopus.com/inward/record.uri?eid=2-s2.0-34248185490&partnerID=40&md5=acc03b7d6df2b8cd9db4c68704184c09
28. Mallett, R., Hagen-Zanker, J., Slater, R., Duvendack, M.: The benefits and challenges of using systematic reviews in international development research. J. Dev. Eff. **4**(3), 445–455 (2012). https://doi.org/10.1080/19439342.2012.711342
29. Department of Mineral Resources and Energy. Renewable Independent Power Producer Programme (REIPPP) | South African Government (2019). https://www.gov.za/about-government/government-programmes/renewable-independent-power-producer-programme. Accessed 1 Mar 2023
30. Department of Mineral Resources and Energy, Intergated Resoruce Plan(IRP)| South African Government (2019). https://www.energy.gov.za/files/irp_frame.html
31. Government of Malawi. Government of Malawi National Energy Policy," no. July, p. 191 (2019)
32. MERA. Malawi Feed-in Tariff policy: Renewable energy Resource Generated Electricity in Malawi, no. September, (2012). http://conrema.org/wp-content/uploads/2019/01/Malawi-feed-in-tariff-policy-final.pdf
33. Rural electrification in Togo (ProEnergie II). https://www.giz.de/en/worldwide/92267.html. Accessed 6 Mar 2023
34. Energypedia. National Energy Efficiency Policy, Strategy and Action Plan in the electricity sector in Cameroon - energypedia (2014). https://energypedia.info/wiki/National_Energy_Efficiency_Policy,_Strategy_and_Action_Plan_in_the_electricity_sector_in_Cameroon. Accessed 3 Mar 2023

35. CEDEAO. Plan d ' Actions National d ' Efficacité Energétique (PANEE)-CI (2016)
36. Cookhouse Windfarm. Cookhouse Wind Farm I Wind farm I Cookhouse Wind FarmI Energy Sheet (2023). https://cookhousewind.co.za/wind-farm/#fact-sheet. Accessed 2 Mar 2023
37. Ademe Enviroearth. Installation of a solar PV mini-grid in Sitolo Village, Malawi ENVIROEARTH (2020). https://clubinternational.ademe.fr/wp-content/uploads/ademe-env iroearth-en.pdf. Accessed 2 Mar 2023
38. EKOenergy. Smart solar kiosks in Togo (2017). https://www.ekoenergy.org/wp-content/upl oads/Climate-Fund-Leaflet-2017-Togo-English.pdf. Accessed 2 Mar 2023
39. UNDP. National Determined contribution of Cote d'Ivoire (2023). https://www.ndcs. undp.org/content/ndc-support-programme/en/home/our-work/geographic/africa/cotedivoire. Accessed 2 Mar 2023
40. Wildpoldsried - photovoltaic/solar/NEH
41. Andrew Bowen. Germany's renewable village – DW – 05/28/2015. 28 May 2015. https:// www.dw.com/en/feldheim-germanys-renewable-village/a-18466800. Accessed 10 Mar 2023
42. Welcome to Wildpoldsried (2023). https://www.wildpoldsried.de/index.html?Energie. Accessed 10 Mar 2023

Smart Energy and Power Systems

Optimal Load Shedding for Smart Power Grid Resilience Enhancement Considering Cyber-Physical Constraints

Sonia Hosseinpour$^{(\boxtimes)}$ and João Martins

NOVA School of Science and Technology, Center of Technology and Systems (UNINOVA-CTS) and Associated Lab of Intelligent Systems (LASI), NOVA University Lisbon, 2829-516 Lisbon, Portugal

`s.hosseinpour@campus.fct.unl.pt, jf.martins@fct.unl.pt`

Abstract. The increasing use of measurement and telecommunication equipment has transformed power systems into smart networks, which have created new challenges in modeling and operation studies. One critical challenge is the transformation of power networks into a vast cyber-physical system, which has made mathematical modeling difficult. Any fault in cyber or physical systems can affect the performance of another part, so the interaction of cyber and physical sectors should be considered in power system studies. Load shedding studies have become important for improving the resilience of power systems, but the interaction of cyber and physical parts in load shedding is rarely studied. This paper proposes a new mathematical model for optimal load shedding in power systems by considering the interaction of cyber and physical parts to improve system resilience. The proposed model is applied to an IEEE RTS-79 power grid and demonstrates its effectiveness in improving resilience by considering cyber-physical constraints.

Keywords: Cyber-Physical Systems · Optimal Load Shedding · Resilience Enhancement · Grey Wolf Optimizer

1 Introduction

A severe disturbance in the power grid, such as a line failure or generator outage, results in an imbalance between production and demand, which can cause instability in the frequency and voltage of the power grid. Modern power grids operate with low operating reserves and stability margins [1], exacerbating the risk of imbalance. When an imbalance occurs, power grid operators take several measures to prevent instability. Optimal load shedding is the last step in maintaining power system stability following a severe disturbance [2–4]. Load shedding is a mechanism used to balance production and demand during energy shortages. However, load shedding faces numerous challenges, particularly in modern power grids. One of the most critical challenges is the impact of cyber-physical constraints on the power grid, which relates to the interdependence of cyber and physical systems.

© IFIP International Federation for Information Processing 2023
Published by Springer Nature Switzerland AG 2023
L. M. Camarinha-Matos and F. Ferrada (Eds.): DoCEIS 2023, IFIP AICT 678, pp. 67–81, 2023.
https://doi.org/10.1007/978-3-031-36007-7_5

With recent developments in the field of smart metering and information and telecommunication technologies, the use of these devices in power systems has increased, turning the power system into an extensive cyber-physical system [5]. While the use of intelligent measurement and telecommunication equipment provides many advantages for the power system, it also faces significant challenges [6]. This equipment offers the possibility of understanding more about the current conditions of the power system and enabling optimal control and load shedding in emergencies. However, the power grid's dependence on the cyber system increases its vulnerability and creates new risks. In recent years, numerous reports have emerged of power grid blackouts in various countries due to cyber-attacks [7, 8]. As a result, studies on improving the resilience of modern power networks by considering the cyber-physical power system have become essential.

In power grids, optimal load shedding requires coordination between the generation, transmission, and distribution systems, which is highly dependent on the cyber system. Therefore, cyber-physical constraints can affect the load-shedding program, and its failure leads to severe disruption in the network. For this reason, the study of load shedding in modern power networks should be done considering cyber-physical constraints. The interaction of cyber and physical parts in power systems can be categorized by methods based on graph theory [9], complex network [10], finite estimation machine [11], and Petri net [12]. In [13] and [14], the graph model is used to model cyber-attacks in cyber-physical systems.

Most studies on the resilience of cyber-physical power systems have focused on only one specific aspect of the system. In early works, power systems have been studied only from the aspect of a physical system or cyber system. In [15], the impact of generation loss on the telecommunication network has been investigated. In some studies, only the cyber side is considered. For example, in [16], the use of an information masking strategy to protect data security in cloud-based energy management systems has been investigated. Many studies have been done on the impact of the cyber network on the power network. The impact of cyber events on the power network [17], the impact of the loss of telecommunications on the power grid [18], and dynamic state estimation based on the risk mitigation strategy to improve the resilience of the network against cyber-attacks [19] have been studied.

Although the above works have tried to study the interactions between physical and cyber networks, the physical and cyber section's mutual dependence has not been considered. It has been tried to model the mutual influence of cyber and physical networks [20–23]. In [22], the impact of cascading failures on the power network coupled with three different types of cyber networks has been evaluated. However, in these works, the physical laws of the power network are not considered [23–26]. In [24] and [26], by adding Kirchhoff's laws, it has been tried to overcome the mentioned weaknesses. However, in these works, only power networks have been modeled, and the proposed models were not enough to cover all the features of the cyber-physical system. The reliability of the cyber-physical power system was evaluated in [27] and [28], but the focus was solely on the impact of cyber-attacks on the power system.

Optimal load shedding with the aim of improving resilience and considering the mutual influence of physical and cyber networks has rarely been studied.

The study in [29] investigates the damage resulting from cyber-attacks on cyber-physical systems while considering the interaction between the cyber and physical sections. The study assumes that the cyber system is backed up by an uninterruptible power supply (UPS) and neglects the effect of the power network on the cyber network. In [30], vulnerability analysis of the coupled power/communication system is performed, considering optimal load shedding to improve resilience. This study also neglects the effect of power loss in the cyber system due to load shedding. In [31], the mutual influence of cyber and physical parts on the load-shedding program has been studied and evaluated to prevent the propagation of faults in the system. The results of this study have shown that the efficiency of the load-shedding program is sensitive to the performance of the cyber domain. Some studies have also focused on the design of the degree of dependence of the cyber and physical sectors [32]. In [33], optimal power flow (OPF) has been studied by considering the mutual influence of cyber and physical networks, however, this model was based on DC OPF and does not provide a suitable criterion for evaluating network voltage stability. In [34], an adaptive-dynamic load-shedding method is presented to improve the frequency resilience of the power grid, but only the physical part of the system is considered. In some works, optimal OPF has been studied by considering cyber-physical constraints and their mutual influence, but it has not been focused on improving resilience [35].

According to the stated content, in this article, an optimal load-shedding program is proposed considering the cyber-physical constraints, in which the mutual influence of the power grid and the cyber network is accurately modeled. In this model, the dependence of the power network on the cyber network and the dependence of the cyber network on the power network are considered. Our goal is to reduce the catastrophic impact of cascading effects on cyber-physical systems, leading to improved power grid resilience. In the proposed model, AC OPF is used so that the physical laws of the power grid are fully applied. For this reason, the final model is a problem with highly nonlinear constraints. To solve this model, the gray wolf optimizer (GWO) algorithm is used along with the Matpower toolbox in Matlab. The proposed model is applied to a standard IEEE system and its efficiency is proved. It is shown by the simulation results that the proposed model can prevent the cascading shutdown of the power network by removing the minimum load. Therefore, this model can improve the resilience of the cyber-physical power system.

2   The Mutual Influence of Cyber and Physical Networks

Figure 1 depicts the cyber-physical structure of a power system, where the lower grid represents the power grid with generator buses, demand buses, and intermediate buses, while the upper grid represents the cyber network with central control and telecommunication nodes. The power grid's objective is to deliver power production from generators to consumers, and the cyber network's objective is to support this process. For stable and optimal operation of the power grid, continuous monitoring and control are necessary, requiring the collection of information from production and load buses and sending it to the central control unit. This process necessitates an interconnected cyber system. In turn, the cyber system requires electrical energy supplied through the power network to carry out telecommunication processes [24]. The power grid and cyber network are interdependent and have a mutual influence on each other.

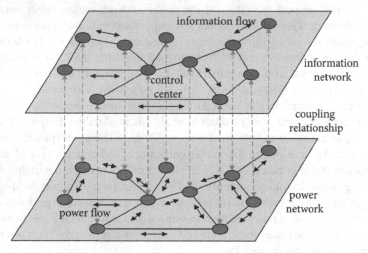

Fig. 1. Cyber-physical structure of a power grid

In traditional power networks, the grid operator does not know the state of the cyber system, and when a failure occurs in the network, he seeks to minimize the load only by considering the state of the power network. In this structure, the power network is operated independently from the cyber network [33]. However, any damage to the cyber network affects the operation of the power network, and the state of the power grid affects the state of the cyber network. On the other hand, in modern power networks, the network operator is fully aware of the state of the cyber network and makes decisions based on measured data in the entire cyber-physical system, considering the mutual influence of cyber and physical networks on each other [33]. This article focuses on the second structure where load shedding during system failure is solved by considering the instantaneous conditions of both cyber and physical networks and their mutual influence.

3   Mathematical Formulation

To study the resilience of the power system, events with low probability but high impacts, such as storms or human attacks, must be considered. These events can cause the failure of one or more transmission lines and disrupt the balance of production and consumption, thus posing a significant threat to the security of the power system. In such situations, the grid operator must ensure the stability of the power grid by implementing optimal load shedding. To achieve this, the problem of optimal load shedding is modeled with the following objective function:

$$\min \ \sum_{i \in I} C^{sh} P_i^{sh} + \sum_{g \in G} \left(a_g P_g^2 + b_g P_g + c_g \right) \tag{1}$$

Where P_i^{sh} is the shedding quantity of load, P_g is the active power output of generator g, and C^{sh} is the shedding price of load. Also, a_g, b_g, and c_g are the cost coefficients of generators. The first part of (1) is related to the cost of load shedding and the second part is the cost of generating power by generators. Based on the AC power flow model, the power grid constraints are presented in the form of the following relations.

$$\sum_{g \in G(i)} P_g - P_i^d + P_i^{sh} = \sum_j P_{i,j}^L , \ i \in I \tag{2}$$

$$\sum_{g \in G(i)} Q_g - Q_i^d + Q_i^{sh} = \sum_j Q_{i,j}^L , \ i \in I \tag{3}$$

$$P_{i,j}^L = V_i \sum_j Y_{i,j} V_j \cos(\delta_i - \delta_j - \theta_{i,j}), \ (i,j) \in \ell \tag{4}$$

$$Q_{i,j}^L = V_i \sum_j Y_{i,j} V_j \sin(\delta_i - \delta_j - \theta_{i,j}), \ (i,j) \in \ell \tag{5}$$

$$\left(P_{i,j}^L\right)^2 + \left(Q_{i,j}^L\right)^2 \leq \left(S_{i,j}^{L,\max}\right)^2, \ (i,j) \in \ell \tag{6}$$

$$P_g^{\min} U_g \leq P_g \leq P_g^{\max} U_g, \ g \in G \tag{7}$$

$$0 \leq P_i^{sh} \leq P_i^d, \ i \in I \tag{8}$$

The variable U_g is a binary representation of the state of generator g, denoting a value of 1 for those generators that are capable of producing power. In the event that a generator becomes disconnected from the grid, either due to physical or cyber-related issues, the corresponding U_g value becomes zero. Q_g is the reactive power output of generator g. $P_{i,j}^L$, $Q_{i,j}^L$ and $S_{i,j}^{L,\max}$ represent the active power flow, reactive power flow, and nominal capacity for transmission line (i,j), respectively. P_i^d and Q_i^d represent the active and reactive power demand of bus i, respectively. V_i and δ_i represent the voltage amplitude and phase angle, while $Y_{i,j}$ and $\theta_{i,j}$ representing the admittance amplitude and angle, respectively. Additionally, $P_g^{\min}$ and $P_g^{\max}$ represent the minimum and maximum active power output limits of the generator g, respectively.

The balance of active and reactive power for each bus is described in Eqs. (2) and (3), respectively. Equations (4) and (5) describe the active and reactive power flowing through the transmission lines, based on the AC power flow model. The thermal limit of the transmission lines, which is determined by their capacity, is described in (6). The output power of each generator is limited by its capacity, as stated in (7). Additionally, the maximum amount of load shedding at each bus is limited, as described in (8), to ensure that it does not exceed the bus's demand.

In the proposed method, the power grid and cyber network are considered separate graphs that depend on each other. If a cyber-node fails, its corresponding buses in the power grid become invisible, and the central control will not be able to monitor or control them. If this happens to buses with generators, the generator will be out of reach and will not produce power [24]. Generator unavailability is the main reason for most power outages [36]. Therefore, the status of the generators depends on the state of the cyber network and must be modeled based on its conditions. To mathematically describe these conditions, a binary variable γ_v is defined that specifies the status of node v in the cyber network. Thus, the generators in the i-th bus of the physical system will be able to produce power only if the corresponding node in the cyber system is in normal conditions. This constraint for the power network is modeled as follows.

$$U_g \leq \gamma_v, \; g \in G(v) \tag{9}$$

Where $G(v)$ represents the set of generators installed in the physical bus that corresponds to the cyber node v. As per Eq. (9), in case the cyber node v, which is connected to the physical bus of generator g, suffers damage, the binary value U_g assumes zero, consequently leading to the generator's incapacity to generate power.

As mentioned earlier, cyber nodes also require energy to function, which must be provided by the physical network. Therefore, the functionality of cyber nodes depends on the working status and connectivity of power buses. If the power supply of a physical bus is interrupted, the corresponding cyber node may become unserviceable due to the lack of sufficient power for the telecommunication system. Hence, it is necessary to determine the value of the variable γ_v based on the status of its corresponding bus in the power grid. To model these conditions, we have used the modified method [15], which is described as follows:

$$\begin{cases} \gamma_v = 1 & if \; P_i^{sh} \leq (1-\alpha).P_i^d \\ \gamma_v = 0 & else \end{cases} \quad v \in \upsilon_i \tag{10}$$

Where υ_i is the set of all cyber nodes connected to the i-th bus in the power network, and α is a parameter in the range [0,1], that indicates the degree of dependence on the cyber network and the power network [15]. Thus, a larger α indicates a greater dependence of the cyber network on the power network.

Unlike the power grid, which must obey Kirchhoff's laws, the cyber grid is much more flexible in operation. In general, if a cyber node maintains its connection with the control center, it has the potential to perform well. However, as previously stated, if the cyber node's energy needs are not supplied by the power grid, it cannot function. In other words, the working state of a cyber node depends not only on its connection to the control center but also on the state of energy support. To apply these conditions, an iterative process is used according to the flowchart presented in Fig. 2.

According to Fig. 2, firstly, the amount of load shedding in each bus and the parameter α are received as input. Based on these parameters, the status of cyber system nodes is determined based on (10). In the next step, the status of cyber nodes is checked in terms of connection to the central control, and the status of isolated cyber nodes is changed to unusable. After the state of all the nodes of the cyber system is determined, the status of the generators is updated based on the status of the cyber nodes and corresponding physical buses. At this stage, the generators whose corresponding nodes are damaged in the cyber system go to the unreachable state, and their U_g value is set to zero. After updating the status of cyber nodes and the status of the generators, if there is a change in

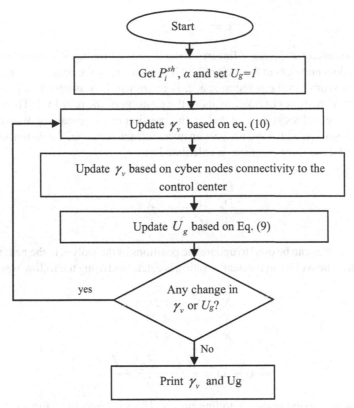

Fig. 2. Flowchart of determining the status of cyber nodes and generators considering cyber-physical systems interaction

the status of cyber nodes or physical buses, the process is repeated. This process continues until there is no change in the value of U_g and γ_v in two consecutive iterations.

4   Solution Methodology

To solve the problem, the GWO is used, which is an algorithm based on artificial intelligence and has a better performance compared to many other algorithms [37]. One of the main advantages of this algorithm is that there is no need for users to set any of its parameters. This algorithm is based on two functions, encircling prey and hunting.

In the prey encircling step, the distance between each wolf and the prey is calculated according to (11), where $\vec{X}_p$ is the prey position vector, $\vec{X}$ is the wolf position vector, t is the number of iterations, and r_1 is a random vector in the range [0,1].

$$\vec{D} = \left| \vec{C}.\vec{X}_p(t) - \vec{X}(t) \right|, \ \vec{C} = 2\vec{r}_1 \tag{11}$$

The hunting stage includes approaching the prey based on the information obtained from the encircling prey. This stage is modeled as follows:

$$\vec{X}(t+1) = \vec{X}_p(t) - \vec{A}.\vec{D} \tag{12}$$

$$\vec{A} = 2\vec{a}.\vec{r}_2 - \vec{a} \tag{13}$$

Where parameter a decrease linearly from 2 to zero during iterations, and r_2 is a vector of random numbers in the range [0,1]. The position of the prey, or in other words, the optimal response in the solution space, is unknown. It is assumed that the wolves α, β, and δ have the best information about the position of the prey [37]. Therefore, the position of these wolves is used to update the position of the remaining wolves. Using these three positions, which are the best answers in each iteration, the distance between each wolf and these three positions is calculated as:

$$\begin{aligned}\vec{D}_\alpha &= |\vec{C}_1.\vec{X}_\alpha - \vec{X}| \\ \vec{D}_\beta &= |\vec{C}_2.\vec{X}_\beta - \vec{X}| \\ \vec{D}_\delta &= |\vec{C}_3.\vec{X}_\delta - \vec{X}|\end{aligned} \tag{14}$$

These distances can be used to update the positions of the wolves in the next iteration. The position of the wolves in the next iteration is calculated using the following relations:

$$\begin{aligned}\vec{X}_1 &= \vec{X}_\alpha - \vec{A}_1.\vec{D}_\alpha \\ \vec{X}_2 &= \vec{X}_\beta - \vec{A}_2.\vec{D}_\beta \\ \vec{X}_3 &= \vec{X}_\delta - \vec{A}_1.\vec{D}_\delta\end{aligned} \tag{15}$$

$$\vec{X}(t+1) = \frac{\vec{X}_1 + \vec{X}_2 + \vec{X}_3}{3} \tag{16}$$

By repeatedly applying the encircling prey and hunting operators, the position of the prey or the best answer is obtained. In the proposed method, for each candidate response of the GWO, which includes the amount of load shedding in each bus, the algorithm in Fig. 2 is applied to determine the status of cyber nodes and generators. Then, considering the state of the cyber-physical system, the OPF is solved. If the total constraints of the problem are met, the results of the OPF and the amount of load shedding are recorded. If the OPF does not converge, a large penalty is sent to the GWO as a cost function. The flowchart of the proposed algorithm for solving the problem is presented in Fig. 3.

5 Simulation Results

The proposed model is applied to the IEEE RTS-79 system for evaluation. Based on [24], it is assumed that each bus of the power network is equipped with a telecommunication node. Additionally, the control center is placed next to the node that has the most connections to other nodes. The simulation is performed on a 3.3 GHz Ryzen 9 5900 hs-based laptop. To solve the problem, the GWO algorithm is implemented in MATLAB, and the Matpower toolbox is used for OPF.

The IEEE RTS-79 system has 12 generators, 36 transmission lines, and 17 load centers. Its complete information is available in [38]. The coupling parameter of the physical and cyber network, α, is set to 0.75 [15]. Figure 4 shows the single-line topology of the power grid along with its cyber network.

To evaluate the resilience of the studied system, various scenarios with different levels of failure have been considered. To this end, ten different levels of severity of failure in the system have been evaluated. For instance, a failure level of "N" implies that N number of system lines have faulted at the same time and are out of service. For each level of failure, ten scenarios are generated. Consequently, by considering ten failure levels and ten scenarios for each level, 100 different modes are obtained, and the problem is solved for each of these modes.

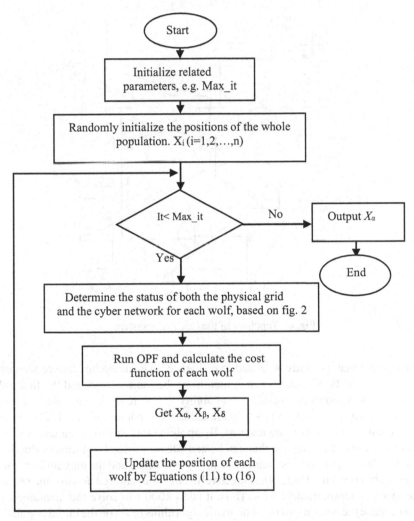

Fig. 3. Proposed strategy for load shedding in cyber-physical system

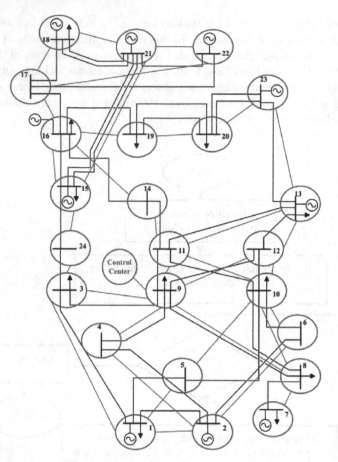

Fig. 4. Topology of the case study system

Considering that the study is related to resilience, to generate line failure scenarios, the failure probability of all lines is assumed to be the same at first, and the first failed line is randomly determined. Next, the probability of failure of the lines that are closer to the failed line is increased, and a second failed line is randomly selected. This process is repeated until ten scenarios are reached. By applying this method, line failures occur in a specific region of the system that can be considered caused by storms or floods.

For the GWO algorithm, the number of wolf populations and the maximum iteration of the algorithm is set to 50 and 50, respectively. The time required to solve the problem for one mode is approximately 80 s. Thus, it takes 8000 s to solve the mentioned 100 situations. Since the outcome of meta-heuristic algorithms relies on the initial population, which is generated randomly, the problem is solved ten times using the GWO algorithm. The best solution obtained from the ten runs is chosen as the final solution.

The problem of optimal load shedding following a disturbance has been solved twice: once by considering the proposed strategy and once without considering the interaction between the physical grid and the cyber network, which is commonly referred to as the traditional strategy. By comparing these two strategies, the impact of considering the interdependence between the cyber and physical networks is determined. Figures 5, 6 and 7 illustrate the simulation results for both strategies.

Figure 5 displays the average total cost value for each fault severity based on (1). This figure is generated by solving the problem for the 100 specified modes and computing the average over the scenarios for each damage severity.

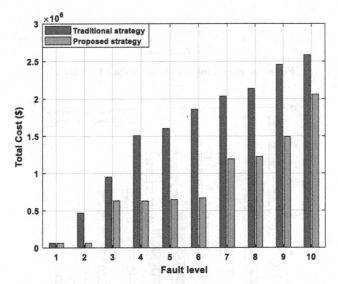

Fig. 5. Average total cost for each failure level

Based on Fig. 5, it is evident that the system cost increases with the increase in the failure level for both methods. As more lines go out of service with increasing failure levels, more loads are isolated or cut off due to the unavailability of generators. However, the proposed strategy shows significantly lower overall cost than the traditional strategy for failure levels 2 and above. The proposed strategy considers load shedding in a way that minimizes the impact on both the physical and cyber networks. In contrast, the traditional method only considers the physical network's conditions, resulting in some load interruptions caused by cyber line failures, reducing power production.

Figure 6 shows the average cost reduction of the proposed strategy compared to the traditional strategy. As shown, for fault level 1, there is no significant cost reduction because this level of fault does not cause widespread failure in the cyber network. It can also be seen that for fault level 2, the overall cost is reduced by nearly 90%. The reason for this is that in the proposed strategy, load shedding is done in such a way that it does not damage the cyber network. For higher fault levels, the cost reduction of the proposed strategy is evident and significant. Figure 7 and 8 display the average number of online cyber nodes and the average interrupted load, respectively, for each failure level.

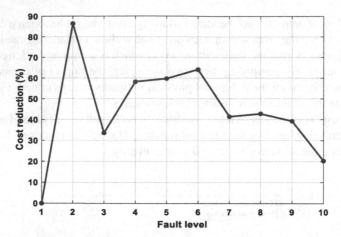

Fig. 6. Average cost reduction for each fault level

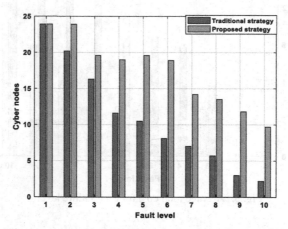

Fig. 7. The average number of cyber nodes in service for each failure level

Figure 7 further supports the benefits of the proposed strategy by showing the number of healthy cyber lines for each fault level. The proposed strategy results in fewer out-of-service cyber lines, indicating that load shedding is performed in a way that preserves the health of the cyber network.

Finally, Fig. 8 displays the average load interruption for each failure level. It is evident that, for failure level 10, the traditional strategy results in over 90% of the system load being cut off (2580 MW), nearly leading to a complete blackout. In contrast, the proposed strategy results in much less load shedding than the traditional method.

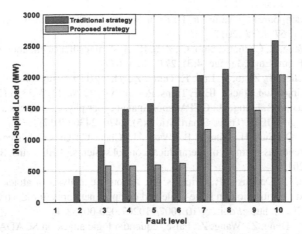

Fig. 8. Amount of interrupted load for each failure level

6 Conclusion

In this study, a novel approach for optimal load shedding was proposed to enhance resilience in cyber-physical power systems. The proposed strategy involved modeling the interaction between the physical and cyber networks and employing AC optimal power flow to accurately represent the physical network rules. The standard IEEE system was used as a case study to evaluate the effectiveness of the proposed strategy. The problem of optimal load shedding was addressed by considering various levels of system failure and scenarios of failed lines in the physical network. The simulation results demonstrated that the proposed strategy can reduce the amount of load shedding during severe disturbances, thereby improving the system's resilience. The results also showed that the proposed strategy can decrease the cost of load shedding compared to conventional methods. This advantage can be attributed to the proposed strategy's simultaneous consideration of both the physical and cyber network conditions during load shedding. Consequently, load shedding is performed with a minimal negative impact on the cyber network, leading to minimal damage to the cyber lines.

References

1. Shekari, T., Gholami, A., Aminifar, F., Sanaye-Pasand, M.: An adaptive wide-area load shedding scheme incorporating power system real-time limitations. IEEE Syst. **12**, 759–767 (2018)
2. Amraee, T., Darebaghi, M.G., Soroudi, A., Keane, A.: Probabilistic under frequency load shedding considering RoCoF relays of distributed generators. IEEE Trans. Power Syst. **33**, 3587–3598 (2018)
3. Yiannis, T., Stelios, T., Elias, K.: Minimal load shedding using the swing equation. IEEE Trans. Power Syst. **32**, 2466–2467 (2017)
4. Reddy, C.P., Chakrabarti, S., Srivastava, S.C.: A sensitivity-based method for under frequency load-shedding. IEEE Trans. Power Syst. **29**, 984–985 (2014)

5. Li, Z., Shahidehpour, M., Aminifar, F.: Cybersecurity in distributed power systems. Proc. IEEE **105**(7), 1367–1388 (2017)
6. Huang, G., Wang, J., Chen, C., Guo, C., Zhu, B.: System resilience enhancement: smart grid and beyond. Front. Eng. Manage. **4**(3), 271–282 (2017)
7. Liang, G., Weller, S., Zhao, J., Luo, F., Dong, Z.: The 2015 Ukraine blackout: Implications for false data injection attacks. IEEE Trans. Power Syst. **32**(4), 3317–3318 (2017)
8. Deng, R., Zhuang, P., Liang, H.: CCPA: coordinated cyber-physical attacks and countermeasures in smart grid. IEEE Trans. Smart Grid **8**(5), 2420–2430 (2017)
9. Xin, S., Guo, Q., Sun, H., Zhang, B., Wang, J., Chen, C.: Cyber-physical modeling and cyber-contingency assessment of hierarchical control systems. IEEE Trans. Smart Grid **6**(5), 2375–2385 (2015)
10. Stergiopoulos, G., Dedousis, P., Gritzalis, D.: Automatic analysis of attack graphs for risk mitigation and prioritization on large-scale and complex networks in Industry 4.0. Int. J. Inf. Secur. 1–23 (2021). https://doi.org/10.1007/s10207-020-00533-4
11. Li, W., Xie, L., Deng, Z., Wang, Z.: False sequential logic attack on SCADA system and its physical impact analysis. Comput. Secur. **58**, 149–159 (2016)
12. Bahrami, M., Fotuhi-Firuzabad, M., Farzin, H.: Reliability evaluation of power grids considering integrity attacks against substation protective IEDs. IEEE Trans. Ind. Inform. **16**(2), 1035–1044 (2020)
13. Lau, P., Wang, L., Liu, Z., Wei, W., Ten, C.-W.: A coalitional cyber-insurance design considering power system reliability and cyber vulnerability. IEEE Trans. Power Syst. **36**(6), 5512–5524 (2021)
14. Zebrowski, P., Couce-Vieira, A., Mancuso, A.: A bayesian framework for the analysis and optimal mitigation of cyber threats to cyber-physical systems. Risk Anal. (2022)
15. Rosato, V., Issacharoff, L., Tiriticco, F., Meloni, S., Porcellinis, S., Setola, R.: Modelling interdependent infrastructures using interacting dynamical models. Int. J. Crit. Infrastruct. **4**(1–2), 63–79 (2008)
16. Xin, S., Guo, Q., Wang, J., Chen, C., Sun, H., Zhang, B.: Information masking theory for data protection in future cloud-based energy management. IEEE Trans. Smart Grid **99**, 1 (2017)
17. Liu, R., Vellaithurai, C., Biswas, S., Gamage, T., Srivastava, A.: Analyzing the cyber-physical impact of cyber events on the power grid. IEEE Trans. Smart Grid **6**(5), 2444–2453 (2015)
18. Parandehgheibi, M., Turitsyn, K., Modiano, E.: Modeling the impact of communication loss on the power grid under emergency control. In: 2015 IEEE International Conference on Smart Grid Communications (SmartGridComm), pp. 356–361 (2015)
19. Taha, A., Qi, J., Wang, J., Panchal, J.: Risk mitigation for dynamic state estimation against cyber attacks and unknown inputs. IEEE Trans. Smart Grid **9**(2), 886–899 (2018)
20. Buldyrev, S., Parshani, R., Paul, G., Stanley, H., Havlin, S.: Catastrophic cascade of failures in interdependent networks. Nature **464**(7291), 1025–1028 (2010)
21. Habib, M., Tornatore, M., Mukherjee, B.: Cascading-failure-resilient interconnection for interdependent power grid-optical networks. In: 2015 Optical Fiber Communications Conference and Exhibition (OFC), pp. 1–3 (2015)
22. Chai, W., Kyritsis, V., Katsaros, K., Pavlou, G.: Resilience of interdependent communication and power distribution networks against cascading failures. In: 2016 IFIP Networking Conference and Workshops (IFIP Networking), pp. 37–45 (2016)
23. Hines, P., Cotilla-Sanchez, E., Blumsack, S.: Do topological models provide good information about electricity infrastructure vulnerability? Chaos Interdiscipl. J. Nonlinear Sci. **20**(3), 033122 (2010)
24. Parandehgheibi, M., Modiano, E., Hay, D.: Mitigating cascading failures in interdependent power grids and communication networks. In: 2014 IEEE International Conference on Smart Grid Communications (SmartGridComm), pp. 242–247 (2014)

25. Wang, Q., Pipattanasomporn, M., Kuzlu, M., Tang, Y., Li, Y., Rahman, S.: Framework for vulnerability assessment of communication systems for electric power grids. IET Gener. Transm. Distrib. **10**(2), 477–548 (2016)
26. Korkali, M., Veneman, J., Tivnan, B., Bagrow, J., Hines, P.: Reducing cascading failure risk by increasing infrastructure network interdependence. Sci. Rep. **7**, 44499 (2017)
27. Rostami, A., Mohammadi, M., Karimipour, H.: Reliability assessment of cyber-physical power systems considering the impact of predicted cyber vulnerabilities. Int. J. Electr. Power Energy Syst. **147**, 108892 (2023)
28. Zhou, B., et al.: Reliability assessment of cyber-physical distribution systems considering cyber disturbances. Appl. Sci. **13**(6), 3452 (2023)
29. Xu, S., Xia, Y., Shen, H.-L.: Analysis of malware-induced cyber attacks in cyber-physical power systems. CIEEE Trans. Circuits Syst. II Express Briefs **67**(12), 3482–3486 (2020)
30. Zhang, Y., et al.: Collaborative stochastic expansion planning of cyber-physical system considering extreme scenarios. IET Generation, Transmission & Distribution (2023)
31. Wei, M., Lu, Z., Tang, Y., Lu, X.: Cyber and physical interactions to combat failure propagation in smart grid: characterization, analysis and evaluation. Comput. Netw. **158**, 184–192 (2019)
32. Shuvro, R.A., Das, P., Hayat, M.M.: Balancing smart grid's performance enhancement and resilience to cyber threat. In 2019 Resilience Week (RWS), Vol. 1, pp. 235–241. IEEE (2019)
33. Huang, G., Wang, J., Chen, C., Guo, C.: Cyber-constrained optimal power flow model for smart grid resilience enhancement. IEEE Trans. Smart Grid **10**(5), 5547–5555 (2018)
34. Kabir, M.A., Chowdhury, A.H.: A dynamic-adaptive load shedding methodology to improve frequency resilience of power systems. Int. J. Electric. Power Energy Syst. **122**, 106169 (2020)
35. Xu, Z., Ge, Y., Lin, Q., Chen, R., Cao, J., Nuo, Y.: Robustness analysis of CPPS considering power flow constraints. Int. Trans. Electric. Energy Syst. **2022**, 1–9 (2022). https://doi.org/10.1155/2022/7385104
36. NERC Resources Subcommittee. Balancing and frequency control. https://www.nerc.com/docs/oc/rs/NERC%20Balancing%20and%20Frequency%20Control%20200405 20111.pdf. Technical Report (2011)
37. Mirjalili, S., Mirjalili, S.M., Lewis, A.: Grey wolf optimizer. Adv. Eng. Softw. **69**, 46–61 (2014)
38. Ordoudis, C., Pinson, P., Morales, J.M., Zugno, M.: An updated version of the IEEE RTS 24-bus system for electricity market and power system operation studies. Technical University of Denmark, 13

Superconducting Saturable Core Reactor as Variable Inductance for Controlling the Power Flow in a Transmission Line

Leonardo Miúdo[1,2]($\boxtimes$), João Murta Pina[1], and Nuno Amaro[1]

[1] NOVA School of Science and Technology, Center of Technology and Systems (UNINOVA-CTS) and Associated Lab of Intelligent Systems (LASI), NOVA University Lisbon, 2829-516 Lisbon, Portugal
l.miudo@campus.fct.unl.pt
[2] Instituto Politécnico, Universidade Katyavala Bwila, 1725 Benguela, Angola

Abstract. Worldwide electric energy consumption is increasing, partially due to the electrification of sectors such as transportation. Simultaneously, there is a need to implement the ongoing energy transition with renewable energy generation, which results in increased transmission capacity needs. This paper uses steady-state simulations (power flow analysis) in an IEEE standard electrical grid of three buses using a saturable core reactor (SCR) with a high-temperature superconducting (HTS) DC coil, on a 2-core model, to optimize the power flow. The SCR-HTS works as a variable inductance, thus having power flow control capabilities, where superconducting materials are used to substantially decrease losses when compared to conventional conductors. Different scenarios are simulated in MATLAB using a developed Newton-Raphson (NR) algorithm and validated using PSSE. Results indicate that the SCR-HTS can effectively control the power flow in transmission lines and can be used as a solution to further integrate renewable energy sources in the electrical grid and to ensure safe operating conditions in contingency cases.

Keywords: Superconducting · Power Flow · Saturable Core Reactor · Transmission Line

1 Introduction

Energy and electricity consumption are related to the growth of the world's population, both increasing significantly [1, 2], with electrification expected economic growth so that global electricity demand will grow rapidly in the coming decades [3]. Renewable energy sources have been one of the solutions to meet the increase in consumption globally as well as one of the main keys to the ongoing energy transition. With the insertion of new energy sources in the grid, existing overhead transmission lines need to have a greater transmission capacity and greater control of power flow. The construction of new energy transport infrastructure is a complex process because aspects such as

L. M. Camarinha-Matos and F. Ferrada (Eds.): DoCEIS 2023, IFIP AICT 678, pp. 82–94, 2023.
https://doi.org/10.1007/978-3-031-36007-7_6

voltage level, number of circuits, provisions of conductors (line geometries), among others, should be considered [4] and, with the existing fast pace of installation of new generations units, there is the risk of having non-optimal solutions.

Dynamic Line Rating (DLR), Flexible AC Transmission System (FACTS), and the Saturable Core Reactor (SCR) with a High-Temperature Superconducting (HTS) DC coil (as an alternative to FACTS for power flow control) have been widely studied and considered effective means to improve capacity and control in power flow to integrate renewable energy and/or in contingency cases. Regarding the thermal limits of over-head lines, the DLR methods still have some limitations in applications. The physical model (Model IEEE Standard 738 and CIGRE Standard [5]) is of simple implementation and versatile, but the accuracy is relatively low. While other models need a lot of data and versatility is limited [6]. For stability reasons, FACTS, the Distributed Static Series Compensator (DSSC) has relatively low cost and high reliability. However, the control capacity is limited because it can only inject reactive power. Combined devices based on Voltage Source Converter (VSC), Unified Power Flow Controller – UPFC and Distributed Power Flow Controller – DPFC, have better power flow control capability and are therefore the most suitable devices. However, its high cost and complexity become the main limitations of its practical application [7]. SCR emerges as an alternative to FACTS, although SCR involves the use of power electronics devices such as FACTS, the most important difference between both is that the AC and DC circuits of the SCR have no direct electrical connection and are coupled simply through the magnetic field in the core. In SCR, there is not power flows along electronic power components. Consequently, only low-voltage electronic components are necessary for control, while FACTS controllers use electronic power components that are also part of the main power circuit [8]. SCR-HTS DC coil is based on the characteristic of materials to have low resistivity in the superconducting state, using a superconducting material with DC coils in the SCR can obtain large DC magnetomotive force with low losses compared to SCR with conventional conductors.

This paper presents a model and prototype of an SCR-HTS, which is used for power flow control purposes in a line. In order to demonstrate the effectiveness of the solution, a three-bus system is simulated, and results are discussed. The structure of this paper is as follows; Sect. 2 presents the contribution of this article seeing the electricity grid as a cyber-physical space. Section 3 takes an SCR-HTS approach as a variable inductance based on the two-core model first presenting the magnetic equations and later the validation of this same approach. Section 4 displays the network model and its data, impedance, voltage, and active and reactive power. As well as the method implemented for power flow analysis. In Sect. 5, the results, of the power flow analysis in the transmission lines are presented using MATLAB and PSSE. Section 6 contains the conclusions and future work.

2 Contribution to Connected Cyber-Physical Spaces

Future electric power grid can be defined as a cyber-physical space (CPS) with two layers; the first layer, physical layer, which is constituted by the electrical energy systems, generators, transmission lines and loads, and a second layer, the cyber layer, where the control and computing devices and communication lines between them are located [9]. The purpose of the cyber layer is to provide control over the electrical grid and improve its performance as well as increase its reliability. The contribution of this paper is the idea of adding to the electrical grid an SCR-HTS as a cyber control to make the transmission line dynamic. SCR-HTS controls power flow and can help in contingency cases for both the integration of renewable energy sources as well as mitigating the market splitting.

3   Superconducting Saturable Core Reactor

In the Publication of the United States Navy [10] a SCR is defined as a device used to control the reactance of an AC coil, through the permeability of the core in which the coil is wound. In other words, a SCR is a ferromagnetic core with windings connected to a DC circuit and a second set of windings connecting an AC circuit, according to the Fig. 1.

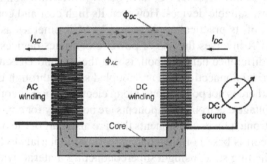

Fig. 1. Basic schematic of a saturable-core reactor [8]

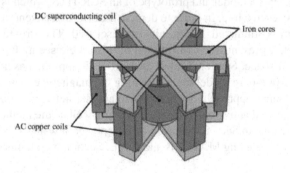

Fig. 2. Design of the SCR with superconducting coil.

In power systems, a SCR can be used in different applications where the effect of a variable reactance is needed, for example, power flow control [11, 12], fault current limiting [13–15], reactive power compensator continuous (with capacitor in series), harmonics filter and to suppress the voltage flicker in power distribution system [8].

SCR-HTS DC coil is based on the characteristic of materials to have low resistivity in the superconducting state. Using a superconducting material with DC coils in the SCR can obtain large DC magnetomotive force with a small loss compared to SCR with conventional conductors. The SCR-HTS usually consists of a superconducting DC coil, non-superconducting AC coils, and an iron core, Fig. 2.

3.1 Two-Core Model of an SCR-HTS

Two-core model approach consists of dividing the three-legged cores into two magnetically decoupled identical core, this is an approach based on the analysis of Saturable-Core Fault Current Limiters (SCFCLs) and was used in the study of SCR in [12] and was the model used in the prototype in [11, 14]. Each magnetic core has a uniform magnetic flux that results from the interaction of the dc and ac flux components.

Magnetic Equations: The mathematical equation that describes the flux interactions and inductance characteristics of model starts with Ampère's law, which is the relationship between current and magnetic field strength:

$$\oint \mathbf{H} \cdot d\mathbf{l} = Ni \tag{1}$$

The integral of a closed contour over the fixed length takes us the expression H as a function of the core length and the magnetomotive force. The relationship between flow intensity and the AC and DC parameters of each core result in the following:

$$H_{core\#1} = \frac{N_{DC}I_{DC} - N_{AC}i_{AC}}{l_1} \qquad H_{core\#2} = \frac{N_{DC}I_{DC} + N_{AC}i_{AC}}{l_2} \tag{2}$$

As the core material has nonlinear magnetic characteristic, then the magnetic field (B) can be expressed as:

$$B = \mu H \tag{3}$$

Considering the uniform magnetic field perpendicular to surface, the total magnetic flux of each magnetic core is obtained by the following:

$$\emptyset = \int_A \vec{B} \cdot \vec{dA} = BA \tag{4}$$

The flux linkage in terms of the AC and DC currents is expressed by:

$$\Psi = N_{AC}\emptyset \rightarrow \Psi = N_{AC}\mu HA \rightarrow \Psi$$
$$= \frac{N_{AC}A}{l}(N_{DC}I_{DC} \pm N_{AC}i_{AC})\mu_{(I_{DC},i_{AC})} \tag{5}$$

The differential inductance results from the combination of the flux linkage and partial derivative in relation to the AC current as follows:

$$L_d = \frac{\partial \Psi(t)}{\partial i_{AC}} = N_{AC}A\frac{\partial\left(\mu_{(I_{DC},i_{AC})}H_{AC}(t)\right)}{\partial i_{AC}} \tag{6}$$

$$L_{d_{total}} = L_{d\_core\#1} + L_{d\_core\#2} \tag{7}$$

$$L_{d\_core\#1} = \frac{N_{AC}^2 A}{l} \mu_{d\_core\#1}(I_{DC}, i_{AC}) \tag{8}$$

$$L_{d\_core\#2} = \frac{N_{AC}^2 A}{l} \mu_{d\_core\#2}(I_{DC}, i_{AC}) \tag{9}$$

Equations 8 and 9 correspond to the inductances as a function of DC saturation current and AC current.

Fig. 3. SCR-HTS with the current source and the LCR meter used to measure inductance [11].

Validation Two-Core Model: Two-core model was validated in [11], who uses the prototype of a three-phase SCR-HTS, as seen in Fig. 3. The DC coil is placed in a cryostat of stainless steel and filled with liquid nitrogen to provides a constant temperature of 77 K, necessary for the HTS tape to maintain a superconducting state. A DC source was used to saturate the cores. The Fig. 4 shows the behavior of the AC coil inductances, as a function of the DC current, the reactance as a function of the current is shown in the Fig. 5. As region 2 is very sensitive the DC current variation results in a high regulation of the power flow. The inductances of the AC coils vary from 8.4 to 58.5 mH, which corresponds to reactance variation of 2.6 to 18.3 Ω. For analysis of the power flow in the transmission line, Sect. 4, the resistance of the SCR-HTS is negligible, thus considered as a pure inductive reactance.

3.2 Other Models

In addition to the two-core model there are other two models for SCR and that can also be applied in SCR-HTS for power flow control, this is the model derived by finite element analysis [16] and gyrator capacitor model [17–19].

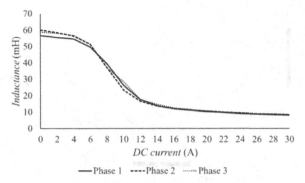

Fig. 4. Inductance of the AC coils [11]

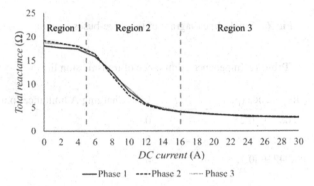

Fig. 5. Reactance of the AC coils [11].

4 Power Flow in Transmission Line

For analysis of the SCR-HTS as a variable inductance for the control of the power flow, a model of a 3-bus grid, consisting of two sources and a load, will be considered. The following Subsect. 4.1, details the grid specifications and methods used for analysis of power flow analysis on the transmission line.

4.1 Electrical Grid Model

The analysis of the power flow will be done in the system represented in Fig. 5, consisting of three buses (IEEE – 3 Bus System). The base power was considered 100 MVA and the base voltage is 60 kV. From these, the base current, 1.67 kA, and base impedance, 36 Ω, are deducted.

The model considers the resistance and reactance of the lines corresponding to 0.1 Ω/km and 0.3 Ω/km. The distance between the lines is line 12–30 km, line 13–26 km, and line 13–15 km, thus resulting, respectively, at the following line impedances Z_{12} = 3.0 + j9.0 Ω, Z_{13} = 2.6 + j7.8 Ω, and Z_{23} = 1.5 + j4.5 Ω. The system impedance and admittance parameters are those indicated in Table 1 and the load and generation data are presented in Table 2, all represented in the per unit system. In line 1–3 the

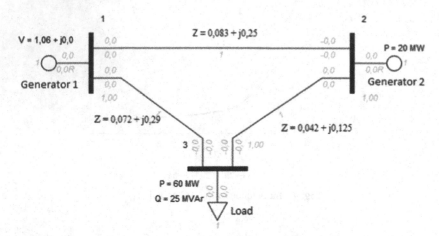

Fig. 6. Single-line diagram of the three-buses system.

Table 1. Impedance admittance of transmission line.

Line	Impedance (p.u.)	Line Charging Admittance (p.u)
1–2	0.083 + j0.25	0
1–3	0.072 + j0.29	0
2–3	0.042 + j0.125	0

impedance value $(0.072 + j0.29)$ Ω is considering the SCR-HTS already inserted in the grid, through the sum of the line reactance and the minimum reactance of the SCR-HTS, 2.6 Ω. This line has a transmission capacity equal to 23 MVA and resistance of SCR-HTS is considered to have a negligible value. The maximum and minimum reactive power generation limits on bus 2 are 35 Mvar and 0, respectively. The analysis of the power flow was made using Newton Raphson (N-R) algorithm in rectangular form in MATLAB, since it allows having a fast convergence thus reducing the simulation time and the number of iterations required in relation to the Gauss and Gauss-Seidel methods.

Table 2. Voltage and powers of generation and specified load.

Bus	Voltage (p.u.)	Generator		Load	
		MW	Mvar	MW	Mvar
1	1.06 + j0.0	—	—	0	0
2	1.00 + j0.0	20	—	0	0
3	—	0	0	60	25

Two scenarios are considered for the analysis of the power flow, first, with an inductive reactance in the line of 1–3 of 0.29 Ω, considering the minimum reactance of the SCR-HTS and, second, with an increased inductive reactance to 0.725 Ω, considering the maximum reactance of the SCR-HTS, according to the values of the previous section obtained in the validation of two core model plotted considering region 2. For each case, the active and reactive powers, losses, capacity, and currents in the lines will be presented and analyzed.

5 Results and Discussion

In this section the analysis of the results will be done by seaming the two scenarios in each of the subsections.

5.1 First Scenario

For the first scenario, NR algorithm implemented in MATLAB converged after four iterations. Obtained power flow results are included in Table 3. As all obtained voltages are in the interval of 0.9 to 1.1 p.u., the system is considered as stable. The reactive power of generator 2 is practically equal to zero. As for the power flow in the transmission lines, the results were calculated and obtained according to Table 4. The powers are represented in the p.u. system, it is worth remembering that the base power is 100 MVA, Table 5 shows the currents that flow in the lines.

Table 3. Analysis results by MATLAB – first scenario.

Bus No.	Bus Type	Voltage	Angle	MW (G)	Mvar (G)	MW (L)	Mvar (L)
1	1	1.06	0	0.41459	0.30065	0	0
2	3	1.0209	-0.024326	0.2	0.0078185	0	0
3	3	0.99389	-0.06189	0	0	0.6	0.25

In the result of system simulation using PSSE software, Fig. 6, the green arrow corresponds to the active power and the orange arrow corresponds to the reactive power represented in the international system (MW and Mvar), the voltages are in p.u. The power when exiting the bus is positive and when entering the bus is negative.

Considering the capacity of line 1–3 equal to 23 MVA, in first scenario the line is overloaded has an apparent power equal to 32.5 MVA that corresponds to about 40% higher than line capacity. As for the losses, adding up to all the lines a total of 1.5 + j5 was obtained and the line that presented the highest amount of loss is line 1–3, 0.7 + j2.8.

Table 4. Power flow in lines – first scenario.

Line	P (p.u.)	Q (p.u.)	I (p.u.)
1–2	0.14481	0.11904	0.17684
1–3	0.26978	0.18161	0.30681
2–3	0.34221	0.11122	0.35247

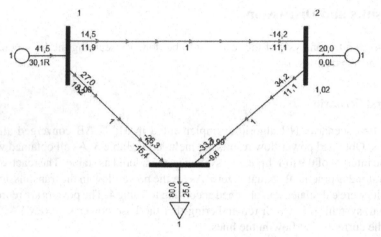

Fig. 7. Power flow for the first scenario.

Table 5. Current in the lines – first scenario.

	Line 1–2	Line 1–3	Line 2–3
I (A)	295.32	512.37	588.62

5.2 Second Scenario

For the second scenario, by increasing the inductive reactance of the SCR-HTS from line 1–3 from 0.29 Ω to 0.725 Ω to reduce the power flow in this line, also after four interactions the results are obtained according to Table 6. The bus voltages for second scenario are acceptable and within the limits set for the analysis as well.

The variation of the reactance of the SCR-HTS will imply the variation of the power flow, the results of the quantities prove this variation by reducing the power flow in line 1–3 and increasing in line 1–2, Table 7.

In the case of the power of the line for this second scenario, it was reduced to 21 MVA which corresponds to 91% of the line capacity. As for the losses there was an increase from 1.5 + j5 to 2 + j8.1 and this increase was compensated by the sources on bus 1 (active power) and bus 2 (reactive power). Line 2–3 is the one with the highest power loss, 1 + j3, as can be seen in Fig. 7. As for the currents in the rows, there was a

Table 6. Analysis results by MATLAB – second scenario.

|Bus No.|	|Bus Type|	|Voltage|	|Angle|	|MW(G)|	|Mvar(G)|	|MW(L)|	|Mvar(L)|
1	1	1.06	0	0.42077	0.33225	0	0
2	3	0.99561	-0.048059	0.2	0.023717	0	0
3	3	0.9568	-0.10085	0	0	0.6	0.25

Table 7. Power flow in lines – second scenario.

Line	P (p.u.)	Q (p.u.)	I (p.u.)
1–2	0.26576	0.18965	0.30801
1–3	0.15501	0.14261	0.1987
2–3	0.45789	0.16593	0.48917

Table 8. Current in the lines – second scenario.

	Line 1–2	Line 1–3	Line 2–3
I (A)	514.37	331.83	816.91

reduction in line 1–3 from 512 A to about 331 A, which causes it to increase in the other lines, Table 8. The SCR-HTS simulation in this paper was for a 60 kV transmission line. One of the barriers to SCR-HTS development has been implementation at high voltage levels, beyond the limits insulation, cooling system development and high complexity and cost [20]. Still there is some research and prototypes in tests of the application of SCR-HTS as a current limiter in 138 kV and 220 kV [21]. The highest voltage found of the SCR-HTS as a current limiter was 500 kV in a single-phase system [21]. Therefore, SCR-HTS has a great advantage that it can work by combining current limiter and power flow controller (Fig. 8).

Analyzing the two scenarios one can see that the integration of the SCR-HTS limited the power flow in line 1–3, which was overloaded. This results in a possible effect in generation, as in a normal operation the generation in Bus 1 would have to be curtailed (without the SCR-HTS) so that the line thermal capacity is respected. By adding the SCR-HTS, it was possible to eliminate the overload situation, thus ensuring that there is no need for curtailment. Assuming that the generator in bus 1 is renewable generation (e.g. wind), is it then possible to conclude that the SCR-HTS would act as a solution to mitigate the need for curtailment and its negative effects in power systems, which included added operation cost (for compensation of curtailment) and environmental impact costs (resulting in the need to produce energy from controllable sources, e.g. thermal).

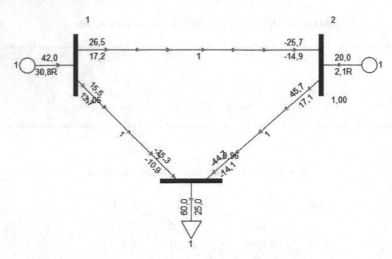

Fig. 8. Power flow for the second scenario.

The SCR-HTS can have improved control over the impedance of the transmission line, giving flexibility in the operation of the grid, allowing optimal management of the power flow, managing grid congestion, and efficiently transferring power from renewable energy sources to other areas of the grid and thus reducing the impact of market division. In addition, in some cases, it is possible to improve the voltage regulation and stability of the network, which helps in the reliability of the power system.

As for the superconducting part of the SCR-HTS, there has been little research on the dynamic voltage on HTS tapes in power applications [22]. In [23] simulations were performed to optimize the energy efficiency in relation to the dynamic voltage in a 4 mm HTS tape with DC currents from 30 A to 60 A, AC magnetic field magnitudes from 90 mT to 360 mT and frequencies from 50 Hz to 1000 Hz.

6   Conclusions and Future Work

The results of the simulations showed that it is possible to control the power flow by varying the inductive reactance of the line using an SCR-HTS through a continuous current. Using a superconducting material with DC coils in the SCR can obtain large DC magnetomotive force with a small loss compared to SCR with conventional conductors. Through this variation of the inductive reactance of the line the SCR-HTS can be inserted into the electrical grid for the control of power flow and current limiter in applications, for example, in contingency cases both for the integration of renewable energy sources as well as mitigating the market splitting. As future work is intended to develop a new model of the SCR-HTS for power flow control based on the characteristic linked magnetic flux (Ψ) and current I from [13] and a new model based on the gyrator capacitor. Subsequently, control the power flow with SCR - HTS in a dynamic line approach of the transmission line based on weather conditions, for example, deterministic model IEEE 738 Standard and/or CIGRE Standard.

Acknowledgments. This research was funded (in part) by the Portuguese FCT program, Center of Technology and Systems (CTS) UIDB/00066/2020 / UIDP/00066/2020 and gratefully thank the Instituto Nacional de Gestão de Bolsas de Estudo (INAGBE) – Angola for financial support.

References

1. Omer, A.M.: Energy, environment and sustainable development. Renew. Sustain. Energy Rev. **12**(9), 2265–2300 (2008). https://doi.org/10.1016/J.RSER.2007.05.001
2. Mekhilef, S., Saidur, R., Safari, A.: A review on solar energy use in industries. Renew. Sustain. Energy Rev. **15**(4), 1777–1790 (2011). https://doi.org/10.1016/J.RSER.2010.12.018
3. Castillo, V.Z., de Boer, H.S., Muñoz, R.M., Gernaat, D.E.H.J., Benders, R., van Vuuren, D.: Future global electricity demand load curves. Energy **258**, 124741 (2022). https://doi.org/10.1016/J.ENERGY.2022.124741
4. Mohd Zainuddin, N., et al.: Review of thermal stress and condition monitoring technologies for overhead transmission lines: issues and challenges. IEEE Access **8**, 120053–120081 (2020). https://doi.org/10.1109/ACCESS.2020.3004578
5. IEEE Power Engineering Society: IEEE standard for calculating the current-temperature relationship of bare overhead conductors, vol. 2006, no. January (2007)
6. Hou, Y., et al.: Research and application of dynamic line rating technology. Energy Rep. **6**, 716–730 (2020). https://doi.org/10.1016/j.egyr.2020.11.140
7. Yuan, Z.: Distributed power-flow controller (DPFC) (2017)
8. Dimitrovski, A., Li, Z., Ozpineci, B.: Applications of Saturable-core Reactors (SCR) in Power Systems, pp. 1–5 (2014)
9. Yohanandhan, R.V., Elavarasan, R.M., Pugazhendhi, R., Premkumar, M., Mihet-Popa, L., Terzija, V.: A holistic review on cyber-physical power system (CPPS) testbeds for secure and sustainable electric power grid – Part – I: background on CPPS and necessity of CPPS testbeds. Int. J. Electr. Power Energy Syst. **136**, 107718 (2022). https://doi.org/10.1016/j.ijepes.2021.107718
10. George Trinkaus - Magnetic Amplifiers - another lost technology - 2000 - includes 1951 US Navy article
11. Varela, D., Oliveira, R., Romba, L., Murta-Pina, J.: A superconducting saturable core reactor for power flow control in transmission grids. In: 9th International Conference on Smart Grid, icSmartGrid 2021, pp. 216–219 (2021). https://doi.org/10.1109/icSmartGrid52357.2021.9551240
12. Aaron, M., Ii, Y.: Saturable Reactor for Power Flow Control in Electric Transmission Saturable Reactor for Power Flow Control in Electric Transmission Systems: Modeling and System Impact Study Systems: Modeling and System Impact Study. https://trace.tennessee.edu/utk_graddiss
13. Vilhena, N.M.G.: Contribution for the Study of the Integration of Inductive Superconducting Fault Current Limiters in Electrical Distribution Grids, no. November (2020)
14. Heidary, A., Radmanesh, H., Rouzbehi, K., Moradi Cheshmehbeigi, H.: A multifunction high-temperature superconductive power flow controller and fault current limiter. IEEE Trans. Appl. Supercond. **30**(5) (2020). https://doi.org/10.1109/TASC.2020.2966685
15. Hayakawa, N., et al.: Feasibility study of superconducting power flow controller and fault current limiter (SPFCL). IEEE Trans. Appl. Supercond. **23**(3), 3–6 (2013). https://doi.org/10.1109/TASC.2012.2230677
16. Young, M., Li, Z., Dimitrovski, A.: Modeling and simulation of continuously variable series reactor for power system transient analysis. In: IEEE Power and Energy Society General Meeting (2016). https://doi.org/10.1109/PESGM.2016.7741766

17. Young, M., Dimitrovski, A., Li, Z., Liu, Y.: Gyrator-capacitor approach to modeling a continuously variable series reactor. IEEE Trans. Power Deliv. **31**(3), 1223–1232 (2016). https://doi.org/10.1109/TPWRD.2015.2510642

18. Hayerikhiyavi, M., Dimitrovski, A.: Gyrator-capacitor modeling of a continuously variable series reactor in different operating modes. In: 2021 IEEE Kansas Power and Energy Conference, KPEC 2021 (2021). https://doi.org/10.1109/KPEC51835.2021.9446236

19. Hayerikhiyavi, M., DImitrovski, A.: Comprehensive analysis of continuously variable series reactor using G-C framework. In: IEEE Power and Energy Society General Meeting (2021). https://doi.org/10.1109/PESGM46819.2021.9637971

20. Safaei, A., Zolfaghari, M., Gilvanejad, M., Gharehpetian, G.B.: A survey on fault current limiters: development and technical aspects. Int. J. Electr. Power Energy Syst. **118**, 105729 (2020). https://doi.org/10.1016/J.IJEPES.2019.105729

21. Zhang, G., Wang, H., Qiu, Q., Zhang, Z., Xiao, L., Lin, L.: Recent progress of superconducting fault current limiter in China. Supercond. Sci. Technol. **34**(1), 013001 (2021). https://doi.org/10.1088/1361-6668/abac1f

22. Shen, B., Chen, X., Fu, L., Hao, L., Coombs, T.: Numerical modelling of the dynamic voltage in HTS materials under the action of DC transport currents and different oscillating magnetic fields. Materials **15**(3), 795 (2022). https://doi.org/10.3390/ma15030795

23. Shen, B., Zhang, M., Bian, X., Chen, X., Fu, L.: Optimisation of energy efficiency: dynamic voltages in superconducting tapes to energise superconducting power/energy applications. Electronics **11**(7), 1098 (2022). https://doi.org/10.3390/electronics11071098

An Overview of the Functions of Smart Grids Associated with Virtual Power Plants Including Cybersecurity Measures

Anas Abdullah Alvi[1(✉)], Enrique Romero-Cadaval[1], Eva González-Romera[1], Jamil Hassan[2], and Dmitri Vinnikov[3]

[1] Electrical, Electronic and Control Engineering Department, University of Extremadura, 06006 Badajoz, Spain
`alvi@unex.es`
[2] Energy Products and Services, Badajoz, Spain
[3] Department of Electrical Power Engineering and Mechatronics, Tallinn University of Technology, 12616 Tallinn, Estonia

Abstract. The use of renewable energy is on the rise and is expanding ever so greatly in this modern age of technology. However, it comes with a new set of challenges to properly integrate these renewable energy-based power plants thus forming a virtual power plant safely and reliably into the power grid in which a smart grid plays an effective role. The main focus of this paper is to review the functions a modern-day smart grid plays in the integration of distributed energy resources to the grid to form a virtual power plant including cybersecurity measures. It also addresses a basic example of the detection of a cyber-attack caused into the grid assuming it to be manipulated by a hacker together with a novel solution and later validated by performing simulation.

Keywords: Virtual Power Plant (VPP) · Smart Grid · Inverter · Cyber-Attack

1 Introduction

The virtual power plant (VPP) is the integration of distributed energy resources (DER) under a single coordinated management. A VPP is an interconnected network of decentralized, small-scale power generating technologies, such as solar panels, wind turbines, energy storage systems and manageable loads that work together under the control of a single control system. Similar to a conventional centralized power plant, the VPP may be regulated to adapt to changes in energy demand and supply and can offer grid services like balancing and stability. The purpose of this integration of dispersed energy resources into a unified utility grid is to improve the energy system's dependability, flexibility, and efficiency [1].

Large centralized generation units were intended to be managed by the power system so that real-time monitoring and control of their safe operation and dependability was possible [2, 3]. Renewable energy sources (RES), such as solar, wind, and hydro power,

L. M. Camarinha-Matos and F. Ferrada (Eds.): DoCEIS 2023, IFIP AICT 678, pp. 95–107, 2023.
https://doi.org/10.1007/978-3-031-36007-7_7

have been growing in popularity due to their environmental benefits and decreasing costs. However, their integration into existing power systems has presented new challenges for control and operation [4]. The overwhelming amount of information including weather forecasts, power demand, and supply, that operators must process in real-time and the dependability of the power electronics-based systems working in parallel, as hundreds of power converters would be simultaneously exchanging energy with the grid, is the main obstacle to increasing the expansion of RES. In practice, it has already been observed that generation systems powered by power converters are having an impact on the stability and dependability of power systems due to the dynamics of the converter not matching well with the dynamics of the grid or due to the introduction of voltage and current harmonics into the power system [5, 6]. Even though distributed RES-based units are currently only considered because of their modest involvement, this will change soon due to the rapid increase in RES integration and the diminishing situation of fossil fuel power facilities [7]. In order to balance generation and demand while also contributing to the stability of power systems, utility-scale renewable power facilities must be designed and operated in a certain method [8, 9].

Cyber-security is another important feature that must be taken into consideration for present-day smart grids. This paper consists of cyber-attack detection along with a novel solution by using islanding mode of operation of the VPPs when an attack takes place in the main grid. It also deals with the contribution of modern-day smart grids in the context of VPPs which are listed as follows:

- Transient Frequency and Voltage Stability
- Inertia Support Capability
- Power quality and stability
- Active and Reactive Power Control
- Fast frequency such as power oscillation and inertia response support, reactive power compensation and grid-forming capability.
- Cyber-security measures associated with smart grids.

2   Relationship with Technological Innovation for Connected Cyber Physical Spaces

The increased implementations of VPPs also comes with the challenges affiliated with data protection, securing physical systems and information privacy. Cybercriminals can now deliberately attack the energy sector to disrupt operations thanks to recent technological breakthroughs. Despite efforts by security researchers to reduce the dangers and vulnerabilities, it is still difficult due to the evolution of VPPs into a cyber-physical based system [10, 11]. This is why it is important to have technological innovation in the cyber physical spaces to keep up with the new and unknown methods of cyber-attacks in the energy sector. The energy sector has recently been one of the most targeted industries. Over time, the attackers' motives have evolved. Table 1 illustrates the increase in other incentives, such as cyberwarfare and causing disruptions, even though money is still the dominant driver [12].

Table 1. Effects of Cyber-Attack.

Name of Cyber Attack	Place	Year	Impact	Vulnerability
BlackEnergy	**Ukraine Power Grid**	2014/2015	In Ukraine, a power disruption for a duration of 6 h occurred which affected almost 230,000 people	Poor infrastructure, corruption, and tensed relations with external countries [13]
Industroyer/Crash Override	**Ukraine Power Grid (North City of Kiev)**	2016	Ukraine lost 1/5 of its electrical capacity due to an hour-long power outage	Direct control of the switches and circuit breakers at power grid substations using four ICS protocols [14]
Triton	**Oil and Gas Plant Saudi Arabia**	2017	The attackers were interested in causing an explosion to spread throughout the entire plant, but their plan was thwarted due to a virus flaw and vulnerability	Malicious TriStation protocol use by a malware framework to target the Triconex Safety Instrumented System (SIS) controllers [15]

3   Functions of Smart Grids

A VPP is a network-based system which combines and controls numerous DERs as if they were a single power plant. The VPP communicates with the grid operator and the combined DER. While physical power is exchanged between DERs and the grid, the VPP communicates with both the grid operator and the aggregated DERs as shown in Fig. 1. Some of the functions of smart grids associated with VPPs are discussed in detail below.

3.1   Inertia Support Capability

The VPP offers inertia support by synchronizing the parameters of grid-forming inverters. Additionally, an online learning-based parameter sets method is created that allows the VPP's inertia to be adjusted. Constant voltage and constant frequency control (V/f control), constant power control (PQ control) and virtual synchronous generator control (VSG control) are the three control techniques that the majority of DERs use to function. Grid-following (GFL) inverters frequently use PQ control, which is dependent on pre-determined frequency and voltage reference values. As a result, it cannot deliver active adjustable inertia support. V/f control, which is commonly adopted in grid-forming (GFM) inverters, can function in a microgrid's islanding mode but cannot supply inertia. A possible method to reduce system inertia is VSG control, which replicates the inertia and damping properties of traditional synchronous generators (SGs). By modifying the GFM inverters' control parameters (i.e., damping coefficient D and the moment of inertia J) in VSG mode, the DERs' inertia can be changed [16].

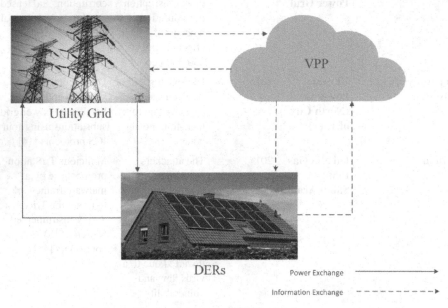

Fig. 1. Overview of VPP interactions.

3.2 Power Quality and Stability

The grid-supportive capabilities of smart grids help the system to maintain power quality and stability. For network managers to directly observe and control every single inverter and DER, however, would not be feasible. VPPs and distribution energy resource management systems (DERMS) are therefore being studied in global states with high penetration of renewable energy. The DERMS software organizes various DERs to achieve local feeder-specific advantages such as optimal power flow, locational capacity relief, and voltage and active power management [17]. The management system can send control signals to smart inverters in DERMS-type applications to control demand-flexible DERs to assist the grid, such as discharging batteries to match the demand or halting electric vehicle (EV) charging to reduce demand. The inverter can function as an interface between the grid and the local energy asset because of its position at the point of intersection in the power network [18].

3.3 Voltage Stability and Transient Frequency Analysis

The flow and control of energy were the main objectives of the VPP models in the past. A dynamic VPP model must be implemented for the system transient response study, a model that works well for system analysis and that the Transmission System Operator (TSO) can use to assess the effect of VPPs in the entire grid. The suggested framework can support the transient response of the vital controllers that comprise the distributed generators that constitute the VPP. The suggested aggregated model's validity is confirmed by comparison with a real-time detailed Electro-Magnetic Transients (EMT) model of the VPP [19].

3.4 Reactive Power Compensation, Frequency Support and Grid-Forming Capability

Transmission system operators (TSOs) are increasingly demanding power plants with power converter interfaces to provide frequency support, reactive power compensation, and grid-forming capabilities. In these plants, a substantial number of converters are run concurrently, and each one must be properly coordinated to offer these services. The virtual synchronous machine (VSM) control approach is frequently used for this purpose. The number of connected converters, their size, control settings, and electrical connections all affect how dynamically the entire plant behaves. Because of this, it is challenging to understand how each VSM affects the plant's response and its aggregated dynamic characteristics [20].

3.5 Fast Frequency Support

System operators have been obliged to tighten grid rules to require renewable power plants (RPPs) to offer fast frequency support, such as power oscillation damping and inertia response, because of the growing contribution of renewables to power systems. This can be achieved by implementing virtual synchronous power plant controller (VSPPC) for RPPs. Since it allows for the reproduction of inertia and offers capabilities for power oscillation damping, the VSPPC benefits the most from replicating the behavior of a SG, particularly in the case of grid events. The primary benefit of the VSPPC is that it avoids the need to modify the converter controllers in the plant, which are frequently controlled as grid-following generation units.

At present, RPPs are required to offer dynamic services like power oscillation damping and inertia response in addition to traditional control services, such as voltage regulation and frequency [21–26]. One of the approaches to establish these newly required services is to use the grid-forming power converters instead of grid-following power converters, which may use a controller based on a virtual synchronous machine [27]. Each power converter that forms a grid can function as a synchronous generator to give the grid damping and synthetic inertia, primarily managing the current or power reference [28, 29]. It has been shown that the implementation of a grid-forming power converter is practical for a single power converter [30, 31]. This strategy might not be financially viable for RPP, though, as it would be necessary to spend more time and money to design a new control system for the power converters. Moreover, the grid-forming power converters' independent parallel functioning may result in problems with power oscillation in the plant [32].

3.6 Active and Reactive Power Control

Distributed generation helps to improve the quality of power. Distributed generation (DG) provides significant advantages for the enhancement of the voltage profile and power factor in places where voltage support is challenging due to constraints on the primary (central) power grid. Large-scale decentralized power generation unit implementation may also cause instability. This is caused by the ineffective power control of the DG units, which also causes reactive power imbalance and fluctuations in the voltage of the power network. These factors make operating DG sources in a regulated environment crucial. As a result, DG control paradigms have been proposed, with MicroGrid and VPP being the two primary ones. For synchronous generators, there are currently no control paradigms that permit independent control of the machine's active and reactive power output. For any network to be stable, the power balance must be maintained. Generator instability, which can include rotor angle instability, voltage instability and frequency instability can be brought on by an improper balance of active and reactive power in the network [33].

4   Cybersecurity Measures in Grids

Modern day smart grids require cyber security measures due to the increasing number of attacks by hackers. There exist different types of solutions regarding cybersecurity measures in grids namely confidentiality, integrity, and availability [34] In this paper, two scenarios of attacks are considered in a VPP. The first one is the attack inside the low voltage grid or the microgrid. The cyber-physical layer of the VPP can monitor the voltage and current in different points of the layer to detect any sudden changes due to external manipulation and hence the system is restored back to normal operation. In the second scenario, the cyber-attack is considered inside the main grid or high voltage side. A novel solution is also proposed regarding this type of threat in detail by using the islanding mode of operation and later validated by performing simulation using MATLAB/Simulink.

4.1   A Basic Example of Determining Cyber Attack in a Micro-grid

A basic example based on Thevenin voltage closed form derivation is demonstrated in the following Fig. 2(a). It comprises of a PV field with 616 solar panel modules coupled in an array of seven series connections and eighty-eight parallel connections with a combined power of 250 kW. 50 Hz is the rated frequency taken into account for the system. In order to successfully reduce the harmonics introduced to an acceptable value and achieve the desired power quality, the PV field is linked to a three-level, neutral point clamping (NPC) inverter that converts DC power to AC and incorporates an LCL filter. A distribution transformer is finally used to link the system to the grid. On the high voltage side, a balanced three phase load rated at 250 kW (at a nominal voltage of $25kV_{RMS}$) is connected. Mainly, in this example, an attack is introduced in the point between the microgrid and distribution grid.

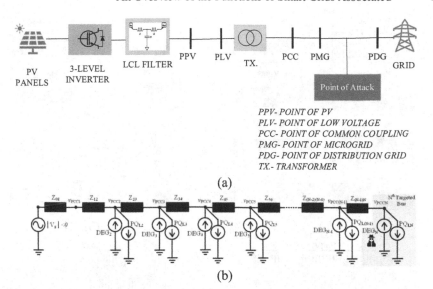

Fig. 2. (a) Block Diagram of the Model under Study (b) An illustration of N-DEGs TVPP for the closed form derivation of Thèvenin voltage

4.1.1 Scenario 1

One of the basic methods of identifying a cyber-attack is determining the manipulation of the voltage and current and as a result the power at different setpoints in a transmission line which are also known as Point of Common Coupling (PCC). The voltage and current in these PCCs are constantly compared with a fixed set of values in the cyber security outer layer. If there is a drastic change in either the voltage or current and as a result, the active power in these PCCs, it should be assumed that there is a high chance of the system being attacked during that period.

In the given illustration of N number of DEGs Technical Virtual Power Plant (TVPP) for the closed form derivation of Thèvenin voltage, the cybersecurity analytics system's methodology for identifying normal operation region serves as the foundation [35]. This region of regular operation is used as a confirmation approach to separate malicious set-points that the network cyber-layer requires. A cyber attacker who controls the set-points for the VPP cyber-layer is the source of these harmful set-points. Based on a derived one-to-one mapping between the cyber-layer generated set-points and the internal PCC bus voltages of the network, the normal operation region is defined. Using internal PCC bus voltage monitoring, this derived mapping is contrasted with an inverse mapping to look for anomalies. The voltage anomaly is caused by an intrusion after the cybersecurity analytics system notices a discrepancy between the one-to-one mapping and the inverse mapping [35].

The system is simulated for a total of 1s by using MATLAB Simulink software as demonstrated in Fig. 3. It is assumed that at 0.5s, the system is attacked by the hacker in between the point of microgrid and distribution grid and as a result the voltage, current and power values are changed from their rated values. From these manipulated values,

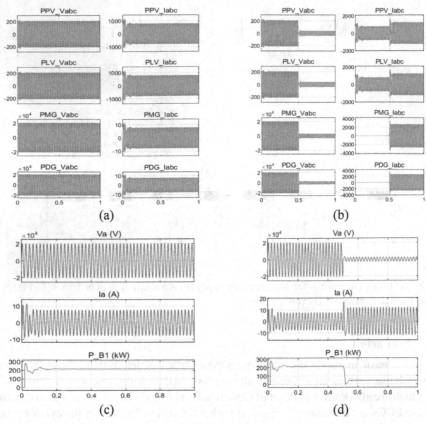

Fig. 3. Voltage (in V) and Current (in A) waveforms in different points of microgrid, as indicated in Fig. 2a (a) during normal condition, (b) after the attack; and Voltage (in V), Current (in A) and Active Power (kW) waveforms of a single phase during (c) normal condition, (d) under attack.

it can be easily identified that the system is under attack by the hacker and necessary steps must be taken to bring the system back to normal operating condition.

4.1.2   Scenario 2

In this case, it is assumed that a cyber-attack takes place in between the main grid and the distribution grid. Often in many circumstances, a hacker has no prior knowledge regarding the total network of VPPs across the whole transmission system. However, the hacker may have the total information regarding the main grid. In this case, the hacker tries to manipulate the data in the main grid system and makes the system unstable and as a result, a blackout may occur. One of the many solutions in this scenario is to isolate the grid from the system and use the islanding mode operation for the microgrid. In this case, the detection takes place if the voltage changes to ±15% and frequency to ±0.1 Hz [36]. In Fig. 4, a flowchart based on the algorithm can be established based on these aforementioned conditions.

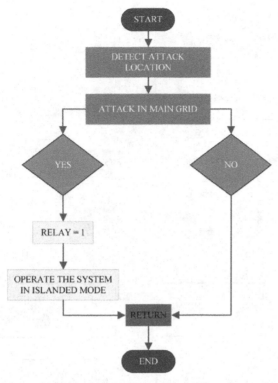

Fig. 4. Flowchart for operating the system in islanded condition due a cyber-attack in the main grid.

In this case in Fig. 5, the simulation results are observed for a total duration of 1s. At 0.5s, a hacker tries to manipulate the system in the main grid location. It can be observed that, if the main grid is not isolated from the grid connected PV based solar power plant, the system becomes unstable and is not able to generate any active power. However, if the grid is disconnected from the system by means of a relay, breakers and using islanding mode of operation, it can be observed that the solar power plant is able to supply active power into the loads and the system remains stable.

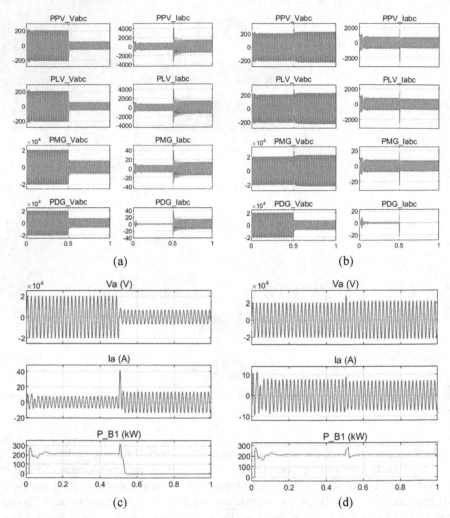

Fig. 5. Voltage (in V) and Current (in A) waveforms in different points of microgrid, as indicated in Fig. 2a (a) before islanding condition, (b) after islanding condition; and Voltage (in V), Current (in A) and Active Power (kW) waveforms of a single phase (c) before islanding condition, (d) after islanding condition.

5   Conclusion

This paper mainly reviewed the different functions along with cybersecurity measures of modern-day smart grids in the context of VPPs. The importance of these functions and the related existing challenges are assessed in different sectors of smart grids and the possible solutions are described. Finally, a case study is performed consisting of a grid connected PV power plant in which a basic detection of cyber-attack together with a novel solution is demonstrated by means of simulation by considering two scenarios of the point of attacks in a power transmission line. It can be observed that, islanding mode of operation of a VPP can be an effective way to supply electrical power to the loads in a microgrid in case there is a cyber-attack in the main generation plant. In the future work, more ways to nullify the effects of cyber-attacks will be assessed along with the improvements of present-day solutions.

Acknowledgement. This project has received funding from the European Union's Horizon 2020 research and innovation programme under the Marie Skłodowska-Curie grant agreement No 955614.

References

1. VPP explained: What is a virtual power plant? VPP explained: What is a Virtual Power Plant? (n.d.). https://www.next-kraftwerke.com/vpp/virtual-power-plant. Accessed 9 Mar 2023
2. Khan, R., et al.: Energy sustainability-survey on technology and control of microgrid, smart grid and virtual power plant. IEEE Access **9**, 104663–104694 (2021). https://doi.org/10.1109/ACCESS.2021.3099941
3. Khorasany, M., Razzaghi, R., Dorri, A., Jurdak, R., Siano, P.: Paving the path for two-sided energy markets: an overview of different approaches. IEEE Access **8**, 223708–223722 (2020). https://doi.org/10.1109/ACCESS.2020.3040391
4. Mao, T., et al.: Virtual power plant platforms and their applications in practice: a brief review. In: 2020 IEEE Sustainable Power and Energy Conference (iSPEC), pp. 2071–2076 (2020). https://doi.org/10.1109/iSPEC50848.2020.9351147
5. Pal, P., Parvathy, A.K., Devabalaji, K.R.: A broad review on optimal operation of Virtual power plant. In: 2019 2nd International Conference on Power and Embedded Drive Control (ICPEDC), pp. 400–405 (2019). https://doi.org/10.1109/ICPEDC47771.2019.9036530
6. Wang, X., Liu, Z., Zhang, H., Zhao, Y., Shi, J., Ding, H.: A review on virtual power plant concept, application and challenges. In: 2019 IEEE Innovative Smart Grid Technologies - Asia (ISGT Asia), pp. 4328–4333 (2019). https://doi.org/10.1109/ISGT-Asia.2019.8881433
7. Xavier, R., Bekker, B., Chihota, M.J.: The value of smart inverter control in distribution energy management systems and virtual power plants, and opportunities for South Africa. In: 2021 56th International Universities Power Engineering Conference (UPEC), pp. 1–6 (2021). https://doi.org/10.1109/UPEC50034.2021.9548163
8. Yu, X., Tang, C., Palensky, P., Colombo, A.W.: Blockchain: what does it mean to industrial electronics?: technologies, challenges, and opportunities. IEEE Ind. Electron. Mag. **16**(2), 4–14 (2022). https://doi.org/10.1109/MIE.2021.3066332
9. Alobaidi, A.H., Fazlhashemi, S.S., Khodayar, M., Wang, J., Khodayar, M.E.: Distribution service restoration with renewable energy sources: a review. IEEE Trans. Sustain. Energy (2022). https://doi.org/10.1109/TSTE.2022.3199161
10. Venkatachary, S.K., Alagappan, A., Andrews, L.J.B.: Cybersecurity challenges in energy sector (virtual power plants) - can edge computing principles be applied to enhance security? Energy Inform. **4**(1), 1–21 (2021). https://doi.org/10.1186/s42162-021-00139-7
11. Adu-Kankam, K.O., Camarinha-Matos, L.M.: Emerging community energy ecosystems: analysis of organizational and governance structures of selected representative cases. In: Camarinha-Matos, L.M., Almeida, R., Oliveira, J. (eds.) DoCEIS 2019. IAICT, vol. 553, pp. 24–40. Springer, Cham (2019). https://doi.org/10.1007/978-3-030-17771-3_3
12. Alghassab, M.: Analyzing the impact of cybersecurity on monitoring and control systems in the energy sector. Energies **15**, 218 (2021). https://doi.org/10.3390/en15010218

13. Duo, W., Zhou, M., Abusorrah, A.: A survey of cyber attacks on cyber physical systems: recent advances and challenges. IEEE/CAA J. Autom. Sinica **9**(5), 784–800 (2022). https://doi.org/10.1109/JAS.2022.105548

14. Win32/industroyer-welivesecurity. https://www.welivesecurity.com/wp-content/uploads/2017/06/Win32_Industroyer.pdf. Accessed 26 Apr 2023

15. International cyber law: interactive toolkit. Triton (2017) - International cyber law: interactive toolkit. International Cyber Law: Interactive Toolkit (2021). https://cyberlaw.ccdcoe.org/wiki/Triton_(2017)

16. Hu, Q., et al.: Grid-forming inverter enabled virtual power plants with inertia support capability. IEEE Trans. Smart Grid **13**(5), 4134–4143 (2022). https://doi.org/10.1109/TSG.2022.3141414

17. Alvi, A.A., Mannan, M.A.: Load flow analysis of dhaka grid using PSAT and ETAP and performance comparison to PGCB Data. AIUB J. Sci. Eng. (AJSE) **18**(3), 81–87 (2019). https://doi.org/10.53799/ajse.v18i3.58

18. Xavier, R., Bekker, B., Chihota, M.J.: The value of smart inverter control in distribution energy management systems and virtual power plants, and opportunities for South Africa. In: 2021 56th International Universities Power Engineering Conference (UPEC), Middlesbrough, United Kingdom, pp. 1–6 (2021). https://doi.org/10.1109/UPEC50034.2021.9548163

19. Chen, J., Liu, M., Milano, F.: Aggregated model of virtual power plants for transient frequency and voltage stability analysis. IEEE Trans. Power Syst. **36**(5), 4366–4375 (2021). https://doi.org/10.1109/TPWRS.2021.3063280

20. González-Cajigas, A., Roldán-Pérez, J., Bueno, E.J.: Design and analysis of parallel-connected grid-forming virtual synchronous machines for island and grid-connected applications. IEEE Trans. Power Electron. **37**(5), 5107–5121 (2022). https://doi.org/10.1109/TPEL.2021.3127463

21. Romero-Cadaval, E., Miñambres-Marcos, V.M., Moreno-Muñoz, A., Real-Calvo, R.J., González de la Rosa, J.J., Sierra-Fernández, J.M.: Active functions implementation in smart inverters for distributed energy resources. In: 2013 International Conference-Workshop Compatibility and Power Electronics, Ljubljana, Slovenia, pp. 52–57 (2013). https://doi.org/10.1109/CPE.2013.6601128

22. Abdollahi, M., Candela, J.I., Rocabert, J., Elsaharty, M.A., Rodriguez, P.: Novel analytical method for dynamic design of renewable SSG SPC unit to mitigate low-frequency electromechanical oscillations. IEEE Trans. Power Electron. **35**(7), 7532–7544 (2020). https://doi.org/10.1109/TPEL.2019.2956397

23. Varma, R.K., Akbari, M.: Simultaneous fast frequency control and power oscillation damping by utilizing PV solar system as PVSTATCOM. IEEE Trans. Sustain. Energy **11**(1), 415–425 (2020). https://doi.org/10.1109/TSTE.2019.2892943

24. Fang, J., Lin, P., Li, H., Yang, Y., Tang, Y.: An improved virtual inertia control for three-phase voltage source converters connected to a weak grid. IEEE Trans. Power Electron. **34**(9), 8660–8670 (2019). https://doi.org/10.1109/TPEL.2018.2885513

25. Baltas, G.N., Lai, N.B., Marin, L., Tarrasó, A., Rodriguez, P.: Grid forming power converters tuned through artificial intelligence to damp sub synchronous interaction. https://doi.org/10.1109/ACCESS.2020.2995298

26. Knuppel, T., Nielsen, J.N., Jensen, K.H., Dixon, A., Østergaard, J.: Power oscillation damping controller for wind power plant utilizing wind turbine inertia as energy storage. In: Proceedings of IEEE Power and Energy Society General Meeting, pp. 1–8 (2011). https://doi.org/10.1109/PES.2011.6038908

27. Chen, Y., Hesse, R., Turschner, D., Beck, H.P.: Dynamic properties of the virtual synchronous machine (VISMA). Renew. Energy Power Qual. J. **1**(9), 755–759 (2011). https://doi.org/10.24084/repqj09.444

28. Zhang, W., Tarraso, A., Rocabert, J., Luna, A., Candela, J.I., Rodriguez, P.: Frequency support properties of the synchronous power control for grid-connected converters. IEEE Trans. Ind. Appl. **55**(5), 5178–5189 (2019). https://doi.org/10.1109/TIA.2019.2928517
29. Mandrile, F., Carpaneto, E., Bojoi, R.: Grid-feeding inverter with simplified virtual synchronous compensator providing grid services and grid support. IEEE Trans. Ind. Appl. **57**(1), 559–569 (2021). https://doi.org/10.1109/TIA.2020.3028334
30. Rodríguez, P., Citro, C., Candela, J.I., Rocabert, J., Luna, A.: Flexible grid connection and islanding of SPC-Based PV power converters. IEEE Trans. Ind. Appl. **54**(3), 2690–2702 (2018). https://doi.org/10.1109/TIA.2018.2800683
31. Verdugo, C., Tarraso, A., Candela, J.I., Rocabert, J., Rodriguez, P.: "Centralized synchronous controller based on load angle regulation for photovoltaic power plants. IEEE J. Emerg. Sel. Top. Power Electron. **9**(1), 485–496 (2020). https://doi.org/10.1109/JESTPE.2020.2995339
32. Tarrasó, A., Lai, N.B., Verdugo, C., Candela, J.I., Rodriguez, P.: Design of controller for virtual synchronous power plant. IEEE Trans. Ind. Appl. **57**(4), 4033–4041 (2021). https://doi.org/10.1109/TIA.2021.3075173
33. Khan, H.A., Bargiev, P., Sreeram, V., Iu, H.H.C., Fernando, T.L., Mishra, Y.: Active and reactive power control of synchronous generator for the realization of a virtual power plant. In: IECON 2012 - 38th Annual Conference on IEEE Industrial Electronics Society, Montreal, QC, Canada, pp. 1204–1210 (2012). https://doi.org/10.1109/IECON.2012.6388599
34. Gunduz, M.Z., Das, R.: Cyber-security on smart grid: threats and potential solutions. Comput. Netw. **169**, 107094 (2020). https://doi.org/10.1016/j.comnet.2019.107094
35. Khan, A., Hosseinzadehtaher, M., Shadmand, M.B., Mazumder, S.K.: Cybersecurity analytics for virtual power plants. In: 2021 IEEE 12th International Symposium on Power Electronics for Distributed Generation Systems (PEDG), Chicago, IL, USA, pp. 1–5 (2021). https://doi.org/10.1109/PEDG51384.2021.9494255
36. EN 50160:2010 Voltage characteristics of electricity supplied by public electricity networks

Intelligent Manufacturing

A Bio-inspired and Altruistic-Based Framework to Support Collaborative Healing in a Smart Manufacturing Shop-Floor

Luis A. Estrada-Jimenez[(✉)], Sepideh Kalateh, Sanaz Nikghadam Hojjati, and Jose Barata

NOVA University of Lisbon, School of Science and Technology, UNINOVA – CTS and LASI, Campus de Caparica, 2829-516 Monte de Caparica, Portugal

{lestrada,sepideh.kalateh,sanaznik}@uninova.pt

Abstract. Biologicalisation defines the analysis of biological patterns as a source of inspiration to model intelligent manufacturing systems. Due to their inherent adaptability, these design representations are highly desirable considering the increasing complexity of modeling current manufacturing solutions. Contributing to the idea of self-organizing and autonomous shop floors, we present a framework that aims to support the collaborative healing of manufacturing resources. This has been inspired on the altruistic behavior of bats in which social care is demonstrated (e.g., in bat colonies) even at the cost of individuals' fitness/health. These ideas are conceptually showcased in an emergent automation manufacturing application, i.e., peer-to-peer energy sharing in automated guided vehicles. Some conclusions, and potential future research are discussed at the end of the paper.

Keywords: Biologicalisation · Self-organization · Smart Manufacturing · Self-healing · Artificial Intelligence · Altruism · Collective Behaviour

1 Introduction

Biologicalisation considers the use of "bio-inspired principles in intelligent manufacturing applications to fulfill their full potential" [1]. The collective intelligence of biological systems can be used as a source of inspiration to design self-organizing, self-adapting, or self-healing mechanisms [2]. Those are key issues in the fourth industrial revolution because of the increasing complexity in their engineering design [3]. Some cases of application include the immune system, where immune cells are used as analogies to define intelligent agents that perform distributed monitoring and diagnosis [4]. Stigmergy, where ant pheromones [5] are used as a mechanism to indirectly coordinate control tasks, or the chemical reaction model where the self-assembly of manufacturing modules is provided similarly to how molecules in a solution react [6].

In healing operations, this collective biological behavior can be used as a source of inspiration to define collaborative self-repair of robots, for providing cures, for sharing

© The Author(s) 2023
L. M. Camarinha-Matos and F. Ferrada (Eds.): DoCEIS 2023, IFIP AICT 678, pp. 111–121, 2023.
https://doi.org/10.1007/978-3-031-36007-7_8

spare parts, or even in peer-to-peer energy-sharing problems. This has been generally elusive considering the context of biologicalisation in smart manufacturing applications.

Thus, the definition and analysis of these ideas in the form of a conceptual framework are the general motivation of this work, where the social altruistic behavior of vampire bats is used as a metaphor to define two basic roles in intelligent manufacturing resources: Altruistic/Donor and Recipients. Those are the base to describe a collaborative healing environment where the ultimate goal of a highly adaptable and flexible manufacturing system can be achieved at the cost of a minor decrease in individual resource fitness. The description of these roles is essential, especially in emergent manufacturing infrastructures e.g., shop floors with flexible transportation of tools and consumables [2, 7]. See Fig. 1 where a basic overview of this idea is shown and applied to a peer-to-peer energy-sharing problem under the context of the matrix production concept [8]. These ideas are also showcased in a simulated scenario using the software NetLogo. Various conclusions and potential future research directions are derived from these results. The next sections of this paper are driven by the following research question (RQ) and hypothesis (H).

- **RQ:** How can a manufacturing framework for healing operations be implemented while denoting autonomous and collaborative collective behavior?
- **H:** A framework with the preceding characteristics can be implemented if certain properties of the reciprocal altruism of vampire bats are studied and represented as a collective healing problem in a shop-floor.

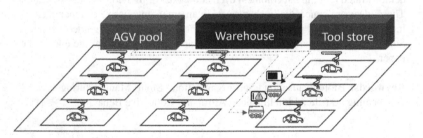

Fig. 1. Peer-to-peer energy sharing in the matrix production concept

2   Relation to Connected Cyber-Physical Spaces

Cyber-physical spaces are defined as" engineered systems operating within physical space with design requirements that depend on space" [9]. Due to their inherent design complexity to generate autonomous and adaptable solutions, i.e., in the context of manufacturing systems, it is necessary to consider new ways of engineering inspiration. Solutions based on collective intelligence, where group intelligence emerges from individual collaboration (e.g., in biological systems) are a promising line of research in this direction. This can generate new ways of adaptability, flexibility, robustness, and resilience for systems that aim to be highly interconnected (i.e., cyber-physical).

3   Altruism in Vampire Bats: A Biologicalisation Concept

This section introduces the origin of the idea of altruism and reciprocal altruism and represents the road-map, and some required technologies in order to model autonomous collaborative healing solutions. Fig. 2 shows the overall concepts and ideas of this section.

- *Altruism and reciprocal altruism:* In one of the genuinely classic articles in the subject of altruism research, Trivers (1971) [10] made the discovery of the reciprocal altruism hypothesis. He coined the term "altruism" to describe actions that benefit someone other than the person acting in an altruistic manner. He uses evolutionary biology to present concepts of costs and gains. He argued that charitable acts frequently result in favors being returned, which can result in a gain for the initial giver. This suggests that doing good actions in strategic networks can result in favors being returned, which would then improve performance both on an individual level and community/social level [11, 12].
- *Reciprocal altruism in Vampire bats:* In situations where there is a risk of death, such as starvation, and it is impossible to predict which individual will be successful on any given occasion, Trivers (1971) [10] argued that reciprocal altruism will become an evolutionarily stable strategy but only if those who are successful in obtaining food get more than they immediately need, and share it with a neighbor.

  One of the noble examples of altruism connection has been observed in vampire bats. These types of bats subsist by sucking the blood off cattle hides, but they frequently go without food. They can survive without food for up to three nights before they perish [13, 14]. Ordinary vampire bats only consume blood and die after 70 hours of fasting, although hungry bats frequently receive food from the regurgitation of their roost-mates. Sharing food among vampire bats is a behavior that happens naturally, is energy-intensive, occurs between kin and non-kin, and may be artificially induced [15]. This behavior has the potential to be a great model for studying the enforcement of cooperation and connection in the societal and industrial domain, as it represents a high level of collaboration, autonomy for individuals, and successful survival especially in the crisis of sufficient supplies.
- *Altruism and reciprocal altruism within the autonomous manufacturing domain:* An autonomous or self-organized manufacturing shop-floor refers to a system that can fulfill its inherent processes (handling, maintenance, control) without human assistance (external intervention). The manufacturing needs are met by autonomous production systems that have the ability to self-manage. Also, an intelligent architecture enables the reuse and sharing of independent task-specific modules which can decrease the manual engineering labor required for configuration and reconfiguration [16, 2].

  Effective communication and collaboration among autonomous vehicles is one of the key criteria in order to fulfill sustainable, self-organized, and collaborative manufacturing, specifically in the time of need for help such as energy ran out, tool repairs, or load sharing. Here is the area in which Altruism has innovative ideas to offer. The intra-group cooperative behavior of reciprocal altruism guarantees that the non-relative agents get assistance in pairs in their time of need [17]. In this way it assures self-management and continuous collaboration within the manufacturing resources, this happens in situations where agents have a solid and stable connection and bond to make autonomous decision-making.

– *Technologies to support altruism and reciprocal altruism:* To make manufacturing processes autonomous, re-configurable, and flexible new technological enablers, and computational tools are constantly being developed. Cooperative altruistic behavior can be assisted by many of these technologies. Intelligent cooperative agents can abstract specific resource awareness and allow distributed communication. Intelligent manufacturing modules can be re-used and shared, providing the capacity of reallocating in case of need. Smart perception systems and artificial intelligence methods allow the monitoring of physical variables to have awareness of the status of individual resources. Hardware like wireless energy chargers may allow the sharing of energy consumption between different resources. Thus, the implementation of altruistic behavior is possible within the current landscape of technologies. However, applying the altruistic model in the context of a smart manufacturing shop-floor requires a concrete framework. This will be discussed in detail in the next section.

4   Framework to Support Altruistic Collaborative Healing

The proposed framework relies on the definition of intelligent agents capable of social ability (communication) and autonomous decision-making. It has been inspired by previous ideas of altruistic behavior for multi-agent systems [18–20] and the context provided of altruism in vampire bats. The main differentiator of the proposed framework is its examination under a self-healing smart manufacturing context. Main roles and components are defined below. In this work an agent can be considered as an entity in the shop-floor capable of performing any manufacturing operation, e.g. transport, assembly or machining. Fig. 3 presents an overview of the conceptual framework for collaborative healing.

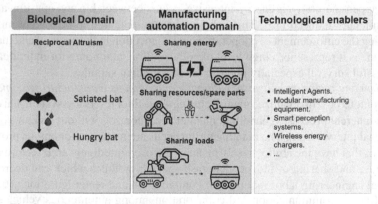

Fig. 2. Bioligalisation of a healing process based on the concept of altruism

4.1   Definition of Agents' Roles

The framework is built under the definition of two main roles.

– *Recipient agent:* Entity that has or is going to have a malfunction or anomaly and requires assistance to continue with its current task.

– *Altruistic/Donor agent:* Entity that in ongoing conditions is capable of assisting a recipient agent, either by providing a cure or by sacrificing part of its fitness while successfully fulfilling its own task.

4.2 Definition of Main Components

The agents of the framework are built within six main functional components:

– *Current task:* Ongoing activity or set of activities assigned to an agent e.g. transportation, assembly, etc. An idle state denotes a momentary stop of the specific task to help or to receive help. See Fig. 4a where a general model of a task is described.
– *Health monitoring:* The element in charge of continuously tracking the health status or a type of potential failure an agent can have. If any problem or failure is identified, an altruistic signal will be emitted looking for a candidate altruistic agent that can provide support. Examples of monitoring units are the remaining energy of an AGV, the remaining useful life of a tool, the inability to carry a load, etc.
– *Remaining altruistic time (lead time):* Time in which an agent can show altruistic behavior. Difference between the estimated time in fulfilling a task and its due date. It can be referred to as the lead time or the maximum allowed cycle time.

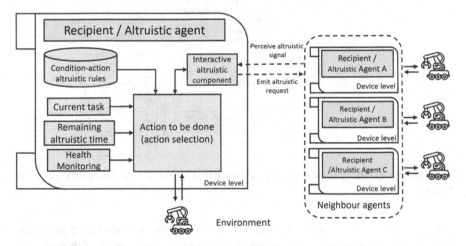

Fig. 3. Framework for collaborative healing based on altruistic behavior

– *Condition-action altruistic rules: a* Set of rules (behaviors) that can be performed by an altruistic agent in order to provide healing support. These are launched once an altruistic signal has been detected and the altruistic task's feasibility has been checked. As there are many different strategies that can be applied in a healing context, this can be treated as a multidimensional decision tree, where each dimension can represent a topic for altruistic support, e.g., energy sharing, load sharing, spare parts tool exchange, etc. These rules should also contemplate restrictions in the applications of certain behaviors. See Fig. 4b where a generic model of decision tree is described.
– *Interactive altruism detection:* Component in charge of both perceiving altruistic signals and emitting altruistic requests.

– *Action to be done:* Main decision-making entity. It takes as input the monitoring component, remaining altruistic time, and interactive altruistic detection to decide if the agent's behavior should be Recipient or Altruistic. Also, it can choose a proper altruistic rule based on the environmental context. It is also the execution unit and interface with the physical resources.

4.3   Execution: Activity Diagram

During the execution of the framework, various stages must be considered.

First, when an anomaly or failure is detected by the health monitoring component, a healing request is launched to the action selection component. This will analyze the feasibility of stopping its primary task. When stopped, a signal will be emitted asking for an altruistic agent and with the necessary requirements for its healing.

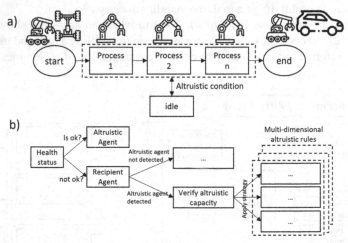

Fig. 4. (a) Task modeling as a sequential process and (b) Decision tree modeling for the condition-action rules

Agents that can perceive this request will decide whether to assist the recipient agent based on their own capabilities i.e., remaining altruistic time, own health monitoring, and current task. If the altruistic request is accepted, the now-called altruistic agent will stop temporarily its current task (idle state). After that and considering the altruistic request, a proper altruistic behavior(s) will be applied from the predefined condition-action rules, and if needed it will approach the recipient agent. Once close enough, the required altruistic behavior will be applied. After that, both the recipient and altruistic agents will continue their normal tasks. Figure 5 summarizes this logic as an activity diagram.

5 Experimental Use Case: Distributed Peer-to-Peer Energy Sharing for Autonomous Mobile Robots

In a shop-floor with flexible transportation mobile robots may have different tasks and therefore different residual energy. Energy can be also restricted by the number and location of charging stations. In extreme conditions (e.g., a rush order) running out of energy can mean a delay or a bottleneck in production. Motivated by this and by previous works in this field [21–24] we decide to showcase the proposed collaborative self-healing framework in this context. Important requirements and assumptions are made to simplify the demonstration of this concept:

- Mobile robots can communicate with each other.
- The collaboration is driven when a specific energy threshold is reached.
- The collaboration is type reactive at this moment.
- There is a priority on sharing energy rather than coming back to a charging station.
- There is instantaneous energy transference with 100% efficiency.

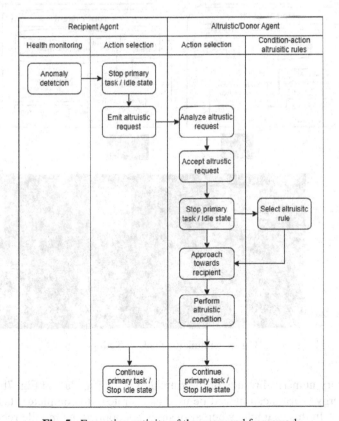

Fig. 5. Execution activity of the proposed framework

The use case consists of two mobile robots. Each of them has a particular task and both tasks must be executed at the same time (transport material to a cell and come back to the home position). One mobile robot has full energy, while the other lacks the energy to complete the task. In this context, the idea is to understand the results of the proposed framework in terms of cycle time and total energy used under 3 scenarios: (1) without altruism, (2) with altruism, (3) with altruism, and with a restriction. In the latter case, the restriction launches the altruistic behavior just when there is a predefined distance between the altruistic and recipient entities.

5.1 Simulation, Results, and Discussion

Previous scenarios were implemented using the software NetLogo, commonly used to study complex behaviors in multi-agent systems. A simple interface was designed to visualize the interaction of the agents, energy consumption, and cycle time in units (u). Figure 6 presents a sketch of the simulation implemented.

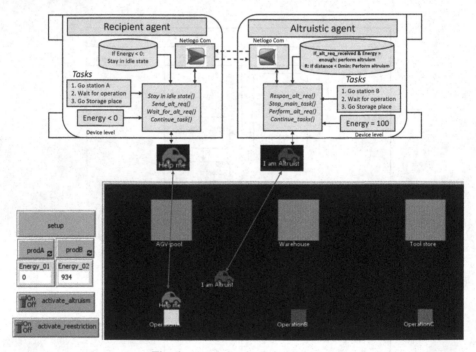

Fig. 6. Simulation made in Netlogo

Preliminary numerical results of the simulation (see Fig. 7a and Fig. 7b) show that altruistic energy sharing can indeed be used as a strategy to complete a task in a case of emergency. In this example, when altruism is not applied the mobile robot 1 cannot autonomously finish its task (which will imply the need for extra manual work). When the altruistic property is applied Robot 1 will be helped by Robot 2 (it will share energy). It is important to note also that, even if altruism is applied, some restrictions are needed to improve the performance of the process (e.g., which is the optimal condition to help another entity while maintaining a certain level of optimal conditions in the process).

In this example, the distance restriction reduced the overall consumption by 49 units (18%) (altruist is activated just when the mobile robot 2 is close enough to the mobile robot 2) compared to the approach that did not use the restriction. A similar result was obtained with the cycle time (time needed for product manufacturing) i.e., 3,37 units of time were reduced in the manufacturing of product 2 (at the cost of a slight increment in the product 1 cycle time). Overall, we can state that these show the potential of this concept. Altruistic collaborative healing can be very effective in emergency situations and can promote higher levels of adaptability and flexibility. More experiments need to be done to understand in detail its potential, possible limitations, and specific scenarios of application.

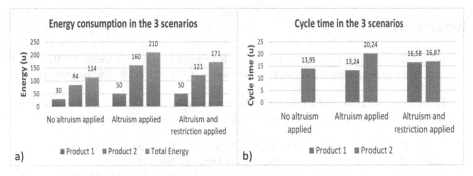

Fig. 7. Simulation results. a) Energy consumption and b) Cycle time

6 Conclusions

The main takeaways of this paper are:

- Introduces a biologicalisation process for collaborative self-healing inspired by the altruistic behavior of bats.
- Presents a framework that conceptualized this idea providing two main roles to the manufacturing resources: Recipient and Altruist.
- Preliminary results of this concept are showcased using the software NetLogo in a distributed peer-to-peer energy sharing problems with autonomous mobile robots.

Future ideas in the direction of the paper include creating an optimization component that can provide the best altruistic rule based on the context of the problem.

Providing a cost-benefit analysis to understand the economic benefits that this idea can provide to a real manufacturing plant. A deeper specification of some components of the framework e.g., "monitoring component" that can be based on a machine learning approach to predict a failure in one of the agents. The contextualization of the approach under a human-centric design [25] is highly relevant considering initiatives like Industry

5.0. This idea needs to be showcased in other applications e.g., load sharing and tool sharing to provide a more generic representation of mutual collaboration (altruism) and also to understand its real potential and possible limitations. Finally, this work can be placed under the context of established control strategies e.g., Holonic manufacturing systems or Evolvable Production Systems. This can make the framework more meaningful in regards the machine control which can be very complex and context dependent.

Acknowledgement. This research is supported by the Digital Manufacturing and Design Training Network (DiManD) project funded by the European Union through the Marie Skl odowska-Curie Innovative Training Networks (H2020-MSCA-ITN-2018) under grant agreement no. 814078. Partial support also from the FCT program UIDB/00066/2020 and UIDP/00066/2020.

References

1. Byrne, G., Dimitrov, D., Monostori, L., Teti, R., van Houten, F., Wertheim, R.: Biological-isation: biological transformation in manufacturing. CIRP J. Manuf. Sci. Technol. **21**, 1–32 (2018)
2. Estrada-Jimenez, L.A., Pulikottil, T.B., Nikghadam-Hojjati, S., Barata, J.: Selforganization in smart manufacturing-background, systematic review, challenges and outlook. IEEE Access (2023)
3. Leitao, P., Karnouskos, S., Ribeiro, L., Lee, J., Strasser, T., Colombo, A.W.: Smart agents in industrial cyber–physical systems. Proc. IEEE **104**(5), 1086–1101 (2016)
4. Rocha, A.D., Lima-Monteiro, P., Parreira-Rocha, M., Barata, J.: Artificial immune systems based multi-agent architecture to perform distributed diagnosis. J. Intell. Manuf. **30**(4), 2025–2037 (2017). https://doi.org/10.1007/s10845-017-1370-y
5. Stock, P., Zuelch, G.: Reactive manufacturing control using the ant colony approach. Int. J. Prod. Res. **50**(21), 6150–6161 (2012)
6. Frei, R., Serugendo, G.D.M.: Self-organizing assembly systems. IEEE Trans. Syst. Man Cybern. Part C (Appl. Rev.) **41**(6), 885–897 (2011)
7. Berger, R.: Rise of the machines – how robots and artificial intelligence are shaping the future of autonomous production. https://www.rolandberger.com/en/Insights/Publications/Autonomousproduction-Rise-of-the-machines.html
8. KUKA: Matrix production: an example for industrie 4.0. https://www.kuka.com/en-de/industries/solutions-database/2016/10/matrixproduction
9. Li, N., Tsigkanos, C., Jin, Z., Hu, Z., Ghezzi, C.: Early validation of cyber–physical space systems via multi-concerns integration. J. Syst. Softw. **170**, 110742 (2020)
10. Trivers, R.L.: The evolution of reciprocal altruism. Q. Rev. Biol. **46**(1), 35–57 (1971)
11. Vuorensyrjä, M.: The rise of reciprocal altruism–a theory based on the centipede game with trivers-payoffs. Evol. Psychol. Sci. **9**(1), 13–25 (2022)
12. Ortqvist, D.: Performance outcomes from reciprocal altruism: a multi-level model. J. Small Bus. Entrep. **32**(3), 227–240 (2020)
13. Layton, R.: Kinship without words. Biol. Theory **16**(3), 135–147 (2021)
14. Hirata, S.: Collaborative behavior. In: Choe, J.C. (ed.) Encyclopedia of Animal Behavior, 2nd edn, pp. 343–348. Academic Press, Oxford (2019)
15. Wilkinson, G.S.: Reciprocal altruism in bats and other mammals. Ethol. Sociobiol. **9**(2–4), 85–100 (1988)

16. Ding, K., Chan, F.T., Zhang, X., Zhou, G., Zhang, F.: Defining a digital twinbased cyber-physical production system for autonomous manufacturing in smart shop floors. Int. J. Prod. Res. **57**(20), 6315–6334 (2019)
17. Maeedi, A., Khan, M.U., İrfanoğlu, B.: Reciprocal altruism-based path planning optimization for multi-agents. In: 2022 International Congress on Human-Computer Interaction, Optimization and Robotic Applications (HORA), pp. 1–9 (2022)
18. Hilaire, V., Gruer, P., Koukam, A., Simonin, O.: Formal driven prototyping approach for multiagent systems. Int. J. Agent-Oriented Softw. Eng. **2**(2), 246–266 (2008)
19. Simonin, O., Ferber, J.: Modeling self satisfaction and altruism to handle action selection and reactive cooperation. In: 6th International Conference on the Simulation of Adaptive Behavior (SAB 2000), vol. 2, pp. 314–323 (2000)
20. Chapelle, J., Simonin, O., Ferber, J.: How situated agents can learn to cooperate by monitoring their neighbors' satisfaction. In: ECAI, vol. 2, pp. 68–78. Lyon (2002)
21. Couture-Beil, A., Vaughan, R.T.: Adaptive mobile charging stations for multirobot systems. In: 2009 IEEE/RSJ International Conference on Intelligent Robots and Systems, pp. 1363–1368. IEEE (2009)
22. Mathew, N., Smith, S.L., Waslander, S.L.: Multirobot rendezvous planning for recharging in persistent tasks. IEEE Trans. Rob. **31**(1), 128–142 (2015)
23. Drenner, A., Janssen, M., Papanikolopoulos, N.: Coordinating recharging of large scale robotic teams. In: 2009 IEEE/RSJ International Conference on Intelligent Robots and Systems, pp. 1357–1362. IEEE (2009)
24. Liang, G., Tu, Y., Zong, L., Chen, J., Lam, T.L.: Energy sharing mechanism for a freeform robotic system-freebot. In: 2022 International Conference on Robotics and Automation (ICRA), pp. 4232–4238. IEEE (2022)
25. Kalateh, S., Estrada-Jimenez, L.A., Pulikottil, T., Hojjati, S.N., Barata, J.: The human role in human-centric industry. In: IECON 2022–48th Annual Conference of the IEEE Industrial Electronics Society, pp. 1–6. IEEE (2022)

Reconfigurable Framework for Data Extraction Using Interoperable Brokers in Manufacturing

Nelson Freitas[✉], Andre Dionisio Rocha, Fábio M-Oliveira, Duarte Alemão,
and José Barata

School of Science and Technology, UNINOVA – CTS and LASI, Nova University of Lisbon,
Campus de Caparica, 2829-516 Monte de Caparica, Portugal
{n.freitas,andre.rocha,fmo,d.alemao,jab}@uninova.pt

Abstract. Technology is an integral part of society and has undergone a great deal of evolution in many different areas, like production or recreation, leading to the emergence of heterogeneous systems. These various systems frequently need to communicate and interact with one another to fully utilize their capabilities and resources, aiming to be as efficient as possible. One such method is the message broker, a useful tool for facilitating communication between multiple and heterogeneous systems. However, message brokers often have a complicated initial setup, besides the necessity of accessing several systems to configure parameters and the lack of automation tools to facilitate it. The proposed solution is creating a tool that can be instantiated on different machines and can control the deployment, configuration, and usage of the message broker, regardless of which one. The results are promising, facilitating data collection from industrial robots and the connection between two different message brokers.

Keywords: Cyber-Physical System · Data Extraction · Interoperability · Kafka · Message Broker · MQTT · Reconfigurable

1 Introduction

In our current day we are surrounded by a multitude of devices that frequently connect to a network, sending several different resources and acting upon the real world through the information received from the network. The fusion of the physical and cyber worlds enables real-time reading and acting upon the physical aspects utilizing the computing and communication power of the cyber aspects. A system capable of using both aspects was given the name of Cyber-Physical Systems (CPS) [1, 2].

However, for some complex infrastructures, a single CPS is insufficient, and a network of CPS is required. This can be true for smart buildings, industry-complex systems, smart cities, among others, where increasingly technological systems are deployed and frequently need to communicate with one another, with CPS being a common example. Being a software-intensive system, the CPS presents dynamic properties that can bring new challenges or exacerbate already existing ones, such as security, safety, and reliability [3].

L. M. Camarinha-Matos and F. Ferrada (Eds.): DoCEIS 2023, IFIP AICT 678, pp. 122–134, 2023.
https://doi.org/10.1007/978-3-031-36007-7_9

A common method of communication between several heterogeneous software, that are often present in CPS, are the message brokers. as they provide fundamental characteristics, such as scalability, easy communication between heterogenous devices, and availability, just to name a few [4]. However, different message brokers often have different characteristics, and some are more suited for certain tasks than others (such as latency, maximum size of message allowed, security protocols, or built-in gateways) [5, 6].

As such the question arrives: "How to create an environment capable of deploying and reconfiguring message brokers for data extraction in an Industrial environment?".

The hypotheses for answering the research question arises as: "Creating a framework capable of automatically and remotely deploy, connect and reconfigure different message brokers for data extraction in Industrial environments".

The proposed solution, therefore, creates a framework capable of handling the concerns of the CPS through the deployment, reconfiguration, and connection of any kind of message broker capable of communicating with the tools. For the implementation of the framework, a Java programming tool comprised of clients and a server, where the clients are deployed on the same machine as the message broker and the master can be deployed on any computer as long as the communication between the master and the clients exists.

The paper is, therefore, divided in: chapter two where the related work is introduced, focused on the communication of CPS. Chapter three where the framework is presented. Chapter four where the tool developed is explained as well as the demonstration case studies. The results are presented and discussed in chapter five. Finally, chapter six contains a conclusion as well as future work.

2 Related Work

As the Internet of Things (IoT) grows in popularity, the CPS is the natural follower as it allows the integration of different physical (such as sensing and actuation) and cyber processes (such as processing and communication). In such a case, a method of communication is required so that IoT devices can communicate with cyberspace [7]. As a result, a CPS can be described by a set of characteristics that allow it to operate and abide by its definition. This set of characteristics is composed of [8]:

- **Autonomy** – CPS are capable of learning on their own and adjusting to their surroundings, and it is the autonomy of the system that makes this possible. The capacity of the system to recover from failures or to adapt to given conditions are all examples of the autonomy of a given system and, consequently, of CPS.
- **Decentralization** - The CPS should be a self-contained system that works with autonomy and independence from all the other processes.
- **Heterogeneity** – CPS should be able to integrate multiple systems as well as meet standards for communication and information exchange. This may include different devices, such as robots, sensors, actuators, production cells, among others.
- **Integration** – This is a fundamental component of the CPS, as it by definition, allows the integration between the physical and the cyber worlds, expanding the capabilities of both.

- **Interconnection** – CPS is a synthesis of physical and cyber elements linked by wired and wireless networks with the objective of constructing intelligence. This makes the interconnection of these different elements essential to achieve the goal.
- **Interoperability** – Interoperability consists of the connection, operation, and communication between the different devices of the CPS, allowing the exchange of relevant data between all the components.
- **Modularity** – CPS are composed of modules that collaborate to adapt to changes, be they in consumer needs, product specifications, or supply chain issues, among other things.

The CPS can, therefore, be divided into three layers that together provide the characteristics mentioned above. These layers are: the physical layer, the network layer, and the application layer, which ultimately comprise the physical and cyber space. The Fig. 1 shows the architecture of a CPS making division between the cyber and physical space as well as each layer providing some examples of each one.

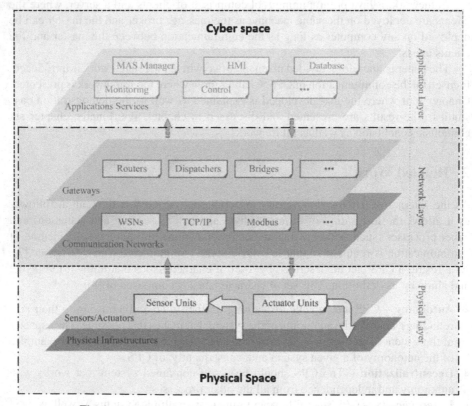

Fig. 1. Architecture of a cyber-physical system. Adapted from [1]

The physical layer is responsible for all the physical infrastructures as well as all the IoT and machinery, such as sensors and actuators. The network layer is responsible for the communication and can have physical elements such as routers and gateways and cyber elements such as communication protocols and technologies. Lastly, the application layer is where all the intelligent systems, such as scheduling software, databases, and monitoring software are deployed.

To be able to satisfy all the previously mentioned characteristics, a CPS needs to be able to communicate between all their different devices and applications. There are numerous communication methods that can be used for communicating between heterogeneous devices over the Intranet and Internet. This can be done with the ICE (Internet Communication Engine), REST, AMQP, MQTT, JMS, among others [7, 9].

MQTT, as Message Queue Telemetry Transport is a publish-subscribe protocol able to receive and send data between multiple publishers and subscribers. The MQTT protocol, created by IBM, quickly gained popularity as a many-to-many communication tool, and the necessity for quick and distributed communication is an essential component for IoT systems. As a result, systems that heavily rely on IoT can use MQTT as a useful tool for enabling them, either alone or in conjunction with other technologies, making it ideal for numerous CPS that work with IoT devices [10]. However, the usage of this protocol should not be used exclusively for IoT systems as work was made with agents regarding the usage of this technology for communication [11, 12]. The message broker is also, often chosen for communication in fog computing it highlights their communication and load balance characteristics [13, 14] and can also be integrated with other important communication protocols, such Open Platform Communications Unified Architecture (OPC UA) [15]. In [16] the authors also use the MQTT message broker approach to handle the security of the transmitted data, making it resilient to cyberattacks.

A message broker is often a tool chosen to act as a publish-subscribe enabler, utilizing the MQTT protocol, among others. There are numerous message brokers available, each of which is unique and specialized in a specific area [14, 17]. As demonstrated, this approach has been largely used and has many benefits for the current CPS architectures. However, a study of the usage and deployment of several message brokers in the same CPS in order to harvest the best characteristics of each message broker, or even an infrastructure of message brokers that allows the multiple CPS to utilize the best characteristics of each message broker to communicate between several components on a CPS, has yet to be made.

3 Proposed Framework

As previously mentioned, different CPS have different characteristics and requisites based on several factors, such as, how many and what type of devices are meant to communicate, number of data extracted and processed, among others. As such, the usage of different message brokers, that have different characteristics, in a given CPS can be the correct decision in order to save resources and make the process modular. With the deployment of several message broker, their configuration, deployment, and reconfiguration become critical factors that can be an arduous job given the different technologies and methods used for each message broker.

The proposed framework focuses on being able to change automatically and remotely, different aspects of the message brokers used to extract data from the physical elements (Fig. 2).

In the proposed framework, three different message brokers are deployed, this can be seen in practice as different work machines in a given CPS, with different characteristics and requirements that need to be complied with. The message brokers are deployed along with a client tool. This client tool is responsible for all the interactions with the message broker regarding different kinds of actions, such as, configuration, deployment, reconfiguration, and termination. All the client tools regarding each CPS should therefore only be accessible by one master tool, which is responsible for giving orders to each client tool to execute each action. This approach can be interpreted as a master tool dictating what should happen for each message broker, while the client tool runs different methods depending on what the master dictates.

The framework can therefore be useful to different degrees, such as load balancing, interconnection or sharing of different information between message brokers, the remote changing of configurations, or even the automatic redeployment of several instances from a unique point.

Finally, it is important to draw attention to the usage of different message brokers in different contexts, which is essential for the correct use of the framework. A simple example can be the usage of low-resource-intensive message brokers, only focused on data extraction on the shop floor (being Broker A and Broker B of Fig. 2), and a message broker with high throughput and scalability (Broker C of Fig. 2). This represents the flexibility of the framework and allows the usage of the best characteristics of each message broker, while the client tool seamlessly interconnects all the message brokers, creating an automatic and continuous flow of data.

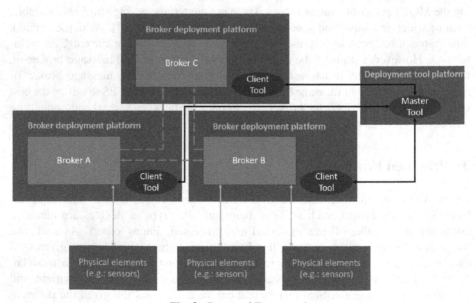

Fig. 2. Proposed Framework

4   Demonstration Scenarios

In this chapter, a master-client tool proposed in the framework is presented, along with two demonstration scenarios. The two demonstration scenarios have different objectives, the first one exemplifies how this connection can and should be done regarding master-client communication and hierarchy, as well as demonstrating in a real-world scenario how all the systems interact. The second demonstration scenario revolves around a deployment and load test of the MQTT Mosquitto software, to accurately see the impact of such a tool on the message broker.

4.1   Master-Client Tool

The master-client tool for the demonstration scenario is made in the Java programming language. The principal reasons for choosing such a language are that Java is one of the most popular languages in the world and can run on most operating systems without the need of changing any code, known as "write once, run anywhere". Both of these reasons allow for the facilitation of the execution of the proposed framework, as the client can be instantiated on almost any machine and the libraries are written in Java, a common programming language.

The tool is made to allow a certain degree of modularity, this means that the user only needs to install the libraries for the specific message broker that they want to communicate with in both the client and the master. This allows for the saving of resources on less capable machines and allows the user to customize the library and the tool. The libraries have five main methods:

- **Start** – Where the desired message broker, referring to the library in question, is deployed with the previous or predefined configurations.
- **Connect** – Used for automatically connecting both equal and different types of message brokers.
- **Config** – Where the configuration of the given message broker should be passed on.
- **Stop** – This method stops all the processes of the given message broker.
- **Restart** – This is a method simply for more convenience where the **Stop** and **Start** methods are combined, for a more straightforward approach.

As previously stated, the tool is made up of a client and a master (Fig. 3). Even though the client has an interface and can run simple commands, this is not necessary, as all actions are made through the master. The master, however, has different and useful tools. It can deploy the message broker, and create topics for each specific one, view all the tool's deployed message brokers, and connect two different message brokers.

The tool communicates between the master and the client with HTTP Post and Get. The master communicates with the client by the same IP as the message broker meant to be created. It assumes that if a broker is meant to be deployed by the tool, the client is already operational on the target machine.

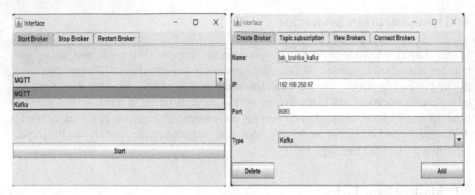

Fig. 3. Client (left) and Master (right) tool.

4.2 Demonstration Scenario: CPS Example

The first demonstration scenario simulates a system where the position of an ABB IRB 120 robot and the energetic consumption of such robot are sent to two different message brokers that are then able to automatically connect and exchange information (Fig. 4). The position of the robot is processed in the Robot Operating System (ROS) and then published on another machine where a Mosquitto message broker is running. In terms of energy consumption, a sensor is linked to a Raspberry Pi, which publishes the data to a Kafka message broker (Fig. 5). The usage of the Kafka message broker is also to demonstrate that powerful event streaming/message broker platforms can be used with this approach, providing a robust and complete integration for data collection corresponding to the necessity of each CPS.

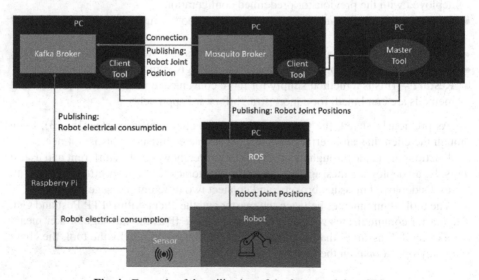

Fig. 4. Example of the utilization of the framework in a CPS

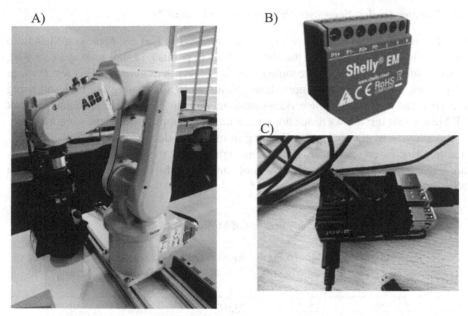

Fig. 5. Hardware used for demonstration. A) ABB IRB 120 Robot. B) Power monitoring Shelly. C) Rasberry PI

It is important to notice that the tool was able to deploy and correctly configure the message brokers so that the other systems can communicate and pass information to the respective brokers. This configuration is all done remotely, with the introduction of the parameters via the graphical interface. The developed system can be further optimized and automated to meet the needs of the user, the company, or the industrial complex. Finally, both the message brokers were connected by the master tool order in the connection tab. This connection allows Mosquitto to send data about the robot's location directly to the Kafka message broker, bypassing the need for any intermediary software.

In summary, the best characteristics of each message broker were made possible: mosquito for data extraction and Kafka for aggregating and storing the information directly in a database. This was also done without any need to know how to deploy and connect the message brokers, as the client/master tool was used.

4.3 Demonstration Scenario: Deployment and Load Tests

For the second demonstration, two tests were made. The first test deploys a Mosquitto message broker without using the tool and tries to publish a small message (<1 Kb), when it succeeds, the time is recorded, and the broker is terminated. This test is made fifty times. After these, two more deployments were made using the tool and using the same test methodology, one via wireless network and the second via cable network (Table 1). This test allows to see how much time both approaches (deploying manually and deploying by the tool) take. Keeping in mind that deploying through the tool has a natural increased delay caused by the network connectivity. Nonetheless, these tests are a reasonable indicator to see if the tool can deploy the message broker remotely in a reasonable time frame.

Table 1. Deployment test of Mosquitto message broker

Type of test	Max delay(ms)	Minimum delay(ms)	Average (ms)	Standard Deviation (ms)	Number of Testes
Local	27	22	23,94	1,06	50
Tool + wireless	417	67	89,09	48,35	50
Tool + cable	88	78	80,07	2,49	50

Despite the increase of the average deploy time by around three-fold in both tests, this can be explained almost entirely by the internet connection of both the sending of the order by the master tool and the publishing of the first message. Comparing the maximum and minimum values, is possible to see how much a connection can affect the time, especially in wireless communication. For comparison, if 5ms are added in the deployment in the local machine for each communication transaction (send the deploy message, receive acknowledge, send publish message, receive acknowledge) it already increases the time by almost two-fold. Regarding this delay, it is still an acceptable time for the deployment of the message broker considering the remote capability. This can also be further justified, considering that this is a task done only when some configuration or problem emerges and not recurrently. Finally, for an easier visualization of the data three graphs of each test were made (Fig. 6).

The second demonstration test was a load capacity test, in which several messages (100,200,300,400 and 500) with reduced size (<1 Kb), were sent to several Mosquitto brokers (1,5,10,25,50 and 100) running on the same machine. The messages were sent at the same time or as close as it was possible. The ratio of message to broker was always one-to-one, but the total number of messages and the total number of brokers vary. Once again, the tests were made wirelessly and by cable (Fig. 7).

In the load test, it is possible to see the great influence that a wireless system has over the average message time. The messages and time of response are small, and as such, the noise of a wireless network has a great influence on the readings, making the graph at the bottom of Fig. 7 have too much delay due to network connectivity to be able to take the load test information. Nevertheless, it serves as a demonstration as why these systems should run on cable environment instead of a wireless one.

The top graph of Fig. 7 shows an interesting characteristic, the number of message brokers can have less influence on the average time than the quantity of messages, but as we increase the number of brokers, this impact becomes less and less noticeable, as the difference between one broker and five brokers is almost the same as the difference from fifty brokers to a hundred brokers. Is possible to see that for the lower number of brokers (1 to 5) the average time of message grows with the deployment of more brokers and the sending of more messages. On the other hand, from the range of 10 to 50 message brokers, some particularities occur, as the deployment of 10 message brokers has worse impact then the 25 or even 50 message brokers. This can indicate that in some instances, a larger deployment of message brokers does not always correlate to a linear worsening of performance. This is, however, still too early to say as more tests should be conducted.

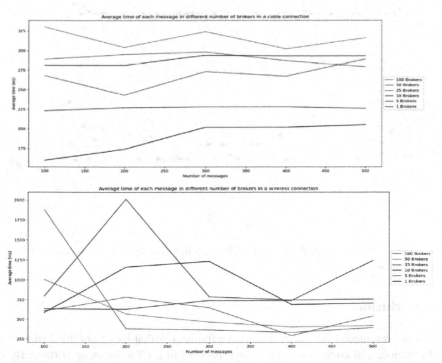

Fig. 6. Load test of Mosquitto message broker, by cable (top) and wireless (bottom)

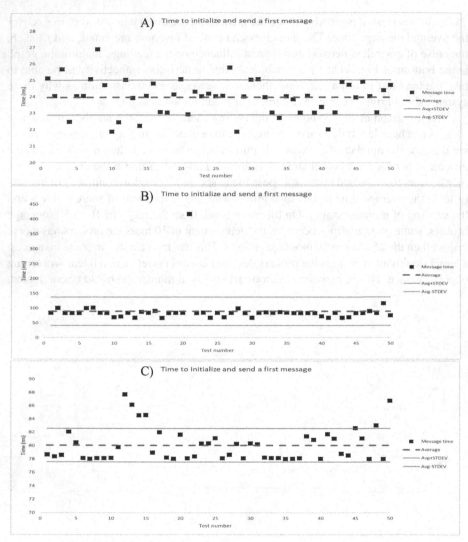

Fig. 7. Deploy tests in a) local without tool, b) with tool remote by wireless, and c) with tool remote by cable.

5   Conclusion

The work presented in this paper proposes a framework that facilitates the deployment, configuration, and connection of message brokers in a CPS, focusing particularly on industrial complex environments. The framework allows for the development of tools capable of incorporating tools either from other users or custom-made tools that facilitate all the configurations needed for the correct utilization of a message broker.

Two demonstration scenarios were presented, the first one regarding an exemplar integration in a CPS industrial environment. A tool programmed in Java was made in order not only to prove the concept but also to serve as a guideline for how to correctly instantiate the tools that would be responsible for all the actions regarding the message brokers. The demonstration also serves as a guide for how to make the program modular so that different libraries with the same standards from different users can be integrated.

The second demonstration scenario shows that despite the slowdown in the deployment of the message broker, this mostly relates to the delays in the network that now play an important role. Despite this, the time that it took still didn't reach a quarter of a second and was deemed acceptable as the time it took to launch the message broker by the tool. In this second demonstration, there were also some load tests that correlated the number of messages and the number of brokers deployed with the time of sending a message. The wireless results of such a study were deemed not useful because the delays in the network overlapped any attempt to interpret such data. Regarding the cable data, it revealed some intriguing results, as the delay caused by broker deployment does not appear to be linear, implying that more brokers deployed have less impact. If this proves true, it can be a useful conclusion for some particular cases, which would benefit from having more brokers given a particular number of messages. Nevertheless, this needs further study, as the test presented does not have enough validation to make a claim, but it is an interesting subject to be studied in future work.

Overall, a framework is presented, capable of extracting the best of each message broker's technologies. However, this approach always has the limitation of utilizing a message broker and consequently the connection of each, which is limited by the advantages and disadvantages of each message broker. The load tests also show that maybe what the authors thought is the best way to use a message broker is not always true. The deployment of several brokers and load balancing between them could be a useful technique although needs further and more intensive testing.

For future work, it is important to test the framework in a real industrial setting and even other environments, as it can be generalized for other use cases. It is important to also make the load and deployment tests with larger messages to see what impact it has and how it differs from the results gathered in this study. Also, to utilize other message brokers, as it can be interesting to see the impact of for example RabitMQ, HiveMQ or even an event streaming like Kafka.

Acknowledgments. The authors acknowledge the Portuguese FCT program UIDB/00066/2020 and UIDP/00066/2020 for providing financial support for this work.

References

1. Januário, F., Cardoso, A., Gil, P.: A distributed multi-agent framework for resilience enhancement in cyber-physical systems. IEEE Access **7**, 31342–31357 (2019). https://doi.org/10.1109/ACCESS.2019.2903629
2. Hoffmann, M.W., et al.: Developing industrial cps: a multi-disciplinary challenge. Sensors **21**(6), 1–28 (2021). https://doi.org/10.3390/s21061991
3. Tsigkanos, C., Kehrer, T., Ghezzi, C.: Modeling and verification of evolving cyber-physical spaces. In: Proceedings of the ACM SIGSOFT Symposium on the Foundations of Software Engineering, Association for Computing Machinery, pp. 38–48 (2017). https://doi.org/10.1145/3106237.3106299

4. Nguyen, C.N., Lee, J., Hwang, S., Kim, J.-S.: On the role of message broker middleware for many-task computing on a big-data platform. Clust. Comput. **22**(1), 2527–2540 (2018). https://doi.org/10.1007/s10586-018-2634-9

5. Mishra, B., Kertesz, A.: The use of MQTT in M2M and IoT systems: a survey. IEEE Access **8**, 201071–201086 (2020). https://doi.org/10.1109/ACCESS.2020.3035849

6. Rocha, A.D., Freitas, N., Alemão, D., Guedes, M., Martins, R., Barata, J.: Event-driven interoperable manufacturing ecosystem for energy consumption monitoring. Energies **14**(12), 3620 (2021). https://doi.org/10.3390/en14123620

7. Pivoto, D.G.S., de Almeida, L.F.F., da Rosa Righi, R., Rodrigues, J.J.P.C., Lugli, A.B., Alberti, A.M.: Cyber-physical systems architectures for industrial internet of things applications in Industry 4.0: a literature review. J. Manufact. Syst. **58**, 176–192 (2021). https://doi.org/10. 1016/j.jmsy.2020.11.017

8. Tonelli, F., Demartini, M., Pacella, M., Lala, R.: Cyber-physical systems (CPS) in supply chain management: from foundations to practical implementation. Procedia CIRP **99**, 598–603 (2021). https://doi.org/10.1016/j.procir.2021.03.080

9. García-Valls, M., Baldoni, R.: Adaptive middleware design for CPS: considerations on the OS, resource managers, and the network run-time. In: Proceedings of the 14th Workshop on Adaptive and Reflective Middleware, ARM 2015 - Collocated with ACM/IFIP/USENIX Middleware 2015. Association for Computing Machinery, Inc. (2015). https://doi.org/10. 1145/2834965.2834968

10. Parto, M., Saldana, C., Kurfess, T.: A novel three-layer IoT architecture for shared, private, scalable, and real-time machine learning from ubiquitous cyber-physical systems. Procedia Manufact. **48**, 959–967 (2020). https://doi.org/10.1016/j.promfg.2020.05.135

11. Gavriluta, C., Boudinet, C., Kupzog, F., Gomez-Exposito, A., Caire, R.: Cyber-physical framework for emulating distributed control systems in smart grids. Int. J. Electr. Power Energy Syst. **114**, 105375 (2020). https://doi.org/10.1016/j.ijepes.2019.06.033

12. Sakurada, L., Barbosa, J., Leitao, P., Alves, G., Borges, A.P., Botelho, P.: Development of agent-based CPS for smart parking systems. In: IECON 2019 - 45th Annual Conference of the IEEE Industrial Electronics Society, pp. 2964–2969. IEEE (2019). https://doi.org/10.1109/ IECON.2019.8926653

13. Naeem, R.Z., Bashir, S., Amjad, M.F., Abbas, H., Afzal, H.: Fog computing in internet of things: practical applications and future directions. Peer Peer Netw. Appl. **12**(5), 1236–1262 (2019). https://doi.org/10.1007/s12083-019-00728-0

14. Bagaskara, A.E., Setyorini, S., Wardana, A.A.: Performance analysis of message broker for communication in fog computing. In: 2020 12th International Conference on Information Technology and Electrical Engineering (ICITEE), pp. 98–103. IEEE (2020). https://doi.org/ 10.1109/ICITEE49829.2020.9271733

15. Hastbacka, D., Kannisto, P., Katkytniemi, A.: Interoperability of OPC UA PubSub with existing message broker integration architectures. In: IECON Proceedings (Industrial Electronics Conference). IEEE Computer Society (2022). https://doi.org/10.1109/IECON49645.2022. 9969039

16. Imran, S.A., Akhtar, S.: Safe and secure communication between two cyber-physical systems: a framework for security. In: Kryvinska, N., Poniszewska-Marańda, A. (eds.) Developments in Information & Knowledge Management for Business Applications. SSDC, vol. 376, pp. 541–558. Springer, Cham (2021). https://doi.org/10.1007/978-3-030-76632-0_19

17. Bertrand-Martinez, E., Dias Feio, P., de Brito Nascimento, V., Kon, F., Abelém, A.: Classification and evaluation of IoT brokers: a methodology. Int. J. Netw. Manag. Wiley (2021). https://doi.org/10.1002/nem.2115

Synthetic Data Generation on Dynamic Industrial Environment for Object Detection, Tracking, and Segmentation CNNs

Danilo G. Schneider[✉] and Marcelo R. Stemmer

Departamento de Automação e Sistemas, Univesidade Federal de Santa Catarina, R. Delfino Conti, S/N, Florianópolis 88040-900, Brazil
danilo_gsch@hotmail.com, marcelo.stemmer@ufsc.br

Abstract. The ability of Convolutional Neural Networks (CNNs) to learn from vast amounts of data and improve accuracy over time makes them an attractive solution for many industrial problems. In the context of Future Assembly Systems such as Line-Less Mobile Assembly Systems, CNNs can be used to monitor the networked system of mobile robots, human operators, and other movable objects that assemble products in flexible environment configurations. This paper explores the use of a simulated industrial environment to autonomously generate training data for object detection, tracking, and segmentation CNNs. The goal is to adapt state-of-the-art CNN solutions to specific industry use cases, where real data annotation can be time-consuming and expensive. The developed algorithm efficiently generates new random image data, allowing accurate object detection, tracking, and segmentation in dynamic industrial scenarios. The results show the effectiveness of this approach in improving the testing of CNNs for industrial applications.

Keywords: Synthetic Data Generation · Convolutional Neural Networks · Object Tracking · Segmentation · Dynamic Industrial Environments

1 Introduction

Convolutional Neural Networks (CNNs) have proven to be a promising solution for various industrial and robotic problems [1–7]. However, training CNNs requires a large and diverse dataset of labeled images, which can be time-consuming and expensive to annotate manually. To address this issue, simulation-based data generation has emerged as a promising solution, where synthetic data can be used to train CNNs for object detection, tracking, and segmentation tasks [2–4].

In future assembly systems, flexibility is increasingly desired. Future factories may be organically configured by spatio-temporal workstations as in the Line-less Mobile Assembly System (LMAS) [8]. Although the high complexity of such system, it is a closed-world environment domain, meaning that all movable instances are known in the production process. In such dynamic environments, a surveillance camera could aid in

L. M. Camarinha-Matos and F. Ferrada (Eds.): DoCEIS 2023, IFIP AICT 678, pp. 135–146, 2023.
https://doi.org/10.1007/978-3-031-36007-7_10

the monitoring of the networked system of mobile robots, human operators, and other movable objects that assemble products in flexible environment configurations.

In this paper, we investigate the following research question: Is it possible to use only synthetic labeled data to train object tracking and segmentation CNNs in a flexible industrial environment and surveillance camera domain? Our hypothesis is that adapting available robotic simulators and state-of-the-art algorithms for navigation and robotic arm manipulation, it is possible to generate large datasets on the source simulation domain similar to the real-world target domain without the real data labeling costs.

Our approach aims to adapt state-of-the-art CNN solutions to a specific industry use case, where real data annotation can be a bottleneck. The innovation achieved is the creation of an algorithm that uses a 2D Mask grid map to spawn and control the moving instances inside the camera field-of-view, assuring the long-term balance of the dataset classes. The developed algorithm efficiently generates new random image data, allowing accurate object detection and instance segmentation in dynamic industrial scenarios. Specifically, we use the generated dataset to train two networks: Fast RCNN for object detection and Mask RCNN for instance segmentation. We evaluate the performance of the trained models on a validation dataset and test the models on unlabeled images, demonstrating the effectiveness of our approach in generating synthetic labeled data in this domain.

2 Relation to Connected Cyber-Physical Spaces

The subject of this research is "Cooperative SLAM in dynamic industrial environments", which we divided in three steps: First, we use a CNN to infer the segmentation of all movable instances in an image. Second, we use the segmented image to transform a depth image in an 2D grid map so the robots can use it to plan paths and navigate. Third, we deal with the data association problem on merging maps from multiple input sources. This paper covers the first step of the PhD research and is directly related to the conference theme of Technological Innovation for Connected Cyber Physical Spaces.

The development of connected cyber-physical spaces has enabled the integration of various machines, robots, and humans to work together seamlessly, increasing the efficiency and productivity of industrial processes. However, this integration requires advanced monitoring and control systems that can handle the complexity of these interconnected systems [9].

Convolutional Neural Networks (CNNs) have emerged as a powerful tool for monitoring and controlling these systems, leveraging vast amounts of data to improve their accuracy over time [4, 5]. Our proposed algorithm provides a cost-effective solution for training CNNs and overcoming the challenges associated with real data annotation. The ability to autonomously generate new random image data that accurately represents dynamic industrial scenarios is an advancement in this field, providing researchers and practitioners with a tool to train and test CNNs efficiently.

In the context of smart manufacturing, synthetic data can be used to improve the accuracy and efficiency of machine learning algorithms for a range of applications, including object detection, tracking, and segmentation in industrial environments [3, 4, 6]. By using synthetic data, researchers can simulate a variety of scenarios that might be difficult or expensive to replicate in the real world, such as rare events, unusual environmental conditions, or equipment failure.

In conclusion, this paper represents a significant contribution to the conference theme of Technological Innovation for Connected Cyber Physical Spaces. The proposed simulation-based data generation approach addresses the challenges associated with monitoring and controlling the behavior of complex interconnected systems and leverages the power of CNNs to improve efficiency and productivity in future assembly systems. This research represents an important step towards the development of advanced monitoring and control systems that can handle the complexity of these interconnected systems.

3 Related Literature

Convolutional Neural Networks (CNNs) are currently the leading approach for object detection, but they often require lengthy training periods. In the context of rapid prototyping production, such as in Smart Manufacturing, the time required to train these networks can exceed the turnaround time required for production. In some cases, this can result in the robot being unable to pick up produced objects before the network has completed training, bringing the entire workflow to a halt. Although there are techniques to accelerate the training of neural networks, the acquisition and labeling of datasets can still add significant delays. Therefore, for workflows with smaller batch sizes, training a robot to detect objects may be infeasible due to these temporal constraints [5].

Object detection and segmentation are two related tasks in computer vision that involve identifying and locating objects within an image or video. Object detection typically involves identifying objects within an image and localizing them by drawing bounding boxes around them. In contrast, object segmentation goes further by accurately delineating the boundaries of objects, allowing for more precise and detailed information about their shape and position. Both tasks have numerous practical applications, including autonomous driving, medical imaging, robotics, and more. Recent advances in deep learning, particularly with Convolutional Neural Networks (CNNs), have led to significant improvements in the performance of object detection and segmentation models, making them a powerful tool for a wide range of computer vision applications. Over the years, techniques like Region Proposal Networks (RPNs) have improved the accuracy and efficiency of object detection models and resulting in popular models like Mask R-CNN [10], which is an instance segmentation CNN that adds a branch for predicting an object mask in parallel with the existing branch for bounding box recognition. For object detection it uses Faster R-CNN [11] as RPN which shares full-image convolutional features with the detection network.

More recently, other models have achieved state-of-the-art in popular benchmark datasets. For object detection, one state-of-the-art network example is YOLOv7 [12], the authors designed several trainable bag-of-freebies methods, so that real-time object detection can greatly improve the detection accuracy without increasing the inference cost and the results show that their model surpasses all known object detectors in both speed and accuracy in the range from 5 FPS to 160 FPS and has the highest accuracy 56.8% AP among all known real-time object detectors with 30 FPS or higher on GPU V100.

For semantic segmentation tasks, other currently relevant network is DeepLabv3+ [13], the authors combined methods of former networks that are able to encode multi-scale contextual information by probing the incoming features with filters or pooling operations at multiple rates and multiple effective fields-of-view, while the latter networks can capture sharper object boundaries by gradually recovering the spatial information.

While benchmark image datasets have been instrumental in advancing the field of computer vision, there are significant differences between these datasets and industrial applications that must be considered. Most benchmark datasets, such as CIFAR-10 [14], ImageNet [15], and COCO [16], contain a wide variety of images depicting everyday objects in static settings. In contrast, industrial applications involve complex environments with movable objects, dynamic lighting conditions, and a wide variety of robots and different scenarios that are difficult to capture in a single dataset.

Regarding the use of synthetic data in training, the authors of [6] developed an automated synthetic data generation pipeline to produce large-scale photo-realistic data with precise annotations, and then formulate an instance segmentation network for object recognition and a 6D pose estimation network for localization. On top of this pipeline, they presented a generic and robust sim-to-real deep-learning-based framework, namely S2R-Pick, for fast and accurate object recognition and localization in industrial robotic bin picking.

The emergence of the digital twin concept and the rise of robotics, driven by the last industrial revolutions and digital transformation, have created a need for updating virtual representations to facilitate appropriate decision-making by system operators. Multi-robot perception capabilities provide an opportunity to enhance object recognition and robot environmental understanding by combining individual observations. However, identifying the most informative camera poses, which play a crucial role in object recognition, is challenging due to the viewing angle dependency.

To address this, the authors of [7] propose a smart view selection approach that maximizes object recognition by determining the most relevant camera poses and the number of informative views. A clustering-based approach on a synthetic view dataset of traditional industrial objects is employed to maximize inter-class distance and minimize intra-class distance. The promising results, presented in terms of F1-score metric, demonstrate the effectiveness of this approach.

The authors of [4] discuss the utilization of Region-based Convolutional Neural Network (CNN) models trained on synthetic images generated from CAD models for part handling applications. The study outlines the development of an automated synthetic data generation process and the training of two CNN models aimed at detecting and distinguishing between similar-looking car components. The performance of these models was evaluated using real images, and the results demonstrate the potential for this approach to be applied to detect various parts in complex backgrounds. The use of synthetic images for CNN training also provides a streamlined process for generating a detector. The conclusion is that generating pictures and training a neural network was overall successful, still, for the high standards of industrial robotics rigorous testing has to be further performed.

Regarding autonomous vehicles, [17] address the problem of class-agnostic instance segmentation. Given the challenging task of providing enough labeled data to cover all possible semantic classes that can appear in an outdoor urban scenario. In the other hand, since we are dealing with a closed-world scenario in this paper, we expect all objects in the production system to be known.

For robotic operations such as bin picking or pick-and-place, explored by [2–4, 6], it is usual to have a training image with the objects positioned randomly, sometimes occluded or upside-down. In our case, as the goal is to track and segment mobile robots, humans and other movable objects, it is not interesting to have upside-down instances in the training data since it does not represent the normal operation target domain.

There are several robotic simulators available. [18] show an extended comparison between Unity3D, V-Rep and Gazebo, pointing that both V-Rep and Gazebo are easier to integrate with ROS. With respect to annotation camera sensors, we found three simulators that have it implemented: Gazebo (since version Fortress) [19], CARLA [20] and Nvidia Isaac Sim [21]. We decided on using Gazebo as it is fully open-source and it seems easier to integrate with ROS2.

4   Method

As the problem formulation, training CNNs lies in the need for large amounts of annotated images arising for each and every new part. In industrial environments there rarely are annotated images of the desired part available, however, construction data in the form of 3D CAD models is almost always available.

The objective of our algorithm is to use meshes information of industrial movable objects, robots and humans to generate large amounts of annotated images for object detection and instance, semantic or panoptic segmentation. While generating data, the goal is to simulate a real industrial navigation scenario and not just placing and dropping models on the environment.

4.1   Software Tools

Our algorithm relies on the Gazebo Simulator (version Garden) [19]. Gazebo is an open-source robotic simulation environment developed by the Open Source Robotics Foundation (OSRF). It provides a platform for researchers and developers to test and evaluate robotic systems in a virtual environment, allowing for faster and more cost-effective development. The simulator includes a physics engine, sensor simulation, and support for various robotic platforms and driving mechanisms, making it a popular choice for a wide range of applications, including robotics, computer vision, and artificial intelligence. The simulator has been used in various research studies, including the development of autonomous robots, navigation systems, and object recognition algorithms.

With the model mashes, it is possible to make a description file with visual, collision and inertial information and add different types of sensors and actuators to use the model in Gazebo. Since the previous version (Fortress), there is a bounding box camera sensor and a segmentation camera sensor that can be used to save annotated images from the simulator, which fits perfectly our purpose.

Moreover, we used the Robot Operating System 2 (version Humble) [22] framework to autonomously navigate the robots and humans in the simulation environment. The Nav2 stack [23] was used for navigation and Moveit2 [24] to control 5 Degrees-of-Freedom (DoF) and 6 DoF robotic arms.

4.2 Data Generation Pipeline

A set of open source online available model meshes were adapted to develop and test the algorithm. Since we used a generic code to navigate and control different models, the models were adapted to have generic joints, transform frames and sensors with the same name. More specifically, 8 different human meshes with walking animations, 8 different object meshes, and 7 different robot meshes were used and are shown in Fig. 1 with the industrial background. For each model, a description file for Gazebo was created with optimized LiDAR sensor and differential or mecanum-wheeled driving systems for the robots. The created models were added to a table with specific parameters to be used in our algorithm. The parameters are shown in Table 1. Those parameters are used to correctly spawn and control the models, label them with their class id and store the number of times this model was already used by the algorithm.

Fig. 1. Every model used for the data generation. Robots on the left side, actors on the middle and movable objects on the right side.

Table 1. Table with configured model parameters with one robot example

Name	Type	Radius	Mode	has_arm	n_uses	class_id
Pioneer3DX	robot	0.3	differential	False	0	10

A configuration file is also needed to setup the algorithm with parameters like maximum simulator iterations per run and maximum number of each model class to spawn. All launch configuration parameters are shown in Table 2.

Table 2. Launch parameters description table.

Parameter	Description
models_df_path	Absolute path for models table
model_resouce_path	Absolute path for Gazebo model files
launch_config_path	Absolute path for data generation configuration files
instance_seg	Loads instance segmentation camera sensor
semantic_seg	Loads semantic segmentation camera sensor
bb2d_vis	Loads 2D visible bounding boxes camera sensor
bb2d_full	Loads 2D full bounding boxes camera sensor
bb3d	Loads 3D bounding boxes camera sensor
save_depth	Loads depth camera sensor
save_path	Path for saving current generated data
camera_pitch	Camera sensor pitch angle
n_max_r	Maximum number of robots to spawn in each iteration
n_max_a	Maximum number of actors to spawn in each iteration
n_max_o	Maximum number of objects to spawn in each iteration
sim_iterations_per_run	Number of simulator iterations for each launcher run (1 iteration = 0.001 s)

Once models and parameters are configured, the full algorithm can be run in one command line in the terminal.

Simplified Pseudo-Algorithm

```
GenerateRandomCameraPose()
RestrictionAreaMask(camera_pose)
models_array[] = SelectSpawnModels(n_max_r,n_max_a,n_max_o)
For (model in models_array[]) do:
  GenerateRandomValidPose()
  Spawn(model)
EndFor
GenerateRandomPoseGoals()
GenerateRandomJointPositions()
For (i = 1 to sim_iterations_per_run) do:
  Run()
  SaveData()
EndFor
Update(n_uses)
```

The first function generates a random pose for the camera sensor using the fixed pitch angle defined in the configuration file. The *RestrictionAreaMask* function creates a binary mask based on the camera pose and its horizontal field of view to restrict the area which the models will spawn and navigate to be inside the camera reach, the mask is applied on top of the empty environment 2D occupancy grid map. An example restriction map generated is show in Fig. 2. Note that the mask has a trapezoidal form that limits the minimum and maximum distance from camera to models by a defined constant, assuring that models will not be too close or too far from the camera during runtime.

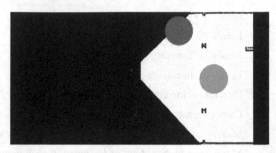

Fig. 2. Example of Restriction Mask. Blue dot represents camera 2D position, red circle represents an invalid generated position for a model and green circle represents a valid generated position for the same model.

Next, the algorithm randomly selects among the less used models, spawns each of them on valid positions using each model radius to assert that they will not spawn on top of each other by marking the occupied area on the restriction mask. Then random joint positions are generated to control the robotic arms and random goal poses for navigation. Finally, the simulator runs for the specified number of iterations saving data and when it is done the number of uses for each model is incremented in the table.

5 Experimental Results and Analysis

Using the proposed algorithm, two datasets were generated composed of 3 category high-level classes annotated (robot, person, object). The first dataset has 5025 images and was used to train a Faster R-CNN model for object detection whereas the second has 2613 images used on Mask R-CNN training.

For training, evaluating and testing we used Detectron2 [25], a next generation library that provides state-of-the-art detection and segmentation algorithms. It is the successor of Detectron and maskrcnn-benchmark. It supports a number of computer vision research projects and production applications in Facebook. Some of the available models are Mask R-CNN, Faster R-CNN and DeepLabv3+. The training step was done following the guidelines on Detectron2 Beginner's Tutorial, which does not use a validation set on training, thus it does not fine-tune the hyper-parameters.

5.1 Faster R-CNN

The first dataset was split into 90% for training and 10% for testing. Faster R-CNN model with ResNet-50 and Group Normalization backbone was used with pre-trained weights obtained with COCO 2017 dataset. The model was trained for 10000 iterations, the total_loss graph and an inference on a test image are shown in Figs. 3 and 4, respectively. Table 3 shows the evaluation using the test dataset.

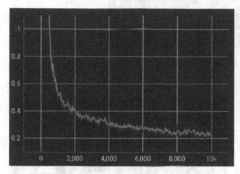

Fig. 3. Graphic of total loss x iterations on Faster R-CNN training.

Fig. 4. Inference of Faster R-CNN on testing image.

Table 3. Table with COCO evaluation metrics using the test dataset.

AP	AP50	AP75	APS	APm	APl
0.521	0.735	0.529	2.649	0.628	0.526

5.2 Mask R-CNN

The second dataset was also split into 90% for training and 10% for testing. Previous Faster R-CNN model was used as a backbone with pre-trained weights obtained with COCO 2017 dataset. The model was trained for 10000 iterations, the total loss graph is shown in Fig. 5.

Inference on a test image and real image are shown in Figs. 6 and 7, respectively.

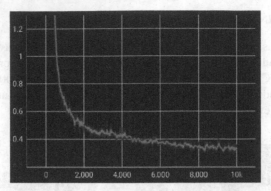

Fig. 5. Graphic of total loss x iterations on MASK R-CNN training.

Fig. 6. Inference of Mask R-CNN on test image.

Fig. 7. Inference of Mask R-CNN on real test image.

5.3 Analysis

The total loss curve flattened in the end of the training, which means that the model has converged and is no longer improving significantly. Although a validation set was not used in the training, the preliminary results indicate the usability of the generated data. A validation dataset is recommended to evaluate the performance of the model during the training process, and to tune the hyper-parameters of the model, such as learning rate, batch size, and the number of epochs. The validation dataset is also used to prevent overfitting, which occurs when the model becomes too complex and starts to memorize the training data instead of generalizing to new data.

The detection evaluation scores on COCO evaluation metric indicate a better performance of the model when the IoU threshold is 0.5.

The inference on test data for both detection and segmentation task show a good prediction for our defined classes, so we are able now to detect and segment instances of robots, persons and objects inside the simulation environment.

The inference on the real image is promising, it detected a robot, human and object although the segmentation does not cover the objects entirely and we can note some false negatives. More similar and realistic instance models or domain adaptations could improve the prediction in the real test image.

6 Conclusion

In conclusion, this paper explores the use of a simulated industrial environment to autonomously generate training data for training CNNs, with the goal of adapting state-of-the-art CNN solutions to specific industry use cases where real data annotation can be time-consuming and expensive. The developed algorithm efficiently generates new random image data, allowing for accurate object detection, tracking, and segmentation in the simulated industrial scenario, but its domain is not similar enough to the real-world application yet. The results of the study demonstrate the effectiveness of this approach in improving the testing of CNNs for industrial applications and suggest that it has the potential to be a valuable tool for enhancing the performance and applicability of CNN-based solutions in the context of future assembly systems. Future research may seek to further refine the algorithm and extend its applicability to other domains. Overall, this study underscores the promise of simulated environments as a means of generating high-quality training data for machine learning applications in industrial settings.

The developed algorithm is available at [26], alongside documentation on usage and new model insertion as well as jupyter notebooks for data registration and training with Detectron2.

Acknowledgments. We would like to acknowledge CAPES (*Coordenação de Aperfeiçoamento de Pessoal de Nível Superior*) for their financial support.

References

1. Rai, R., Tiwari, M. K., Ivanov, D., Dolgui, A.: Machine learning in manufacturing and industry 4.0 applications. Int. J. Prod. Res. **59**(16), 4773–4778 (2021). https://doi.org/10.1080/002 07543.2021.1956675
2. Danielczuk, M., et al.: Segmenting unknown 3D objects from real depth images using mask R-CNN trained on synthetic data. In: International Conference on Robotics and Automation (ICRA), pp. 7283–7290. IEE/Canada (2019). https://doi.org/10.1109/ICRA.2019.8793744
3. Tobin, J., Fong, R., Ray, A., Schneider, J., Zaremba, W., Abbeel, P.: Domain randomization for transferring deep neural networks from simulation to the real world. In: International Conference on Intelligent Robots and Systems – IROS, pp. 23–30. IEEE/RSJ (2017). https://doi.org/10.1109/IROS.2017.8202133
4. Andulkar, M., Hodapp, J., Reichling, T., Reichenbach, M., Berger, U.: Training CNNs from synthetic data for part handling in industrial environments. In: 14th International Conference on Automation Science and Engineering (CASE), Germany. IEEE (2018). https://doi.org/10.1109/COASE.2018.8560470
5. Schnieders, B., Luo, S., Palmer, G., Tuyls, K.: Fully Convolutional One-Shot Object Segmentation for Industrial Robotics. arXiv preprint arXiv:1903.00683 (2019). https://doi.org/10.48550/arXiv.1903.00683
6. Li, X., et al.: A sim-to-real object recognition and localization framework for industrial robotic bin picking. IEEE Robot. Autom. Lett. **7**(2), 3961–3968 (2022). https://doi.org/10.1109/LRA.2022.3149026

7. Xu, K., Ragot, N., Dupuis, Y.: View selection for industrial object recognition. In: 48th Annual Conference of the IEEE Industrial Electronics Society – IECON, Belgium, pp. 1–6. IEEE (2022). 1109/IECON49645.2022.9969121
8. Buckhorst, A.F., do Canto, M.K.B., Schmitt, R.H.: The line-less mobile assembly system simultaneous scheduling and location problem. Procedia CIRP **106**, 203–208 (2022). https://doi.org/10.1016/j.procir.2022.02.179
9. Villalonga, A., et al.: A decision-making framework for dynamic scheduling of cyber-physical production systems based on digital twins. Annu. Rev. Control. **51**, 357–373 (2021). https://doi.org/10.1016/j.arcontrol.2021.04.008
10. He, K., Gkioxari, G., Dollár, P., Girshick, R.: Mask R-CNN. In: Proceedings of the IEEE International Conference on Computer Vision – ICCV, pp. 2961–2969 (2017). https://doi.org/10.48550/arXiv.1703.06870
11. Ren, S., He, K., Girshick, R., Sun, J.: Faster R-CNN: towards real-time object detection with region proposal networks. In: Cortes, C., Lawrence, N., Lee, D., Sugiyama, M., Garnett, R. (eds.) Advances in Neural Information Processing Systems – NIPS, vol. 28 (2015). ISBN 9781510825024
12. Wang, C.Y., Bochkovskiy, A., Liao, H.Y.M.: YOLOv7: Trainable Bag-of-Freebies Sets New State-Of-The-Art for Real-Time Object Detectors. arXiv preprint arXiv:2207.02696 (2022). https://doi.org/10.48550/arXiv.2207.02696
13. Chen, L.-C., Zhu, Y., Papandreou, G., Schroff, F., Adam, H.: Encoder-decoder with atrous separable convolution for semantic image segmentation. In: Ferrari, V., Hebert, M., Sminchisescu, C., Weiss, Y. (eds.) ECCV 2018. LNCS, vol. 11211, pp. 833–851. Springer, Cham (2018). https://doi.org/10.1007/978-3-030-01234-2_49
14. The CIFAR-10 dataset. https://www.cs.toronto.edu/~kriz/cifar.html. Accessed 30 Apr 2023
15. ImageNET. https://www.image-net.org/. Accessed 30 Apr 2023
16. COCO Dataset. https://cocodataset.org/#home. Accessed 30 Apr 2023
17. Nunes, L., et al.: Unsupervised class-agnostic instance segmentation of 3D LiDAR data for autonomous vehicles. IEEE Robot. Autom. Lett. **7**(4), 8713–8720 (2022). https://doi.org/10.1109/LRA.2022.3187872
18. De Melo, M.S.P., da Silva Neto, J.G., Da Silva, P.J.L., Teixeira, J.M.X.N., Teichrieb, V.: Analysis and comparison of robotics 3D simulators. In: 21st Symposium on Virtual and Augmented Reality – SVR, pp. 242–251, Brazil. IEEE (2019). https://doi.org/10.1109/SVR.2019.00049
19. Gazebo Simulator. https://gazebosim.org/home. Accessed 30 Apr 2023
20. Dosovitskiy, A., Ros, G., Codevilla, F., Lopez, A., Koltun, V.: CARLA: an open urban driving simulator. In: Conference on Robot Learning – PMLR, pp. 1–16. (2017). https://proceedings.mlr.press/v78/dosovitskiy17a.html. Accessed 30 Apr 2023
21. Nvidia Isaac Sim. https://developer.nvidia.com/isaac-sim. Accessed 30 Apr 2023
22. Macenski, S., Foote, T., Gerkey, B., Lalancette, C., Woodall, W.: Robot operating system 2: design, architecture, and uses in the wild. Sci. Robot. **7**(66), eabm6074 (2022). https://www.science.org/doi/abs/10.1126/scirobotics.abm6074
23. Macenski, S., Martín, F., White, R., Ginés Clavero, J.: The marathon 2: a navigation system. In: 2020 IEEE/RSJ International Conference on Intelligent Robots and Systems (IROS) (2020). https://github.com/ros-planning/navigation2, https://arxiv.org/abs/2003.00368
24. Moveit2 package. https://moveit.ros.org/. Accessed 30 Apr 2023
25. Wu, Y., Kirillov, A., Massa, F., Lo, W.Y., Girshick, R.: Detectron2 (2019). https://github.com/facebookresearch/detectron2
26. Data generation on Ignition Gazebo (Garden) for Segmentation and Object Tracking CNN's. https://github.com/danilogsch/Coop-SLAM. Accessed 30 Apr 2023

Health and Biomedical Information Systems

Cleaning ECG with Deep Learning: A Denoiser Based on Gated Recurrent Units

Mariana Dias$^{(\boxtimes)}$, Phillip Probst, Luís Silva, and Hugo Gamboa

LIBPhys (Laboratory for Instrumentation, Biomedical Engineering, and Radiation Physics),
NOVA School of Science and Technology, NOVA University Lisbon, 2829-516 Caparica,
Lisbon, Portugal
{mag.dias,p.probst}@campus.fct.unl.pt, {lmd.silva,
hgamboa}@fct.unl.pt

Abstract. The electrocardiogram (ECG) is an established exam to diagnose cardiovascular disease. Due to the increasing popularity of wearables, a wide part of the population has now access to (self-)monitorization of cardiovascular activity. Wearable ECG acquisition systems are prone to noise sources stemming from surrounding muscle activation, electrode movement, and baseline wander. Hence, many attempts have been made to develop algorithms that clean the signal, but their performance falls short when applied to very noisy signals. Acknowledging the demonstrated power of Deep Learning on timeseries processing, we propose a ECG denoiser based on Gated Recurrent Units (GRU). Noisy ECG samples were created by adding noise from the MIT-BIH Noise Stress Test database to ECG samples from the PTB-XL database. The trained network proves to remove various common noise types resulting in high quality ECG signals, while having a much smaller number of parameters compared to state-of-the-art DL approaches.

Keywords: ECG · Signal Processing · Deep Learning · Denoiser · GRU

1 Introduction

The electrocardiogram (ECG) records the electrical activity of the heart and is a widely used exam to diagnose cardiovascular diseases. A healthy heartbeat signal is represented in Fig. 1(a), being composed of: i) a P wave generated by the atrial depolarization, ii) the QRS complex generated by the ventricular depolarization, and iii) a T wave generated by ventricular re-polarization [1].

ECG monitoring allows capturing information regarding cardiac events, such as arrhythmia, anomalous heartbeats, or fluctuations in heart rate variability. Due to the increasing popularity of wearables, ECG assessments have become more accessible enabling a wide part of the population to (self-)monitor cardiovascular activity. While ECG is relatively straight-forward to capture, acquisition systems are prone to different types of noise that might influence a correct analysis and interpretation. The most common sources of noise in ECG signals are surrounding muscle activation (MA), electrode

© IFIP International Federation for Information Processing 2023
Published by Springer Nature Switzerland AG 2023
L. M. Camarinha-Matos and F. Ferrada (Eds.): DoCEIS 2023, IFIP AICT 678, pp. 149–160, 2023.
https://doi.org/10.1007/978-3-031-36007-7_11

movement (EM), and baseline wander (BW) [2]. Artifacts that overlap with the frequency spectrum of the ECG signal (~[1 Hz, 45 Hz]) are especially challenging because these cannot be removed with linear filters (low-, band-, nor high-pass filters) [1].

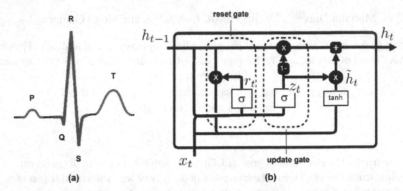

Fig. 1. (a) A normal heartbeat ECG and annotated waves. (b) Schematic representation of a GRU cell.

Traditional noise removal techniques include empirical mode decomposition, wavelets, sparsity-based models, Bayesian filters, and hybrid models [3]. Recently, Deep Neural Networks have shown enhanced performance in ECG denoising [4] just like in several other tasks regarding automatic ECG processing and classification [5].

Recurrent Neural Networks (RNNs) are a family of neural networks for processing sequential data, such as physiological signals. RNNs include feedback connections among hidden units, which allow a "memory" of previous inputs to persist in the network's internal state. The mathematical challenge of learning long-term dependencies is that gradients propagated over many timesteps tend to vanish. A variation of an RNN that addresses this problem is the GRU [6]. The basis behind the GRU architecture is a cell (illustrated in Fig. 1(b)) which can maintain its state over time due to two non-linear gates that regulate the information flow into and out of the cell: the reset and update gates. An advantage of the GRU architecture in comparison with other gated RNN architectures (such as the Long Short-Term Memory) is its lower computational complexity.

In this work, we propose a bidirectional GRU-based model for removing MA, EM and BW noise from ECG data. For its development, noisy ECG samples were created by adding noise from the MIT-BIT Noise Stress Test database [7] to ECG samples from the PTB-XL database [8]. This database contains records from more than 18 thousand subjects, both healthy individuals and patients with a variety of CVDs. Employing heterogeneous datasets is a crucial factor as a major difficulty in denoising is preserving the trace of abnormal signals of patients while removing noise. As such, in the present work, the goal was to investigate whether it was possible to build a GRU-based denoiser effective in removing the most common types of noise from ECG signals with diverse characteristics, including healthy and unhealthy patterns.

The main contribution and novelty of our work can be summarized as follows: i) we are the first using a GRU-based network to perform ECG denoising, ii) we are the first using the PTB-XL database in the task of removing MA, EM and BW noise from

ECG signals, and iii) in our approach, we try to mimic noise patterns that are closer to real-world scenarios, e.g., introducing MA and EM as noise bursts instead of corrupting the entire signal.

2 Related Work: Deep Learning for ECG Denoising

In recent years Deep Learning (DL) methods have been successfully applied to ECG denoising leading to state-of-the-art results. Extensive reviews of methods that do not use DL can be found in [9] and [3]. Most ECG denoising approaches that employ DL focus on autoencoders (DAE), for which several model architectures have been published, including feed forward neural networks (NN), convolutional neural networks (CNN), and long short-term memory (LSTM).

Rodrigues and Couto [10] presented a feed forward NN and showed that a variety of QRS detectors perform better after using it to denoise ECG signals. In [11] fully connected DAEs were tested on real ECG signals to which Gaussian white noise was added. Arsene, Hankins, and Yin [12] proposed both a CNN and a LSTM based model for ECG denoising which were tested on synthetic and real data and compared with a traditional wavelet approach, showing that the CNN model outperformed the LSTM and the wavelet approach.

Antczack [13] developed an architecture that consists of a LSTM cell followed by several ReLU layers. Their network was pre-trained with synthetic data to find an optimized architecture and subsequently fine-tuned with real data. Both datasets were corrupted by white noise. They compared their network to a wavelet approach and a bandpass filter and their model outperformed these approaches. A DAE that combines CNN and LSTM was proposed by Dasan and Panneerselvam [14]. Their model consists of several convolutional layers followed by a LSTM cell and a dense fully connected layer. The encoded representation is then decoded by convolutional layers and a dense layer that reconstructs the signal.

Recently an approach using a generative adversarial network (GAN) was proposed in [4]. The generator of the GAN receives signals corrupted with noise and is set to recreate the original noise-free signal. The discriminator receives either the output of the generator or a real noise-free ECG signal. It is set to distinguish if the provided input is either a real noise-free signal or a denoised signal. The network was compared to several other DAEs as well as traditional models, managing to outperform all comparative approaches on real ECG data that was exposed to different noise levels and noise types such as EM, MA, BW.

While the presented approaches are all valid, they have certain limitations. With the exception of [11] and [13], all presented papers use either synthetic data and/or the MIT-BIH Arrhythmia database [15], which consists of data from only 47 subjects. There is the possibility that these networks are biased towards arrythmia signals and their denoising results would not translate to other pathologies. Furthermore, in all works noise was applied to the entire sample, which is not necessarily representative of real-world scenarios (e.g., motion or muscle artifacts do generally appear for short amounts of time, unless the subject is moving constantly). Finally, while [11] and [13] used the PTB-XL database they only applied white noise to their ECG samples. This shows that there is a lack of models that are trained with more diverse datasets (i.e., containing more pathologies and data from healthy subjects) as well as with realistic noise characteristics.

3 Contribution to Connected Cyber Physical Spaces

The efforts of digitalization in the industry sector together with recent technological advancements in ubiquitous computing have opened up research opportunities for work-flow and process optimization that also focus on worker health. Within this context the project OPERATOR was initiated. The project aims to take a holistic approach at the industry 4.0 workplace with a major focus on the mental and physical well-being of workers ultimately creating a more human-centered workplace. Part of this project is to develop innovative frameworks that collect quantitative and qualitative data through ubiquitous computing devices, such as wearables, and health-oriented questionnaires. The gathered data will be used to implement decision support systems that help man-ufactures optimize processes under three perspectives: ergonomics, cognition, and pro-ductivity. A key component to track worker health is the ECG as it can indicate how the different work processes influence the cardiac cycle. This allows us to not only see immediate changes in cardiac activity (for example, changes in the heart rate variability due to the presence of fatigue [16]) but also see how cardiac health is affected over longer periods of time. However, acquiring ECG signals in industrial settings comes with its challenges. As workers in this sector are often exposed to work tasks that involve high amounts of movement, recorded ECG signals are prone to motion and muscle artifacts. Hence, it is necessary to develop robust noise removal techniques that can be integrated into the data processing pipeline. The proposed denoiser thus contributes to the topic of "Connected Cyber Phyisical Spaces" as it will be an essential part of the data acquisition pipeline, ensuring high quality standards for the collected data and in turn the validity of the developed decision support systems.

4 Methods

4.1 Databases

In this work two databases were used, the PTB-XL database [8] and the MIT-BIH Noise Stress Test database [7], both publicly available in PhysioBank [17].

The PTB-XL database consists of 21 837 clinical 10-s ECG records that were acquired from 18 885 patients with an age range between 0–95 years and gender evenly distributed. Signals were originally acquired at 400 Hz using a 12-lead ECG. An upsampled version at 500 Hz and a downsampled version at 100 Hz are provided. The database covers pathologies with regards to conduction disturbance, myocardial infarction, hypertrophy, and ST/T change. Additionally, 9528 instances (43.6%) of normal ECG are provided. The data is, according to the authors, of highest quality, with only some instances containing static noise (14.9%), baseline drift (7.4%), burst noise (2.8%), or electrode problems (0.1%).

The MIT-BIH Noise Stress Test database contains three half-hour recordings of BW, MA, and EM noise. Two channels of noise were collected at 250 Hz, by placing the electrodes in such a way that the ECG is not visible.

4.2 The Creation of Our Dataset

Data Pre-processing. The following pre-processing steps were applied to the ECG data. The 500 Hz version of the PTB-XL database was downsampled to 360 Hz (same as MIT-BIH Arrhythmia database). As some records contained small amounts of noise, a second order bandpass butterworth filter was applied to all ECG signals, with high pass cut-off frequency of 1 Hz and low pass cut-off frequency of 45 Hz for high frequency noise elimination [1]. Lastly, a *Min-Max* normalization was performed (normalization based on the minimum and maximum values of each record). The noise data was also resampled to 360 Hz.

Training, Validation, and Test Sets. The ECG data from PTB-XL was divided in training, validation, and test sets, with a proportion of 70%, 15%, and 15%, respectively. For each signal, the three leads with the lowest number of peaks were selected and, for the training set, the 3 leads were used, as separate signals; for the validation and test sets, 1 of the 3 leads was randomly selected. The rationale is: as all leads are records of the same heart activity, a higher number of peaks in one lead is likely due to the presence of noise. This way, we had 45777 (15259 $\times$ 3 leads) ECG samples for training, 3270 for validation, and 3270 for testing. Regarding the noise data, both provided channels were used, totaling 60 min of BW, MA, and EM noise. 80% (48 min) was used for training, 10% (6 min) for validation, and the remaining 10% for testing.

The Model's Input: Creation of Noisy Samples. For training our model, we added to each 10-s clean ECG signal a random portion of noise, with a length of 2 to 6 s. The EM and MA noises were added to a random part of the clean ECG signal while the BW noise was always added to the entire 10 s, as illustrated in Fig. 2. Additionally, to some records, mixed samples of different types of noise were added. The set of all possible combinations was: (MA, EM, BW, BW + MA, BW + EM, MA + EM, BW + MA + EM). There was a probability of 1/3 that the added noise was MA, of 1/3 that the added noise was EM and of 1/3 that the added noise was either BW or any combination. The reason for this is the fact that BW noise is the easiest to remove and having combinations of different noise simultaneously is less likely in the real-world scenarios. In the training set, as we used separately 3 leads from the same signal, a different type of noise was added to each lead. In the training and validation sets, in order to include different proportions of noise, the noise was multiplied by a randomly chosen factor between [0.7, 1.5] before being added to the ECG signal. These boundaries were chosen to ensure that the model was exposed to neither too low nor unrealistically high amounts of noise. Regarding the test set, the added noise had known SNR_{in} values of either 0, 5, 7, or 10 dB. The reasoning for this procedure was that the model should be prepared to handle a wide range of noise but at the same time should be tested in a way that would allow for a comparison with the results found in the literature.

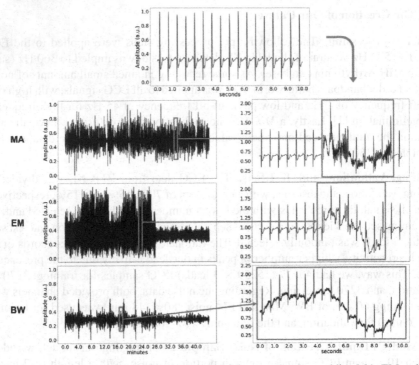

Fig. 2. Schematic representation of the creation of noisy samples from adding MA, EM and BW noise to the clean ECG samples from PTB-XL.

4.3 The GRU-Based Denoiser

Throughout the development of the GRU model, different architectures were tested. The optimized hyperparameters are presented in Table 1 and the two main versions of the architecture are illustrated in Fig. 3: the unidirectional and the bidirectional GRU. The model had as input the ECG signals after the pre-processing and noise addition steps. A Min-Max normalization was performed to the input, prior giving the data to the model. This way, the input consisted of sequences with a length 3600 samples (10 s recorded at 360 Hz) with values between [0, 1]. The desired output was the clean signals after preprocessing.

While the number of layers, neurons, and the dropout rate (applied to the output of GRU layers with the exception of the last) were optimized, there were some parameters of the model that were chosen *a priori*. In the bidirectional approach, only the first or first two (in the cases where there were three) GRU layers were bidirectional. The loss function used was the Root Mean Square Error between the predicted and desired outputs. All models were trained using the *Adam* optimizer, for 130 epochs with a batch size of 256 and an initial learning rate of 0.005. For each approach, the model's parameters from the epoch with the lowest validation loss during training were saved. Finally, validation losses were compared and the model achieving the lowest value was tested on the test set.

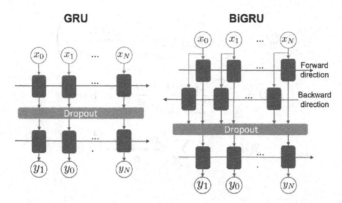

Fig. 3. Overview of the proposed GRU based framework for ECG denoising.

Table 1. Hyperparameters of the model and corresponding optimized values.

Hyperparameter	Tested values
Number of layers	$\{2, 3\}$
Number of neurons	$\{32, 64, 128, 256\}$
Dropout rate	$\{0, 0.3\}$
Bidirectional	$\{True, False\}$

4.4 Metrics

To evaluate model performance, common metrics found in the literature were used: the Root-Mean-Square Error (RMSE), the improvement in the Signal-to-Noise Ratio (SNR_{imp}), and the Percentage-Root-Mean-Square Difference (PRD) [3]. Equations 1 to 5 describe tese metrics, where **y** is the original clean ECG signal, $\tilde{y}$ is the noisy signal, and $\hat{y}$ is the denoised signal. Additionally, we used a signal quality metric, the kurtosis (SQI_{kur}). It is a statistical measure, that describes the distribution of the signal data throughout the mean [18]. As ECG data follows a Gaussian distribution, the higher the SQI_{kur} value, the higher the quality of the signal and, typically, a $SQI_{kur} > 5$ indicates a noise-free signal [18]. It can be computed using Eq. 6, where x(n) denotes the sample point n of the signal **x**, and μ_x and σ_x are, respectively, the mean and the standard deviation of **x**. The equations that define the used metrics are the following:

$$RMSE = \sqrt{\frac{1}{N} \sum_{n=1}^{N} [y(n) - \hat{y}(n)]^2} \tag{1}$$

$$SNR_{imp} = SNR_{out} - SNR_{in} \tag{2}$$

$$SNR_{in} = 10 \times \log_{10} \left(\frac{\sum_{n=1}^{N} [y(n)]^2}{\sum_{n=1}^{N} [\tilde{y}(n) - y(n)]^2} \right) \tag{3}$$

$$SNR_{out} = 10 \times \log_{10}\left(\frac{\sum_{n=1}^{N}[y(n)]^2}{\sum_{n=1}^{N}[\hat{y}(n) - y(n)]^2}\right) \tag{4}$$

$$PRD = \sqrt{\frac{\sum_{n=1}^{N}[\hat{y}(n) - y(n)]^2}{\sum_{n=1}^{N}[y(n)]^2}} \times 100\% \tag{5}$$

$$SQI_{kur} = \frac{1}{N}\sum_{n=1}^{N}\left[\frac{x(n) - \mu_x}{\sigma_x}\right]^4 \tag{6}$$

5   Results and Discussion

Given that we are the first to PTB-XL database as basis for developing a GRU-based denoiser there are no benchmarks available to which our results can be compared. Thus, we opted for comparing our models to traditional denoising approaches and perform a qualitative comparison with state-of-the-art models. From the models described in Sect. 4.3, the one that achieved the lowest RMSE on the validation set was the bidirectional GRU with 2 layers of 64 hidden units with 0 dropout rate. This model has 26121 parameters and achieved the best performance on the validation set after training for 58 epochs. Figure 4 illustrates the evolution of the model performance throughout the training phase: after the first epoch, the model outputs a timeseries that is almost entirely the same as the input; after 10 epochs it gets closer to the clean signal and after training for 58 epochs the noise is essentially removed from the input signal. Figure 5 shows some examples of the performance of the final model on different signals from the test set, corrupted with each type of noise and combination of different noises.

Table 2 demonstrates the mean results over all test signals according to the SNR_{in}. When higher amounts of noise are added to the input (i.e., lower SNR_{in}) the SNR_{imp} is higher. However, PRD and RMSE increase while SQI_{kur} decreases, indicating that the output has a higher denoising error and is of lower quality.

Regarding the model's performance on different types of noise, described in Table 3, the results show that the model is most and least effective in cleaning BW and EM, respectively. This is in accordance with results found in the literature. Unexpectedly, the model's performance does not necessarily decline when more than one type of noise corrupts the data. For example, when denoising MA + BW noise, the RMSE is lower than when removing just MA noise and higher than when removing just BW noise. This can be interpreted as if the denoiser removes each type of noise independently and, for the same amount of SNR_{in}, when multiple noise sources are present, the error is around the mean of the obtained error for each type of noise alone.

In Fig. 6 we compare our model's performance with two traditional denoising methods: the *Neurokit* filter (a 0.5 Hz high-pass butterworth filter of 5th order, followed by powerline filtering) and the Pan-Tompkins algorithm. These denoisers are implemented and publicly available in the Neurokit Python Toolbox [19]. The RMSE is 0.029, 0.393, and 0.405 when using the proposed GRU model, the Neurokit and the Pan-Tompkins denoisers, respectively, which shows that our model clearly outperforms these traditional denoisers.

The proposed GRU model achieves good results removing MA, EM and BW noise from ECG signals, as the output signals have a $SQI_{kur} > 11$. Comparing our results with state-of-the-art DL models (CDAE-LSTM [14] and GAN [4]), although our mean values of SNR_{imp} and RMSE do not outperform those approaches, our tests were performed on a significantly higher number of records (3270) with diverse characteristics, achieving SNR_{imp} values of up to 30.6, 28.5, 26.5, and 24.2 dB on records with SNR_{in} of 0, 5, 7 and 10 dB, respectively. Regarding the computational expense of these DL approaches, our model contains only 2.6×10^4 parameters, more than 10 times less than the parameters of the GAN (2.8×10^4) and around 500 times less comparing with the CDAE-LSTM (1.1×10^7). This is a crucial advantage, as the testing time, especially in light weight devices, increases exponentially with the number of parameters.

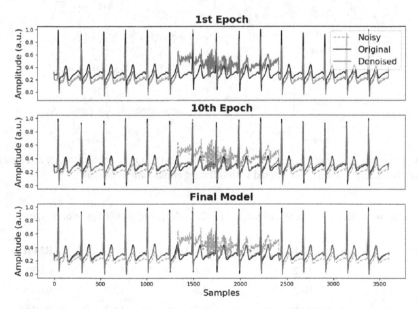

Fig. 4. Denoiser perfomance after the first, the tenth and the 58th (best) epochs.

Table 2. Mean results obtained (SNR_{imp}, PRD, SQI_{kur}, and RMSE) for each SNR_{in}.

SNR_{in} (dB)	SNR_{imp} (dB)	PRD (%)	SQI_{kur}	RMSE
0	21.7	8.9	12.0	0.041
5	19.5	6.5	12.2	0.029
7	18.6	5.7	12.4	0.025
10	16.5	5.4	12.5	0.023

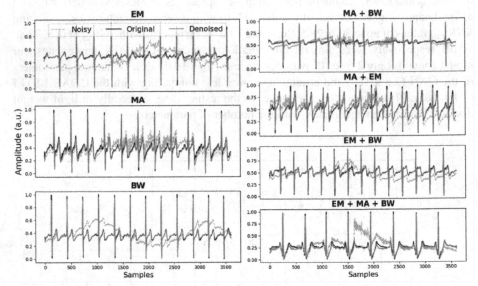

Fig. 5. Denoiser performance. Left: electrode motion (EM), muscle artifact (MA), and baseline wander (BW). Right: samples corrupted with different combinations of noise.

Table 3. Results obtained (SNR_{imp}, PRD, SQI_{kur}, and RMSE) per noise type.

Noise type	SNR_{imp} (dB)	PRD (%)	SQI_{kur}	RMSE
MA	19.2	6.4	12.4	0.029
EM	18.2	7.0	12.1	0.032
BW	20.6	5.5	13.3	0.024
MA + BW	19.4	6.5	11.8	0.027
EM + BW	19.5	6.1	12.3	0.027
MA + EM	19.2	6.4	11.7	0.029
MA + EM + BW	18.9	6.6	12.8	0.029

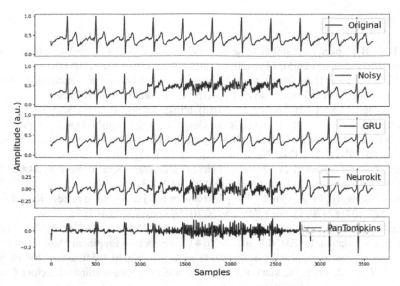

Fig. 6. Comparative results of the proposed denoiser (GRU) and two denoisers publicly available through the Neurokit Python toolbox [19]: *Neurokit* and Pan-Tompkins.

6 Conclusions and Future Work

In this work, a simple GRU-based DL architecture is proposed to execute the task of ECG denoising. For the first time, a DL denoiser was trained and tested on the PTB-XL database for the task of removing MA, EM and BW noise from ECG signals. The developed approach cleans noisy ECG signals and outputs signals with good quality, based on the SQI_{kur}, while simultaneously preserving the trace of abnormal signals of patients. Comparing with the state of the art approaches, the proposed model contains an at least 10 times lower number of parameters, which makes it comparatively much more suitable for automatic real time processing of data, useful in contexts of ECG monitoring using wearable sensors. As future work, it would be interesting to understand why the denoiser behaves better in some signals than in others. Furthermore, we will fine-tune the developed model to other types of noise to make it more robust to any situation.

Acknowledgments. This work was supported by Project OPERATOR (NORTE01-0247-FEDER-045910), cofinanced by the European Regional Development Fund through the North Portugal Regional Operational Program and Lisbon Regional Operational Program and by the Portuguese Foundation for Science and Technology, under the MIT Portugal Program. M. Dias and P. Probst were supported by the doctoral Grants SFRH/BD/151375/2021 and RT/BD/152843/2021, respectively, financed by the Portuguese Foundation for Science and Technology (FCT), and with funds from State Budget, under the MIT Portugal Program.

References

1. Li, H.Z., Boulanger, P.: A survey of heart anomaly detection using ambulatory electrocardiogram (ECG). Sensors **20**(5), 1461 (2020). https://doi.org/10.3390/S20051461
2. Joshi, S.L., Vatti, R.A., Tornekar, R.V.: A survey on ECG signal denoising techniques. In: Proceedings - 2013 International Conference on Communication Systems and Network Technologies, CSNT 2013, pp. 60–64 (2013). https://doi.org/10.1109/CSNT.2013.22
3. Chatterjee, S., Thakur, R.S., Yadav, R.N., Gupta, L., Raghuvanshi, D.K.: Review of noise removal techniques in ECG signals. IET Signal Process. **14**(9), 569–590 (2020). https://doi.org/10.1049/IET-SPR.2020.0104
4. Wang, J., et al.: Adversarial de-noising of electrocardiogram. Neurocomputing **349**, 212–224 (2019). https://doi.org/10.1016/J.NEUCOM.2019.03.083
5. Liu, X., Wang, H., Li, Z., Qin, L.: Deep learning in ECG diagnosis: a review. Knowl.-Based Syst. **227**, 107187 (2021). https://doi.org/10.1016/j.knosys.2021.107187
6. Cho, K., et al.: Learning phrase representations using RNN encoder-decoder for statistical machine translation. In: EMNLP 2014 - 2014 Conference on Empirical Methods in Natural Language Processing, pp. 1724–1734 (2014). https://doi.org/10.48550/arxiv.1406.1078
7. Moody, G.B., Muldrow, W., Mark, R.G.: A noise stress test for arrhythmia detectors. Comput. Cardiol. **11**(3), 381–384 (1984)
8. Wagner, P., et al.: PTB-XL, a large publicly available electrocardiography dataset. Sci. Data **7**(1), 1–15 (2020). https://doi.org/10.1038/s41597-020-0495-6
9. Tripathi, P.M., Kumar, A., Komaragiri, R., Kumar, M.: A review on computational methods for denoising and detecting ECG signals to detect cardiovascular diseases. Arch. Comput. Methods Eng. 1–40 (2021). https://doi.org/10.1007/s11831-021-09642-2
10. Rodrigues, R., Couto, P.: A neural network approach to ECG denoising, arXiv (2012). https://doi.org/10.48550/arXiv.1212.5217
11. Marwan, B., Samann, F., Schaanze, T.: Denoising of ECG with single and multiple hidden layer autoencoders. In: Current Directions in Biomedical Engineering, pp. 652–655 (2022). https://doi.org/10.1515/cdbme-2022-1166
12. Arsene, C.T.C., Hankins, R., Yin, H.: Deep learning models for denoising ECG signals. In: European Signal Processing Conference, vol. 2019 (2019). https://doi.org/10.23919/EUSIPCO.2019.8902833
13. Antczak, K.: Deep Recurrent Neural Networks for ECG Signal Denoising (2018). https://doi.org/10.48550/arxiv.1807.11551
14. Dasan, E., Panneerselvam, I.: A novel dimensionality reduction approach for ECG signal via convolutional denoising autoencoder with LSTM. Biomed. Signal Process. Control **63**, 102225 (2021). https://doi.org/10.1016/J.BSPC.2020.102225
15. Moody, G.B., Mark, R.G.: The impact of the MIT-BIH arrhythmia database. IEEE Eng. Med. Biol. Mag. **20**(3), 45–50 (2001). https://doi.org/10.1109/51.932724
16. Carvalho, D., et al.: Cardiovascular reactivity (CVR) during repetitive work in the presence of fatigue. Intell. Hum. Syst. Integr. (IHSI 2023) Integr. People Intell. Syst. **69**(69) (2023). https://doi.org/10.54941/ahfe1002833
17. Goldberger, A.L., et al.: PhysioBank, PhysioToolkit, and PhysioNet: components of a new research resource for complex physiologic signals. Circulation **101**(23), e215–e220 (2000)
18. Karmakar, C., Rahman, S., Natgunanathan, I., Yearwood, J., Palaniswami, M.: Robustness of electrocardiogram signal quality indices (2022). https://doi.org/10.1098/rsif.2022.0012
19. Makowski, D., et al.: NeuroKit2: a Python toolbox for neurophysiological signal processing. Behav. Res. Methods **53**(4), 1689–1696 (2021). https://doi.org/10.3758/s13428-020-01516-y

Exploring Kolmogorov Complexity Approximations for Data Analysis: Insights and Applications

Jorge Miguel Silva[1]([⊠]) [iD], Diogo Pratas[1,2,3] [iD], and Sérgio Matos[1,2] [iD]

[1] IEETA, Institute of Electronics and Informatics Engineering of Aveiro and LASI, Intelligent Systems Associate Laboratory, University of Aveiro, Aveiro, Portugal
jorge.miguel.ferreira.silva@ua.pt
[2] DETI, Department of Electronics, Telecommunications and Informatics, University of Aveiro, Aveiro, Portugal
[3] DoV, Department of Virology, University of Helsinki, Helsinki, Finland

Abstract. This paper presents a PhD research project focused on investigating the use of Kolmogorov complexity approximations as descriptors for various data types, with the aim of addressing inversion problems. The research explores the application of these approximations across different domains while considering the relationship between algorithmic and probabilistic complexities. The study starts with genomic data analysis, where specialized data compressors are employed to improve taxonomic identification, classification, and organization. The research then extends to analysing artistic paintings, utilizing information-based measures to attribute authorship, categorize styles, and describe the content. Additionally, the research examines Turing Machine-generated data, providing insights into the relationship between algorithmic and probabilistic complexities. A method for increasing probabilistic complexity without affecting algorithmic complexity is also proposed. Lastly, a methodology for identifying programs capable of generating outputs approximating given input strings is introduced, offering potential solutions to inversion problems. The paper highlights this research's diverse applications and findings, contributing to understanding the relationship between algorithmic and probabilistic complexities in data analysis.

Keywords: Algorithmic-Statistical Information · Kolmogorov Complexity · Data Compression

1 Introduction

The rapid growth of data and computational power in recent years has led to an increased focus on understanding the interplay between computation and information. This has fueled significant advancements in Algorithmic Information Theory (AIT), which investigates the properties of algorithms and their relationship with the information content of their inputs and outputs [1]. AIT is a field of study that explores the measurement of an object's complexity in terms of the minimum number of bits required for a program to compute it and halt without loss of information.

© IFIP International Federation for Information Processing 2023
Published by Springer Nature Switzerland AG 2023
L. M. Camarinha-Matos and F. Ferrada (Eds.): DoCEIS 2023, IFIP AICT 678, pp. 161–174, 2023.
https://doi.org/10.1007/978-3-031-36007-7_12

The potential applications of AIT span many fields, including bioinformatics [2], data compression [3], machine learning [4, 5], cryptography [6, 7], and even art [8]. In bioinformatics, AIT facilitates the analysis of genomic sequences [9], aiding in tasks such as identifying conserved regions [10], uncovering functional elements [11], and understanding evolutionary processes [12].

For data compression, AIT plays a crucial role in informing the development of more efficient compression algorithms through algorithmic modelling. By modeling the algorithmic structure of data, AIT-based methods can achieve superior compression rates by capturing the inherent patterns and redundancies in various data types, such as text, images, video, and audio streams.

In machine learning, AIT can potentially enhance model interpretability and performance by providing more concise representations of the learned patterns [13, 14]. This can lead to better generalization, reduce overfitting, and improve the understanding of the underlying mechanisms driving the data. Furthermore, AIT-inspired techniques can be employed for feature selection, model comparison, and complexity regularization, ensuring more robust and efficient learning processes [15].

AIT has also found applications in cryptography, where it has been used to analyze the randomness and security of cryptographic primitives [16, 17]. By quantifying the information content of keys and ciphertexts, AIT can help assess the strength of encryption schemes and guide the development of more secure protocols [18].

AIT has been employed in art to analyze and classify artistic styles, offering an objective and quantitative approach to understanding the creative process. By examining the complexity of artistic elements, researchers have been able to identify patterns, trace influences, and uncover the evolution of styles over time. This has opened up new avenues for interdisciplinary research at the intersection of art, computation, and information theory [8].

The primary motivation for this work was to investigate the usage of Kolmogorov Complexity approximations, particularly its usage in 1d and 2d digital objects such as genomic sequences, images, and algorithmically generated sequences, advancing knowledge in these areas, as well as investigate how these approximations can be used to solve the inversion problem. Therefore, our exploration's central research question was: "How can Kolmogorov complexity approximations be employed as descriptors of different data types and be used to solve inversion problems?".

This paper explores the use of approximations of Kolmogorov complexity as descriptors for a wide range of data types, including genomic sequences and artistic paintings. Our investigation led to the creation of new methodological advancements and provided fresh insights into these fields.

Afterwards, we investigate the relationship between probabilistic and algorithmic complexity using Turing Machines' tapes. Finally, we investigate how these methods can solve inversion problems through approximations.

The paper is organized as follows: Section II offers background information on Kolmogorov complexity and Algorithmic Information Theory, presenting their key concepts and mathematical foundations. Section III discusses AIT applications in genomics, providing a detailed account of its contributions to sequence analysis and viral classification. Section IV delves into the applications of AIT in art, exploring the use of Kolmogorov complexity to analyze and classify artistic styles and the detection of artists' influencing relationships. Section V investigates the relationship between probabilistic and algorithmic complexity and how this relationship can be used to approximate a possible solution to the inversion problem.

Finally, section VI summarises our findings and concludes with a discussion of future research directions in AIT, highlighting emerging trends and open questions that emerged at the end of the doctorate.

2 Kolmogorov Complexity, Algorithmic Information Theory, and Applications

Kolmogorov complexity, a fundamental concept in computer science and information theory, provides a means of quantifying the information content of an object [19]. The complexity is defined as the length of a shortest program capable of generating the object, typically using a fixed reference universal Turing machine [9]. By capturing the size of the most concise description of an object, Kolmogorov complexity inherently considers the structure and regularities within the object [20].

Algorithmic Information Theory delves into the interplay between computation and information [21]. It integrates Kolmogorov complexity with Shannon's information theory to establish a mathematical framework for evaluating the information content of individual objects. While Shannon's information theory concerns the average information content of message ensembles, AIT focuses on the intrinsic algorithmic properties of specific objects, providing a deeper understanding of their structure and complexity [9, 20].

Data compression, one of the primary applications of Kolmogorov complexity and AIT relies on the principle that a more compact program describing an object enables compression into a smaller size without any loss of information [9]. Lossless data compression, in particular, seeks to minimize data size while preserving the ability to reconstruct the original data perfectly [22]. By leveraging the structure and regularities within the data, AIT-based compression methods can achieve high compression rates for various data types, including text [23], images [24], and genomic sequences [3].

In addition to data compression, Kolmogorov complexity and AIT find applications in several domains, including data analysis, pattern recognition, feature selection, model comparison, and anomaly detection [9]. These applications benefit from the insights of measuring an object's Kolmogorov complexity, which can reveal information about its inherent structure and patterns. For instance, identifying high or low-complexity regions within a dataset can help detect distinct patterns or features, which may be helpful in tasks such as sequence alignment, classification, or clustering [25–27].

Furthermore, AIT-based methods can facilitate the comparison of models or algorithms, providing a robust means of assessing their performance and complexity [13]. In machine learning, for example, AIT can be applied to model selection, guiding the choice of an optimal model based on the trade-off between complexity and fitting of the data [28]. In the context of algorithm analysis, AIT can study algorithms' efficiency and resource requirements, offering insights into their time and space complexity [29].

In recent years, AIT has been increasingly used to address challenges in diverse fields, such as genomics [30], neuroscience [31], and art classification [8]. This paper provides a comprehensive overview of Kolmogorov complexity, Algorithmic Information Theory, and their diverse applications. By delving into the theoretical foundations and practical use cases, we aim to highlight the potential of AIT to advance our understanding of the information content and structure inherent in a wide range of data types, ultimately contributing to developing novel methods and techniques across various domains.

3   Genomic Sequence Analysis Using Kolmogorov Complexity Approximations

This section explores the application of Kolmogorov complexity approximations in genomic sequence analysis. The primary goals include developing novel computational methods for analyzing and classifying viral genomes, identifying unique features in viral sequences, and contributing to a better understanding of the relationships between different viral families and genera. The work was validated in the following articles [26, 30, 32]. Furthermore, we also contributed with the following open-source repositories [33–35] as well as a web-page [36].

3.1   Methodology

The methodology employed in this research centers on efficiently approximating the Kolmogorov complexity with data compression algorithms, specifically GeCo3, to analyze natural genomic sequences. The Normalized Compression (NC) was used to approximate the Kolmogorov complexity of genomic sequences, mathematically described as follows:

$$NC(x) = \frac{C(x)}{|x|\log_2|\theta|} \tag{1}$$

where x is the string, C(x) represents the number of bits needed by the lossless data compression program to represent the string x, $|\theta|$ is the size of the alphabet and $|x|$ is the length of the string x.

The lower the value of NC, the higher the sequence's redundancy (or lower complexity).

To evaluate the effectiveness of GeCo3 in quantifying regions described by simple algorithmic sources, it was benchmarked against other high compression ratio general-purpose data compressors (PAQ and cmix) and a measure that combines small algorithmic programs and Shannon entropy (Block Decomposition Method or BDM). The analysis revealed that GeCo3 could efficiently address and quantify regions properly described by simple algorithmic sources, such as inverted repeats (exact and approximate), among other characteristics. GeCo3 was used with three different configurations to detect inverted repeats (IRs) and quantify their abundance in each genome:

A configuration with a specific module to detect IRs (GeCo3-IR). A configuration without the module to detect IRs (GeCo3-noIR). A configuration that used both modules during compression (GeCo3-both). By comparing the NC values computed using each configuration, the abundance of IRs in each genome was quantified. The detection of IRs was fundamental to the research, as it served as an essential criterion for characterizing the genomic sequences.

The main objectives of this research were to develop a method for taxonomic classification using compression-based measures by approximating the Kolmogorov complexity of genomic sequences and comparing them to a reference database of known sequences, identify the structural description of the viral genome using minimal bidirectional complexity profiles to visualize the distribution of complexity locally and describe structural regions detected in the genome with other methods, and analyze rich genomic features to correctly identify viruses and archaea's taxon by examining the frequency of occurrence of specific motifs or patterns in genomes.

3.2 Viral Complexity Landscape

Our study aimed to explore the diversity of viruses in terms of genome size, structure, and content while addressing the limitations of traditional virus classification methods that often rely on phenotypic characteristics. To achieve this, we employed efficient approximations of the Kolmogorov complexity to analyze the complexity landscape of viral genomes and elucidate the relationships between different viral families and genera from a computational perspective.

Our findings revealed that, on average, dsDNA viruses are the most redundant (least complex) according to their size. This result is consistent with that dsDNA viruses typically have larger genomes. Conversely, we found that ssDNA viruses are the least redundant, indicating that they have more complex genomes despite their smaller sizes. Interestingly, we also discovered that dsRNA viruses show lower redundancy than ssRNA viruses, an intriguing finding considering the RNA viruses' rapid evolution and adaptation capabilities.

By examining the complexity landscape according to genome type, our study highlights the differences between various viral groups, such as dsDNA, ssDNA, dsRNA, and ssRNA viruses. The results demonstrate that smaller genomes, such as ssDNA and dsRNA, tend to have higher complexity, while larger genomes, such as dsDNA, are less complex. These findings are consistent with the inverse correlation observed between genome size and normalized compression (NC), a measure used to compare the proportions of the absence of redundancy independently from the sizes of the genomes.

Furthermore, we analyzed the complexity landscape according to taxonomic levels, such as Realm, Kingdom, Phylum, Class, Order, Family, and Genus. This approach allowed us to observe patterns and associations among viral taxa and understand the role of inverted repeats (IRs) in viral genomes. We found that certain viral families, such as Adnaviria, Varidnaviria, and Duplodnaviria, have low complexity due to their larger genome sizes and dsDNA nature. However, within these groups, some realms, like Adnaviria, exhibit higher complexity, suggesting that they are more complex than other dsDNA viruses.

Additionally, we explored the complexity landscape of specific viral families, such as Herpesviridae. Our results revealed a significant variation between the genera in this family, with some exhibiting high levels of inverted repeats (IRs). In contrast, others showed very low compression with the IR detection subprogram. We postulate that these variations in complexity could be related to different rates of evolution within these genomes.

3.3 Classification Performance and Impact of Normalized Compression

In this study, we examined the classification performance of our feature-based method, focusing on the impact of normalized compression (NC) as a genomic descriptor, which approximates Kolmogorov complexity. The primary goal was to determine if NC and Kolmogorov complexity approximations are effective data descriptors for classifying viral and archaea genomes.

Our results demonstrate that the NC feature significantly contributes to the classification performance. When used alone, the NC achieves relatively high accuracy and F1-score compared to the other individual features, indicating that the information derived from NC effectively captures essential genomic characteristics.

In our experiments, we observed that the accuracy and F1-score of the XGBoost classifier improved substantially when combining all features (NC, GC-content, and sequence length) compared to using only the NC feature. This improvement is observed across different taxonomic classification tasks in viral and archaea domains. This finding suggests that the NC feature, as an approximation of Kolmogorov complexity, is a robust data descriptor that can be employed in genomic sequence classification.

Furthermore, combining NC with other features, such as GC content and sequence length (SL), further enhances the classification performance. This improvement demonstrates a synergistic effect between these features, capturing complementary information that enhances the classification process.

3.4 Insights

This section delved into applying Kolmogorov complexity approximations in genomic sequence analysis.

We found that Kolmogorov complexity approximations, specifically normalized compression (NC), are suitable for analysing and classifying viral genomes. The developed classification method's effectiveness in classifying viral and archaea genomes at various taxonomic levels demonstrates the potential of leveraging Kolmogorov complexity approximations for genomic classification tasks. Furthermore, we observed a synergistic effect achieved by combining NC with other genomic features, such as GC content and sequence length. This significantly improved the classification performance, suggesting that incorporating multiple complementary features can lead to more accurate and reliable classification outcomes. These insights showcase the potential of using Kolmogorov complexity approximations for genomic sequence analysis, particularly for classifying viral genomes. The results contribute to the ongoing advancement of genomic analysis techniques and provide a foundation for developing more accurate, comprehensive, and robust classification methods in the future.

4   2D Data Analysis Using Kolmogorov Complexity Approximations

This section focused on applying Kolmogorov complexity approximations to 2D data analysis, specifically for artistic paintings. We present our findings by comparing complexity measures, their application in artistic paintings, and the potential improvements to existing classification methodologies. The work was validated in [27]. Furthermore, we also contributed with the following open-source repositories [37] as well as a web-page [38].

4.1   Comparison of Complexity Measures

Our analysis began with comparing Normalized Compression (NC), and Block Decomposition Method (BDM) measures to understand their respective strengths and weaknesses in measuring image complexity. We conducted experiments on different types of images, including cellular automata, X-ray images, paintings, and others, to assess the performance of each measure under various conditions. BDM was found to help identify data content similar to simple algorithms but had difficulty dealing with uniform pixel edition and lossless information quantification due to block representability. This limitation affected its performance when applied to highly uniformed images or where information was distributed unevenly. Conversely, NC was more robust to data alterations, such as pixel edition and quantization, and was better suitable for measuring the quantity of information in artistic paintings without underestimating it. This robustness made NC more suitable for a broader range of image types, including those with varying degrees of complexity and uniformity.

4.2   Applications of Complexity Measures in Artistic Paintings

Using these complexity measures, we investigated their application in the context of artistic paintings. We assessed the potential of NC as a stylistic descriptor by combining it with the roughness exponent α. This combination effectively identified hidden patterns and relationships in paintings with the same complexity range, providing valuable insights into the similarities and differences between various art styles.

In addition to using NC as a stylistic descriptor, we explored the concept of complexity fingerprints to explain art content and aid art authorship attribution and validation. By examining how each artist typically distributes content on canvas, we could discern unique patterns that enabled to differentiate between artists and validate their authorship.

4.3   Revealing Relationships Between Artists Using Complexity Measures

Moreover, our study discovered interesting links between artists based on the distance between their regional complexity. This approach highlighted shared techniques and stylistic influences, suggesting that complexity measures can be used to relate artists and provide insights into their stylistic connections and potential influences on each other's work. The relationships revealed by these complexity measures could be valuable for art historians and researchers studying the evolution of art styles and the impact of individual artists on their contemporaries.

4.4 Improving Classifications Methodologies with Regional Complexity and HDC Function

Lastly, we examined whether the regional complexity and the Height Difference Correlation (HDC) function of paintings could be used as additional features to improve existing author and style classification methodologies. To test this hypothesis, we integrated these features into a classification pipeline and evaluated their performance on a dataset of artistic paintings.

Our results showed that incorporating regional complexity and HDC features led to a significant increase in classification accuracy, indicating that these measures can effectively extract information that differs from non-handcrafted features. This finding supports the potential of complexity measures to improve current methodologies in classifying artistic paintings and emphasizes the relevance of regional complexity as a descriptor of images in this context.

4.5 Summary

In summary, our exploration of 2D data analysis using Kolmogorov complexity approximations in the field of artistic paintings has led to several noteworthy findings. We demonstrated the strengths and weaknesses of NC and BDM measures in measuring image complexity and assessed their sensitivity to data alterations. Furthermore, we showed that the combination of NC and the roughness exponent α could be an adequate stylistic descriptor and that complexity fingerprints can be valuable for art content explanation, authorship attribution, and validation. Additionally, our study highlighted the potential of complexity measures to reveal relationships between artists based on shared techniques and stylistic influences.

Finally, we provided evidence that was incorporating regional complexity and HDC function as additional features can improve existing classification methodologies for artistic paintings. These findings aid in the development of computer-based analysis techniques for art and open new avenues for future research in this field.

5 Evolving Probabilistic Complexity in Turing Machines

In this section, we explore the evolution of probabilistic complexity in Turing Machine (TM) tapes, maintaining the same level of algorithmic complexity. We demonstrate its potential applications by devising a methodology to increase probabilistic complexity. The content of this section is validated in [39]. Additionally, we discuss a new approach to approximate the inverse problem in Turing machines, comparing different search strategies and addressing the challenges and limitations in this context. For this section we also contributed with the following open-source repositories [40–43].

5.1 Analyzing Probabilistic Complexity in TM Tapes

Our investigation began by analyzing TMs with low algorithmic complexity, i.e., a small number of states and alphabet. Then, we employed a compression-based measure, approximated by the best-order Markov model, to quantify the probabilistic complexity of the generated tapes. By examining the compression-based approach concerning symbol editions and block transformations, we identified two distinct regions with higher Normalized Compression (NC) patterns in the tapes produced by TMs with the same number of states and alphabet. These regions were associated with repetitive short cycles in the configuration matrix, resulting from sequential modifications in the matrix and leading to shorter tapes.

5.2 Complexity Profiles

We introduced normal and dynamic complexity profiles as approximate measures to quantify local complexity. Normal complexity profiles allow us to localize higher and lower probabilistic complexity areas in machines that reached the external halting condition. In contrast, dynamic complexity profiles enable us to track the temporal dynamics of probabilistic complexity through the tape's modification cycles. By applying both profiles, we could draw meaningful insights regarding global quantities.

We also compared a measure incorporating algorithmic and probabilistic approaches (Block Decomposition Method or BDM) to analyze the tapes. Although BDM was found to be an efficient describer of the tapes generated by TMs with specific conditions, for a higher number of states, our methodology progressively approximated the BDM.

5.3 Increasing Probabilistic Complexity

We developed an algorithm capable of progressively increasing a tape's probabilistic complexity. This algorithm generates a tape that evolves through a stochastic optimization rule matrix, modified according to the quantification of the NC. Consequently, this algorithm can be adapted to vary the value of the NC. By implementing and comparing two methods to increase probabilistic complexity, we found that the second method was more effective at systematically increasing the probabilistic complexity of TMs while retaining algorithmic complexity.

5.4 Potential Applications and Implications

Our algorithm for increasing probabilistic complexity while maintaining algorithmic complexity has several potential applications in bioinformatics. For instance, the output of these TMs can be used as input to test and quantify the accuracy of genome assembly algorithms for different complexities from nonstationary sources. Another application involves simulating progressive mutations in metagenomic communities or complementing absent regions of genome viruses due to sequencing limitations or DNA/RNA degradation. A broader application includes benchmarking compression algorithms used to localize complexity in the data, considering possible algorithmic sources. These applications demonstrate the significance of our findings in understanding and manipulating probabilistic complexity in Turing Machines.

5.5   Approximating the Inverse Problem in Turing Machines

Building upon our exploration of probabilistic complexity in TM tapes, we introduce a methodology to approximate the inverse problem in Turing machines, which aims to find programs capable of generating given strings. By defining a search space with the specific alphabet and state cardinalities, we focus on candidate programs more likely to produce the target string.

We generate candidate Turing machines within the search space and simulate their execution for a predetermined number of iterations. Upon halting, we compare the output strings to the target string using a loss function based on the Kullback-Leibler divergence, which measures the dissimilarity between probability distributions.

We employ a Guided search approach inspired by the A* search algorithm to navigate the vast search space efficiently. This heuristic-driven method prioritizes candidate programs more likely to produce the target string and iteratively refines the search parameters and the number of iterations for enhanced approximation.

Our methodology for addressing the inverse problem in Turing machines connects with the complexity profiles and the algorithm for increasing probabilistic complexity. It provides a framework to discover programs that generate strings with desired complexity properties. By combining loss function minimization, Guided search, and an iterative search strategy, we present a comprehensive approach to identify Turing machines that best represent given strings.

5.6   Comparing Search Strategies

To evaluate the effectiveness of our methodology, we compared three search strategies for finding candidate programs that represent the strings: sequential search, Monte Carlo search, and Guided search. Sequential search explores the search space systematically, Monte Carlo search employs random sampling, and Guided search uses heuristics to prioritize promising candidates.

Our comparison results demonstrated that Guided search consistently outperformed the other two methods regarding minimal average loss and the number of found solutions. This finding highlights the potential advantage of Guided search in approximating the inverse problem in Turing machines, suggesting that incorporating heuristic information can significantly improve the search process.

5.7   Challenges and Limitations

Despite the promising results, our methodology faced some challenges and limitations. The vastness of the search space required a time-constrained evaluation method, which limited the search for small tapes. As a result, the compression suffered in many cases, as more bits were required to represent the program than those needed to represent the target string.

Additionally, our methodology's performance was tested only on synthetically generated data, which may not accurately represent the complexity of real-world data. Therefore, further research and testing are needed to address these challenges, refine the methodology for broader applications, and validate its effectiveness in more complex and noisy data.

These new findings, combined with our existing work on evolving probabilistic complexity in Turing machines, contribute to our understanding of the relationship between algorithmic and probabilistic complexity and offer potential applications in bioinformatics, compression algorithms, and other fields where data complexity plays a crucial role.

5.8 Conclusions and Future Work

This doctorate explores the use of Kolmogorov complexity approximations for data description and classification. We apply it to various data types, such as 1D genomic sequences, 2D paintings, and algorithmic data. Our findings demonstrate the importance and versatility of these approximations in improving classification results for artistic paintings, taxonomic identification, and author and style attribution. We also provide insights into the redundancy of viral genomes and the complexity spectrum of paintings. Limitations and future directions include improving block representability, exploring other data types, and refining compression-based measures to better detect programs and improve classifications. Overall, this study lays a strong foundation for future applications of Kolmogorov complexity approximations in diverse domains.

6   Relationship to Connected Cyber-Physical Spaces

Our research on Kolmogorov complexity approximations explores potential advancements in data analysis for interconnected systems found in connected cyber-physical spaces. These spaces require efficient data management and analysis for optimal performance and reliability, as they integrate computational and physical processes for seamless communication, data exchange, and real-time analytics.

Though our study focuses on genomic data and artistic paintings, the underlying concepts and techniques could apply to other domains within cyber-physical spaces. Additionally, our research emphasizes the development of specialized data compressors, which could enhance efficient data storage and transmission, a crucial aspect for maintaining high-speed communication in interconnected systems.

Our proposed methodology for solving inversion problems aims to identify programs that generate outputs similar to given input strings. This approach can be used to tackle challenges such as reconstructing original data from compressed or noisy versions, which could have implications in various domains within Connected Cyber-Physical Spaces, including error detection and correction in communication systems.

In conclusion, our research on Kolmogorov complexity approximations contributes to developing innovative data representation, compression, and problem-solving approaches, potentially supporting more efficient, reliable, and secure interconnected systems within the cyber-physical domain.

Acknowledgments. This work was partially funded by National Funds through the FCT - Foundation for Science and Technology, in the context of the project UIDB/00127/2020. Furthermore, this work has received funding from the EC under grant agreement 101081813, Genomic Data Infrastructure. J.M.S. acknowledges the FCT grant SFRH/BD/141851/2018. National funds funded D.P. through FCT – Fundação para a Ciência e a Tecnologia, I.P., under the Scientific Employment Stimulus - Institutional Call - reference CEECINST/00026/2018.

References

1. Hutter, M.: Algorithmic information theory. Scholarpedia **2**, 2519 (2007)
2. Nalbantoglu, Ö., Russell, D., Sayood, K.: Data compression concepts and algorithms and their applications to bioinformatics. Entropy **12**(1), 34–52 (2009). https://doi.org/10.3390/e12010034
3. Silva, M., Pratas, D., Pinho, A.J.: Efficient DNA sequence compression with neural networks. GigaScience **9**(11), giaa119 (2020). https://doi.org/10.1093/gigascience/giaa119
4. MacKay, D.J.C., Mac Kay, D.J.C.: Information theory, inference and learning algorithms. Cambridge University Press, Cambridge (2003)
5. Cohen, A.R., Bjornsson, C.S., Temple, S., Banker, G., Roysam, B.: Automatic summarization of changes in biological image sequences using algorithmic information theory. IEEE Trans. Pattern Anal. Mach. Intell. **31**(8), 1386–1403 (2009). https://doi.org/10.1109/TPAMI.2008.162
6. Maurer, U.: Information-theoretic cryptography. In: Wiener, M. (ed.) Advances in Cryptology — CRYPTO' 99. LNCS, vol. 1666, pp. 47–65. Springer, Heidelberg (1999). https://doi.org/10.1007/3-540-48405-1_4
7. Yeboah-Ofori, A., Agbodza, C.K., Opoku-Boateng, F.A., Darvishi, I., Sbai, F.: Applied cryptography in network systems security for cyberattack prevention. In: 2021 International Conference on Cyber Security and Internet of Things (ICSIoT), pp. 43–48 (2021)
8. Tenreiro Machado, J., Lopes, A.M.: Artistic painting: a fractional calculus perspective. Appl. Math. Model. **65**, 614–626 (2019)
9. Li, M., Vitanyi, P.: An Introduction to Kolmogorov Complexity and its Applications. TCS, Springer, New York (2008). https://doi.org/10.1007/978-0-387-49820-1
10. Voss, R.F.: Evolution of long-range fractal correlations and 1/f noise in DNA base sequences. Phys. Rev. Lett. **68**(25), 3805–3808 (1992). https://doi.org/10.1103/PhysRevLett.68.3805
11. Ciliberti, S., Martin, O.C., Wagner, A.: Innovation and robustness in complex regulatory gene networks. Proc. Natl. Acad. Sci. **104**(34), 13591–13596 (2007). https://doi.org/10.1073/pnas.0705396104
12. Adami, C., Ofria, C., Collier, T.C.: Evolution of biological complexity. Proc. Natl. Acad. Sci. **97**(9), 4463–4468 (2000). https://doi.org/10.1073/pnas.97.9.4463
13. Rissanen, J.: Modeling by shortest data description. Automatica **14**(5), 465–471 (1978)
14. RossQuinlan, J., Rivest, R.L.: Inferring decision trees using the minimum description length principle. Inf. Comput. **80**(3), 227–248 (1989). https://doi.org/10.1016/0890-5401(89)90010-2
15. Davies, D.L., Bouldin, D.W.: A cluster separation measure. IEEE Trans. Pattern Anal. Mach. Intell. **PAMI-1**(2), 224–227 (1979). https://doi.org/10.1109/TPAMI.1979.4766909
16. Dodis, Y., Reyzin, L., Smith, A.: Fuzzy extractors: how to generate strong keys from biometrics and other noisy data. In: Cachin, C., Camenisch, J.L. (eds.) Advances in Cryptology - EUROCRYPT 2004. LNCS, vol. 3027, pp. 523–540. Springer, Heidelberg (2004). https://doi.org/10.1007/978-3-540-24676-3_31
17. Chaitin, G.J.: Algorithmic information theory. IBM J. Res. Dev. **21**(4), 350–359 (1977)
18. Bruce, S.: Applied cryptography: Protocols, Algorthms, and Source Code in c.-2nd (1996)

19. Kolmogorov, A.N.: Three approaches to the quantitative definition of information. Probl. Inf. Trans. **1**(1), 1–7 (1965)
20. Chaitin, G.J.: On the length of programs for computing finite binary sequences: statistical considerations. J. ACM (JACM). **16**(1), 145–159 (1969)
21. Calude, C.S.: Information and Randomness: An Algorithmic Perspective. Springer Science & Business Media, Heidelberg (2002). https://doi.org/10.1007/978-3-662-03049-3
22. Sayood, K.: Introduction. In: Introduction to data compression, pp. 1–10. Elsevier (2018). https://doi.org/10.1016/B978-0-12-809474-7.00001-X
23. Moffat, A.: Word-based text compression. Softw. Pract. Exp. **19**(2), 185–198 (1989). https://doi.org/10.1002/spe.4380190207
24. Knoll, B., de Freitas, N.: A machine learning perspective on predictive coding with PAQ8. In: 2012 Data Compression Conference, pp. 377–386. IEEE (2012)
25. Carrasco, R.C., Oncina, J.: Learning stochastic regular grammars by means of a state merging method. In: Carrasco, R.C., Oncina, J. (eds.) Grammatical Inference and Applications. LNCS, vol. 862, pp. 139–152. Springer, Heidelberg (1994). https://doi.org/10.1007/3-540-58473-0_144
26. Silva, J.M., Pratas, D., Caetano, T., Matos, S.: The complexity landscape of viral genomes. GigaScience **11**, 1–16 (2022). https://doi.org/10.1093/gigascience/giac079
27. Silva, J.M., Pratas, D., Antunes, R., Matos, S., Pinho, A.J.: Automatic analysis of artistic paintings using information-based measures. Pattern Recogn. **114**, 107864 (2021). https://doi.org/10.1016/j.patcog.2021.107864
28. Wallace, C.S.: Minimum message length and kolmogorov complexity. Comput. J. **42**(4), 270–283 (1999). https://doi.org/10.1093/comjnl/42.4.270
29. Hutter, M.: Universal algorithmic intelligence: a mathematical top→down approach. In: Goertzel, B., Pennachin, C. (eds.) Artificial general intelligence, pp. 227–290. Springer Berlin Heidelberg, Heidelberg (2007). https://doi.org/10.1007/978-3-540-68677-4_8
30. Silva, J.M., Almeida, J.R.: The value of compression for taxonomic identification. In: 2022 IEEE 35th International Symposium on Computer-Based Medical Systems (CBMS), pp. 276–281. IEEE (2022)
31. Zenil, H., Delahaye, J.-P.: An algorithmic information theoretic approach to the behaviour of financial markets. J. Econ. Surv. **25**(3), 431–463 (2011)
32. Silva, J.M., Pratas, D., Caetano, T., Matos, S.: Feature-based classification of archaeal sequences using compression-based methods. In: Pinho, A.J., Georgieva, P., Teixeira, L.F., Sánchez, J.A. (eds.) Pattern Recognition and Image Analysis, pp. 309–320. Springer International Publishing, Cham (2022). https://doi.org/10.1007/978-3-031-04881-4_25
33. jorgeMFS. Complexity ANalysis VirAl Sequences (C.A.N.V.A.S.) Repository (2021). https://github.com/jorgeMFS/canvas
34. jorgeMFS. Classification and identification of Archaea (ARCHAEA2) Repository (2021). https://github.com/jorgeMFS/Archaea2
35. bioinformatics ua. COMPressor tAxonomic ClassificaTion (C.O.M.P.A.C.T.) Repository (2021). https://github.com/bioinformatics-ua/COMPACT
36. CANVAS Website. CANVAS Website (2021). https://asilab.github.io/canvas/
37. asilab. Measuring probabilistic-algorithmic information of artistic paintings (PANTHER) Repository (2021). https://github.com/asilab/panther
38. PANTHER Website. PANTHER Website (2021). http://panther.web.ua.pt/
39. Silva, J.M., Pinho, E., Matos, S., Pratas, D.: Statistical complexity analysis of turing machine tapes with fixed algorithmic complexity using the best-order Markov model. Entropy. **22**(1), 105 (2020)
40. asilab. TMCompression Repository (2021). https://github.com/asilab/TMCompression
41. jorgeMFS.Turing Machine Recreator (TMRecreator) (2021). https://github.com/jorgeMFS/TMRecreator

42. jorgeMFS. SPTTM (2021). https://github.com/jorgeMFS/spttm
43. bioinformatics ua. TM Neural Finder (2021). https://github.com/bioinformatics-ua/TM-Neural-Finder

Clinical Data Integration Strategies for Multicenter Studies

João Rafael Almeida[1,2]([✉]), Alejandro Pazos[2], and José Luís Oliveira[1]

[1] DETI/IEETA, LASI, University of Aveiro, Aveiro, Portugal
{joao.rafael.almeida,jlo}@ua.pt
[2] Department of Computation, University of A Coruña, A Coruña, Spain
apazos@udc.es

Abstract. Multicenter health studies are important to enrich the outcomes of medical research findings due to the number of subjects that they can engage. To simplify the execution of these studies, the data-sharing process should be effortless, for instance, using interoperable databases. However, achieving this interoperability is still an ongoing research topic. In the first stage of this work, we propose methodologies to optimize the harmonization pipelines of health databases, considering the OMOP CDM as the destination schema. In the following stage, aiming to enrich the information stored in OMOP CDM databases, we have investigated solutions to extract clinical concepts from unstructured narratives. In the final stage, we aimed to simplify the protocol execution of multicenter studies, by proposing novel solutions for facilitating the discovery of databases. The developed solutions are currently being used in European projects aiming to create federated networks of health databases across Europe.

Keywords: Health Data · Database Profiling · Data Integration · Text Mining · OMOP CDM

1 Introduction

The efforts made to increase health treatments have encouraged numerous medical research investigations, including different types of clinical studies (observation and trial) [1]. The clinical trials are conducted by splitting patients into groups, in which some perform an active protocol while others are taking a placebo. This strategy aims to study the efficacy of the treatments in specific clinical conditions [2]. In these studies, health professionals have a direct intervention with the patients, which may not be always possible [3]. Another type of study, in which researchers do not perform any active intervention with patients is the observational study. In this case, the exposure occurs naturally or through other factors, *i.e.*, a group of patients suffer from a specific condition while others with similar conditions are healthy [1]. The research is made by documenting the relationship between the exposure and the outcome of the study by analyzing data [2].

© IFIP International Federation for Information Processing 2023
Published by Springer Nature Switzerland AG 2023
L. M. Camarinha-Matos and F. Ferrada (Eds.): DoCEIS 2023, IFIP AICT 678, pp. 175–190, 2023.
https://doi.org/10.1007/978-3-031-36007-7_13

Observational studies employ diverse strategies and are established by defining a set of inclusion and exclusion criteria for subjects participating in the study. These studies also observe several features that are identified and monitored over a period of time [4]. Certain initiatives aim to reuse data that was already collected by health professionals during follow-up visits to carry out observational studies. This approach not only saves time but also allows for a pre-verification of the number of subjects before beginning the analysis [5]. In case of certain diseases, it becomes necessary to gather more data about the selected subjects. For those situations the data is recorded based on the study guidelines, and various solutions can be employed for data storage, such as the institutional Electronic Health Record (EHR) system [6]. The dependence on technical teams is a major barrier when there is a need to extract data for analysis. Many other ethical and technical issues are raised when one wants to combine datasets from distinct organizations. This is the case of multicenter studies with the goal of increasing the population size, that may impact the power of the statistical evidence, and thereby the study's findings [7].

The process of integrating data sources is more than a technological issue. There are some Extraction, Transformation and Load (ETL) tools capable of performing this task using large amounts of data. The non-technical problem of this aggregation is the data domain, *i.e.,* identifying the concepts in the data and combine correctly the information associated with them that was extracted from multiple sources. Healthcare databases belong to one of the domains in which this is a concerning problem, due to the variety of concepts to represent similar procedures and medical terms. Solving these problems is helpful to optimize studies, but sharing patient-level data still raises some issues, specifically related with the subjects' privacy [8]. The data contains very sensitive information, and the disruption of this privacy has consequences for several entities involved in the process [9, 10]. The legislation of the different countries raises more challenges regarding the analysis of multiple data sources without exposing sensitive data.

Researchers are driven by the potential impact of multicenter studies to look for more reliable and reusable solutions to combine knowledge from distributed health datasets [1]. Organizations and methodologies were established to explore clinical databases by reusing existent data [5]. One of these efforts aims to create a strategy to reuse EHR databases using a homogeneous schema, to facilitate the interoperability between databases. This integration is currently possible using open-source frameworks that help support the whole process [1].

The research objectives of this work can be paraphrased into several questions focused in addressing specific problems. We recognize that multicenter medical studies may raise additional issues that will not be considered in this work, mainly due to the data types used on these. For instance, research studies based on biomarkers that are correlated with DNA information, or studies primarily focused on using medical images. Therefore, to achieve a scenario capable of supporting distributed health studies using multiple data sources from distinct institutions, we limited the scope to EHR databases. This objective will be accomplished by answering the following research questions:

1. *How to execute a database query over a network of heterogeneous health databases?*
   The lack of interoperability is the main problem in this scenario. An ecosystem with

heterogeneous databases may not share the same data schema, which invalidates the query-sharing. Besides this problem, the healthcare domain contains huge amounts of medical concepts, that may differ between institutions, at the national or international level. A methodology to harmonize such databases is required, which converts them into an interoperable format. This process may have different stages and components, and some of them will be automatized aiming to reduce the cost and time of executing this procedure. This may result in a new software solution.

2. *How to enrich patients' health history using information available in clinical notes?* The free format of this type of information raises several challenges in terms of named-entity recognition and normalization. Currently, the research lines focused on NLP, may lead to new solutions that can enrich this field. In this work, we aim to investigate a solution capable of improving the quality of information stored in the relational databases. This solution will be a software solution capable of processing clinical free text and storing this information in a relational database, following the harmonization principles defined in the ETL procedures for EHR databases.

3. *How to select the most adequate health databases for a specific research study?* This question can be addressed from different perspectives. However, by correlating it with the previous statements, we identified that the main problems medical researchers meet are: i) the discovery of databases of interest; and ii) the access to those databases without violating privacy policies and ethical regulations. The solution to these problems is too complex to be solved by a software application alone. To answer this question, it is necessary to create an ecosystem of tools and methodologies, in which data owners can feel confident in sharing characteristics about their databases, while researchers can have enough information to select the databases that fit better their needs. Therefore, the solution proposed for this problem will be a portal that integrates: i) a web catalogue of database characteristics; ii) tools to visualize and compare these characteristics; and iii) tools for orchestrating distributed studies.

In this manuscript, we describe an extended overview of a PhD thesis focused on enriching information extraction pipelines in clinical decision support systems. The main goal of this work was to investigate a new strategy to use medical data from distributed databases to conduct multicenter health studies.

2 Contribution to Technological Innovation for Connected Cyber Physical Spaces

One of the most important parts of a medical study is the patients' information correlated to the study scope. The patient's characteristics are crucial to the success of medical studies since it is estimated that up to 50% of trials are not completed due to insufficient enrollment [11]. When collecting these characteristics, the procedure is achieved to a specific goal, resulting in distinct data types. For instance, distinct medical tests can be performed on the subjects, such as medical imaging, blood analysis and electrocardiogram, to identify any health issue. The information extracted from these sources can contribute to the clinical history of each person, which can be a valuable insight for making more precise diagnostics [12]. However, the digital data formats for those records can be different.

To address the challenge of managing different digital data formats for medical records, technological innovation for connected cyber-physical spaces can play a crucial role. By integrating several medical data sources, healthcare researchers can collect or questioning different institutions based on a study scope. This has the potential of increasing the number of subjects in the study, improving its findings. Overall, technological innovation for connected cyber-physical spaces can support the integration and analysis of patient data, leading to improved healthcare outcomes and better understanding of human health.

3 Secondary Use of Clinical Data

The secondary use of medical data to conduct research studies has become a common practice. These studies have provided complementary support to generate new insights and knowledge, namely in pragmatic trials using records collected from routine clinical care visits, comparative effectiveness studies or patient-centered outcomes research [13]. These data were not primarily generated to support research or secondary analysis. This concept refers to the use of data for purposes other than those that it was originally collected [14]. However, over the last few years, the clinical research community recognized that recruiting patients to record their medical characteristics over time is challenging. Although this practice is required in some types of studies, medical research is currently not limited to them. Therefore, this section presents an overview of the most relevant data types in the medical domain.

3.1 Electronic Health Records

An EHR is a digital version of the data collected about a patient. Hospitals usually have a EHR system to make the information available in real-time to the health professionals of the institution [15]. Besides patient data, there is an amount of additional information regarding patients' medical conditions that are also stored in such systems. EHR aims to simplify the data management and data exchange within the institution, between different services, resulting in higher quality and safer care for patients.

Some of the data stored in these systems follow a tabular structure, following the principles of relational databases [16]. Although there are some efforts in having interoperable databases supporting the EHR systems, each vendor has its own data schema. Over the last years, several EHR standards were developed, namely the CEN ISO 13606 [17], OpenEHR [18], OMOP CDM from OHDSI [5, 19] and HL7 standards (CIMI, HL7-CDA HL7-FHIR) [16]. The HL7 standards were proposed to simplify the processes of exchanging of data between software applications provided by distinct vendors that are used by different healthcare providers. They define guidelines and methodologies to support the communication between various healthcare systems [20].

Utilizing the data from the EHR system to answer healthcare questions differs from the traditional approach based on collecting data after defining a question [15]. The tabular data can help medical researchers conduct different types of studies, namely by identifying patient populations with specific healthcare interventions and outcomes, e.g., related to drug exposure, procedures, and conditions, among others. The parameters available to characterize these patient populations are various, including demographic information, morbidities, utilization and cost, healthcare delivery, treatments, and disease natural history.

Although EHR has been used for many years, as well as the idea of secondary use of this data, the process of reutilizing its data still raises some challenges. These challenges include limitations of processing ability [21, 22], interoperability [23, 24], inability to extract the required information [25, 26], and security and privacy concerns [27].

EHR can be a strategy for federating biomedical data using a particular data view. Some information may not be possible to represent in this format, such as medical images or omics data. However, this tabular format already contains valuable information to be used for conducting medical studies.

3.2 Clinical Notes

EHR systems can have repositories of non-tabular patients' information, e.g., clinical notes. The text data contained in these notes is typically subdivided into main categories, depending on whether they are structured or not. The structured notes, as the name indicates, integrate some structured format, for instance, a form. Examples of this data are the diagnosis forms or the laboratory analysis results. Alternatively, unstructured notes refer to notes that contain free-text, for instance, some of the physician's notes transcripts [28]. Free text notes are characterized by their vast variability, especially due to their heterogeneity. EHR contains agglomerates of different types of medical narratives (for progress, admission, operative, primary care, and discharge, among others), with different dimensions (from very short to very long) [29]. Structuring the information available in medical narratives is challenging due to this reason, but also because those are often ungrammatical. They contain short telegraphic sentences, plenty of misspellings, and are filled with abbreviations. In some cases, these abbreviations refer to local dialectal shorthand expressions, which may overload the use of acronyms, *i.e.,* the same group of letters with different meanings [28].

One strategy to introduce some kind of structure in these notes is making use of pseudo-templates or integrating tabular data into the narratives, for instance, the laboratory results. This pseudo-structure is not generalized, and nothing ensures that this is used in all narratives present in the system. Besides, the adoption can vary between physicians, services, or institutions [28]. A different attempt to increase the readability of free-text notes was through the adoption of standard lexicons to encode the information present in the narratives [30].

Despite clinical text being of significant interest, extracting pertinent information from it has traditionally relied on clinical experts manually reviewing clinical notes. However, various approaches have been developed to automate this process and extract relevant information. There are challenges associated to these processes since that cannot scale with the growing rate of generation of medical data [31], much research has been made during the past years in domains such as clinical NLP to create systems for automatically extract data from clinical notes [32].

The use of unprocessed narratives for conducting multicenter studies raises several challenges, namely regarding patients' privacy and data interoperability. Mapping the clinical concepts to their standard definition can solve the latter issue but raises other challenges since this task can become time-consuming. Additionally, it is acknowledged that the challenging nature of the free text can difficult the development of solutions for retrieving data from medical [33].

4 Semi-automatic Translation of Data Sources into a Common Schema

The challenges to define and implement ETL workflows collaboratively can be more complex in specific application domains. In medical scenarios that handle with sensitive data and requires the harmonization of the data into a common data schema, it requires the collaboration between technical teams and medical specialists [34]. This collaboration can be necessary in different stages, namely design, implementation, and validation. In each stage, there are some challenges that we addressed in this work.

4.1 Methodology for Cohort Harmonization

We proposed a methodology that is based on OHDSI ETL principles. During the extraction stage, the chosen data source is obtained from one or multiple data sources using a dedicated process. This strategy aims to get the data from the source systems without interfering with their usual performance since in health databases, the medical system should not be overloaded with tasks that can be scheduled. Therefore, the data is exported to a tabular format.

Out of all the stages, the transformation stage is the most complex component. This stage requires the mapping of the source database into the target schema, as well as the harmonization of the content. For a data source, this procedure requires full mapping, which is time-consuming and requires specialized entities to validate the mappings. Custom operations on the data may be necessary, depending on the source of the data. Clinical databases contain a broad range of clinical concepts that require harmonization using standard vocabularies. Although certain parts of this stage have been automated, we rely on manual approval by a specialized medical entity, ensuring that all mapped data is accurate.

The loading stage completes the process by inserting the data into the OMOP CDM database. These databases are loaded with data that is pseudo-anonymized to protect the patient's privacy rights. Furthermore, when data is migrated to this schema, the original raw data can also be validated, and issues can be detected. The pipeline includes quality mechanisms that verify whether loaded data adhere to the attributes for each concept.

4.2 Proposed Tools

The technical components of the proposed ETL methodology were first implemented in a Python-based tool [1, 35]. This tool considers all the three stages of the ETL operations, *i.e.* the operations from the original source data into the OMOP CDM database, as presented in Fig. 1. In this implementation, we split these stages to enable their execution in an isolated manner. We also adopted some open-source tools to support some of the stages of this workflow. WhiteRabbit and Usagi are tools from the OHDSI ETL ecosystem. WhiteRabbit is responsible for collecting information about the data sources' structure, namely columns and attributes. While Usagi is used to map concepts into their standard definition. This last offers an intuitive GUI that helps the medical specialist to validate these mappings.

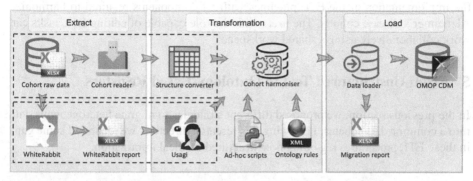

Fig. 1. The proposed methodology, that also includes some of the ETL OHDSI tools, facilitating the migration workflow of raw data to the OMOP CDM structure. This process comprises three primary stages, with two processes running in parallel (indicated by a red box). The initial stage involves the extraction of cohort information and its subsequent loading into the system. Next, the transformation stage employs mappings combined with ontology rules to perform all the necessary operations on the raw data. Finally, the loading stage inserts the processed data into the database, generating a migration report highlighting any issues with the original data [1]. (Color figure online)

The implementation of some components raised some challenges due to the data sensibility of the proposed research application. Dealing with health data demands a deep understanding of the data source to perform accurate harmonization. Besides, there is another challenge is the task to define custom transformation on each data source. This is because the data collection strategy was not standardized, making it difficult to work with the original data. This lack of interoperability when recording the data complicated the implementation of the migration workflow.

The data quality is another advantage of using this workflow. When an ETL procedure is finished, a report is generated which includes statistical data related to the migrated data, i.e., typing errors when recording the raw data.

BIcenter is a web based ETL tool capable of covering some of the existent limitations currently found in multi-institution environments that require the collaboration for building and managing ETL workflows [36]. This application can simplify the development of these workflows due to its intuitive GUI, namely users without technical expertise. BIcenter replicates the Kettle features in a web environment, which creates a more user-friendly environment.

The use of BIcenter leveraged the proposed methodology to new possibilities, leading to a collaborative and multi-institutional environment. This tool was initially proposed to simplify the management of the distinct roles assigned to different institutions. However, the system can be installed locally and used internally with invited users to support the definition of these pipelines. The RBAC mechanisms of this tool can support the definition of rules associated with the different features of this tool.

BIcenter-AD was proposed to be an extension of BIcenter applied to Alzheimer's disease datasets [37]. This tool provided a collaborative environment that was focused in the ETL Task Editor. With this component, a workspace is created that allows the implementation of the ETL pipelines with all components required to harmonize Alzheimer's disease cohorts. The users with the role capable of editing ETL tasks can work collaboratively using a shared workspace.

5   From Unstructured Text to Ontology-Based Registers

In the previous section, we proposed different strategies to migrate heterogeneous data into a common data schema. Following this research direction, we identified some gaps in these ETL procedures regarding non-structured medical information.

5.1   Extract and Harmonize Drug Mentions

The first proposal for extracting medical information from non-structured data was a two-stage workflow, denominated DrAC [38]. The initial stage involves extracting prescriptions found in patients' narratives. Subsequently, the extracted information is harmonized into standard definitions during the second stage, before being stored in a shared database schema known as the OMOP CDM.

To implement the reader component, a factory programming pattern was used. This simplifies the adoption of this tool a new dataset of clinical notes is used. Once the clinical notes have been read, the annotator is employed to extract the medication concepts present in each narrative. The annotations are then stored and subject to post-processing. The tool used for this was Neji, an open-source and modular framework designed for processing text and retrieving medical annotation [39].

Neji was configured as a medication annotator using three drug-related medical terminologies from the UMLS Metathesaurus [40]: AOD, DrugBank and RxNorm. These terminologies encompass several semantic types and groups. Therefore, we narrowed the content of these dictionaries by only retaining entries from the "Chemicals & Drugs" semantic group. After cleaning these dictionaries, they were imported to an instance of the Neji server and a new service was configured. Once all of these notes were loaded into the proposed system, it uses the Neji endpoints to annotate the medication entities and the extracted information was stored in a matrix structured by patient, drug and values for this relation.

Therefore, each cell contains the strength, dosage, and route for each drug annotated and associated with the patient. This particular format was adopted since it is similar to the one used in one of the stages of the ETL workflows, proposed for harmonizing cohort studies into an OMOP CDM database.

5.2 Multi-language Concept Normalization

One of the challenges posed by ETL procedures is the definition of the transformation rules. The task for mapping original concepts into their standard definitions is time-consuming and requires specialized teams. Although there are various automatic mapping solutions available to assist this process, these are more complex when working with multilingual databases, resulting in a substantial manual effort for translation and mapping. The proposed component defines a strategy that combines language detection techniques with text mining algorithms to optimize the ETL workflows [41]. This component is intended to be integrated into existing harmonization pipelines.

The proposed component employs two open-source tools: i) a web collaborative platform capable of simplifying the management of the ontologies used in this proposal; and ii) a tool with a user interface to support the mapping validation. Usagi was used as the interface for validating the mappings. This tool provides a straightforward and user-friendly interface to validate mappings using word similarity and suggestive associations. While Usagi's suggestions only compare concepts with the standard vocabulary, resulting in some incorrect mappings that require manual modification, the user interface is user-friendly and can be reused for our proposed approach. Currently, it is used in several migration workflows, including those proposed in the previous section.

6 Scalable Database Profiling for Multicenter Studies

One of the challenges when reusing health databases for research is the correct selection of the data sources. This is a complex problem since it requires strategies to characterize data sources without revealing their content, and platforms for disseminating the databases' characteristics [42, 43]. For the database characterization issue, there are already some guidelines when dealing with this type of data. Depending on the project or institution's policies, the data owners can share aggregated information about their data. This can provide a summarization of the patients in the databases. Other characteristics can also be provided, namely data governance policies and contact details. These summarization guidelines are not standard and may differ depending on the context. For instance, a community focused on studying Alzheimer's Disease would have datasets with different characteristics compared with a more generic domain [44].

Profiling databases (or fingerprinting) is the action of representing a database using a set of characteristics that combined can create a singular conception of the database. Defining these characteristics raises some issues that vary depending on the project scope. While these issues have complex solutions, we propose a different strategy to help the discovery of medical databases. It aims to provide enough information about the databases, that can characterize them at a deeper level, without sharing sensitive information. Figure 2 represents the main idea of the concept of this summarization, which is defined as fingerprinting.

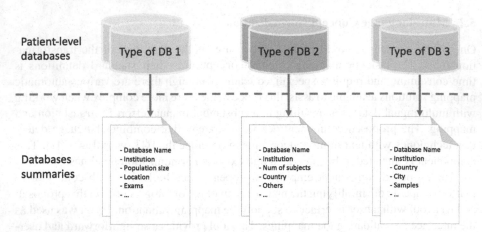

Fig. 2. The concept of fingerprinting databases focuses on extracting characterizes from databases of the same type.

6.1 Framework for Profiling Databases

The MONTRA 2 framework was developed as a solution for enabling biomedical data sharing through the creation of web-based environments for research purposes. The database catalogue can be considered one of the core features of MONTRA 2. In this catalogue, it is represented each database through the concept of fingerprinting, as was already described. Therefore, the data owners can define the catalogue structure that better fits their needs in that scope, and the system generates the web catalogue based on that file. The skeleton structure is flexible and contains fields (questions) to be filled by the data owners. Several questions can be aggregated in a "QuestionSet", creating a hierarchical data representation. Each question can store different types of data, for instance, dates, numbers, strings, multiple-choice values, geographic location, among others. These fields, which represent the metadata about the health databases in the catalogue, are used for free text search, advanced search, dataset comparison, and other features of the catalogue.

MONTRA 2 was implemented to also support the creation of an environment to integrate distinct tools in a centralized platform. The goal of this paradigm was to provide the researchers with a workplace with all required tools to: i) compare and identify the databases of interest for clinical studies; ii) streamline a study over the network; and iii) retrieve the results and aggregate them. All these tools are protected under a federated SSO mechanism with profile verification. MONTRA 2 is currently used to support different other projects. The system has three instances in production, to support different platforms, namely the EHDEN Portal, EMIF Catalogue and MSDA Portal.

6.2 Exploring Distributed Patient-Level Databases

The proposed component with the goal of streamlining multicenter studies is based on MONTRA 2. To accomplish this, we developed an additional tool that was integrated in MONTRA 2 as a plugin [45]. It aims to simplify the execution of health studies as well as centralize and coordinate the operations between all the entities involved. The proposed system, designated as Study Manager, adopted the same technologies used in MONTRA 2, namely Django in its core. To simplify the integration between systems, this tool was implemented to be compliant with the MONTRA SDK, following a MVC software pattern. This pattern segregates the application logic into three main elements: i) the model, responsible for handling the data storage; ii) the view, that generates the data representation for the client; and iii) the controller, which contains the business layer.

With all the proposed solutions in the previous sections, including MONTRA 2 framework, the process of conducting multicenter medical studies is currently a reality. Medical researchers have identified some challenges and opportunities when sharing biomedical data. The component proposed in this part of this work aims to empower these opportunities, which may increase the impact of the outcome of such medical studies. Therefore, the proposed strategies aim to facilitate the exploration of patient-level databases, while minimizing the risk of violating the patient's privacy.

7   Results and Discussion

Enriching information extraction pipelines in clinical decision support systems is a research topic that can be addressed from different points of view. In this work, we tried to enrich these pipelines starting by working on the foundations of clinical decision support systems. We recognised that to increase the quality of the treatments, researchers need to study the impact of new drugs, or the efficiency of current treatments. These findings can originate new treatment protocols that can be integrated into the decision-support systems of healthcare institutions. Therefore, in this work, we focused on creating methodologies and tools to help medical researchers conduct more impactful findings, to improve the source of these systems.

We started by specifying the scope of this work, based on the biomedical data formats that we could use. Motivated by EHDEN project, we focused this work on EHR relational data, that we tried to supplement with data extracted from medical narratives. Then, in the later stage, after defining strategies to have an interoperable network of data sources, we proposed solutions to support research using these data sources. In short, we presented some software solutions to integrate medical data sources, and the final product is a platform to simplify the data analysis across distributed databases [46].

The first hypothesis addressed the lack of interoperability between health databases. However, as we find during this work, the problem was not the lack of standard solutions to interconnect these databases. Instead, the problem was the effort required to adopt one of these standards. To answer this problem, we proposed solutions to simplify the migration of EHR data to one of the standard data schemas currently used in medical studies. We validated these solutions using heterogeneous cohorts of patients' data suffering from Alzheimer's disease. After harmonizing these datasets, the data of 6,669 subjects were combined considering the information of 172 clinical concepts. The interoperability was ensured by converting data sources to the OMOP CDM data schema [1].

The second hypothesis was about enriching the information stored in the databases, using unstructured data present in clinical narratives. For this, we proposed a solution capable of extracting medical concepts and storing them in an OMOP CDM database. Part of this solution is supported by the work done to answer the first hypothesis. We validated the proposed NLP strategies using scientific challenges, namely organized by n2c2 organization [38].

Finally, the third hypothesis was focused on finding the most adequate health databases for specific research studies. To answer this question, we have collaborated during this doctoral program with the EHDEN partners aiming to propose and adjust a solution based on real needs. The result was a flexible framework capable of being extended to support complementary tools. This work was validated in the context of the EHDEN project [46]. This portal currently contains information about 93 EHR databases, which are publicly accessible to all the 750 registered. Additionally, it also replaced old technologies that have supported the EMIF project in the past. This tool was validated with thousands of users. Overall, all these platforms have a real impact on medical environments since researchers can easily identify databases of interest to conduct multicenter studies.

8 Conclusions and Future Work

Enriching information extraction pipelines in clinical decision support systems is a research topic that can be addressed from different points of view. In this work, we tried to enrich these pipelines starting by working on the foundations of clinical decision support systems. We recognized that to increase the quality of the treatments, researchers need to study the impact of new drugs, or the efficiency of current treatments. These findings can originate new treatment protocols that can be integrated into the decision-support systems of healthcare institutions. Therefore, in this work, we focused on creating methodologies and tools to help medical researchers conduct more impactful findings, to improve the source of these systems.

We started by specifying the scope of this work, based on the biomedical data formats that we could use. Motivated by EHDEN project, we focused this work on EHR relational data, that we tried to supplement with data extracted from medical narratives. Then, in the later stage, after defining strategies to have an interoperable network of data sources, we proposed solutions to support research using these data sources. In short, we presented several software solutions to integrate medical data sources, and the final product is a platform to support the analysis of biomedical data across distributed databases.

With this research, we identified some future work and research directions, namely by analyzing some of the limitations of the proposed solutions. Herein, we present and discuss some of the possible research lines for future work:

1. Standardizing a fingerprinting schema: A lot of efforts have been conducted to ensure interoperability between data sources, as well as to publish their metadata to facilitate discovery. This resulted in several health database catalogues that cannot communicate and exchange information between them. There are already some initiatives to create federated catalogues in specific domains, however, this is only the beginning. Standard schemas and ontologies to federate this communication is a possible research direction to optimize the creation of health database catalogues.

2. Automatic definition of ETL workflows: Automatically establishing the mappings between the inial data schema to the target is an open research direction that can be applied beyond the health domain. This can be simplified and focused on the medical domain, by using OMOP CDM as the target data schema. In this work, we proposed semi-automatic methodologies, but this proposal can be optimized at different levels.
3. Extending OMOP CDM to incorporate other data types: Over the years some initiatives tried to extend the OMOP CDM to incorporate more information. The adoption of these initiatives at a large scale fails due to several issues (ensuring data privacy in complex data formats, breaking the schema interoperability, and raising issues when sharing results, among others). Investing in this direction may leverage medical research to new levels, namely by allowing distributed studies using DICOM images, or genomic data.
4. Secure FAIR data: The objective of FAIR principles is to optimize the reutilization of data. The principles highlight the importance of machine-actionability, which refers to the ability of computational systems to independently discover, access, interoperate, and reuse data with minimal or without manual intervention [47]. However, we identified a research line in this topic, by combining it with security, *i.e.* applying the FAIR principles following secure guidelines to ensure safe machine-to-machine communication.

Considering the increasing impact of technology in healthcare, along with the rapid developments in this field, we firmly believe in the importance of the presented research topics.

Acknowledgments. This work has received support from the EU/EFPIA Innovative Medicines Initiative 2 Joint Undertaking under grant agreement No 806968. JRA has been funded by FCT (Foundation for Science and Technology) under the grant SFRH/BD/147837/2019.

References

1. Almeida, J.R., Silva, L.B., Bos, I., Visser, P.J., Oliveira, J.L.: A methodology for cohort harmonisation in multicentre clinical research. Inform. Med. Unlocked **27**, 100760 (2021). https://doi.org/10.1016/j.imu.2021.100760
2. Ranganathan, P., Aggarwal, R.: Study designs: part 1–an overview and classification. Perspect. Clin. Res. **9**(4), 184 (2018). https://doi.org/10.4103/picr.PICR_124_18
3. Song, J.W., Chung, K.C.: Observational studies: cohort and casecontrol studies. Plast. Reconstr. Surg. **126**(6), 2234 (2010). https://doi.org/10.1097/PRS.0b013e3181f44abc
4. Carlson, M.D., Morrison, R.S.: Study design, precision, and validity in observational studies. J. Palliat. Med. **12**(1), 77–82 (2009). https://doi.org/10.1089/jpm.2008.9690
5. Hripcsak, G., Duke, J.D., Shah, N.H., et al.: Observational health data sciences and informatics (OHDSI): opportunities for observational researchers. Stud. Health Technol. Inform. **216**, 574 (2015). https://doi.org/10.3233/978-1-61499-564-7-574
6. Harris, P.A., Taylor, R., Thielke, R., Payne, J., Gonzalez, N., Conde, J.G.: Research electronic data capture (REDCap)—a metadata-driven methodology and workflow process for providing translational research informatics support. J. Biomed. Inform. **42**(2), 377–381 (2009). https://doi.org/10.1016/j.jbi.2008.08.010

7. Brown, C.H., Sloboda, Z., Faggiano, F., et al.: Methods for synthesizing findings on moderation effects across multiple randomized trials. Prev. Sci. **14**(2), 144–156 (2013). https://doi.org/10.1007/s11121-011-0207-8

8. Cushman, R., Froomkin, A.M., Cava, A., Abril, P., Goodman, K.W.: Ethical, legal and social issues for personal health records and applications. J. Biomed. Inform. **43**(5), S51–S55 (2010). https://doi.org/10.1016/j.jbi.2010.05.003

9. Fox, G.: "To protect my health or to protect my health privacy?" A mixedmethods investigation of the privacy paradox. J. Am. Soc. Inf. Sci. **71**(9), 1015–1029 (2020). https://doi.org/10.1002/asi.24369

10. Meystre, S.M., Lovis, C., Bürkle, T., Tognola, G., Budrionis, A., Lehmann, C.U.: Clinical data reuse or secondary use: current status and potential future progress. Yearb. Med. Inform. **26**(01), 38–52 (2017). https://doi.org/10.15265/IY-2017-007

11. Topaloglu, U., Topaloglu, M.B.: Using a federated network of realworld data to optimize clinical trials operations. JCO Clin. Cancer Inform. **2**, 1–10 (2018). https://doi.org/10.1200/CCI.17.00067

12. Kaelber, D.C., Jha, A.K., Johnston, D., Middleton, B., Bates, D.W.: A research agenda for personal health records (PHRs). J. Am. Med. Inform. Assoc. **15**(6), 729–736 (2008). https://doi.org/10.1197/jamia.M2547

13. Kahn, M.G., Callahan, T.J., Barnard, J., et al.: A harmonized data quality assessment terminology and framework for the secondary use of electronic health record data. Egems **4**(1) (2016). https://doi.org/10.13063/2327-9214.1244

14. Weiskopf, N.G., Hripcsak, G., Swaminathan, S., Weng, C.: Defining and measuring completeness of electronic health records for secondary use. J. Biomed. Inform. **46**(5), 830–836 (2013). https://doi.org/10.1016/j.jbi.2013.06.010

15. Ross, M., Wei, W., Ohno-Machado, L.: "Big data" and the electronic health record. Yearb. Med. Inform. **23**(01), 97–104 (2014). https://doi.org/10.15265/IY-2014-0003

16. Gamal, A., Barakat, S., Rezk, A.: Standardized electronic health record data modeling and persistence: a comparative review. J. Biomed. Inform. **114**, 103670 (2021). https://doi.org/10.1016/j.jbi.2020.103670

17. Muñoz, P., Trigo, J.D., Martínez, I., Muñoz, A., Escayola, J., García, J.: The ISO/EN 13606 standard for the interoperable exchange of electronic health records. J. Healthc. Eng. **2**(1), 1–24 (2011). https://doi.org/10.1260/2040-2295.2.1.1

18. Ulriksen, G.-H., Pedersen, R., Ellingsen, G.: Infrastructuring in healthcare through the OpenEHR architecture. Comput. Support. Coop. Work (CSCW) **26**(1–2), 33–69 (2017). https://doi.org/10.1007/s10606-017-9269-x

19. Hripcsak, G., et al.: The Book of OHDSI: Observational Health Data Sciences and Informatics. OHDSI (2019)

20. Rodrigues, J.J.: Health Information Systems: Concepts, Methodologies, Tools, and Applications: Concepts, Methodologies, Tools, and Applications, vol. 1. IGI Global (2009)

21. Fernandes, L.M., O'Connor, M., Weaver, V.: Big data, bigger outcomes. J. AHIMA **83**(10), 38–43 (2012)

22. Rehman, A., Naz, S., Razzak, I.: Leveraging big data analytics in healthcare enhancement: trends, challenges and opportunities. Multimedia Syst. **28**, 1339–1371 (2021). https://doi.org/10.1007/s00530-020-00736-8

23. Murdoch, T.B., Detsky, A.S.: The inevitable application of big data to health care. JAMA **309**(13), 1351–1352 (2013). https://doi.org/10.1001/jama.2013.393

24. Abraham, L., Vilanilam, G.C., et al.: Big data in clinical sciences-value, impact, and fallacies. Arch. Med. Health Sci. **10**(1), 112 (2022). https://doi.org/10.4103/amhs.amhs_296_21

25. Jensen, P.B., Jensen, L.J., Brunak, S.: Mining electronic health records: towards better research applications and clinical care. Nat. Rev. Genet. **13**(6), 395–405 (2012). https://doi.org/10.1038/nrg3208

26. Xu, J., Glicksberg, B.S., Su, C., Walker, P., Bian, J., Wang, F.: Federated learning for healthcare informatics. J. Healthc. Inform. Res. **5**(1), 1–19 (2020). https://doi.org/10.1007/s41666-020-00082-4

27. Fung, B.C., Wang, K., Chen, R., Yu, P.S.: Privacy-preserving data publishing: a survey of recent developments. ACM Comput. Surv. (CSUR) **42**(4), 1–53 (2010). https://doi.org/10.1145/1749603.1749605

28. Meystre, S.M., Savova, G.K., Kipper-Schuler, K.C., Hurdle, J.F.: Extracting information from textual documents in the electronic health record: a review of recent research. Yearb. Med. Inform. **17**(01), 128–144 (2008). https://doi.org/10.1055/s-0038-1638592

29. Wang, Y., Wang, L., Rastegar-Mojarad, M., et al.: Clinical information extraction applications: a literature review. J. Biomed. Inform. **77**, 34–49 (2018). https://doi.org/10.1016/j.jbi.2017.11.011

30. Ford, E., Carroll, J.A., Smith, H.E., Scott, D., Cassell, J.A.: Extracting information from the text of electronic medical records to improve case detection: a systematic review. J. Am. Med. Inform. Assoc. **23**(5), 1007–1015 (2016). https://doi.org/10.1093/jamia/ocv180

31. Sheikhalishahi, S., Miotto, R., Dudley, J.T., Lavelli, A., Rinaldi, F., Osmani, V., et al.: Natural language processing of clinical notes on chronic diseases: systematic review. JMIR Med. Inform. **7**(2), e12239 (2019). https://doi.org/10.2196/12239

32. Pivovarov, R., Elhadad, N.: Automated methods for the summarization of electronic health records. J. Am. Med. Inform. Assoc. **22**(5), 938–947 (2015). https://doi.org/10.1093/jamia/ocv032

33. Neustein, A., Imambi, S.S., Rodrigues, M., Teixeira, A., Ferreira, L.: Application of text mining to biomedical knowledge extraction: analyzing clinical narratives and medical literature. In: Text Mining of Web-Based Medical Content, pp. 3–32 (2014). https://doi.org/10.1515/9781614513902

34. Hripcsak, G., Ryan, P.B., Duke, J.D., et al.: Characterizing treatment pathways at scale using the OHDSI network. Proc. Natl. Acad. Sci. **113**(27), 7329–7336 (2016). https://doi.org/10.1073/pnas.1510502113

35. Almeida, J.R., Silva, L.B., Pazos, A., Oliveira, J.L.: Combining heterogeneous patient-level data into transMART to support multicentre studies. In: 2022 IEEE 35th International Symposium on Computer-Based Medical Systems (CBMS), pp. 62–65 (2022). https://doi.org/10.1109/CBMS55023.2022.00018

36. Almeida, J.R., Coelho, L., Oliveira, J.L.: BIcenter: a collaborative web ETL solution based on a reflective software approach. SoftwareX **16**, 100892 (2021). ISSN: 2352-7110. https://doi.org/10.1016/j.softx.2021.100892

37. Almeida, J.R., Pazos, A., Oliveira, J.L.: BIcenter-AD: harmonising Alzheimer's disease cohorts using a common ETL tool. Inform. Med. Unlocked **35**, 101133 (2022). ISSN: 2352-9148. https://doi.org/10.1016/j.imu.2022.101133

38. Almeida, J.R., Silva, J.F., Matos, S., Oliveira, J.L.: A two-stage workflow to extract and harmonize drug mentions from clinical notes into observational databases. J. Biomed. Inform. **120**, 103849 (2021). https://doi.org/10.1016/j.jbi.2021.103849

39. Matos, S.: Configurable web-services for biomedical document annotation. J. Cheminform. **10**(1), 68 (2018). https://doi.org/10.1186/s13321-018-0317-4

40. Bodenreider, O.: The unified medical language system (UMLS): integrating biomedical terminology. Nucleic Acids Res. **32**(suppl 1), D267–D270 (2004). https://doi.org/10.1093/nar/gkh061

41. Almeida, J.R., Oliveira, J.L.: Multi-language concept normalisation of clinical cohorts. In: 2020 IEEE 33rd International Symposium on Computer-Based Medical Systems (CBMS), pp. 261–264. IEEE (2020). https://doi.org/10.1109/CBMS49503.2020.00056

42. Lovestone, S., Consortium, E.: The European medical information framework: a novel ecosystem for sharing healthcare data across Europe. Learn. Health Syst. **4**(2), e10214 (2020). https://doi.org/10.1002/lrh2.10214
43. Oliveira, J.L., Trifan, A., Silva, L.A.B.: EMIF Catalogue: a collaborative platform for sharing and reusing biomedical data. Int. J. Med. Inform. **126**, 35–45 (2019). https://doi.org/10.1016/j.ijmedinf.2019.02.006
44. Bos, I., Vos, S., Vandenberghe, R., et al.: The EMIF-AD Multimodal Biomarker Discovery study: design, methods and cohort characteristics. Alzheimer's Res. Ther. **10**(1), 64 (2018). https://doi.org/10.1186/s13195-018-0396-5
45. Almeida, J.R., Barraca, J.P., Oliveira, J.L.: A secure architecture for exploring patient-level databases from distributed institutions. In: 2022 IEEE 35th International Symposium on Computer-Based Medical Systems (CBMS), pp. 447–452. IEEE (2022). https://doi.org/10.1109/CBMS55023.2022.00086
46. Almeida, J.R., Silva, J.M., Oliveira, J.L.: A FAIR approach to real-world health data management and analysis. In: 2023 IEEE 36th International Symposium on Computer-Based Medical Systems (CBMS). IEEE (2023)
47. Wilkinson, M.D., et al.: The FAIR Guiding Principles for scientific data management and stewardship. Scientific data **3.1**, 1–9 (2016). (vid. págs. 142, 151)

Support Operation and Maintenance of Power Wheelchairs with Digital Twins: The IoT and Cloud-Based Data Exchange

Carolina Lagartinho-Oliveira$^{(\boxtimes)}$, Filipe Moutinho, and Luís Gomes

NOVA School of Science and Technology, Center of Technology and Systems (UNINOVA-CTS) and Associated Lab of Intelligent Systems (LASI), NOVA University Lisbon, 2829-516 Caparica, Portugal

ci.oliveira@campus.fct.unl.pt, {fcm,lugo}@fct.unl.pt

Abstract. Digital twins are becoming popular in a wide range of industries for the monitoring, control, and optimization of physical objects, processes, and systems. Its growing demand is related to its potential to improve efficiency, reduce costs and increase safety in different applications. As a result, a variety of approaches, modeling processes, technologies, and tools have been used to develop and deploy digital twins. The choice of which to use often depends on the specific application area, case study, available resources, and expertise. This paper explores the idea of using the digital twin concept applied to power wheelchair systems, to supervise and improve their operation and maintenance. In particular, it focuses on data flow and connectivity within the digital twin, proposing an IoT and cloud-based data exchange to enable efficient cyber-physical connection and easy data management. For this work, a small-scale prototype of a power wheelchair was built with some sensors and actuators interfaced with a microcontroller, and the data exchange with a ROS-based virtual entity was performed via cloud under the MQTT protocol.

Keywords: Data Acquisition · Data Management · HiveMQ Cloud · InfluxDB · MQTT · NXT

1 Introduction

Power wheelchairs and related devices are available on the market to assist people with severe mobility impairments [1, 2]. As they often allow for the augmentation and replacement of functions and devices, they can also deal with speech, hearing, and vision problems. This means that two power wheelchairs are unlikely to be alike, making the market relatively limited. This, associated with manufacturers having to comply with all relevant legislation, contributes to the high cost of power wheelchairs, which can be as expensive as a car [3, 4]. So, it is important to properly maintain and preserve a power wheelchair to help to extend its lifespan and guarantee that it continues to provide safe and reliable mobility for its user. This can include regular cleaning and inspections, prompt repairs and replacements of any worn or damaged components, as well as adjustments to some wheelchair parameters, such as acceleration, forward speed, joystick throw or steer correction.

© IFIP International Federation for Information Processing 2023
Published by Springer Nature Switzerland AG 2023
L. M. Camarinha-Matos and F. Ferrada (Eds.): DoCEIS 2023, IFIP AICT 678, pp. 191–202, 2023.
https://doi.org/10.1007/978-3-031-36007-7_14

To make this easier, some companies in the sector have begun to explore ways to remotely connect their latest models of power wheelchairs with their service centers. Invacare's MyLiNX app [5] establishes a bluetooth connection with the wheelchair's control unit, and transmits data via Wi-Fi to a cloud accessed by the provider's portal. In the case of Permobil wheelchairs, they have a built in SIM card to communicate data with the MyPermobil app [6] and the fleet management portal [7].

These types of software applications provide users and technicians with valuable data on wheelchair usage and performance, and important information on wheelchair condition to improve remote diagnostics. Examples are battery charge status, number of charging cycles, undertaken drive time, and fault codes. With real-time metrics, technicians can identify and diagnose issues before an appointment, sometimes aided by suggestions to help with troubleshooting. With Quantum Rehab's Interactive Assist app [8], technicians can also access a real-time image of the wheelchair's electronic display to proceed with remote resolutions, as updating software or adjusting settings. Basically, these are the initial steps in employing digital twins for wheelchairs.

The authors of this paper intend to further study the use of digital twins for power wheelchair systems, to supervise them and make their operation and maintenance more efficient. A digital twin allows a physical asset or prototype to be represented in the virtual world, with physical and virtual entities connected and sharing the same properties, characteristics and behavior by means of data and information [9]. In this regard, this paper proposes an IoT and cloud-based data exchange to enable seamless connection between entities and to support data management; the question also posed is: "How can digital twin, along with an IoT and cloud-based data exchange, support the operation and maintenance of power wheelchairs?".

This work builds on the standard MQTT messaging protocol that facilitates communication for IoT devices, and the HiveMQ cloud native IoT messaging broker, which efficiently forwards data to and from a small-scale prototype of a power wheelchair. The prototype was equipped with some sensors and actuators interfaced with a microcontroller, and its virtual entity, responsible for storing data in an InfluxDB database, was based in ROS. Power wheelchairs face some challenges, and this section talked about some innovations on the market for their follow-up and maintenance.

Throughout the paper, the authors also contribute with some considerations about the state-of-the-art in the remaining topics of this work. Section 2 explains how this paper contributes towards the development of connected cyber-physical spaces. Section 3 details the proposal; describes the experimental prototype, and presents some results. Section 4 presents some discussion around the proposal; and Sect. 5 presents the conclusions and future work.

2   Contribution for Connected Cyber-Physical Spaces

A digital twin (DT) can simply be composed of three elements [9]: a real space, corresponding to the physical world where physical entities (PEs) exist; a virtual space that exists within the domain of the cyber space and where virtual entities can mirror the PEs; and a bidirectional path that allows data synchronization between the two spaces. In this paper, the focus is on the third element specifically on the connection between a power wheelchair prototype and a virtual entity, and on the management of related data. This focus is due to two factors: firstly, VE mirroring with PE is driven by real-time or near-real-time data; secondly, the VE relies on the data to compute control actions and send instructions to the PE.

To support data flow and connectivity within DT, internet of things (IoT) transmission technologies can be used together with appropriate network architectures, communication and security protocols, middleware platforms, etc. [10]. A middleware platform for IoT helps manage and process the large amounts of data generated by IoT devices. In particular, message-oriented middleware (MOM) platforms [11] allow devices to communicate asynchronously using a message broker, such as ActiveMQ, RabbitMQ, Mosquitto, VerneMQ, EMQX, and HiveMQ. These popular brokers support the Message Queuing Telemetry Transport (MQTT) protocol, which allows topics to be published and subscribed between distributed client nodes [12]. There are also cloud-based platforms available to manage these brokers' clusters, providing better scalability and accessibility.

Additionally, when accepting an MQTT client or connecting to external resources like a database, these brokers can establish secure connections via SSL/TLS and various authentication mechanisms. The relevant data that is exchanged in the DT – including its context, location and time – must be stored to ensure its future accessibility, so that if the PE changes, it can be analyzed in a specific time frame [13]. The data can be used later to understand and predict the PE behavior within its original context or in a new one. Such data can be collected as time series.

Big data storage technologies such as distributed file storage, NoSQL database and NewSQL database are getting more attention and can also be used to store and manage large volumes of data, including time series data [14]; examples of used tools are: Couchbase, MongoDB, RavenDB, and Cassandra. However, time series databases (TSDBs) are specially designed to store and retrieve large volumes of timestamped data, and provide additional features such as indexing, compression and aggregation. Examples of TSDB are: Prometheus, TimescaleDB, OpenTSDB, kdb+, KairosDB, and InfluxDB.

The following section presents the materials and methods associated with the deployment of the IoT and cloud-based data exchange for two-way connection of cyber-physical spaces, and data management in the context of power wheelchairs. It also includes a description of the experimental prototype, as well as the presentation of results.

3   Proposed IoT and Cloud-Based Data Exchange

The aim of this work is to support the research being conducted to use digital twins for power wheelchairs [15–17]. This envisions a seamless and secure remote connection between power wheelchairs and digital counterparts, which could ideally be implemented in service centers of companies in the sector.

The architecture underlying this proposal is represented in the diagram of Fig. 1. PE and VE in this diagram are represented by the prototype and the digital image, respectively. They are connected in a bidirectional manner through the HiveMQ cloud [18] acting as an MQTT broker, which also sends data to an on-premise InfluxDB [19] database using a Telegraf agent. In order to materialize this approach, an experimental prototype of a wheelchair was created with LEGO components, while the digital image was deployed using the ROS framework [20].

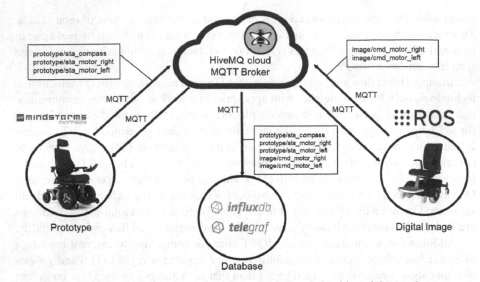

Fig. 1. Digital twin for a power wheelchair with IoT and cloud-based data exchange.

3.1 Power Wheelchair Experimental Prototype and Digital Image

As no real wheelchair was available at the time of this work, a small experimental prototype was developed using LEGO Mindstorms NXT components. This provided a simple yet effective way to test and verify the proposal. The prototype mainly focused on the power system elements that make the wheelchair capable of propelling; that is, the drive and caster wheels, the drive motor, the batteries and the controller.

An L293D motor drive IC interfaced with an ESP32 microcontroller (running micropython) was used to monitor and control the speed and steering of two 9 V DC NXT drive motors using modified RJ-12 cables. A compass was also integrated to monitor changes in tilt and rotation of the wheelchair. To power the prototype, a bank of 8 1.2 V Ni-MH batteries was used, providing a sufficient power source for the motors; as well as an additional bank of 4 batteries for the IC and ESP32. The ESP Wi-Fi module established a connection with the MQTT broker and transmitted the wheelchair motion values and its rotation around each axis. It also received commands from virtual entity to change the speed and state of the motors.

Several models can be considered for VE to replicate PE [21]. In order to deploy the digital image of the prototype, the virtual entity was modeled using a combination of geometric and physical models. While the geometric model represents the overall solid appearance of the VE using data structures that contain topological and geometric information, the physical model reflects the physical characteristics of the PWC. Concretely, a unified robot description format (URDF) XML file was described to represent the visual and physical aspects of the wheelchair digital image in the ROS environment. This model was visible in 3D in Gazebo and closely resembles a real wheelchair.

Then, and most importantly, a python script node was implemented to establish the MQTT connection with the broker and manage the transmission and reception of data. It was also used to monitor the status of the prototype so that any changes could be replicated and animated by the VE in the Gazebo simulator; as well as used to manage the commands to affect and control the physical prototype.

3.2 Data Exchange and Data Storage

A private HiveMQ cloud cluster was used to connect MQTT clients to a cloud native IoT messaging broker hosted on Amazon Web Services. At no cost, the cluster provides a maximum of 100 MQTT client sessions and can handle up to 10 GB of data traffic per month; however, in this particular scenario, it was only necessary to configure the access credentials of 3 clients, so that the power wheelchair, the digital image, and the database could publish and subscribe to the cluster.

The broker effectively gathers information published on specific topics and distributes it to the clients who have subscribed to those topics. The wheelchair prototype sends messages to the digital image by publishing to topics "prototype/#" and receives messages from the digital image by subscribing to "image/#". For bidirectional communication between the prototype and the digital image, each client sends messages to the other by publishing on the topic that the other client is subscribed to. To receive the data from both clients, the InfluxDB database simply subscribed to the prototype and digital image topics using the Telegraf agent.

All communications were secured using the TLS protocol, which provided encryption and authentication to ensure data was transmitted securely; and messages were sent with a quality of service (QoS) level of 1 to ensure they arrived at least once, even in the presence of network outages. In this setup, the InfluxDB and the digital image were installed on the same computer, as the cloud-based version of InfluxDB only has a maximum data retention period of 30 days. Yet, data needs to be saved for a longer period for potential future services.

3.3 Outcome

To validate the proposal, two types of procedures were considered. Firstly, a test web client was defined at HiveMQ cloud cluster to publish and subscribe to all topics. This allowed to test the communication with each client individually under the different topics, as well as determine the impact of the messages on each client. Secondly, all the clients were launched and establish communication with the HiveMQ cloud broker.

From top to bottom, Fig. 2 presents the successful connection of Telegraf, ROS, and ESP, with the subscription of topics from both prototype and digital image. In the ESP terminal, it is possible to see the first publish of data, "Publishing status", with data from compass, namely the pitch ("p") and roll ("r"), and data speed and motion values of each motor. In turn, we see in ROS terminal, that the messages were correctly parsed.

From InfluxDB it is possible to better inspect the results obtained. Figure 3, 4 and 5, depict all the messages received during approximately 1 min. Figure 3 corresponds to the values from compass. Here we see the first values from pitch and roll to be the same as those shown in terminals from Fig. 2.

Fig. 2. Connection, publish and subscribe of clients.

Since no remote controller like a joystick was used, the prototype waited for commands from ROS node to change its state. So, for Fig. 4 and 5 the results focused are the ones in which we can see that the commands sent to "prototype/#" affected the status of motors, updated previously with the status send by "image/#".

Finally, it was also possible verify the correct mirroring between that both entities, which functioned identically, in Gazebo and in real prototype.

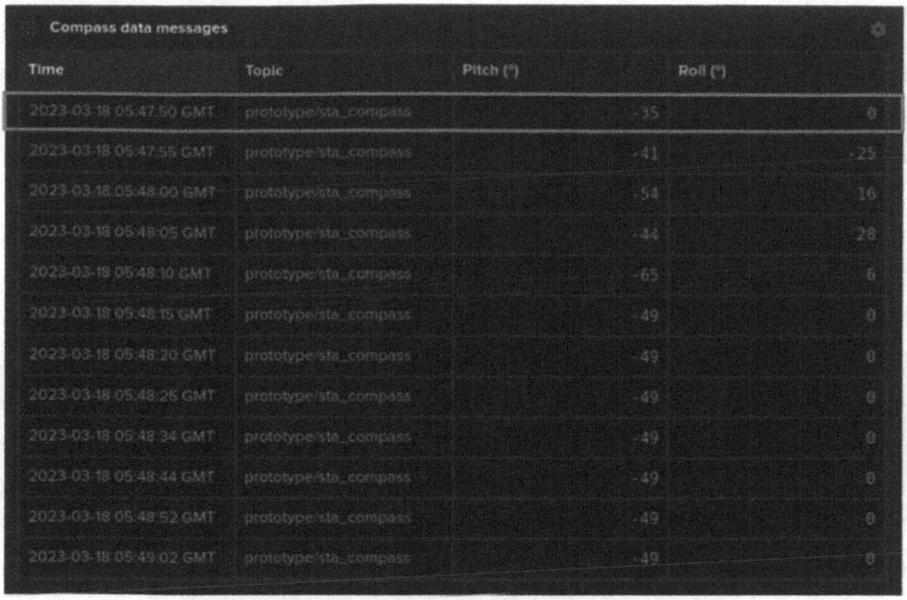

Compass data messages

Time	Topic	Pitch (°)	Roll (°)
2023-03-18 05:47:50 GMT	prototype/sta_compass	-35	0
2023-03-18 05:47:55 GMT	prototype/sta_compass	-41	-25
2023-03-18 05:48:00 GMT	prototype/sta_compass	-54	16
2023-03-18 05:48:05 GMT	prototype/sta_compass	-44	28
2023-03-18 05:48:10 GMT	prototype/sta_compass	-65	6
2023-03-18 05:48:15 GMT	prototype/sta_compass	-49	0
2023-03-18 05:48:20 GMT	prototype/sta_compass	-49	0
2023-03-18 05:48:25 GMT	prototype/sta_compass	-49	6
2023-03-18 05:48:34 GMT	prototype/sta_compass	-49	0
2023-03-18 05:48:44 GMT	prototype/sta_compass	-49	0
2023-03-18 05:48:52 GMT	prototype/sta_compass	-49	0
2023-03-18 05:49:02 GMT	prototype/sta_compass	-49	0

Fig. 3. Messages from ESP in prototype/sta_compass topic.

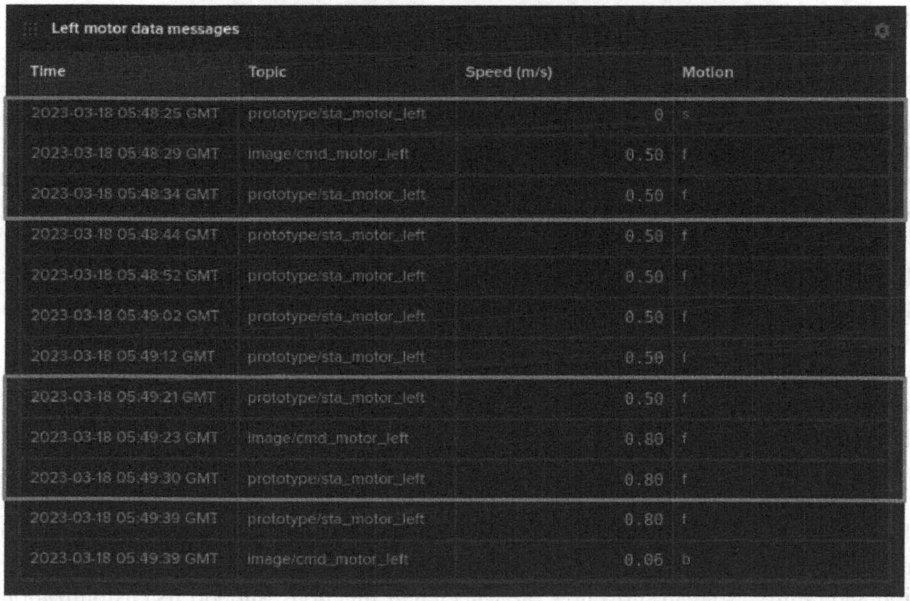

Left motor data messages

Time	Topic	Speed (m/s)	Motion
2023-03-18 05:48:25 GMT	prototype/sta_motor_left	0	s
2023-03-18 05:48:29 GMT	image/cmd_motor_left	0.50	f
2023-03-18 05:48:34 GMT	prototype/sta_motor_left	0.50	f
2023-03-18 05:48:44 GMT	prototype/sta_motor_left	0.50	f
2023-03-18 05:48:52 GMT	prototype/sta_motor_left	0.50	f
2023-03-18 05:49:02 GMT	prototype/sta_motor_left	0.50	f
2023-03-18 05:49:12 GMT	prototype/sta_motor_left	0.50	f
2023-03-18 05:49:21 GMT	prototype/sta_motor_left	0.50	f
2023-03-18 05:49:23 GMT	image/cmd_motor_left	0.80	f
2023-03-18 05:49:30 GMT	prototype/sta_motor_left	0.80	f
2023-03-18 05:49:39 GMT	prototype/sta_motor_left	0.80	f
2023-03-18 05:49:39 GMT	image/cmd_motor_left	0.06	b

Fig. 4. Messages from ESP and ROS in prototype/sta_motor_left and image/cmd_motor_left.

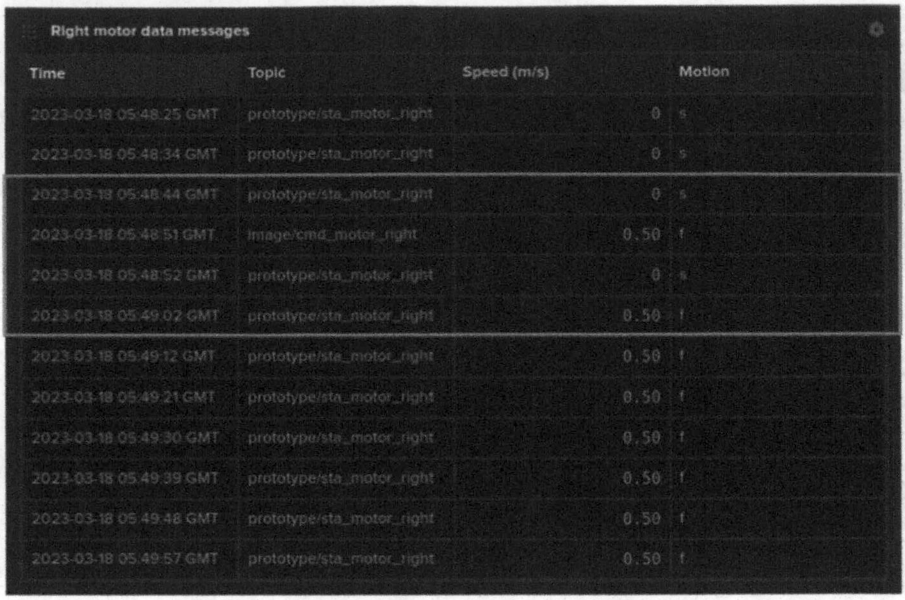

Right motor data messages

Time	Topic	Speed (m/s)	Motion
2023-03-18 05:48:25 GMT	prototype/sta_motor_right	0	s
2023-03-18 05:48:34 GMT	prototype/sta_motor_right	0	s
2023-03-18 05:48:44 GMT	prototype/sta_motor_right	0	s
2023-03-18 05:48:51 GMT	image/cmd_motor_right	0.50	f
2023-03-18 05:48:52 GMT	prototype/sta_motor_right	0	s
2023-03-18 05:49:02 GMT	prototype/sta_motor_right	0.50	f
2023-03-18 05:49:12 GMT	prototype/sta_motor_right	0.50	f
2023-03-18 05:49:21 GMT	prototype/sta_motor_right	0.50	f
2023-03-18 05:49:30 GMT	prototype/sta_motor_right	0.50	f
2023-03-18 05:49:39 GMT	prototype/sta_motor_right	0.50	f
2023-03-18 05:49:48 GMT	prototype/sta_motor_right	0.50	f
2023-03-18 05:49:57 GMT	prototype/sta_motor_right	0.50	f

Fig. 5. Messages from ESP and ROS in prototype/sta_motor_right and image/cmd_motor_right.

4 Discussion

The increasing complexity of current systems has been a motivation for the use of appropriate techniques to verify and validate their dependability, especially with regard to safety-critical systems (SCSs). A SCS is any kind of system where non-desired properties can endanger people's lives and the environment, as well as lead to financial losses. Power wheelchair systems fall precisely within the scope of SCSs.

As stated before, power wheelchairs have their own set of issues and problems and despite the efforts of companies to provide follow-up and maintenance services for them, there is still room for improvement. For instance, Quantum Rehab's Interactive Assist app [8] enables technicians to remotely access a real-time mirror image of the wheelchair's electronic display to resolve issues such as updating software or adjusting settings. However, they have limited control over the actual wheelchair. In many cases, they rely on customers and caregivers to follow technicians' instructions on how to proceed.

In this sense, we acknowledge the potential benefits in the use of digital twins in the power wheelchair industry, like what already happens in other sectors, such as the automobile industry. As an example, a digital twin can be useful for wheelchair preparation and fitting, as it can show how the wheelchair functions, support its customization and adaptation, and help in planning and testing different scenarios. The DT can also be applied to justify, design, and validate new or existing wheelchair features, services, and parts, as well as simulating the health conditions of the wheelchair, to detect and prevent the sources of problems and unwanted situations. The digital twin can also predict the performance of the power wheelchair, including the occurrence of unexpected scenarios.

As the digital twin can collect real-time operational data from the power wheelchair, it can provide insights into possible outcomes of its use, or trigger alerts during follow-up, maintenance, and repair so that a problem can be diagnosed. With the DT, wheelchair repair can be facilitated through remote analysis and real-time power wheelchair intervention. Here are some ways digital twin, along with an IoT and cloud-based data exchange, support the operation and maintenance of power wheelchairs.

The architecture depicted in Fig. 6 presents how digital twins can be used by service providers in real-time connectivity with their wheelchairs.

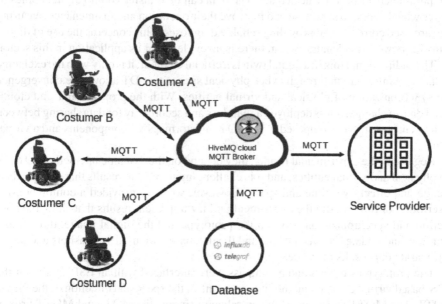

Fig. 6. Monitoring of multiple wheelchairs with IoT and cloud-based data exchange.

The proposed architecture facilitates flexible communication among multiple devices, with each client capable of communicating with one or more other clients as required. It can also be applied in a scenario where a provider center monitors multiple wheelchairs to support their operation and maintenance.

In future, this proposal can be improved to enhance the following services:

- Real-time monitoring of power wheelchair locations;
- The collection of information about each user's driving style and use;
- Engaging with users by sharing tips about their driving;
- Access wheelchair data and information on how to optimize its performance;
- Sending instructions or updates directly to the power wheelchair;
- Establish a maintenance schedule and perform pre-diagnostics;
- Generation of cost simulations based on required maintenance;
- Based on the information from used wheelchairs, configure new or replacement wheelchairs;

- Automatic report generation or downloaded on demand.

In the following section, the concluding remarks of this study will be presented, and emphasis will be given to future research.

5   Conclusions and Further Work

This paper explores a solution to support the operation and maintenance of power wheelchairs. One solution can be based on sensors that gather data to monitor important parameters of power wheelchairs. The data can be transferred into digital copies of power wheelchairs, to supervise and improve their operation and maintenance, ensuring they are used correctly and providing reliable diagnoses. This concerns the use of digital twins for power wheelchairs. So far, there is no evidence of its application in this sector.

The bidirectional link in a digital twin is a crucial element; it is only with the exchange of data and information through cyber-physical spaces that DT allows the convergence and synchronization of physical and virtual entities. With the proposed IoT and cloud-based data exchange, it was deployed a seamless and secure way for data sharing between a wheelchair prototype composed of LEGO Mindstorms NXT components and a virtual entity.

Regarding the experimental results, they depend on the dynamic interaction between the physical and virtual entities, and it is challenging to present results that capture their change and effect over time and space. However, we have provided a comprehensive description of how we did the experiment and try to present results that show the connection and synchronization between the prototype and the digital image, through the data flow and updates between them (and the database); we used screenshots and tables to illustrate our results more clearly.

The prototype's motors and a compass were interfaced with an ESP32, so that the ROS-based virtual entity could monitor and control the speed and direction of the PE via MQTT. The MQTT messages were centralized using a HiveMQ Cloud MQTT broker, and the relevant data was stored in an InfluxDB time-series database to support future services. This facilitates distributed communication between nodes that are located remotely and opens up unexplored possibilities for the wheelchair market.

The next phase of this study involves the use of an actual power wheelchair, an Invacare Fox [22]. Among other things, it will be necessary to modify the digital twin to accommodate the LiNX electronics found in Invacare's wheelchairs [23]. In addition, other sensors will be assembled to provide useful data in the given context.

On the virtual entity side, the authors also plan to extend and use a new high-level Petri net [24] to specify both the behavioral state model and the rule model. It is intended that this model can meet specific requirements, such as defining and establishing secure MQTT connections. The improvement of the VE geometric model is also a point to work on; and finally, real use case scenarios will be defined so that the digital twin has validation in the real wheelchair.

Acknowledgments. This work had the support of the Portuguese Agency FCT ("Fundação para a Ciência e a Tecnologia"), in the framework of project UID/EEA/00066/2020, and under the PhD scholarship 2020.08462.BD.

References

1. Mobility Management. Power Wheelchairs: Compare 29 Companies. https://buyersguide. mobilitymgmt.com/category/power-wheelchairs. Accessed 07 Mar 2023
2. Permobil: F3 Corpus Order form. https://permobilwebcdn.azureedge.net/media/l24h2z3x/ noprice-f3-corpus_model-2019-dd-15-07-2021.pdf. Accessed 07 Mar 2023
3. Permobil: 2023 MAP Pricing. https://hub.permobil.com/us/map-pricing. Accessed 07 Mar 2023
4. Invacare: Mobility products price list. https://www.invacare.co.uk/mobility-products-price-list. Accessed 07 Mar 2023
5. Invacare: MyLiNX - the helpful app to check your powerchair status! (2018). https://www.inv acare.co.uk/events-news/news/mylinx-helpful-app-check-your-powerchair-status. Accessed 06 Mar 2023
6. Permobil: MyPermobil. https://permobilwebcdn.azureedge.net/media/v5vgqmbp/myperm obil_brochure_uk_200525_web.pdf. Accessed 06 Mar 2023
7. Permobil: Power Wheelchairs Fleet Management. https://permobilwebcdn.azureedge.net/ media/tyen1e5w/fleet-management-brochure.pdf. Accessed 06 Mar 2023
8. Quantum Rehab: Interactive Assist. https://www.quantumrehab.com/quantum-electronics/int eractive-assist.asp. Accessed 06 Mar 2023
9. Grieves, M.W.: Product lifecycle management: the new paradigm for enterprises. Int. J. Prod. Dev. **2**(1–2), 71–84 (2005). https://doi.org/10.1504/IJPD.2005.006669
10. Lim, K.Y.H., Zheng, P., Chen, C.-H.: A state-of-the-art survey of Digital Twin: techniques, engineering product lifecycle management and business innovation perspectives. J. Intell. Manuf. **31**(6), 1313–1337 (2019). https://doi.org/10.1007/s10845-019-01512-w
11. Yongguo, J., Qiang, L., Changshuai, Q., Jian, S., Qianqian, L.: Message-oriented middleware: a review. In: Proceedings of 2019 5th International Conference on Big Data Computing and Communications (BIGCOM), QingDao, China, pp. 88–97 (2019). https://doi.org/10.1109/ BIGCOM.2019.00023
12. Bender, M., Kirdan, E., Pahl, M.-O., Carle, G.: Open-source MQTT evaluation. In: Proceedings of 2021 IEEE 18th Annual Consumer Communications & Networking Conference (CCNC), Las Vegas (2021). https://doi.org/10.1109/CCNC49032.2021.9369499
13. Minerva, R., Lee, G.M., Crespi, N.: Digital twin in the IoT context: a survey on technical features, scenarios, and architectural models. Proc. IEEE **108**(10), 1785–1824 (2020). https:// doi.org/10.1109/JPROC.2020.2998530
14. Namiot, D.: Time series databases. In: Proceeding of Data Analytics and Management in Data Intensive Domains (DAMDID), Obninsk, Russia, pp. 132–137 (2015). https://ceur-ws. org/Vol-1536/paper20.pdf. Accessed 07 Mar 2023
15. Lagartinho-Oliveira, C., Moutinho, F., Gomes, L.: Towards digital twin in the context of power wheelchairs provision and support. In: Camarinha-Matos, L.M. (ed.) Technological Innovation for Digitalization and Virtualization, DoCEIS 2022, vol. 649, pp. 95–102. Springer, Cham (2022). https://doi.org/10.1007/978-3-031-07520-9_9
16. Lagartinho-Oliveira, C., Moutinho, F., Gomes, L.: Digital twin in the provision of power wheelchairs context: support for technical phases and conceptual model. Computers **11**(11), 166–180 (2022). https://doi.org/10.3390/computers11110166
17. Alves, A., Lagartinho-Oliveira, C., Moutinho, F., Gomes, L.: ROS-based digital twin for power wheelchair. In: Proceedings of 1st IEEE Industrial Electronics Society Annual On-Line Conference (ONCON) (2022). https://ies-oncon.com/OnConPapers2022.pdf. Accessed 08 Mar 2023
18. HiveMQ: HiveMQ Cloud – Free Fully Managed MQTT Platform (2023). https://www.hiv emq.com/mqtt-cloud-broker/. Accessed 01 Mar 2023

19. InfluxData: InfluxDB Times Series Data Platform (2023). https://www.influxdata.com. Accessed 01 Mar 2023
20. Open Robotics: ROS – Robot Operating System (2023). https://www.ros.org. Accessed 20 Feb 2023
21. Qi, Q., et al.: Enabling technologies and tools for digital twin. J. Manuf. Syst. **58**(part B), 3–21 (2021). https://doi.org/10.1016/j.jmsy.2019.10.001
22. Invacare: Invacare – Fox – Brochure – Powerwheelchair (2017). https://www.invacare.co.uk/sites/gb/files/csv_migration/product_docs/sales_docs/DSAL009475_4P_Fox_Modulite_UK.pdf. Accessed 06 Mar 2023
23. Invacare: Invacare – LiNX – Brochure – Power Wheelchair GB (2017). https://www.invacare.co.uk/sites/gb/files/csv_migration/product_docs/sales_docs/DSAL009476_6P_LINX_UK_2017.pdf. Accessed 06 Mar 2023
24. Girault, C., Valk, R.: Petri Nets for Systems Engineering – A Guide to Modeling, Verification, and Applications, 1st edn. Springer, Heidelberg (2002). https://doi.org/10.1007/978-3-662-05324-9

Intelligent Computational Systems

Preliminary Verification of Liveness in a Control Part of Cyber-Physical Systems Modeled by a Petri Net

Mateusz Popławski[1](✉), Remigiusz Wiśniewski[1], Grzegorz Bazydło[1], and Maxim Maliński[2]

[1] Institute of Control and Computation Engineering, University of Zielona Góra, 65-516 Zielona Góra, Poland
{m.poplawski,r.wisniewski,g.bazydlo}@issi.uz.zgora.pl
[2] University of Zielona Góra, 65-516 Zielona Góra, Poland
98881@g.elearn.uz.zgora.pl

Abstract. This paper proposes a novel approach for the liveness verification of a Petri net-based cyber-physical system (CPS). The idea is based on the reduction of the initial Petri net and further analysis of its structure in order to identify the sequences of places and transitions that may affect the liveness of the system. In particular, the technique searches for the sequences in the Petri net in order to determine whether the system may not be live, or, (in certain cases) it is definitely not live. The proposed method is mainly aimed at accelerating the process of initial verification of the control part of CPS. The main benefit of the presented technique is its polynomial computational complexity (the method runs in polynomial time). Therefore, the technique permits rapid checking of the system. Although this method is oriented toward CPSs, it can also be applied to other Petri net-based systems where liveness is especially important (e.g., concurrent control systems). The proposed technique was examined experimentally with a set of 242 benchmarks.

Keywords: Liveness · Control Part of the Cyber-Physical System · Petri Net

1 Introduction

Currently, on the market an increasing demand can be observed for new-generation systems, which combine the execution part (physical process) with cyber components. The behavior of such a system is defined by the physical part but also by the control (cyber) component. Such systems in the literature are called Cyber-Physical Systems (CPS) [1, 2]. CPSs are all around us: smart home automation devices [3], healthcare systems [4], power electronic converters [5], manufacturing systems [6], transportation systems [7], etc. CPSs permit to perform operations concurrently, which makes them possible to execute several operations at the same time [8]. The increasing number of components (as well as their complexity), and the growing use of advanced sensors and

© IFIP International Federation for Information Processing 2023
Published by Springer Nature Switzerland AG 2023
L. M. Camarinha-Matos and F. Ferrada (Eds.): DoCEIS 2023, IFIP AICT 678, pp. 205–215, 2023.
https://doi.org/10.1007/978-3-031-36007-7_15

actuators cause a serious challenge related to the design and verification of modern CPS [9]. Petri nets [10] are one of the most efficient solutions for modeling and verification of CPSs [11], combining their graphical and readable notation with the intuitive expression of parallel behavior of the designed CPS [12]. Furthermore, their application in modeling of CPSs (or more generally – concurrent systems) has abounding benefits over other modeling techniques. The visualization of Petri nets using simple graphic elements (circles, rectangles, arrows) makes the models relatively readable and flexible. Moreover, well-developed verification techniques (e.g., invariants, reachability tree or graph analysis) allow for effective detection of most errors of CPS model [13, 14].

Petri nets are widely supported by several mathematical techniques. Therefore, the designer can perform the examination of the CPS at the early modelling stage. The main properties of a Petri net-based CPS are liveness, boundedness, and safeness [10]. Examination of those properties permits avoiding malfunctions of the modeled system, such as deadlocks, and redundant or unreachable states. The main problem with the traditional analysis techniques of a Petri net is exponential computational complexity, which makes their use in large and complex Petri nets extremely difficult. Therefore, it is worth developing methods that can simplify the analysis (unfortunately, the results may not be unambiguous, but from the other side they can indicate the path of further analysis).

The design of a CPS modelled by a Petri net consists of several stages, including modeling, verification, and analysis, as well as further hardware implementation [14, 15]. Petri net-based methods allow for the examination of the robustness and reliability of the CPS at the specification stage [16, 17], which may meaningly affect the costs and time and of the designed CPS. There are various verification techniques, including concurrency and sequentiality relations analysis, as well as Petri net properties examination, such as liveness, safeness and boundedness [12, 18–23]. Verification of such crucial attributes prevents deadlocks in the system and helps avoid redundancy (unreachable states) [24]. Unfortunately, verification and analysis of Petri net-based CPSs, especially liveness property, are not trivial tasks. The main bottleneck refers to the computational complexity of the existing algorithms. From one side, exact methods, such as those that apply the reachability tree/graph are effective and able to obtain optimal results. However, they do usually have exponential computational complexity, which means that the solution may never be found within the assumed time. On the other hand, the approximate algorithms are much more efficient (their run-time is executed within the assumed time), but the result may not be optimal. Therefore, there is very hard to find a comprehensive solution, and the existing techniques balance the optimal results (effectiveness) and reasonable computation time (efficiency) [15]. In the paper we propose a polynomial-time algorithm for preliminary liveness verification of the Petri net-based CPS. The main contributions are summarized as follows:

- a novel Petri net-based analysis technique is proposed, which allows the initial liveness examination of the model in order to determine whether the system *may not* be live, or, (in certain cases) it is *definitely not* live;
- a short computation time is the main benefit of the proposed solution;

- the presented technique was experimentally validated with a set of 242 benchmarks (test cases).

This paper is oriented on the preliminary liveness verification of a Petri net-based CPS (or more precisely the control part of CPS). After the initial reduction of the net [10], the defined sequences of places and transitions are searched in the system. In particular, the method determines whether the given net may be dead and in special cases shows lack of liveness). Let us underline that this paper is focused on the control part of CPSs. In opposite to the traditional concurrent systems, the control part of the CPS (also called the "cyber part") is strictly joined with the "physical" (execution) part. Such a combination can be observed in other works published by authors, including manufacturing systems [6], integrated systems [5, 25], and distributed systems [26]. However, in our previous papers, boundedness and safeness analysis was emphasized [27]. This paper deals with the liveness examination of the control part of CPS.

The rest of the paper is structured as follows. Section 2 presents the relation of the presented research with technological innovation for connected cyber-physical spaces. Section 3 introduces the necessary definitions and notations. The idea of the proposed technique is presented in Sect. 4. Section 5 presents the experimental results of the proposed method, and the final conclusion can be found in Sect. 6.

2 Technological Innovation for Connected Cyber-Physical Spaces

The continuous technological development in recent years, additionally intensified by the coronavirus pandemic [28], has meant that our current environment is now filled with various types of *smart* systems and electronic services. We live in *smart* cities, in *smart* buildings, controlled by *smart* home systems. We watch *smart* TV and use *smart*phones. We are a *smart* society [29]. We are increasingly using artificial intelligence systems to make our lives safer, more convenient, cheaper, and more efficient. Many people cannot imagine functioning in everyday life without using electronic devices or smart gadgets.

We live in environments, where both physical and cyber spaces intersect. Nowadays, we are encompassed by countless CPSs. In addition, present-day CPSs are anticipated to be viably securing personal information, energy effective, small in size, valuable, effectively versatile, and secure. In particular, the last mentioned prerequisite is requesting since these days CPS are complex, progressive, and exceptionally regularly concurrent. The possibility of making a mistake by designing such complex systems is natural and large. Removal of such errors revealed only in the implementation phase can be very expensive. Moreover, unrelated errors can be dangerous for people (think about defective medical devices). Therefore, there is an urgent need for the development of methods and techniques which can analyze the model in the first stages of the CPS design process. Petri nets are one of the promising modeling techniques because they are simple and effective. Moreover, they are supported by a set of methods for model analysis (e.g., invariants, reachability tree analysis, deadlock search) that allow for the detection of the design errors at the model stage.

The analysis technique proposed in the paper is oriented on the preliminary liveness verification of a Petri net-based CPS (more precisely, the control part of CPS). The presented method, after the initial reduction of the Petri net, analyzes the model in order to find the particular sequences of places and transitions. Finally, the method determines whether the Petri net is not live. Such an approach fits into the current trend of developing systems that are smarter with increasing levels of cognition and autonomy, oriented to solve societal problems with a human-centric perspective.

3   Main Definitions, Notations, and Reduction Techniques

This section presents the main definitions and notations for better clarification of the proposed method [10, 12, 13, 15, 17–19, 21–23]. Moreover, it also briefly introduces the reduction techniques applied in the proposed approach.

Definition 1 *(Petri net)*. A Petri net N is a 4-tuple – Eq. (1):

$$N = (P, T, F, M_0) \tag{1}$$

where P is a finite set of places, T is a finite set of transitions, $F \subset (P \times T) \cup (T \times P)$ is a finite set of arcs, M_0 is an initial marking.

Definition 2 *(Input (output) places (transitions))*. Sets of input and output places of a transition are defined respectively as follows: $\bullet t = \{p \in P : (p, t) \in F\}$, $t \bullet = \{p \in P : (t; p) \in F\}$. The sets of input and output transitions of a place are defined: $\bullet p = \{t \in T : (t, p) \in F\}$, $p \bullet = \{p \in P : (p, t) \in F\}$.

Definition 3 *(Marking)*. A marking *(state)* M of a Petri net is a distribution of tokens in the net places. If a place contains one or more tokens, it is called a marked place. A marking can be changed by means of firing (execution) of a transition.

Definition 4 *(Firing)*. A transition t is *enabled* and can *fire* (be executed), if every of its input places contains a token. Transition firing removes one token from each input place and adds one token to each output place.

Definition 5 *(Reachability)*. Marking M_j is reachable from marking M_i, if M_i can be changed to M_j by a sequence of transition firings.

Definition 6 *(Incidence matrix)*. Matrix $A_{m \times n}$ is an incidence matrix of a Petri net $N = (P, T, F, M_0)$ with $|P|$ columns and $|T|$ rows of integers, given by – Eq. (2):

$$a_{ij} = \begin{cases} -1, & (p_j, t_i) \in F \\ 1, & (t_i, p_j) \in F \\ 0, & \text{otherwise} \end{cases} \tag{2}$$

Definition 7 (Liveness). Petri net N is live if it is possible to fire any transition from any reachable marking by a sequence of firings of other transitions.

Please note that the above definition refers to the strictest condition of liveness. There exist also other liveness definitions, which are more relax (denoted by "liveness levels"), cf. [10].

Finally, let us present the reduction techniques applied in the paper. Reduction techniques allows for the simplification of the Petri net structure [9]. It is worth mentioning that such operations preserve the main properties of the analyzed system, including liveness. In general, the reductions can be divided into four groups: Fusion of Series Places (FSP) (Fig. 1a), Fusion of Series Transitions (FST) (Fig. 1b), Fusion of Parallel Places (FPP) (Fig. 1c), Fusion of Parallel Transitions (FPT) (Fig. 1d). Let us briefly describe them.

The first reduction method (FSP) combines places that are modeled as a sequence. There is a restriction in regard to the places that are initially marked (with tokens), which cannot be reduced (Fig. 1a). Similarly, the FST reduction is executed. This technique also has a restriction, thus the places initially marked cannot be reduced (Fig. 1b). Third reduction method (FPP) is based on the elimination of the places that are modeled as parallelly. The method can be applied if each of reduced places contains a token, or none of them contains a token (Fig. 1c). Finally, the FPT is executed in the similar way. However, in this case, there are no restrictions on marked places (Fig. 1d).

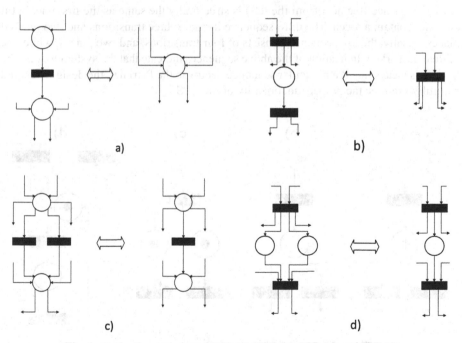

Fig. 1. Reduction techniques: FSP (a), FST (b), FPP (c), and FPT (d)

4   The Idea of the Proposed Technique

This section presents the proposed liveness verification technique of the control part of CPS. The system is initially reduced with the set of techniques presented within Sect. 3 (Fig. 1). In the proposed liveness verification technique, the above four methods are executed periodically until there is a possibility for further reductions. The main aim of the applied reductions is simplification of the Petri net structure with preservation of the liveness property. Such reductions influence on the second part of the proposed technique, since the specific sequences may be detected in easier way.

The main idea of the proposed technique refers to the searching of the certain sequences of places and transitions in the system. The presented methods are divided into two main groups. The algorithms presented in the first group indicate that the system *may not* be live. This means that the Petri net contains sequences of places that may lead to e.g., deadlock or not reachable states, but we are not sure about it. Therefore, the designer ought to perform additional verification or validation (simulation) of the system. In opposite, detection of the second group of sequences indicates that the Petri net is definitely not live. Hence, no further examinations are required.

The first group consists of four types of sequences, as shown in Fig. 2. The first case (most from the left) consists of three transitions and a single marked place. The second sequence (the next from the left) is structurally the same as the first one, but it does not contain a token. The third sequence includes three transitions and two marked places. Finally, the last sequence consists of four transitions, and two places, while one of them is marked. Indication of the above sequences indicate that the system *may not* be live. This means that if a particular sequence occurs in the Petri net, the designer should carefully examine the proper functionality of the CPS.

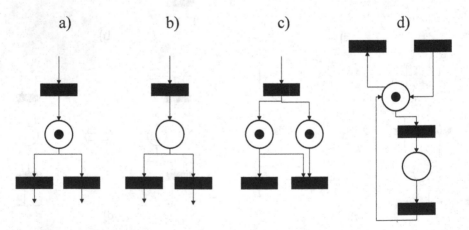

Fig. 2. Sequences indicating that the system *may not* be live

The second group of sequences includes two cases, as shown in Fig. 3. Existence of each of them assures that the examined Petri net is not live. The first case (shown in Fig. 3 on the left) consists of a marked place (with a token), and a transition. Similarly, the second sequence contains a place (but without a token), and a transition.

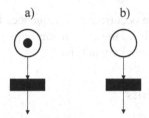

Fig. 3. Sequences indicating that the system is not live

Let us now present the technique that permit to find the above cases. The method that detects sequences from both first group is divided into two main steps. Firstly, the algorithm checks the occurrence of the sequences from the first group: first, second, and third cases (Fig. 2a, 2b, 2c). Subsequently, the fourth case from the first group is investigated (Fig. 2d), moreover, the algorithm searches for the sequences from the second group (Fig. 3). As the input, the algorithm reads the incidence matrix of a Petri net (after reductions). Existence of the above sequences indicates that the system is definitely not live. This means that no further examinations are required and the Petri net ought to be revised (re-modelled). It should be noted that the designer is able to locate the improper areas of the Petri net (detected by the proposed algorithm).

Moving into details the algorithm comprises the following stages:

1. For each transition t:
   a) if $(|\bullet t| = 1$ and $|t\bullet| = 1)$ then:
      - if $|t \bullet \bullet| = 2$ and $|t\bullet|$ is marked then the Petri net contains a sequence from the first group, first case (shown in Fig. 2a);
      - if $|t \bullet \bullet| = 2$ and $|t\bullet|$ is not marked then the Petri net contains a sequence from the first group, second case (shown in Fig. 2b);
   b) if $(|\bullet t| = 1$ and $|t\bullet| = 2)$ then:
      - if both output places p_1 and p_2 of t are marked and additionally $(|p_1\bullet| = 2$ and $|p_2\bullet| = 1)$ such that $(p_2\bullet) = (p_1\bullet)$ then the Petri net contains a sequence from the first group, third case (Fig. 2c);

2. For each place p:
   a) if $(|\bullet p| = 2$ and $|p\bullet| = 2$ and p is marked) then:
      - if there exists $(p' = p \bullet \bullet)$ such that $[(p\bullet) = (\bullet p')$ and $(p'\bullet) = (\bullet p)$ and $(|\bullet p'|=|p'\bullet| = 1)$ then the Petri net contains a sequence from the first group, fourth case (shown in Fig. 2d);

b) if $(|\bullet p| = 0)$ and $|p\bullet| = 1$ then:

- if p is marked then the Petri net contains a sequence from the second group, first case (shown in Fig. 3a);
- if p is not marked then the Petri net contains a sequence from the second group, second case (shown in Fig. 3b).

As already mentioned, the occurrence of sequences from the first group indicates that the system *may not* be live. However, if the sequence from the second group is detected then the Petri net is definitely not live.

5   Results of Experiments

In this part, the results of experimental research will be presented and discussed. The proposed technique was examined in terms of its efficiency (run-time) and effectiveness (proper results). The method was tested on the dedicated laptop with the use of an Intel® Core® i7-1165G7@2.8 GHz processor and 32 GB of RAM. The set of benchmarks contains 242 Petri nets that describe theoretical and real-life CPSs, control systems, manufacturing systems, discrete systems, etc. The tests are available at: http://www.hippo.uz.zgora.pl.

Table 1. Results of the experiments for selected benchmarks.

Benchmark name	Number of places in the context of reduction		Number of transitions in the context of reduction		1st Group of sequences		2nd Group of sequences		Reachability graph	
	pre	after	pre	after	Result	Runtime [ms]	Result	Runtime [ms]	Result	Runtime [ms]
CNC_machine	7	5	2	1	Not occurs	0,016	Not live	0,013	Not live	21,241
tank_heating	4	4	2	1	Not occurs	0,014	Not live	0,012	Not live	121,881
lnet_p8n1	51	40	3	2	Not occurs	0,024	Not live	0,018	Not live	44192,545
s_net_copy_milling_machine_subprocess	31	28	5	6	Potentially not live	0,167	Not occurs	0,086	Not live	697,037
bause1	11	11	9	9	Potentially not live	0,978	Not occurs	0,319	Not live	44,087
balduzzi1	18	16	18	16	Potentially not live	13,862	Not occurs	2,820	Not live	31,324
esparza1	11	10	10	9	Potentially not live	0,537	Not occurs	0,261	Not live	94,952

Table 1 shows the experimental results for the selected benchmarks. The obtained results of these tests were compared to a full liveness analysis using the state reachability graph [10]. In the "Benchmark" column are the names of the analyzed systems. The next two columns show the number of places and transitions before and after the reduction. The result of the first group of sequences was denoted either by "potentially not live" (if the sequence was detected) or "not occurs" (in another case). The result of the second group "not live" indicates that the sequence was found, while the opposite case is denoted by "not occurs".

The experiments show that the presented approach has potential. The time of the proposed method is shorter than the reference method used for comparison. It should be emphasized that the occurrence of sequences from the first group means that the system *may not* be live (but it does not have to be). The occurrence of sequences from the second group means that the tested Petri Net is definitely not live. Going into detail, the sequence from the first group was found in 36 systems, while 17 of them were indeed not live. This means that 47% of detected Petri nets were not live. Let us underline that this is relatively high result, since almost half of the indicated systems contain errors, which are usually very hard to detect (the traditional methods based on the reachability tree/graph are often insufficient due to the exponential computational complexity). Moving on to the second group of sequences, they were found in 18 tested cases. It should be noted that all of them were indeed not live. This means that the experimental results fully confirmed the theoretical expectations.

6 Conclusions

A method of preliminary liveness verification of Petri net-based CPSs was proposed in the paper. The technique includes the initial reduction of the Petri net, and further searching for the particular sequences of places and transitions in the system. Two kinds of such sequences are proposed and analyzed. The occurrence of the first of them indicates that the system *may not* be live. Furthermore, existence of the second group of sequences assures that the Petri net is not live.

The experimental results confirm the efficiency and effectiveness of the proposed method. The sequences from the first group were obtained for 36 Petri nets (out of 242 analyzed), while 17 of them are indeed not live. Furthermore, 18 systems contain the sequences from the second group, and all of them were not live. On the other hand, there are limitations of the proposed algorithm. First of all, the method is oriented on the preliminary verification of the system, thus it is not able to indicate all Petri nets that are not live. Furthermore, detection of a sequence from the the first group requires additional analysis. Even if such a sequence is detected, it does not mean that the system is not live, and further verification/validation is required. However, let us point out, that such an analysis is very fast (confirmed by experimental results). Moreover, such an information can be extremely useful, especially in the case of relatively large CPS.

Future work includes further development of the proposed technique. Firstly, the proposed ideas are going to be proved formally, including their functionality, as well as computational complexity. Moreover, it is planned to include linear algebra techniques in order to combine the presented method with boundedness verification and deadlocks detection.

Acknowledgments. This work is supported by the National Science Centre, Poland, under Grant number 2019/35/B/ST6/01683.

References

1. Ryalat, M., ElMoaqet, H., AlFaouri, M.: Design of a smart factory based on cyber-physical systems and Internet of Things towards Industry 4.0. Appl. Sci. **13**, 2156 (2023). https://doi.org/10.3390/app13042156
2. Lee, E.A., Seshia, S.A.: Introduction to Embedded Systems: A Cyber-Physical Systems Approach. MIT Press, Cambridge (2017)
3. Shih, C.-S., Chou, J.-J., Reijers, N., Kuo, T.-W.: Designing CPS/IoT applications for smart buildings and cities. IET Cyber-Phys. Syst. Theory Appl. **1**, 3–12 (2016). https://doi.org/10.1049/iet-cps.2016.0025
4. Dey, N., Ashour, A.S., Shi, F., Fong, S.J., Tavares, J.M.R.S.: Medical cyber-physical systems: a survey. J. Med. Syst. **42**, 74 (2018). https://doi.org/10.1007/s10916-018-0921-x
5. Wiśniewski, R., Bazydło, G., Szcześniak, P.: Low-cost FPGA hardware implementation of matrix converter switch control. IEEE Trans. Circ. Syst. II Express Briefs **66**, 1177–1181 (2019). https://doi.org/10.1109/TCSII.2018.2875589
6. Patalas-Maliszewska, J., Posdzich, M., Skrzypek, K.: Modelling Information for the burnishing process in a cyber–physical production system. Int. J. Appl. Math. Comput. Sci. **32**, 345–354 (2022). https://doi.org/10.34768/amcs-2022-0025
7. Guo, Y., Hu, X., Hu, B., Cheng, J., Zhou, M., Kwok, R.Y.K.: Mobile cyber physical systems: current challenges and future networking applications. IEEE Access **6**, 12360–12368 (2018). https://doi.org/10.1109/ACCESS.2017.2782881
8. Lee, E.A.: Cyber physical systems: design challenges. In: 2008 11th IEEE International Symposium on Object and Component-Oriented Real-Time Distributed Computing (ISORC), pp. 363–369 (2008). https://doi.org/10.1109/ISORC.2008.25
9. Wiśniewski, R., Wojnakowski, M., Li, Z.: Design and verification of Petri-net-based cyberphysical systems oriented toward implementation in field-programmable gate arrays—a case study example. Energies **16**, 67 (2023). https://doi.org/10.3390/en16010067
10. Murata, T.: Petri nets: properties, analysis and applications. Proc. IEEE **77**, 541–580 (1989). https://doi.org/10.1109/5.24143
11. Liu, Z., Hu, L., Hu, W., Tan, J.: Petri nets-based modeling solution for cyber-physical product control considering scheduling, deployment, and data-driven monitoring. IEEE Trans. Syst. Man Cybern. Syst. **53**, 990–1002 (2023). https://doi.org/10.1109/TSMC.2022.3170489
12. Wojnakowski, M., Wiśniewski, R., Bazydło, G., Popławski, M.: Analysis of safeness in a Petri net-based specification of the control part of cyber-physical systems. Int. J. Appl. Math. Comput. Sci. **31**, 647–657 (2021). https://doi.org/10.34768/amcs-2021-0045
13. Girault, C., Valk, R.: Petri Nets for Systems Engineering. Springer, Heidelberg (2003). https://doi.org/10.1007/978-3-662-05324-9
14. Wiśniewski, R., Bazydło, G., Gomes, L., Costa, A., Wojnakowski, M.: Analysis and design automation of cyber-physical system with hippo and IOPT-tools. In: IECON 2019 - 45th Annual Conference of the IEEE Industrial Electronics Society, Lisbon, Portugal, pp. 5843–5848. IEEE Press (2019). https://doi.org/10.1109/IECON.2019.8926692
15. Wiśniewski, R.: Prototyping of Concurrent Control Systems Implemented in FPGA Devices. Springer, Cham (2017). https://doi.org/10.1007/978-3-319-45811-3
16. Li, B., Khlif-Bouassida, M., Toguyéni, A.: On–the–fly diagnosability analysis of bounded and unbounded labeled Petri nets using verifier nets. Int. J. Appl. Math. Comput. Sci. **28**, 269–281 (2018). https://doi.org/10.2478/amcs-2018-0019
17. Karatkevich, A.: Dynamic Analysis of Petri Net-Based Discrete Systems. Springer, Heidelberg (2007). https://doi.org/10.1007/978-3-540-71560-3
18. Best, E., Devillers, R., Koutny, M.: Petri Net Algebra. Springer, Heidelberg (2001). https://doi.org/10.1007/978-3-662-04457-5

19. David, R., Alla, H.: Bases of petri nets. In: David, R., Alla, H. (eds.) Discrete, Continuous, and Hybrid Petri Nets, pp. 1–20. Springer, Heidelberg (2010). https://doi.org/10.1007/978-3-642-10669-9_1

20. Wojnakowski, M., Wiśniewski, R.: Verification of the boundedness property in a Petri net-based specification of the control part of cyber-physical systems. In: Camarinha-Matos, L.M., Ferreira, P., Brito, G. (eds.) DoCEIS 2021. IAICT, vol. 626, pp. 83–91. Springer, Cham (2021). https://doi.org/10.1007/978-3-030-78288-7_8

21. Silva, M., Colom, J.M., Campos, J.: Linear algebraic techniques for the analysis of Petri nets. In: Recent Advances in Mathematical Theory of Systems, Control, Networks, and Signal Processing II, Tokyo, Japan, pp. 35–42. Mita Press (1992)

22. Esparza, J., Silva, M.: A polynomial-time algorithm to decide liveness of bounded free choice nets. Theor. Comput. Sci. **102**, 185–205 (1992). https://doi.org/10.1016/0304-3975(92)902 99-U

23. Barkaoui, K., Minoux, M.: A polynomial-time graph algorithm to decide liveness of some basic classes of bounded Petri nets. In: Jensen, K. (ed.) ICATPN 1992. LNCS, vol. 616, pp. 62–75. Springer, Heidelberg (1992). https://doi.org/10.1007/3-540-55676-1_4

24. Guo, X., Wang, S., You, D., Li, Z., Jiang, X.: A siphon-based deadlock prevention strategy for S^3PR. IEEE Access **7**, 86863–86873 (2019). https://doi.org/10.1109/ACCESS.2019.292 0677

25. Wiśniewski, R., Bazydło, G., Szcześniak, P., Wojnakowski, M.: Petri net-based specification of cyber-physical systems oriented to control direct matrix converters with space vector modulation. IEEE Access **7**, 23407–23420 (2019). https://doi.org/10.1109/ACCESS.2019. 2899316

26. Grobelna, I., Wiśniewski, R., Grobelny, M., Wiśniewska, M.: Design and verification of real-life processes with application of Petri nets. IEEE Trans. Syst. Man Cybern. Syst. **47**, 2856–2869 (2017). https://doi.org/10.1109/TSMC.2016.2531673

27. Wojnakowski, M., Popławski, M., Wiśniewski, R., Bazydło, G.: Hippo-CPS: verification of boundedness, safeness and liveness of Petri net-based cyber-physical systems. In: Camarinha-Matos, L.M. (ed.) Technological Innovation for Digitalization and Virtualization, pp. 74–82. Springer, Cham (2022). https://doi.org/10.1007/978-3-031-07520-9_7

28. He, W., Zhang(Justin), Z., Li, W.: Information technology solutions, challenges, and suggestions for tackling the COVID-19 pandemic. Int. J. Inf. Manag. **57**, 102287 (2021). https://doi.org/10.1016/j.ijinfomgt.2020.102287

29. Foresti, R., Rossi, S., Magnani, M., Guarino Lo Bianco, C., Delmonte, N.: Smart society and artificial intelligence: big data scheduling and the global standard method applied to smart maintenance. Engineering **6**, 835–846 (2020). https://doi.org/10.1016/j.eng.2019.11.014

QiBERT - Classifying Online Conversations

Messages with BERT as a Feature

Bruno D. Ferreira-Saraiva[1,2]([✉]), Manuel Marques-Pita[1,2],
João Pedro Matos-Carvalho[1,2], and Zuil Pirola[1,2]

[1] COPELABS, Universidade Lusófona, Campo Grande 376, 1749 - 024 Lisboa, Portugal
{bruno.saraiva,manuel.pita,joao.matos.carvalho,
zuil.pirola}@ulusofona.pt
[2] CICANT, Universidade Lusófona, Campo Grande 376, 1749 - 024 Lisboa, Portugal

Abstract. Recent developments in online communication and their usage in everyday life have caused an explosion in the amount of a new genre of text data, short text. Thus, the need to classify this type of text based on its content has a significant implication in many areas. Online debates are no exception, once these provide access to information about opinions, positions and preferences of its users. This paper aims to use data obtained from online social conversations in Portuguese schools (short text) to observe behavioural trends and to see if students remain engaged in the discussion when stimulated. This project used the state of the art (SoA) Machine Learning (ML) algorithms and methods, through BERT based models to classify if utterances are in or out of the debate subject. Using SBERT embeddings as a feature, with supervised learning, the proposed model achieved results above 0.95 average accuracy for classifying online messages. Such improvements can help social scientists better understand human communication, behaviour, discussion and persuasion.

Keywords: Natural Language Processing (NLP) · Short Text · Text Classification · Sentence Embeddings · Supervised Learning · Online Conversation

1 Introduction

Influenced by social networks based on short and fast content such as Twitter and TikTok, the digitalized post-pandemic school can adapt, emulating these types of networks and motivating the participation of students in the discussion of current topics [1]. One of the possibilities is the use of multi-participant chat, a form of chat with several participants talking synchronously through textual communication [2]. Chats, and their integration with teaching, have already been studied [3, 4] Despite their implementation advantages, these are increasingly being incorporated into the range of teaching tools, and it is important to know whether or not students are engaged with the themes proposed.

© IFIP International Federation for Information Processing 2023
Published by Springer Nature Switzerland AG 2023
L. M. Camarinha-Matos and F. Ferrada (Eds.): DoCEIS 2023, IFIP AICT 678, pp. 216–229, 2023.
https://doi.org/10.1007/978-3-031-36007-7_16

Natural Language Processing (NLP) tools can assist in the analysis and even in the classification of these data as useful or not useful. Recently, several studies have investigated the classification of short texts [5–9].

However, conventional text classification tools are not directly suited to this type of medium with short texts [2]. This inadequacy is mainly due to the characteristic difference between the two types of text. Short texts mainly present sparsity, ambiguity, shortness and incompleteness.

In general, those studies follow the conventional classification pipeline containing four levels: Features extraction, Dimensionality Reduction, Classification Techniques and Evaluation [10].

For this study, we intend to replicate this pipeline and focus on the analysis of chat conversations in order to understand whether or not the students are talking about the subject they were stimulated.

The goal is to be able to classify the messages as "on the subject" or "off the subject". For that, we will use multilingual BERT models [11, 12] trained in multiple languages, including Portuguese (European), which will be applied to sentence units via SBERT [13]. It is expected that these models can effectively capture the semantics of the analysed messages with the least amount of training data possible.

This paper is organised as follows: Section 2 describes the state-of-the-art (SoA). Sections 3 and 4 will present the characteristics and the way in which the analysed data were acquired, including the annotation procedure. In Sect. 5 the proposed method will be presented, in Sect. 6 the results are shown discussed and in Sect. 7 the conclusions and the future work are presented.

2 Contribution to Connected Cyber Physical Spaces

Online debates are crucial to providing important data for the interpretation and classification of ML models. In this study, it was analyzed whether a given debate subject was maintained throughout the conversation, and to this end, different feature extraction models and ML algorithms were studied to classify whether or not the subject in question was discussed during the conversation. The presented work focuses on Connected Cyber Physical Spaces, especially on intelligent NLP models developed through ML algorithms.

3 Related Work

Online conversations come in many different formats. There are studies on data such as discussion forums [14], specific messages from platforms such as Facebook [15, 16], or Twitter [7]. Although all these studies involve short texts, they have significantly different structures. Replies to a tweet may come shortly after it is posted, but they can be made days later. Discussion forums can last for years and have features like quotes and replies. Among these and other differences, this paper focuses specifically on chats, where all participants in the conversation are simultaneously exposed to a virtual environment to discuss, in our case, the topic of racism.

The analysis of multi-participant chats, their problems, and their relationship to computational techniques has been widely studied [2]. Computational models can even help social studies through Conversation Analysis (CA) [17–19]. However, for this, it is crucial to understand what the participants are talking about in order to improve the reading and perception of the messages sent.

We intend to explore the classification of chat messages. Short texts in chat rooms could have a few words, presence of abbreviations, spelling errors, or texts being supplemented in subsequent messages. All these characteristics, in addition to other factors, make feature extraction difficult. As a solution, the authors complement the short text with external knowledge. Liu [20] used external knowledge to enrich the semantic representations to develop a model based on TCN and CNN. Hu [8], augmented the vector representations of the text by combining information from the message actors to generate mental features.

Danilov [6] proposed 27 parameterised PubMedBERT options and new models for classifying academic texts. There was also the use of BERT to classify political discourse [21] in short texts on Facebook and Twitter. With the application of BERT and other vector representations (Glove), Khatri [22] used binary classification to classify sarcasm in tweets. BERT was also used to create a graph convolutional network for classifying short texts [23].

Motivated by the discussions above, in this work we aim to classify text messages present in a chat using conventional classification techniques and contribute to the discussion as follows:

- It is possible to classify texts from chat messages, even if they only have short features (short texts);
- With a small amount of training data, supervised learning models have high accuracy;
- Using pre-trained BERT models in combination with the sentence embedding framework (SBERT) to train a robust sentence classification model.
- Use of feature selections to reduce the dimensionality of the model inputs.

4 Data Gathering

The data for this research was collected from instant multi-participant messaging chat under the project "Debaqi - Factors for promoting dialogue and healthy behaviours in online school communities". Users were placed to debate in a private virtual environment and interactions were synchronous where any participant can contribute to the conversation at any time.

The online conversations took place in a virtual environment involving Portuguese state high schools. There were 25 rooms, with 309 participants. The messages sent are predominantly short-text and have a median of five tokens (Table 1). The participant's ages were between 15 and 19 and we obtained previous consent from their parents for them to participate in the chat room debates.

The students may or may not know each other and the chat application guarantees the anonymity of participants. Platform anonymity means that participants know that something was said by a particular user, but they do not know who the user is in the school context.

Table 1. Data summary.

Item	Number
Rooms	25.0
Messages with Moderator	5303.0
Messages without Moderator	4044.0
Users	309.0
Average Messages Length (chars)	61.4
Median Messages Length (chars)	28.0
Average Messages Length (tokens)	10.1
Median Messages Length (tokens)	5.0

At the beginning of the conversation, students were stimulated through a video and the moderator also contributed through questions launched at a given time according to a moderation script. There is no way to set a certain conversation path or set a certain topic, so there is the possibility of students following the theme, changing the theme, creating sub-themes or even ignoring the proposed theme in order to boycott.

5 Annotation

In supervised models, as foreseen in this work, the classification model demands annotated data. The most convenient way to generate this annotated data is to use annotators that do it manually. It is important to define an annotation method that guarantees good inter-agreement [24, 25] between annotators and that can reliably transmit the annotated data to the classifier. The annotation criteria used in this work were:

- Label 1 - Messages that were about the topic/subject *"Racismo e Esteri´otipos"*. Sentences containing words such as "racism", "racist", "stereo-types", "culture", "prejudice", "black/white" were considered, as well as sentences like "we are all equal/human";
- Label 0 - All messages that do not have a defined subject like greetings ("good morning", "hi"…), agreements/disagreements ("yes", "no", "agree", "disagree", "maybe"). All messages that have a defined subject, but are not directly linked to "Racismo e Esteri´otipos" topic.

In a pilot annotation phase, only two rooms were randomly chosen and assigned to 3 annotators, where we obtained an average inter-agreement above 0.7 of Krippendorff's alpha as expected [24]. Therefore, the simple annotation criteria proposed was well understood among the annotators and can be implemented in the total pool of rooms. Despite having access to the entire conversational sequence of messages, annotators do not consider the context. There may be messages that talk about racism or that were related (reply or quote) to a message about racism but do not necessarily have words that cite the topic directly. In this case, they were not annotated as messages of racism.

In the second annotation phase, the other 23 rooms were submitted to the same three annotators. The average *Krippendorff's alpha* value for the three annotators, at the 25 rooms, was 0.77.

6 Proposed Method

In this section, we describe the methods used to build the models for the online text classification task.

6.1 Feature Extraction

In the model-building process, feature extraction is crucial. Word and sentence embeddings are commonly used to represent language features in the field of Natural Language Processing (NLP) [26–28]. Sentence embedding refers to a group of feature learning techniques used in NLP to map words or sentences from a lexicon to vectors of real numbers. For the feature extraction stage of our study, we used embeddings from a pre-trained model[1] from SBERT framework [13]. SBERT outperformed the previous (SoA) models for all common semantic textual similarity tasks since it produces sentence embeddings, so there is no need to perform a whole inference computation for every sentence-pair comparison. This framework is a useful tool for generating sentence embeddings where each sentence is represented as a size 768 vector (Fig. 1). This embeddings are based on BERT [27], so they are contextual. Once the embeddings were extracted for the training data, the sequence of embeddings was ready to feed the machine learning models.

6.2 Training and Predictions

After extracting the sentences embeddings we followed into two different approaches:

- We trained the six ML algorithms, mentioned above, with the raw embeddings (768 features);

- A feature selection method [30] was used in order to remove the less important features, before training the algorithms.

For the first approach, we follow the dashed path of the pipeline (Fig. 2), where after extracting the embeddings, we move directly to the classification algorithms.

---

[1] SBERT Model: *paraphrase-multilingual-mpnet-base-v2*. Multi-lingual model of paraphrase-mpnet-base-v2, extended to 50 + languages.https://huggingface.co/sentence-transformers/paraphrase-mpnet-base-v2.

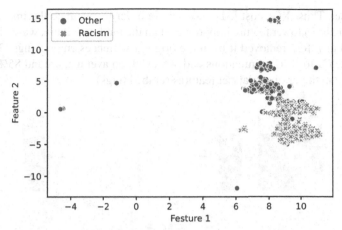

Fig. 1. Comparison between "Racism" and "Other" subject sentence embeddings. To be possible to visualise the sentences embeddings, UMAP [29] was used to reduce the vector's 768 dimensions for two.

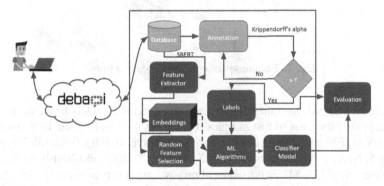

Fig. 2. Proposed system architecture.

For the second approach, we have an intermediate step, before moving towards the classification algorithms stage, that aims to select the most important features (blue path of pipeline), in order to try to reduce memory usage as much as possible and maintain the proposed system performance. For that purpose, given the sentences embeddings, created before, known as X and a target (annotation) Y, a random vector V was created and appended as a new feature of X: $X' = [X, V]$. Now, with that data (X', Y), the next step was to train a Supervised Learning algorithm with with a relevant feature importance measure (Fig. 3). Generally, importance provides a score that indicates how useful or valuable each feature was in the model's construction and is calculated explicitly for each attribute in the provided dataset, allowing attributes to be ranked and compared to each other. Thus, XGBoost [31] was used in order to calculate the importance. If a given feature has a lower feature importance than the random feature, we set it as useless feature and therefore removed it from the original sentences embeddings [30]. We ran 1000 Monte Carlo (MC) simulations and achieved, on average, around 85% of feature reduction from the original dataset features (embeddings).

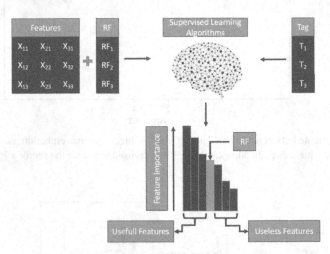

Fig. 3. Feature selector method. Adapted from [30].

The next step was to train different machine learning models to create a classifier that can predict the class of test samples. Classifiers such as Logistic Regression (LR), Support Vector Machine (SVM), Gaussian Naive Bayes (GNB), Bernoulli Naive Bayes (BNB), K-Nearest Neighbours (KNN), XGBoost (XGB), and Multi-layer Perceptron (MLP) were used [32–34]. Scikit-learn library was used to train these models. Sentence embeddings were obtained for the test dataset in the same way as mentioned before. This way, they got ready for predictions.

7   Experiments and Results

The first developed experiment was directly related to the data annotation. Since there were three annotators, it was expected that they would not always agree, and for that reason two different models were investigated:

- A model in which all three annotators agreed (Complete Agreement (CAg)).
- A model in which at least two of the annotators agreed (Majority Agreement (MAg)).

For the CAg model there was a total of 2334 messages annotated in concordance, from which only 17% were annotated with a value "1" that indicated that the students' sentences were explicitly addressing the subject of *"Racismo e Esteri´otipos"*, as explained before. For the MAg model, there was a total of 3727 annotated messages in which at least two of the annotators were in agreement. 18% out of those had been annotated with the value "1". Thus, in order for the data not to be biased, only 790 sentences were used for CAg model training and 1300 for MAg model training. This way, around 50% of the messages would have been annotated with value "1" and the remaining 50% were annotated with zero.

For this experiment, the ML algorithm choice was not the true focus. The main goal was to realise that annotated data, in which three of the annotators were in agreement, obtained better results than with only two annotators in agreement. SVM was the selected ML algorithm and the training and testing sizes were set to 66% and 33%, respectively.

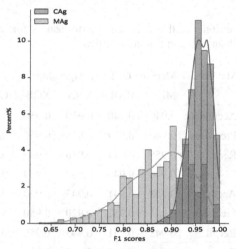

Fig. 4. Comparison between Complete (CAg) and Majority (MAg) Agreement. Inspired from [34–37].

As it can be seen in Fig. 4, we can intuitively perceive that the model CAg was much superior in the evaluation metrics chosen by the authors, than the MAg model. The former obtained an average of 0.96 F1-score, whereas the latter got 0.88 F1-score. This is understandable because, in the training phase, CAg only puts a sentence at 1 when all annotators agree, while MAg connotates 1 when the majority agrees. Therefore, there is much more noise in MAg than in CAg.

The second experiment performed a comparison between several ML algorithms in order to understand which one or ones would get better results in classifying short messages. For this purpose, it was defined that the CAg annotation reading model would be used, along with testing the two sentence embeddings possibilities (raw sentence embeddings and feature reduced sentence embeddings).

As we can see in both Fig. 5 and Table 2, after 1000 MC's simulations, the values of the two models are similar. It is also visible that all tested algorithms obtained average results above 0.93 for all (accuracy, precision, recall, f1-score) evaluation metrics and that the most prominent algorithm, for both approaches was the Support Vector Machine.

The first approach had no embedding reduction, whereas the second one got embeddings randomly reduced. They both turned out with a median and average f1-scores values of 0.956 and 0.955, respectively. In Fig. 6, it is possible to compare the behaviour of these two approaches (embeddings with and without reduction) for the SVM algorithm over the 1000 MC simulations.

Table 2. Accuracy, precision, recall and f1-score performances for different set of machine learning algorithms, with and without feature reduction.

Data	Metrics	Machine Learning Algorithms						
		MLP	BNB	KNN	XGB	GNB	SVM	LR
Without Reduction	Accuracy	0.946	0.940	0.930	0.950	0.945	**0.957**	0.953
	Precision	0.940	0.939	0.895	0.952	0.950	**0.964**	0.956
	Recall	0.955	0.944	**0.976**	0.950	0.941	0.950	0.951
	F1-score	0.946	0.940	0.932	0.949	0.944	**0.956**	0.952
With Reduction	Accuracy	0.948	0.941	0.943	0.950	0.944	**0.955**	0.948
	Precision	0.945	0.952	0.920	0.950	**0.961**	0.960	0.955
	Recall	0.948	0.941	0.943	0.950	0.944	**0.955**	0.948
	F1-score	0.949	0.941	0.945	0.950	0.944	**0.955**	0.948

After reaching such positive results for the randomly selected features model, we studied how the amount of training data in a estimator would affect its results. For this matter, the CAg annotation reading model was selected, as well as SVM algorithm that had obtained the best results. We determined a training dataset minimum and maximum of 5% and 95%, respectively, and obtained the results illustrated in Fig. 7.

We can observe that, even with a low amount of training data, we achieved optimal results regarding the classification of text messages. We also obtained an average f1-score results of 0.94 for training data between 15% and 25%.

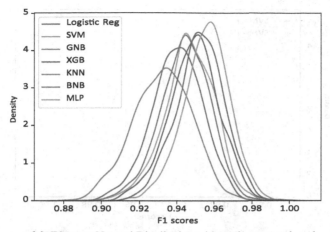

(a) F1-score Normal Distribution without features reduced

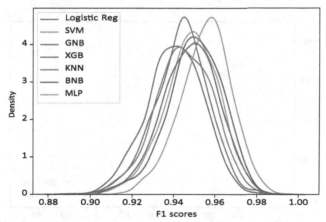

(b) F1-score Normal Distribution with features reduced. Inspired from [38-44].

Fig. 5. Comparison between different Machine Learning Models: a) without features reduced and b) features reduced.

Finally, in order to evaluate the model, we performed cross-validation [44]. Cross-validation is used to evaluate the performance of the estimator and allows the model to learn and be tested on different data. This is important because a model that simply repeated the labels of the samples it had just seen would produce a perfect result, but it would not make useful predictions for data not yet seen. Thus, we defined, once again, that the annotation reading type would be CAg. The ML algorithm would be SVM and that the sentence embeddings features would be randomly selected, as previously explained. The number of re-shuffling and splitting iterations was set to 10 and the number of training data to 20% of the dataset. With scikit-learn library's help to calculate the cross-validation, we obtained the average result of 0.95 f1-score with a standard deviation of 0.01.

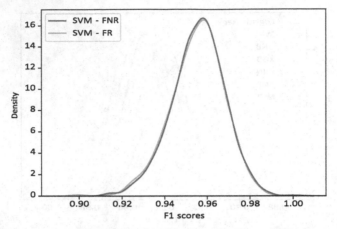

Fig. 6. Comparison between SVM results with (FR) and without (FNR) features reduced.

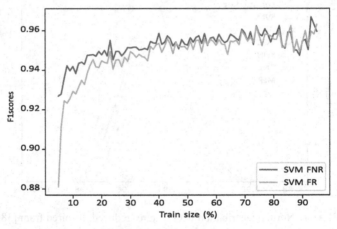

Fig. 7. Train Size Analysis.

8   Conclusion and Future Work

Our study demonstrates that it is feasible to use SBERT as a feature for classifying short messages in online chat conversations. This research aims to aid social science researchers and educators in gauging the level of engagement of online chat participants on a particular subject. Although our pipeline was developed using only one theme, we believe that it has potential for incorporation into future work, in other subjects. Our results suggest that utilizing BERTbased techniques to classify online chat room messages from online conversations can considerably enhance machine classification outcomes. Additionally, we have demonstrated that reducing the number of embeddings features by approximately 85% can produce similar outcomes to training algorithms with raw embeddings with 768 dimensions. Lastly, we have proven that by training machine learning algorithms with a smaller percentage of training data (approximately 20% of the dataset), we can achieve results that surpass our expectations: an average f1-score of 0.94 with a standard deviation of 0.01.

This work will be continued with further developments on the modules presented in this paper. Other techniques, like Deep learning are very promising in terms of further supporting social scientists in better understanding human communication and persuasion in online chat rooms. Although its use may have significant limitations in a few categories, the overall advances are encouraging. As guidelines for future work, the list below enumerates some of the main topics that will provide novel contributions:

- Chat rooms messages temporal analysis with deep learning temporal networks.
- Turn shift analysis, during the debate.
- An increase in the dataset size for other ages and data types sources.

Acknowledgment. This research was partially funded by Fundação para a Ciência e a Tecnologia under Projects "Factors for promoting dialogue and healthy behaviours in online school communities" with reference DSAIPA/DS/0102/2019 and developed at the R&D Unit CICANT - Research Center for Applied Communication, Culture and New Technologies, UIDB/04111/2020, UIDB/50008/2020 as well as Instituto Lusófono de Investigação e Desenvolvimento (ILIND) under Project COFAC/ILIND/COPELABS/1/2022.

References

1. Careaga-Butter, M., Mar´ıa Graciela, B.Q., Carolina, F.H.: Critical and prospective analysis of online education in pandemic and post-pandemic contexts: digital tools and resources to support teaching in synchronous and asynchronous learning modalities. Aloma: revista de psicologia, ci'encies de l'educacio´ i de l'esport Blanquerna **38**(2), 23–32 (2020). https://raco.cat/index.php/Aloma/article/view/377756
2. Uthus, D.C., Aha, D. W.: Multiparticipant chat analysis: a survey, 106–121 (2013)
3. Anjewierden, A., Kolloffel, B., Hulshof, C.: Towards educational data mining: using data mining methods for automated chat analysis to understand and support inquiry learning processes (2007)
4. Trausan-Matu, S., Rebedea, T., Dragan, A., Alexandru, C.: Visualisation of learners' contributions in chat conversations, 217–226 (2007). https://www.researchgate.net/publication/2102418955.
5. Alsmadi, I., Gan, K.H.: Review of short-text classification, 155–182 (2019)
6. Danilov, G., Ishankulov, T., Kotik, K., Orlov, Y., Shifrin, M., Potapov, A.: The classification of short scientific texts using pretrained BERT model, pp. 83–87, July 2021
7. Demirsoz, O., Ozcan, R.: Classification of news-related tweets. J. Inf. Sci. **43**, 509–524 (2017)
8. Hu, Y., Ding, J., Dou, Z., Chang, H.: Short-text classification detector: a BERT-based mental approach. Comput. Intell. Neurosci. **2022** (2022)
9. Lee, J.Y., Dernoncourt, F.: Sequential short-text classification with recurrent and convolutional neural networks, March 2016. http://arxiv.org/abs/1603.03827
10. Kowsari, K., Jafari Meimandi, K., Heidarysafa, M., Mendu, S., Barnes, L., Brown, D.: Text classification algorithms: a survey (2019)
11. Devlin, J., Chang, M.-W., Lee, K., Google, K.T., Language, A.I.: BERT: pre-training of deep bidirectional transformers for language understanding (2018). https://github.com/tensorflow/tensor2tensor

12. Lin, Y.H., et al.: Choosing transfer languages for cross-lingual learning. In: ACL 2019 - 57th Annual Meeting of the Association for Computational Linguistics, Proceedings of the Conference, pp. 3125–3135 (2020)
13. Reimers, N., Gurevych, I.: Sentence-BERT: sentence embeddings using siamese BERT-networks. CoRR, vol. abs/1908.10084, 2019. http://arxiv.org/abs/1908.10084
14. Hidey, C., Musi, E., Hwang, A., Muresan, S., McKeown, K.: Analyzing the semantic types of claims and premises in an online persuasive forum, pp. 11–21 (2017)
15. Meredith, J., Stokoe, E.: Repair: comparing Facebook 'chat' with spoken interaction. Discourse Commun. **8**, 181–207 (2014)
16. Huynh, H.X., Nguyen, V.T., Duong-Trung, N., Pham, V.H., Phan, C.T.: Distributed framework for automating opinion discretization from text corpora on facebook. IEEE Access **7**, 78675–78684 (2019)
17. Jucker, A.H.: Methodological issues in digital conversation analysis, August 2021
18. Meredith, J.: Conversation analysis and online interaction. Res. Lang. Soc. Inter. **52**, 241–256 (2019). https://doi.org/10.1080/08351813.2019.1631040
19. Paulus, T., Warren, A., Lester, J.N.: Applying conversation analysis methods to online talk: a literature review. Discourse, Context Media **12**, 1–10 (2016). https://doi.org/10.1016/j.dcm.2016.04.001
20. Liu, Y., Li, P., Hu, X.: Combining context-relevant features with multi-stage attention network for short text classification. Comput. Speech Lang. **71**, 1 (2022)
21. Gupta, S., Bolden, S., Kachhadia, J., Korsunska, A., Stromer-Galley, J.: PoliBERT: classifying political social media messages with BERT (2020)
22. Khatri, A., Kumar, A.: Sarcasm detection in tweets with BERT and glove embeddings (2020)
23. Ye, Z., Jiang, G., Liu, Y., Li, Z., Yuan, J.: Document and word representations generated by graph convolutional network and BERT for short text classification, vol. 325, pp. 2275–2281. IOS Press BV, August 2020
24. Landis, J.R., Koch, G.G.: The measurement of observer agreement for categorical data. Biometrics **33**(1), 159–174 (1977). http://www.jstor.org/stable/2529310
25. Krippendorff, K., Mathet, Y., Bouvry, S., Widlo¨cher, A.: On the reliability of unitizing textual continua further: developments. Qual. Quant. **50**, 2347–2364 (2016). https://doi.org/10.1007/s11135015-0266-1
26. Goldberg, Y., Levy, O.: word2vec explained: deriving mikolov et al.'s negativesampling word-embedding method. arXiv preprint: arXiv:1402.3722 (2014)
27. Devlin, J., Chang, M., Lee, K., Toutanova, K.: BERT: pre-training of deep bidirectional transformers for language understanding. CoRR, vol. abs/1810.04805 (2018). http://arxiv.org/abs/1810.04805
28. Levy, O., Goldberg, Y.: Dependency-based word embeddings. In: Proceedings of the 52nd Annual Meeting of the Association for Computational Linguistics (Volume 2: Short Papers), pp. 302–308 (2014)
29. McInnes, L., Healy, J., Melville, J.: Umap: Uniform manifold approximation and projection for dimension reduction (2018). https://arxiv.org/abs/1802.03426
30. Stoppiglia, H., Dreyfus, G., Dubois, R., Oussar, Y.: Ranking a random feature for variable and feature selection. J. Mach. Learn. Res. **3**, 1399–1414 (2003)
31. Chen, T., Guestrin, C.: XGBoost. In: Proceedings of the 22nd ACM SIGKDD International Conference on Knowledge Discovery and Data Mining. ACM, August 2016. https://doi.org/10.1145/2F2939672.2939785
32. Mestre, G., Matos-Carvalho, J.P., Tavares, R.M.: Irrigation management system using artificial intelligence algorithms. In: 2022 International Young Engineers Forum (YEF-ECE), pp. 69–74 (2022)
33. Cristianini, N., Ricci, E.: Support Vector Machines. Springer, Boston, pp. 928–932 (2008). https://doi.org/10.1007/978-0-387-30162-4_415

34. Matos-Carvalho, J.P., et al.: Static and dynamic algorithms for terrain classification in uav aerial imagery. Remote Sens. **11**(21), 2501 (2019). https://doi.org/10.3390/rs11212501
35. Sulemane, S., Matos-Carvalho, J.P., Pedro, D., Moutinho, F., Correia, S.D.: Vineyard gap detection by convolutional neural networks fed by multi-spectral images. Algorithms **15**(12), 440 (2022)
36. Santos, R., Matos-Carvalho, J.P., Tomic, S., Beko, M., Correia, S.D.: Applying deep neural networks to improve UAV navigation in satelliteless environments.In: 2022 International Young Engineers Forum (YEFECE), pp. 63–68 (2022)
37. Pedro, D., Matos-Carvalho, J.P., Fonseca, J.M., Mora, A.: Collision avoidance on unmanned aerial vehicles using neural network pipelines and flow clustering techniques. Remote Sens. **13**(13), 2643 (2021)
38. Matos-Carvalho, J.P., et al.: Static and dynamic algorithms for terrain classification in UAV aerial imagery. Remote Sens. **11**(21), 2501 (2019)
39. Nakama, J., Parada, R., Matos-Carvalho, J.P., Azevedo, F., Pedro, D., Campos, L.: Autonomous environment generator for UAV-based simulation. Appl. Sci. **11**(5), 2185 (2021)
40. Pedro, D., Mora, A., Carvalho, J., Azevedo, F., Fonseca, J.: Colanet: a UAV collision avoidance dataset. In: Camarinha-Matos, L.M., Farhadi, N., Lopes, F., Pereira, H. (eds.) DoCEIS 2020. IAICT, vol. 577, pp. 53–62. Springer, Cham (2020). https://doi.org/10.1007/978-3-030-451 24-0_5
41. Salvado, A.B., et al.: Semantic navigation mapping from aerial multispectral imagery. In: 2019 IEEE 28th International Symposium on Industrial Electronics (ISIE), pp. 1192–1197 (2019)
42. Matos-Carvalho, J.P., Correia, S.D., Tomic, S.: Sensitivity analysis of LSTM networks for fall detection wearable sensors. In: 2023 6th Conference on Cloud and Internet of Things (CIoT), Lisbon, Portugal, pp. 112–118 (2023) https://doi.org/10.1109/CIoT57267.2023.100 84906
43. Vong, A., et al.: How to build a 2D and 3D aerial multispectral map?—All steps deeply explained. Remote Sens. **13**(16), 3227 (2021). https://doi.org/10.3390/rs13163227
44. Stone, M.: Cross-validatory choice and assessment of statistical predictions. J. R. Stat. Soc. Ser B (Methodological) 36(2), 111–147 (1974). http://www.jstor.org/stable/2984809

Supply Chain Quality Improvement Based on Customer Compliance

Rene Maas[1,2(✉)], Eduard Shevtshenko[1,2], and Tatjana Karaulova[1,3]

[1] University of Tartu, Ülikooli 18, 50090 Tartu, Estonia
{Rene.Maas,Eduard.Sevtsenko,Tatjana.Karaulova}@tktk.ee
[2] TTK UAS, Pärnu Mnt 62A, 10135 Tallinn, Estonia
[3] Tallinn University of Technology, Ehitajate Tee 5, 19086 Tallinn, Estonia

Abstract. Current research is focused on topics of interest in the digital transformation of the supply chain, data analytics and system automation perspectives. The study aims to test the hypothesis that real-time information on the supply chain could be used to improve customer service quality and lead to a more reliable supply chain. Research is done to analyse supply chain performance using SCOR-based KPI model. The Integration of the methods presented in the study focuses on a solution that minimises supply chain failures, decreases failure elimination time, and improves customer satisfaction. Originality is that the proposed mechanism, is based on the Supply Chain Operations Reference (SCOR) model and Bayesian Belief Network (BBN) to estimate the influence of KPI metrics improvements on Supply Chain efficiency. Along that using the network of interconnected KPI-s, solution will show which operational level best practices influence the strategic level metrices the most.

Keywords: Supply Chain Operations Reference (SCOR) · Key Performance Indicators (KPIs) · Bayesian Belief Network (BBN) · Digitalisation · Reliability · Customer Service Quality

1 Introduction

Digitalising the supply chain is essential to eliminate the communication barriers between supply chain stakeholders. Digital Supply Chains share data and work together to guarantee that processes are seamless and free of bottlenecks, disruptions, and failures. Indeed, effective communication supported by real-time information over digital platforms enables prompt decision-making for improved supply chain performance. Digital technologies characterising industry 4.0 present a new strategy for increasing product quality and enhancing process efficiency [1].

Businesses can use the SCOR model to analyse the supply chain performance and how well processes are aligned with business objectives [2]. The SCOR reference model can be applied to define process architecture that aligns with essential business functions and goals [3, 4].

© IFIP International Federation for Information Processing 2023
Published by Springer Nature Switzerland AG 2023
L. M. Camarinha-Matos and F. Ferrada (Eds.): DoCEIS 2023, IFIP AICT 678, pp. 230–242, 2023.
https://doi.org/10.1007/978-3-031-36007-7_17

The authors suggest measuring its performance by key performance indicators built based on the SCOR v12.0 model. It may be achieved by developing the SCOR database to establish the links between processes with performance metrics and best practices [5]. The suggested approach can be used across industries using standard definitions for any supply chain process.

The innovative Digital Customer feedback mechanism supports the selection of SCOR-based KPIs to measure the reliability of the Supply Chain. It enables joint analysis of internal and external business process on customer satisfaction and help the decision-makers select the best practices and tools to improve the overall customer journey in the garment and electronics industries.

The authors developed a generic model that enables measuring the current level of the Supply Chain reliability based on data collected from companies. The authors developed the SCOR database to map the description of problems with SCOR business processes, measure the most critical processes to be improved by SCOR third level KPI-is, select the possible corrective actions by applying the SCOR best practices, and assess their influence on Supply Chain reliability improvement by Bayesian Belief Network before implementation.

1.1 Contribution to Connected Cyber Physical Spaces

Cyber physical space consists of cyber physical systems. Cyber-Physical Systems (CPS) could be defined as technologies that manage interconnected systems and helps to change information between physical assets and digital systems [6, 7] that deal with the physical and informational aspects of the system [8].

The supply chain and proposed mechanism for digitalising it contribute to cyber physical spaces in many aspects. First, it means that physical forms of the supply chain also have a cyber part. We could easily find the relation between manufacturing 4.0 and digitalising the supply chain. In each step of the physical supply chain, background functions that are called in literature cyber supply chain processes to add value through information generation and analyse and optimise processes [9]. Cyber physical manufacturing faces challenges in the digital supply chain and the support of decision making. The proposed mechanism will help make quick decisions on improvement needed processes.

There are intentions to find a bonding solution with e-commerce logistics and cloud-based solutions for better utilisation of resources while reducing waiting and wastage [10]. It is essential to understand the solutions for bonding physical and cyberspace using accurate- time information as we will propose mechanisms that will sense reclamations in a real-time manner and monitor processes that are affected by the reclamations.

As part of the supply chain, there is manufacturing; recent research focuses on the Digital twins that are mentioned as one of the constructors of cyber physical systems in the context of industry 4.0 [11, 12]. It also means more decision systems are server based and will manage resources in a more centralised manner.

Industry 4.0 context is necessary to add key performance metrics for a sustainable supply chain [13]. It shows the importance of using the KPIs for greener and more sustainable production in the supply chain context. The proposed solution digitises supply chain metrics that will help identify chain problems faster and solutions that have proven successful.

Using cyber physical systems in supply chain management has shown promising results in performance in the chain [14]. The importance of digitalised side of the supply chain [15] states that it will help support supply chain performance and contribute to overall business performance.

As the supply chain idea is to direct manufacturing towards producing consumer value [16–18], digital solutions for consumers are needed. The proposed mechanism will cover consumer journeys and help to inform them of supply disturbances in advance.

In current research, authors propose a solution to collect physical items claims information, assess their influence on supply chain SCOR based performance metrics, consider the previously made decisions, and discover the best corrective actions to improve the existing business processes. Authors believe that the supply chain performance metrics could be fed with data with automated data collection or sensors. Authors introduce how physical items collected data could be used to construct a supply chain BBN model with standardised processes and metrics to assess process improvement efficiency.

1.2 SCOR Concept

The Supply Chain Council (SCC) takes the Supply Chain Operations Reference (SCOR) as the official supply chain management diagnostics standard. This is why we used it as a base for our research. The best practices and people skills sections of SCOR introduces the skills management framework within SCOR.

The critical point of the model is the ability to visualise the interconnections between all Supply Chain partners business processes to speed up the feedback provided to customers and select the most efficient improvement actions. Thus, the SCOR model effectively controls and diagnoses supply chains. For example, the SCOR framework for "Perfect Order Fulfilment" measured by second and third-level KPI-s metrics clearly shows bottlenecks and possible alternative solutions for building up a system for enterprises reliability level monitoring and efficient management.

1.3 Problem Description

Due to the supply chain complexity, failures frequently appear. The problem to be addressed through the research is that supply chain processes improvement and on-time, accurate delivery for customers are not achieved. Until now, enterprises track the reclamations and returns but do it from their company's perspective. For the enterprises it is unknown, how will different level KPI-s change, when particular process is improved. For the customer, it is unknown that when reclamation is submitted, are the reorders free of the same problems.

Problems that occur in the enterprise will change the KPI metrices. Our mechanism will find the processes that is related with the metrices and what best practice to implement to improve process and through it the KPI-s itself.

The research questions are:

Does mechanism give improvement of reliability in sustainable supply chain by faster and more accurate process improvement?

Does the mechanism give faster response about defects and confidence that defects do not occur on re order?

Hypothesis for thesis:

The suggested mechanism increases customer service quality and supports quick decision making for entire supply chain participants, which gives economic relations between enterprises.

2 Main Idea of Research and Used Methods

The mechanism suggested in the current research includes integration of the methods for supply chain failure minimisation and to decrease the failure elimination time.

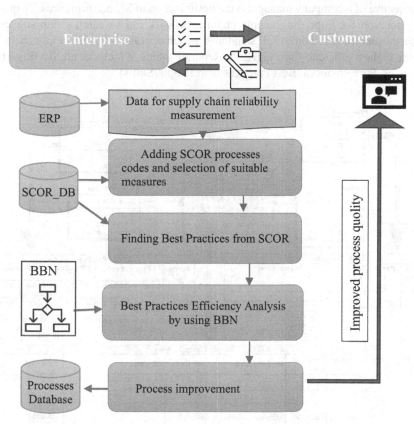

Fig. 1. Processes improvement based on customer feedback

The suggested mechanism is applied in the following order:

1. SCOR database development
2. Select the list of complaints resulting from improper use of products and faults in their delivery from the ERP system.
3. Connecting the list of complaints with SCOR process codes from SCOR-DB.

4. Efficiency analysis of SCOR best practices by using BBN. We should select the most suitable techniques from the suggested best practices from SCOR and analyse their influence on the supply chain effectiveness. For this aim we suggest use metrics of the considered supply chain processes.

Based on customer complaints, Fig. 1 visualises the steps for eliminating product defects and delivery accuracy in the supply chain. The decisions for more efficient use of a supply chain should be taken using the BBN analysis.

2.1 SCOR Database Development

The objective of a company manager is the optimisation of SC performances. To quickly find a solution for improving supply chain processes, our research group suggests a database structure based on SCOR standards, which operates with the supply chain data with the highest efficiency, see Fig. 2. As separate tables, it includes all SCOR sections (Processes, Performances, Best Practices, and People/Skills).

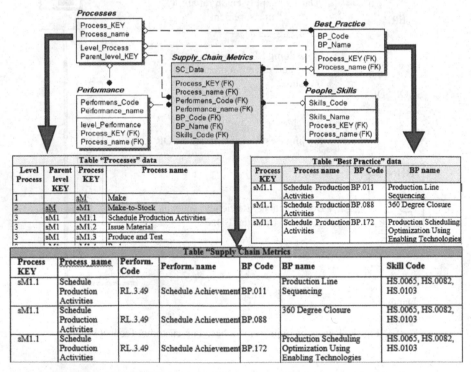

Fig. 2. SCOR-DB structure with an example of database tables filling

The benefits of using the SCOR database are:

- The database allows quickly find a needed process due to the process's hierarchical structure and the SCOR attributes.
- The database suggests all applicable best practices for processes, metrics, and practice reference components (see Table 1.).
- SCOR database allows determining the impact of changing one metric on another performance metric.
- The database allows the addition of new processes and attributes to a specific process based on enterprise skills.
- DB techniques make maintaining large volumes of information more accessible and apply other data analysis methods.

Table 1. Example of SCOR-DB data

Process KEY SCOR name	Reliability	Best Practices
sD.13 Receive and verify Product by Customer	RL.2.4 Perfect Condition RL.3.12% Of Faultless Installations **RL.3.55 Warranty and Returns RL 3.42 Orders Delivered Defect Free Conformance**	BP.147 Receiving Goods Inspection BP.089 Perfect Pick Put away

3   Validation of Customer Feedback Mechanism

The authors compare factors influencing the customer journey experience in garment and automotive electronics production. There are considerable differences between those sectors, as automotive electronics products are sold based on long lasting contracts to customers, and garments are a high mix low volume product, where the sales in driven by replenishment processes. The order amounts, product quality and delivery precision in those sectors vary significantly.

The authors use a scientific study based on qualitative and quantitative research methodology. During the research, the authors collected and analysed the data provided by commonly used internal processes related to delivery precision and external processes related to customer complaints, applied appropriate reliability KPIs and investigated the predicted efficiency of selected best practices implementation on the reliability measures of the company by using the BBN model.

3.1 Case Study from Garment and Electronics Industries

The authors analysed the data from four small garments and one automotive electronics production company. In both companies, the defects are usually discovered by the final consumer. In the garment sector, the defect can be caused by applying the wrong care procedures; either the products are destroyed by inappropriate use. Technological defects are avoided by quality checking in the production process and before delivery.

Every electronic device is checked thoroughly before delivery to achieve the high-quality level required by customers. Defects found should be corrected, and failed components should be replaced. Any deviation in quality causes a delay in payment or price reduction in the worst cases. External defects can be found in some cases by the end customer. It can be a defect when wrong care procedures are used or physical damage happens. Technical faults are avoided by quality checking in the production process and before delivery.

The number of defects is not similar. Defects are presented as a percentage of the total amount of orders (see Table 2.).

Table 2. Empirical data received from garment and automotive electronics companies

	Reliability target 99,5%						
	Internal Processes and CDA			External (Complaints)			
Garment Enterprise data	RL 3.45 Payment documentation accuracy	RL 3.43 Other required documentation accuracy		RL 3.55 Warranty and Returns	RL 3.42 Orders Delivered Defect Free Conformance		RL.3.24 % Orders/ lines received damage Free
Failures indexing	99%	98%		92,5%	95%		97%
Electronics Enterprise data	RL 3.49 Lack of production capacity	RL 3.20 Lack of material from an external source	RL 3.27 Increased customer demand near the time	RL 3.55 Warranty and Returns	RL 3.12 % Of Faultless Installations	RL 3.21 % Orders/ lines received with the correct content	RL.3.24 % Orders/ lines received damage Free
Failures indexing	12/32 37,5%	11/32 34,4%	6/32 8,1%	11/26 42,3%	12/26 46,2%	1/26 3,8%	2/26 7,7%
% of failures for the total amount	12*100/6935 = 0,17%	11*100/6935 = 0,15%	9*100/6935 = 0,13%	11*100/6935 = 0,15%	12*100/6935 = 0,17%	1*100/6935 = 0,01%	2*100/6935 = 0,02%

Reclaims/returns were aligned with SCOR model processes. After that, the performance metrics for the process are picked from the database. Performance metrics are divided into sections; this case study implements only the Reliability section, offering a view of supply chain reliability.

Third level SCOR KPIs were calculated based on the reclamations and were entered into the BBN model. The authors investigated third-level KPI impact to second-level KPI and, finally Perfect order fulfilment strategic target. Third-level KPI are connected to related business processes and the best practices applied to improve them.

Analysing third-level KPIs authors found out that both companies had reclamations, it could be found electronics producing company case has a lower percentage (0.15%) compared to the garment (7,5%). "Orders On Time in Full" KPI has shown better results in electronics companies (99,41%) compared to garment (92.5%.) It means garment companies had more reclamations and less on time and full complete orders deliveries. Overall, electronics manufacturing companies showed better results due to excellent quality management and developed standards in this sector. Also, the requirements for suppliers in the automotive industry are significantly higher than in the garment industry.

Technological defects cover the cases when non-appropriate components are used. Those defects usually are avoided by visual testing and repair process to avoid appearing at functional and final testing.

Table 3. shows the complaints that require consideration and action for their correction. For more effective supply chain it is necessary to complement the list of reclaims with the SCOR process code (KEY) and its name.

Table 3. Fragment of List of complaints with Reliability Performances (RL) and Best Practices (BP) in electronic company

Case Nr	Product	Quantity	Customer complaint	Root cause analysis	SCOR Process KEY/Name	SCOR Perform. Code/Name	SCOR Best Practices Code/Name
Case 1	Prod 1	2	Function failure	Component 1 component damaged, suspect that it happened in the router, monitoring	sM1.3: Produce and Test	RL.3.55 Warranty and Returns	BP.152 Automated Data Capture (ADC)

Figure 3 shows the generic model with processes and metrics suitable for the garment and automotive electronics industries. The model allows selecting enterprise specific processes and KPI-s using SCOR standard model. Everything that is not needed could take out of the model. It will give reusability aspects. Many enterprises could use the same model structure as the baseline to collect best practices and data. When new enterprises start using the model, already used best practices could be included and added (see Fig. 1).

Accordingly, to the SCOR model, every process has their best practices to improve it. On Fig. 3, they are shown on the bottom. Processes are found on the next tier, named "processes level". When using the BP that is connected with the process by the arrow, showing the relationship, it should improve that process. Every process is related to many levels of metrics. In Fig. 3, they are shown from level 3 – 1, from bottom to top. Metrics could be fed with many kinds of data, in this paper, it is fed with reclamations, showing how many orders there were and how many of them had the defect. Those defects could situate with processes that influenced again the metrics above them.

For example, when a defect occurs on process "sD1.14 install product" and reclamations are submitted, the data is inserted about the reclamation to the named process.

Next, we could see on the network what is the best practice to improve the process and when it is improved, subsequent orders should be free of those defects. At the same time, we could see from the network how reclamations change the KPI-s that are situated with it.

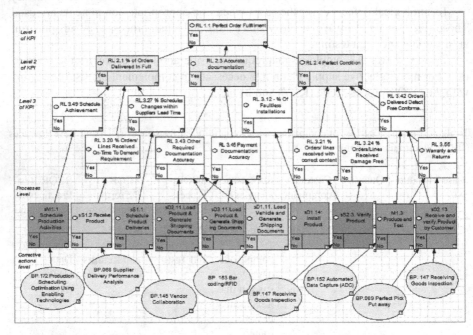

Fig. 3. BBN structure generic model based on Fig. 2

Figure 4 shows a case study specific model with reclamations data for textile industry. Percentages indicate the metrics influence level. A higher level means the influence on the second and first levels of metrics is significant. The highest impact on the second-level KPI for the textile case study is the third-level KPI, "RL 3.55 Warranty and Returns". The SCOR recommends applying the "BP.089 -Perfect Pick Put away" and B.147 Receiving Goods Inspection. After implementing those practices in Textile industry, it is expected to increase the Perfect Order Fulfilment from 54% to 56% eliminate the problems related to current returns (see Fig. 4).

The main challenge that small and medium electronics-producing enterprises face is an expectation of 99,8% of orders fulfilment in time. The total order amount for the electronics company during the considered period (one year) was 6935. The number of defects is not similar. Defects are presented as a percentage of the total failure for every SCOR process KEY (see Table 2.).

The highest impact on the second-level KPI for the current case study is the third-level KPI, "RL 3.49 Schedule Achievement", RL 3.21 and RL3.24. The SCOR recommends applying the "BP.0172 -Production Scheduling Optimisation" and B.147 best practices. After implementing those practices in Electronics industry, it is expected to increase

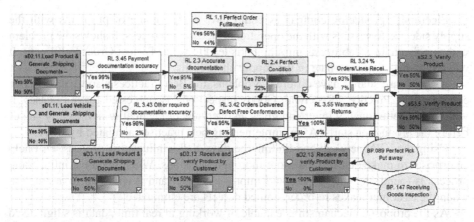

Fig. 4. Evaluation of processes KPI BBN network after best-practice tools implementation for the Textile industry

the Perfect Order Fulfilment from 99,56% to 99,61% eliminate the problems related to current returns (see Fig. 5).

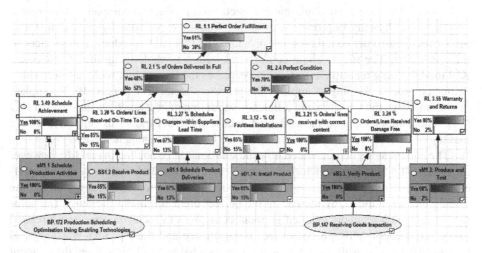

Fig. 5. Evaluation of processes KPI BBN network after best-practice implementation for the Electronics industry

4 Discussion

Garment production faces more external defects than electronics companies [19, 20]. It could be better-quality management, but it could also be that the number of problems is more frequently rising in production. Internal difficulties in garment production are related to finishing products, as electronics are associated mainly with a lack of materials.

Electronics producing companies could have a higher rate of problems with the supply side and few issues with the operational side of the process. It shows the problem with supply chain reliability as missing parts lead to worse Perfect Order Fulfilment. It will mean that issues resonate in the supply chain [20].

As both case studies have different problems, the Best Practices also vary. Still, one common Best Practice, "Receiving Goods Inspection," is suggested for both cases. It will lead to better quality input and gives an overview of the quality in the early stages before the production starts. After implementing best practise calculated by BBN.

Using the BBN network and finding the most KPI-s influencing process, will help enterprises to make quicker and more thorough decisions. When the most influencing process is found, the enterprise could improve it faster and it will lead to a situation when the customer makes re-order, named defects are eliminated.

As the proposed mechanism is capable of working in real time, data is sdigitalised and processes are connected with reclamations, it will give a customer a sense of security that re-ordering does not contain the same defects in the future.

5 Conclusions

The supply chain digitalisation mechanism and generic BBN template were developed and validated in garment and automotive electronics production companies.We present how to solve digitally improve the customer journey experience by providing faster responses to customer complaints and providing better quality products and services to the consumers. The supply chain could be viewed as a whole using the SCOR-based KPI model. Using real-time information decreases the time to link reclamations with a dedicated process, helping to improve the processes faster. The generic BBN template model improves the selection and efficiency validation of best practices on selected KPI [21]. The authors supplied the collected data to the BBN model to support decision making of what process improvement gives the best results on named KPIs.

The current study demonstrated how the solution can be applied in real life, however the study is limited to manufacturing companies, future research will study model applicability to different sector companies. The introduced solution enabled to increase the Supply chain reliability, by increasing the perfect order fulfilment measure. The solution developed by authors enabled garment companies to focus on core issues related to RL3.42 Orders delivered defect free conformance and the RL 3.55 Warranty and returns. After applying the best practices recommended by SCOR improved the garment company reliability by 4% and electronical company reliability by 0,5%.

It should be done to clear out similarities and specificities. Future work is to obtain more operational data for quantitative analysis. The current case study recommends implementing a digital solution that guarantees the "Perfect Pick and Put Away" and "Receiving Goods Inspection". Authors validated that those best practices can be successfully applied to improve the strategic targets of garment and automotive electronics companies.

Acknowledgement. This research has been financed by the European Social Fund via the IT Academy programme.

References

1. Tortorella, G.L., Fettermann, D.: Implementation of industry 40 and lean production in Brazilian manufacturing companies. International Journal of Production Research **56**(8), 2975–2987 (2017)
2. Lockamy, A., McCormack, K.: Modelling supplier risks using Bayesian networks. Ind. Manag. Data Syst. **112**(2), 313–333 (2012). https://doi.org/10.1108/02635571211204317
3. Taghizadeh, H., Hafezi, E.: The investigation of supply chain's reliability measure: a case study. J. Industr. Eng. Int. **8**, 22 (2012). https://doi.org/10.1186/2251-712X-8-22
4. APICS, Supply Chain Operations Reference Model SCOR, Version 12.0, 2017 APICS
5. Shevtshenko, E., Mahmood, K., Karaulova, T., Raji, I.O.: Multitier digital twin approach for agile supply chain management. In: Proceedings of the 2020 ASME International Mechanical Engineering Congress and Exposition, pp. 1–10 (2020)
6. Lee, J., Bagheri, B., Kao, H.A.: A Cyber-Physical Systems architecture for Industry 4.0-based manufacturing systems. Manufact. Lett. **3**, 18–23 (2015). https://doi.org/10.1016/j.mfglet.2014.12.001
7. Baheti, R., H. G.: Cyber-physical systems. Impact Control Technol. **12**(1), 161–166 (2011)
8. Chen, L., Dui, H., Zhang, C.: A resilience measure for supply chain systems considering the interruption with the cyber-physical systems. Reliab. Eng. Syst. Saf. **199** (2020). https://doi.org/10.1016/j.ress.2020.106869
9. Panetto, H., Iung, B., Ivanov, D., Weichhart, G., Wang, X.: Challenges for the cyber-physical manufacturing enterprises of the future. Annual Rev. Control **47**, 200–213 (2019). https://doi.org/10.1016/j.arcontrol.2019.02.002
10. Kong, X.T.R., et al.: Cyber physical ecommerce logistics system: an implementation case in Hong Kong. Comput. Industr. Eng. 139 (2020).https://doi.org/10.1016/j.cie.2019.106170
11. Park, K.T., Son, Y.H., Noh, S.D.: The architectural framework of a cyber physical logistics system for digital-twin-based supply chain control. Int. J. Prod. Res, 1–22 (2020). https://doi.org/10.1080/00207543.2020.1788738
12. Tao, F., Qi, Q., Wang, L., Nee, A.Y.C.: Digital twins and cyber–physical systems toward smart manufacturing and industry 4.0: correlation and comparison. Engineering, 5(4), 653–661 (2019). https://doi.org/10.1016/j.eng.2019.01.014
13. Morella, P., Lambán, M.P., Royo, J., Sánchez, J.C., Corrales, L.D.C.N.: Development of a new green indicator and its implementation in a cyber–physical system for a green supply chain. Sustainability (Switzerland) **12**(20), 1–19 (2020). https://doi.org/10.3390/su12208629
14. Frazzon, E.M., Silva, L.S., Hurtado, P.A.: Synchronising and improving supply chains through the application of cyber-physical systems. IFAC-PapersOnLine **28**(3), 2059–2064 (2015). https://doi.org/10.1016/j.ifacol.2015.06.392
15. Lee, K.L., Azmi, N.A.N., Hanaysha, J.R., Alzoubi, H.M., Alshurideh, M.T.: The effect of digital supply chain on sorganisational performance: an empirical study in Malaysia manufacturing industry. Uncertain Supply Chain Manag. **10**(2), 495–510 (2022). https://doi.org/10.5267/j.uscm.2021.12.002
16. Esper, T. L., et al.: Everything old is new again: the age of consumer-centric supply chain management. J. Bus. Logist. **41**(4), 286–293 (2020). https://doi.org/10.1111/jbl.12267
17. Min, S., Zacharia, Z.G., Smith, C.D.: Defining supply chain management: in the past, present, and future. J. Bus. Logist. **40**(1), 44–55 (2019). https://doi.org/10.1111/jbl.12201
18. Stolze, H.J., Mollenkopf, D.A., Flint, D.J.: What is the right supply chain for your shopper? Exploring the shopper service ecosystem. J. Bus. Logist. **37**(2), 185–197 (2016). https://doi.org/10.1111/jbl.12122
19. Murumaa, L., Shevtshenko, E., Karaulova, T., Mahmood, K., Popell, J.: Supply chain digitalisation framework for servive/product satisfaction, modern materials and manufacturing.

In: IOP Conference Series, Materials Science and Engineering; Bristol, vol. 1140, p. 012041 (2021). https://doi.org/10.1088/1757-99X/1140/1/012041

20. Shevtshenko, E., Maas, R., Murumaa, L., Karaulova, T., Raji, I.O., Popell, J.: Digitalisation of supply chain management system for customer quality service improvement. J. Mach. Eng. **22**

21. Shevtshenko, E., Wang, Y.: Decision support under uncertainties based on robust Bayesian networks in reverse logistics management. Int. J. Comput. (2009)

Monte Carlo Simulation Applicable for Predictive Algorithm Analysis in Aerospace

Jorge Bautista-Hernández[1,2]([envelope]) [iD] and María Ángeles Martín-Prats[1] [iD]

[1] Electronics Engineering Department, University of Seville, 41092 Seville, Spain
jorbauher@alum.us.es, mmprats@us.es
[2] Aerospace Electrical Engineering Department, Airbus Poland, 02-256 Warsaw, Poland

Abstract. Safety investigations about electrical wiring harness caused by failures in electrical systems establish that origin of these accidents are related to electrical installation. Predictive techniques which mitigate and reduce risk of the occurrence of errors to enhance safety shall be considered. The development of machine learning has evolved towards the creation of innovative predictive algorithms which show high performance in data analysis and making predictions in the context of artificial intelligence. The Monte Carlo approach is used to validate the model performance. In this paper, Monte Carlo simulation was used to evaluate the level of the uncertainty of the selected parameters over 1000 runs. This study analyzes the reliability of the predictive algorithm in order to be implemented as an automatic error predictor in aerospace. The results obtained are within the expected range suggesting that the model used is accurate and reliable.

Keyword: Monte Carlo Simulation · Predictive Algorithms · Sensitivity Analysis · System Reliability · Automatic Error Predictor

1 Introduction

Safety is a pillar in our lives. It has been evaluated in aerospace that major accidents are consequential from human errors which can contribute to up to 80% of the total accidents. Human errors can never be eliminated completely but they can be reduced to the minimum by implementing predictive and automatic algorithms which are focus upon the risk rather than on the error elimination. An analysis of dataset is encouraged to be performed in order to better identify relevant indicators and situations which are vulnerable to create an error in order to implement measures to avoid potential failures.

Human errors in aerospace are considered as a multi-event and can be mainly generated from design (e.g. models errors), manufacturing (incorrect procedures), installation issues (incorrect assembly) and operational errors of the aircraft (miscommunication or poor decisions). Furthermore, some of these errors are likely to generate a hazard. The complex process for error generation needs to be better analyzed in order to show a holistic view of one indicator towards the creation of the error [1]. Based on the aviation authorities investigation the main cause for accident creation was the failures generated in the electrical harness installation. Thus, quantification of the main parameters that

L. M. Camarinha-Matos and F. Ferrada (Eds.): DoCEIS 2023, IFIP AICT 678, pp. 243–256, 2023.
https://doi.org/10.1007/978-3-031-36007-7_18

exist in the electrical system of an aircraft and used predictive techniques to predict uncertainties are necessary. Advanced technology such as cyber-physical systems and automation are effective strategies to prevent errors [2].

Cyber-physical systems (CPS) are based on computational and physical elements which can be used to monitor processes in order to prevent errors before they occur. For example, in electrical manufacturing, the risk matrix can be used as an outcome of the predictive algorithm in order to detect in real time any anomalies before they cause a failure. Additionally, automation can be used to prevent errors and reduce the risk of human error creation.

The main goal is to implement an innovative methodology to keep the aerospace industry at the greatest level of safety and potentially analyses its applicability to other disciplines such as energy, health care, transportation or infrastructure. Thus, the research question established in this paper is: What can be the benefit of introducing this novel methodology in the industry?

To answer to this question requires to give evidences to the following assumptions:

- Time assessment during the creation of the manufacturing engineering processes,
- Mitigation errors in the end-to-end process,
- Positive impact in safety in order to keep aviation standards at the highest level.

The quantification of the successful results have generated a decreased of 93% in manufacturing time and 90% in potential errors creation during creation of applicable manufacturing engineering processes.

This specific paper aims to assess reliability and validation for the model system engineering represented in Fig. 1 by using a Monte Carlo simulation. This technique can be used as a proper method to assess reliability for a system engineering. The model in Fig. 1 presents a level of uncertainty in the three input parameters selected in this simulation. The Monte Carlo method will solve this uncertainty by running 1000 samples for each parameter and representing the result using the probabilistic function. This function represents the probability of the possible outcomes values are below a threshold. The aim of the study is to investigate the level of sensitivity of the key parameters used for the prediction to consider them as good indicators [3, 4].The impact of varying these parameters on model with 1000 runs simulation will define the robustness of the model as a tool to be implemented as an auto-failure detector. Thus, the model uncertainties are identify towards a more reliable system in order to improve predictions in the future [3].

The remainder of this paper is as follows. The review of the relationship to connected cyber physical spaces is in Sect. 2, Sect. 3 addresses the research methodology related to the validation model. The main results are presented in Sect. 4. Discussions are in Sect. 5 and finally to summarize in Sect. 6 conclusions and future work.

2 Relationship to Connected Cyber Physical Spaces

The motivation to implement this novel and innovative methodology based on the proposed automatic and predictive algorithm in the electrical manufacturing processes is fundamental in order to keep aerospace safety at the greatest level. The advanced technologies such as Big Data and the increasing system complexity together with the necessity that the data needs to be fast analyzed to provide the best solution, enable the creation of a Cyber Space Model to respond to this necessity [2]. Cyber-Physical systems provide feedback in real time and present very good adaptive and predictive capacity. The latest research in the aerospace framework shows these systems not only have a positive impact on the aviation safety but also enhancing efficiency, integration and autonomy of the next generation aerospace systems.

The solution approach proposal based on this hybrid and predictive algorithm contributes to connect Cyber Physical Spaces through the use of machine learning techniques. The automatic manufacturing processes and predictive tasks enable engineering systems to execute activities independently with minimum human actions. Therefore the mitigation error is guaranteed. Additionally, the assessment in real time of the error creation by using the risk matrix not only decrease the probability of create a failure, but it also ensures the correct decision provided by the automatic system. This situation generates a positive impact in the electrical harness built process. Thus, automation process and predictive tasks are references towards connected Cyber Physical Spaces.

This emerging and innovative methodology convergences on the new technologies used in the new dynamic manufacturing industry. The required multi-interaction to satisfy the demand of systems complexity establish better collaboration between academic engineering disciplines and industry since cyber-physical systems also requires more elements to be inter-connected and easy adaptability to this new technology and future applications.

3 Methods

3.1 The Algorithm Overview

The innovative procedure using predictive algorithms has been developed in aerospace not only to mitigate the errors but also to predict the error creation in the electrical manufacturing engineering processes in the aerospace context by using innovative machine learning techniques. The Fig. 1 represents the algorithm structure and is based on the following elements.

The risk matrix mechanism that assess the probability of error creation in each specific harness. It determinates five main categories from 'very low' to 'very high' probability of error creation [5]. The automation tool is developed to avoid manual tasks during creation of the engineering documentation. Thus, it mitigates creation of an error during the engineering process. The dendrogram is using the hierarchical agglomerative method which creates groups with similar objects within the data set. The clusters data provides information about the critical groups which require special attention. The logistic regression estimates the parameters by establishing relationships between the input data and the outcomes according to a mathematic criterion. The confusion matrix will define the accuracy of the algorithm by table of contingency. Finally, the computation time will be the minimum necessary to define the optimal number of iterations using the method of gradient descent after regression logistic is applied to the categorical variable.

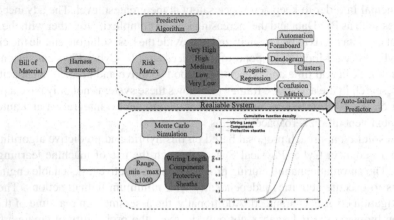

Fig. 1. Diagram representation of the predictive algorithm and Monte Carlo simulation

3.2 The Input Parameters

The first step in the creation of the predictive algorithm is to define the parameters. These are based on the electrical configuration of the harness to be manufactured and eventually installed on the aircraft. These are the number of zones (Z), number of wires (H) and number of electrical components (N) which define the risk matrix ϕ. Such criteria defines each harness category based on these parameters. The risk matrix function defines the probability of creating an error during the manufacturing process of electrical harness as part of the outcomes from predictive algorithms. The risk matrix as a function can be expressed as follows:

$$\phi = \phi(Z, H, N) \tag{1}$$

Scores assigned to each parameter will be evaluated on a scale from 1 to 5, being 1 the simplest geometry and 5 the most complex. A detailed description of the model has been recently proposed by Bautista Hernández and Martín Prats assessing its performance towards introduction in aerospace applications [6].

The baseline parameters for the Monte Carlo simulation will be based on the following relevant metrics, p_1 for wiring length, p_2 for number of electrical components and p_3 for the protective sheath quantities present in the 'bill of material' on each harness for a military aircraft. The Monte Carlo function determinates the performance of the model for implementation purposes. The generic function for Monte Carlo simulation λ, is expressed as follows:

$$\lambda = \lambda(p_1, p_2, p_3) \tag{2}$$

The C295 aircraft dataset with a total of 221 electrical harness to fully define the electrical system of this aircraft. In total in this case study, 157 harness considered are presenting the following parameters, 18523.95 m of the total wiring length, 21200.55 electrical components and 250.84 m of protective sheath length. The baseline run Monte Carlo simulation was executed 1000 times across a range between maximum and minimum values of meters of wiring length (0.29–2374.79), units of number of components (4–2243) and meters of protective sheath (0.06–22.59).

3.3 Sensitivity Analysis

The sensitivity analysis was carried out to understand the correlation between the input parameters and indicate the importance for the outcomes. Additionally, this analysis evaluates the model performance by considering the response of the input variables parameters after simulation [7]. The high correlation between the variables indicates that increasing of their values will enhance outcomes values. Thus, the probability of creating an error will be also higher [8].

The outcomes presented were analyzed to understand the impact of the maximum and minimum values within the dataset suggesting that the model performs well. In this medium-light size aircraft the predicted outcomes after 1000 runs were within the range of expected values.

The box-plots performed for the chosen parameters represented in Fig. 2 aim to analyze the data set and demonstrate the spread of numerical data through their quartiles follows one of the known distributions probabilistic. The Fig. 2 shows the dataset distribution associated to each parameter defined by the generic function Monte Carlo in a logarithmic scale.

In the first case related to the p_1, the first quartile $Q_1 = e^{0.9} = 2.45$ m marks one quarter (25%) of the ordered dataset and the value 1.5 IQR (-) below the first quartile is 1.5 IQR (-) $= e^{0.1} = 1.01$ m.

The maximum value in the dataset is 2374 m and the value for 1.5 IQR (+) $= e^{6.3} = 544.21$ m above the $Q_3 = e^{3.2} = 24.52$ m, which marks three quarter (75%) of the ordered dataset. The maximum value is above the 1.5 IQR (+), so in this case the maximum is an outlier which may indicate the measurements are not in the center of the data.

In the second case related to the p_2, the first quartile $Q_1 = e^{2.4} = 11.02$ components and the value 1.5 IQR (-) $= e^{1.4} = 4.05$ components.

The maximum value of the dataset is 2243 components. In this case, this maximum value is above the 1.5 IQR (+) $= e^{6.9} = 991$ components showing outliers.

In the third case related to the p_3, the first quartile $Q_1 = e^{0.1} = 1.1$ m and the 1.5 IQR (+) $= e^{2.3} = 9.97$ m below the maximum value of this parameter in the dataset which is 22.59 m.

The analytical results estimate the input data for the three parameters selected can be fitted to a normal distribution.

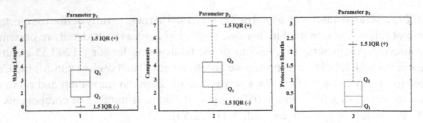

Fig. 2. Box-plots representation for input metrics p_1, p_2, p_3 on the Monte Carlo function λ

3.4 Monte Carlo Simulation

The Monte Carlo simulation is a method to assess reliability of an engineering system. The simulation uses as input parameters the p_1, p_2, p_3 values. These values are randomly assigned 1000 times variating within the range of the maximum and minimum values defined from the entire dataset in a logarithmic scale shown in the Table 1.

This simulation is used to obtain outcomes estimation from a set of stochastic trial from proper definition quantities [4].

Table 1. Minimum, maximum, mean and standard deviation values of the input parameters used in Monte Carlo simulation

Description	parameter	min	max	mean	std	units
Wiring length	p_1	0.1	7.77	2.46	1.90	m
Number of components	p_2	1.38	7.71	3.66	1.36	–
Protective sheath	p_3	0.1	3.11	0.44	0.74	m

Such statistical distributions are used within the range of the lower and the higher end value for each parameter to estimate the outcomes across a Monte Carlo simulation with 1000 runs. Probabilistic distributions are considered for probability calculations within the dataset. The assignment for calculation of the probability in each individual run was carried out using the normal function from the random Python xlwings library within the given interval. As the input dataset variable X is log-normally distributed then the input values were transformed to a distribution $Y = \ln(X)$ for representation [9].

The simulation is defined by generation of a stochastic trial to each of the input parameters on each of 157 electrical harness on a C295 military aircraft following a probabilistic function normally distributed. After simulation using random combination of the input variables the output is calculated for each parameter. Finally, the outcomes are represented with the probabilistic function distribution and the cumulative function of density.

3.5 Method of Gradient Descent

The regression logistic used to predict the categorical variable needs 144 iterations until the algorithm converges. This situation requires a high computation time. The method of gradient descent can be used to find the optimal solutions by proper adjustment of the parameters which minimize the function in order to reach the global minimum faster and the convergence of algorithm [10].

Being $f : \Omega \subset R^n \rightarrow R$, this method can find $\theta \subset \Omega / f(\theta)$ min. The Eqs. 3, 4 and 5 define the best solution path in order to find the optimal solution.

$$\theta \in \arg\min \, f(\theta) \tag{3}$$

$$\theta_{t+1} = \theta_t - \delta_t \nabla f(\theta_t) \tag{4}$$

$$\nabla f(\theta_t) = (\partial f / \partial x_1(\theta), \ldots, \partial f / \partial x_n(\theta)) \tag{5}$$

δ_t is the learning rate which determinates the number of iterations until the algorithm converges. The convenient value of δ guarantees minimize the number of iterations improving the computation time.

The use of this method allows the algorithm to perform faster. Thus, the number of iterations decrease to 41 generating significantly benefit in the computation time.

4 Results

The tendency of each parameter presents a linear relation between the parameters chosen for the Monte Carlo simulation (length, number of electrical components and protection sheaths). The correlation of these parameters is quantified by the correlation matrix shown in table 2. A positive value of the coefficient means an increase of this parameter necessary involves an increase in the other parameter. The strongest correlation occurs when the absolute value of the coefficient is as close as possible to 1. From the correlation matrix we observed that p_1 and p_3, as well as parameters p_2 with p_3 have lower positive correlation coefficients, but still indicate some degree of correlation between these variables.

Table 2. Correlation matrix for the input parameters used for the Monte Carlo simulation

Description	Parameter	Length	Components	Protection
Wiring length	p_1	1.0000000	0.928046	0.470757
Number of components	p_2	0.928046	1.0000000	0.471076
Protective sheath	p_3	0.470757	0.471076	1.0000000

The Monte Carlo simulation has performed 1000 runs and the output parameters as a result of the new predicted values for the wiring length, numbers of electrical components and protective sheath are normally distributed. The cumulative distribution function shows the probability that each parameter value stays below specific threshold.

4.1 First Output - Wiring Length

The Eqs. (6–7) quantify through the probabilistic distribution function the prediction of the outputs in a new harness. As a first output of the new parameter for the wiring length, the p_1 will be between 2.01 and 3.00 m with a probability of occurrence between 50 and 90% (Fig. 3).

$$P(0.5) \rightarrow X_1 = e^{0.7} = 2.01\,\text{m} \tag{6}$$

$$P(0.9) \rightarrow X_2 = e^{1.1} = 3.00\,\text{m} \tag{7}$$

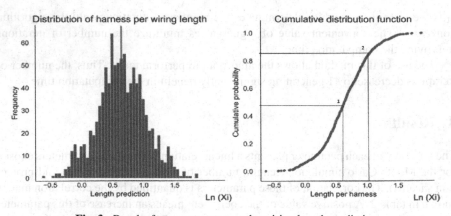

Fig. 3. Results for p_1 outcomes on the wiring length prediction

4.2 Second Output – Number of Components

The Eqs. (8–9) quantify through the probabilistic distribution function the prediction of the outputs in a new harness. As a second output of the new parameter for the number of components, the p_2 will stay between 45 and 245 units with a probability of occurrence between 50 and 90% (Fig. 4).

$$P(0.5) \rightarrow X_1 = e^{3.8} = 45\,\text{units} \tag{8}$$

$$P(0.9) \rightarrow X_2 = e^{5.5} = 245\,\text{units} \tag{9}$$

4.3 Third Output – Protective Textile Sheaths

The Eqs. (8–9) quantify through the probabilistic distribution function the prediction of the outputs in a new harness. As a third output of the new parameter protective sheath

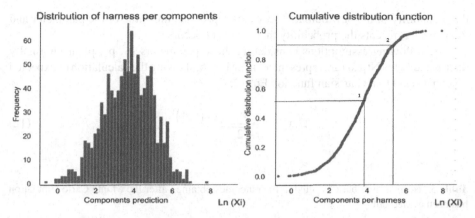

Fig. 4. Results for p_2 outcomes on the number of electrical components prediction

length, the p_3 in a new harness will be between 1.49 and 4.48 m with a probability of occurrence between 50 and 90% (Fig. 5).

$$P(0.5) \rightarrow X_1 = e^{0.4} = 1.49\,\text{m} \tag{10}$$

$$P(0.9) \rightarrow X_2 = e^{1.5} = 4.48\,\text{m} \tag{11}$$

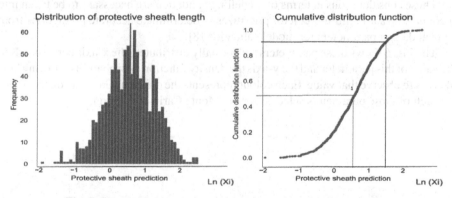

Fig. 5. Results for p_3 outcomes on the protective sheath prediction

The reliability assessment at each parameter level is needed to calculate the probability that a new component does not exceed a limit defined through the cumulative distribution function [11].

The previous figures refer to the Monte Carlo simulation represent the random values of the parameters which are variating from maximum to the minimum within the three parameters. The distribution function shows the outcomes predicted are normally distributed. The y-axis shows the frequencies where a parameter appears and the x-axis the value of that parameter at that frequency. The cumulative distribution function estimates the probability of the new output. The x-axis represents the value of the parameter and the y-axis represents the probability that the event occurs.

The following assumptions considering those parameters p_1, p_2, p_3 are normally distributed / $\Omega \sim N(\mu,\sigma)$ are represented in the Fig. 6, showing the calculation of expected outcomes lead to a Gaussian function Eq. 12.

$$\Omega(x) = \frac{1}{\sigma\sqrt{2\pi}}e^{-\frac{1}{2}\left(\frac{x-\mu}{\sigma}\right)^2} \tag{12}$$

Table 3. Normal distributions fitted to the outcomes obtained after the Monte Carlo simulation has been carried out

Description	Parameter	Normal distribution
Wiring length	p_1	N (2.46, 1.89)
Number of components	p_2	N (3.66, 1.36)
Protective sheath	p_3	N (0.61, 0.74)

The purpose of the normal distributions is to obtain a probability function to help to understand the variability of the system simulated and to give an evidence of its reliability. In the future, they can also be useful to make predictions of the parameters.

These considerations in terms of modelling validation are necessary to be taken into account. The auto failure-predictor prioritizes to determinate accurate predictions from a given dataset parameters for model validation [8].

The Fig. 6 shows these parameters are normally distributed, the x-axis corresponds to the value of this parameter and the y-axis the density function of probability showing how likely is to observe that value. Each colour represents the different Gaussian distributions for each of those parameters selected for the Monte Carlo simulation.

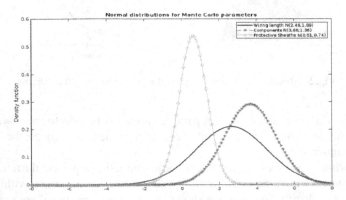

Fig. 6. Normal or Gaussians distribution for the dataset parameters p_1, p_2, p_3

The Fig. 7 depicts the dataset within the time and frequency domain. The series of points in left figure are referred to the parameters of the model and show the signal changes within time. The blue line represents the first parameter p_1, which is the wiring length. The red line represents the second parameter p_2, which is the number of electrical components and the third parameter p_3, represents by the orange line is the protection sheaths. The 'y axis' refers to the amplitude of the signal what is the scale of each point of the dataset. The 'x axis' refers to each point of the dataset on a single harness out of 157. The information obtained from wiring length and number of components show that the harness with more wiring length will also present more number of electrical components, so these parameters are positively correlated. It is also observed they have similar amplitude between peaks. In harness with longer wiring length it is shown that the blue line is above the red line showing that in this group of harness the amplitude of this parameter is greater than the number of components. This type of harness are the most critical harness since the present high risk matrix. From the orange line, the protective sheath is the unpredictable parameter, in some points the dataset has 'zero values' what it means there are harness which are not in presence of this parameter. This parameter is also in phase with the other two parameters, what it means, if the parameter value is greater than 0, the increasing of the wiring length and number of electrical components will also reflect an increasing of the protective sheath parameter. The use of this representation helps to predict future values based on the previous history data.

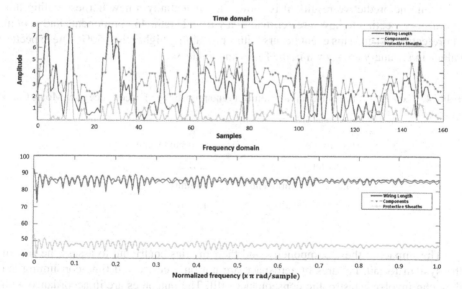

Fig. 7. Time/frequency domain representation for the dataset parameters p_1, p_2, p_3

From the representation in the frequency domain, the right Fig. 7 shows how much the amplitude of the signal is present in each frequency interval. The times series analysis and the observed values are represented in a data spectrum. The information from this representation includes in detail the phase difference between the signals. The wiring length and number of components are in phase. There is a minimal difference in phase at low frequency (f = 0.05 Hz). At this frequency the wiring length decreases, however the number of electrical components increases. In this specific situation it is expected that the number of electrical components should increase as well. This situation occurs in avionics harness where the number of components is in percentage very closed to the wiring length percentage. There are many electronic devices to be connected in a very small area.

At f = 0.35 Hz is another particular case where the signals are not in phase and there is a difference between the phases on both signals. This situation illustrates only one electrical harness presents more components than wiring length.

The protective sheaths parameter is presented in a constant rate and the information obtained shows is an unpredicted parameter, concluding that this parameter should not be considered as a relevant parameter for validation of the model.

5 Discussion

For the purpose to validate the system, the Monte Carlo simulation is a proper method to analyse how the performance is affected by the parameters. The input parameters are stochastically assigned for each dataset. The random behaviour of the components aim to define sensitivities indexes to quantify the outcomes and inform about the importance of variation in the features of the system.

From the predictive results, it is shown that potentially a new harness within this aircraft is expecting to have greater than 2 m wiring length, 45 components and 1.49 m of protective sheath. This event occurs with a probability higher than 50%. The expected values in summary are shown in the following Table 3.

Table 4. Expected values of the input parameters and probability of occurrence after Monte Carlo simulation

Description	Expected value
Wiring length	2.01 m
Number of components	45 units
Protective sheath	1.49 m

The impact of these components and their metrics contribute to assess the risk of the system to fail. Failures in aerospace are not only costly and time-consuming but they can involve catastrophic consequences [9]. The outcomes are in accordance with the expected values and within the range for this aircraft. The correct behaviour of the outcomes is relevant to consider the system as a reliable and a safe system. This represents the best model prediction (Table 4).

From the risk matrix, this type of harness is defined as a medium-low risk what it means there is low probability to create an error during the creation of manufacturing process. This situation shows very reliable results since mostly harness in this medium light aircraft are medium size presenting not a high risk in terms of error creation. This information provided in advanced generate a lot of benefits, such as better performance on the end-to-end process shortening the potential error creation between stages. Additionally, the whole process system gets more reliable providing a full visibility of the entire process.

The aging effect on these parameters is also important to take into consideration. The wiring length aging can influence to the wiring properties and make them shorter. The number of components can be also reduced due to material wear decreasing components efficiency. The protection sheaths aging can increase the risk of short circuit after damaging the wires.

Additionally, the accuracy of the model is ensured by calculation of the minimum square error. The results show a value of 0.13 what implies that the model is predicting well the outcomes for the given input parameters. The expected values obtained from the cumulative function of density in Table 3 are also good metrics to ensure accuracy of the modelling parameters.

6 Conclusions

Safety is a main priority and necessary to be established between all main actors involved in the end-to-end process. The positive communication enhances not only safety but also commitment with high requirements in order to anticipate before the undesirable situations occur. Starting from this research developed within aerospace the aim is to define the sensitivity respect three main inputs parameters which are the most relevant for electrical harness in order to define the model as reliable to be used as a reliable model. The importance of these parameters defines effectiveness for the risk matrix calculation and sensitivity analysis. In this paper we presented evidences that the model used for prediction of errors creation in a military aircraft case study is a reliable auto-failure detector. The model has used the following relevant parameters in the electrical harness definition such as wiring length, number of electrical components and length of protective sheaths. For the sensitivity analysis the sample size used n = 1000 for these factors were modelled in a Monte Carlo simulation. After analysis, results show these parameters are highly correlated, showing that the wiring length and number of components are proportional and reliable parameters to be used to define the risk matrix of the model. Additionally, we observed the avionics harness are critical presenting both parameters in very similar proportion. The protection sheath shows an unpredictable behaviour and to be used as an estimator of the risk matrix needs to be consider together with another parameter, either wiring length or number or components. The dataset has been validated using real data manufactured by one of the main aircrafts making this system as reliable model and safe. This research also establishes future trends applicability to keep safety at the highest level, not only in aerospace but also in other disciplines. This is the first milestone in order to be implemented in the industry. The results show that the model can be implemented as an auto-failure predictor and can be used to make realistic estimation of these parameters.

Acknowledgments. The authors acknowledge the contributions to the automatic and electronic engineering department from the Seville University and to Airbus Poland for supporting this work with their research facilities and resources.

References

1. Authority, C.A.: CAP 716: aviation maintenance human factors (EASA/JAR145 Approved Organisations): guidance material on the UK CAA interpretation of part 145 human factors and error management requirements. Hum. Factors (2006)
2. Lin, W.D., Low, Y.H., Chong, Y.T., Teo, C.L.: Integrated cyber physical simulation modelling environment for manufacturing 4.0. In: 2018 IEEE International Conference on Industrial Engineering and Engineering Management (IEEM), pp. 1861–1865. IEEE (2018)
3. Rao, K.D., Gopika, V., Rao, V.S., Kushwaha, H., Verma, A.K., Srividya, A.: Dynamic fault tree analysis using Monte Carlo simulation in probabilistic safety assessment. Reliab. Eng. Syst. Saf. **94**(4), 872–883 (2009)
4. Marseguerra, M., Zio, E.: Monte Carlo estimation of the differential importance measure: application to the protection system of a nuclear reactor. Reliab. Eng. Syst. Saf. **86**(1), 11–24 (2004)
5. Barr, et al., L.C.: Preliminary risk assessment for small unmanned aircraft systems. In: 17th AIAA Aviation Technology, Integration, and Operations Conference, p. 3272 (2017)
6. Bautista-Hernández, J., Martín-Prats, M.Á.: Innovative procedure using predictive algorithms for cutting-edge approach in technology (2023). [Manuscript in preparation]
7. Saltelli, A., Marivoet, J.: Non-parametric statistics in sensitivity analysis for model output: a comparison of selected techniques. Reliab. Eng. Syst. Saf. **28**(2), 229–253 (1990)
8. Goda, T.: A simple algorithm for global sensitivity analysis with Shapley effects. Reliab. Eng. Syst. Saf. **213**, 107702 (2021)
9. Burmaster, D.E., Hull, D.A.: Using lognormal distributions and lognormal probability plots in probabilistic risk assessments. Hum. Ecol. Risk Assess. **3**(2), 235–255 (1997)
10. Ruder, S.: An overview of gradient descent optimization algorithms. arXiv preprint: arXiv: 1609.04747 (2016)
11. van Casteren, J.F., Bollen, M.H., Schmieg, M.E.: Reliability assessment in electrical power systems: the Weibull-Markov stochastic model. IEEE Trans. Ind. Appl. **36**(3), 911–915 (2000)

Electronics and Communications

A Load Balancing Mechanism for 3D Network-on-Chip with Partially Vertically Connected Links

Shiva Majidzadeh[✉]

NOVA School of Science and Technology, UNINOVA-CTS and LASI, NOVA University
Lisbon, 2829-516 Caparica, Portugal
s.majidzadeh@campus.fct.unl.pt

Abstract. 3D integrated circuit was presented as a new solution to enhance the efficiency and expand the capabilities of modern integrated circuit as well. Studies have shown that in comparison with 2D NoCs, the proposed 3D NoC offers a lower power consumption, shorter delay and high performance due to the reduction of the connection length in 3D NoCs. In this article, we present a routing algorithm for heterogeneous 3D NoC which distributes the chip traffic in the whole network based on the global congestion information. This is achieved by finding the least congested minimal path between the communicating nodes. For vertical connections, we consider the Through-Silicon-Vias (TSV) and to avoid deadlock, we use two virtual channels. The results show that the proposed mechanism is superior in comparison with the Elevator-First algorithm in the similar working condition.

Keywords: 3D integration · Vertical Channels · Load-balancing · Latency · Thermal Distribution

1 Introduction

Due to power performance advantages of 3D technologies, they have been considered as a feasible solution by industry. 3D integration technology can be established with multiple silicon layers that are stacked and used TSVs [1, 2] as a vertical connection. 3D integrations can cause bandwidth widening and die area reduction by shortening the length of the connections on the chip [3–6]. Vertical links in 3D Networks-on-Chips (3D NoCs) are the shortest ones in the network which reduce both the latency and power consumption. However, the disadvantages of vertical links using TSVs are their expensive manufacturing process and low yield [7]. So, if we have a tradeoff between performance and reduction of the vertical links, we can decrease the total cost of 3D NoC and make it suitable for market [8].

So far, there are some articles about the load-balancing in 3D NoCs but only a few of them addressed the vertically partially connected networks. For routing, the local information was used where it does not reduce the possibility of dealing with congestion in the future. In this paper, we present the global load balanced (GLB) deadlock-free

L. M. Camarinha-Matos and F. Ferrada (Eds.): DoCEIS 2023, IFIP AICT 678, pp. 259–267, 2023.
https://doi.org/10.1007/978-3-031-36007-7_19

distributed routing algorithm in vertically partially connected 3D NoC equipped with an efficient load-balancing mechanism. This method checks the available load on all links and then selects the less congested path for sending the packet from its source.

One of the major issues in 3D NoCs is thermal distribution problem. The reason for this occurrence is high power density due to the stacking structure of 3D ICs. Although in 3D ICs, power consumption is less than of 2D ICs because of reduced length of connection, reduced chip area increases power density and affects operating frequency of the chip. These factors along with other factors such as cooling problem lead high temperature. In 3D architectures, power consumption rises with growing number of stacked layers; therefore, the possibilities of overheating increase. Thermal dissipation path from silicon layers to the surroundings is provided through convection method through heat sinks is located in the lowest surface [9–11].

This paper is organized as following. After discussing the related work in Sect. 2, in Sect. 3, we will present our global load-balancing technique in detail. The experiment setup and results will be described and analyzed in Sect. 4, and finally, in Sect. 5, we conclude the work.

2   Related Work

In [10] an oblivious routing algorithm has been presented, called Randomized Partially Minimal (RPM) which balances the network traffic in order to avoid the creation of hotspots in the network. RPM first sends packets randomly to one of layers then use XY and YX routing with equal probability. Finally, the packets will be sent to the final destination in Z dimension. RPM is not always a minimal routing and the number of hop count will be increased which can increase the latency, particularly in large networks.

To guarantee the minimal path with keeping the simplicity of routing, most of the 3D NoCs use the conventional Dimension Ordered Routing (DOR). [13] is an extended version of DOR for 3D networks known as Balanced Dimension Ordered Routing (BDOR). Considering the relative position of source and destination with one another, the BDOR routes the packets with one of the XY or YX methods to improve the balance of routes in networks.

In [14] the problem of TSVs large-scaled dimension in 3D NoC and the necessity of using a smaller number of TSVs to reduce the chip size have been studied. In the article, an adaptive routing algorithm is presented which distributes the traffic on the network by considering the limited bandwidth of vertical connections. In this method, they use an adaptive routing with non-minimal path which distributes the traffic locally due to the lack of global information related to the network congestion. To avoid the long path within each router a certain weight is assigned to all directions, so based on the traffic the priority of every direction can be calculated and then the routing can be done according to these priorities. In this algorithm, the input buffer space of neighboring nodes with the routers was used as the congestion status.

Elevator-First [15] is a deterministic distributed algorithm for partially vertically connected [16] was presented where the routing selection is taken locally. This algorithm is not only deadlock and livelock free but also independent of vertical link's location. This algorithm includes two states:

State 1: If source and destination nodes are in the same layer, the deterministic routing algorithm will be executed and packets will be assigned randomly to one of the virtual channels $Z+$ or $Z-$.

State 2: If source and destination nodes are in different layers, the deterministic algorithm is responsible for routing the packets to the nearest elevator. Once the destination is on upper/lower layer of the source, packets will be assigned to $Z+$ /$Z-$ virtual channels to be routed to the upper/lower layer.

3   Load-Balancing Algorithm

The proposed approach is based on the Elevator-First algorithm but the routing is done adaptively and has a complete view of the congestion status of the whole network following two conditions:

- Minimal path.
- Less congested path.

In the proposed algorithm, Global Load Balance (GLB), each node calculates the number of packets traverses through output ports. Every time packets sent out from the related link, the rate of sending to that link should be added based on the rate of passing flit, so each router can record the sending rate of its output ports. If we assume the mesh network as a graph, the sending rate of each link, will be considered as the weight of each edge in the graph. So, the packets are always sent though the lower weight to keep the network balanced.

We used Dijkstra algorithm [17] for finding shortest path. Dijkstra picks the path with less congested value within the all minimal paths. This method can be used for all the destinations. In addition, since the decision is carried out in parallel with the routine activities in the network, we can ignore the algorithm overhead and hardware overhead as explained in Sect. 4.

Deadlock in the network causes system stopping due to a cyclic dependency for resources. [18] proposed a method preventing a cyclic waiting of buffer in routers and proved that the turn model is deadlock-free based on Channel Dependency Graph (CDG) [16]. CDG shows whether a network is deadlock-free or not. For providing a deadlock-free routing algorithm, channel dependency graph should contain no cycle in a network.

We analyze our algorithm based on Elevator-First algorithm for deadlock-free and consider two virtual channels per physical link in x dimension. Additionally, in y and z dimension, if the packet is sent to the ascending/descending links, the assigned virtual channel will be called $Z+$ /$Z-$ that is fully independent of $Z-$/$Z+$ and in x dimension can choose $Z+$ or $Z-$. Selection of virtual channel is done statically on the source router. Thus, its allocation never changes during routing. The proof is similar to [15, 18]. Accordingly, a cyclic dependency of input buffer usage is broken.

The GLB router microarchitecture has been shown in Fig. 1. The below components are added to a baseline adaptive router [19] in order to obtain the proper route path between two nodes which are:

1. **Traffic Map**: This can store the congestion information of the entire network links and is being updated in the traffic map router of the requester after the ACK transmitted

by router and credit receives. It keeps just the information from every hop. However, in some cases like that the source and destination are on the same layer, there is no need for traffic storage and information updates of the nodes of other layers.

2. **Local Traffic Values**: It will store the congestion rate of output links of the source router in all directions.

3. **Route Computation**: The stored values in the traffic map will be transferred to this part in order to calculate and find the most proper output port of each router. When the route computation algorithm is being executed, it will estimate the cost of the route to reach one node and will choose the best route.

4. **Best output port table**: The result from the route computation stored in this section.

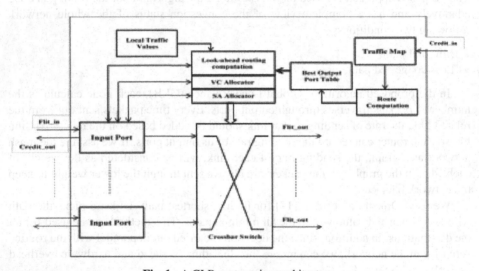

Fig. 1. A GLB router microarchitecture.

In order to find the minimum route, number of hops between source and destination is being determined and then updating process of traffic map and route computation is being done in a way that the hops between the source and destination are minimum. As an example, shown in Fig. 2, node 1 is supposed to transmit data to node 8 and the minimum distance between source and destination nodes is 3 hops, then the updating process for traffic map for node 1 is three steps.

At first, node 1 will calculate the output ports traffic in all directions and puts them in the local traffic values, then calculates the all minimal adaptive routing for one node in 2 hops from the source. It means that the source node can use nodes 3, 5 and 7 to reach the destination. And as a result, the traffic map of node 1 is being updated and then the route computation is conducting the minimum traffic to find the shortest route in the network in a way that the traffic from node 1 to 5 contains:

$Path1 - 2 - 5 : 2/E + 1 = 3/E$ and $Path1 - 4 - 5 : 3/S + 2 = 5/S$.

And the traffic rate from node 1 to 3 contains:

$Path1 - 0 - 3 : 1/W + 3 = 4/W$ and $Path1 - 4 - 3 : 3/S + 2 = 5/S$.

Therefore, route $1 - 2 - 5$, $1 - 0 - 3$ and $1 - 4 - 7$ are placed in the best output port table and in the next step calculations for the nodes in 3 hops from source node are being calculated and the traffic map is being updated. Node 6 is not transferred to the route computation since it is not a destination node. So, the source node can use node 5 or 7 to reach the destination. As a result, the computation is being done in the route computation and since traffic rate from node 5 to 8 is equal to $3/E + 4 = 7/E$ and from node 7 to 8 is $3/S + 1 = 4/S$, therefore, the route of $1 - 4 - 7 - 8$ being selected and placed in the best output port table.

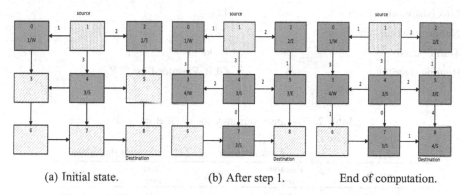

(a) Initial state.	(b) After step 1.	End of computation.

Fig. 2. An illustration of the GLB router technique for a 3x3 2-D mesh.

The congestion information of each link needs five bits to store in a router, in which two bits for free buffers and three bits for the directions of links. Since our link is 128 bits then the flit size is 128 as well. If we consider the size of network $8 \times 8 \times 4$, in order to store congestion values in a 7-port router, we will need maximum three buffers (12 flits). With regards to the routers with 5 and 6-ports, less buffer space is needed to store link congestion and directions information due to the reduction in the number of links (In 5-ports router, 2 bits are enough to store the directions) for this reason, they have less area overhead and power consumption.

4 Experimental Results

For the evaluation of the proposed algorithm in 3D NoC, the simulation tool of Access-Noxim [20] is used. We consider XYZ and Elevator-First [15] as baseline algorithms in our simulation comparisons, 10% of the vertical links are removed randomly in both synthetic and realistic traffic profiles also design parameters are shown in Table 1.

4.1 Performance Evaluation

The results of reduced latency and increased throughput in mesh topologies with different sizes are presented in Table 2, showing that the GLB latency has been reduced considerably before the saturation point, compared to the other two approaches.

Table 1. Design parameters.

Subject	Description
Topology	3D mesh
Switching mechanism	Wormhole
Packet size(flit)	8
Buffer length (flit)	4
Flit length (bit)	128
Link bandwidth (Gbps)	128
Number of virtual channels	2
Traffic pattern	Random
Routing algorithm	GLB, Elevator-First, XYZ

Table 2. The improvement value of GLB method.

mesh	Average latency		Average throughput	
	Elevator-First	XYZ	Elevator-First	XYZ
4x4x4	34%	7%	12%	-
8x8x2	42%	15%	14%	2%
8x8x4	46%	19%	30%	3.8%

4.2 Thermal Model

Top layers are farther from heat sink in 3D NoC, so thermal conductivity path lengthens and processing elements in these layers have more heating potential than bottom layers that generate new thermal hotspots, amplify available thermal hotspots and make thermal variation in different parts of the chip [21, 22].

The experiments are on an $8 \times 8 \times 4$ with 64 tiles in each layer and the tile model is from 80-core NoC system and the ambient temperature is set to 45 °C.

In Fig. 3, the packet injection rate is set in this traffic pattern to 0.05. The thermal map shows that Elevator-First algorithm has the imbalance thermal state under random traffic pattern and each layer has different thermal characteristics with respect its distance of heat sink. The bottom layer, which is close to the heat sink, has the lowest temperature while the top layer is at the highest temperature due to the high-power density. Unbalanced traffic makes thermal hotspots in middle tiles that distribute from high to low of top layer to bottom layer and corner tiles are at a lower temperature than the middle tiles because the corner traffic is less congested under the random traffic. Using GLB algorithm leads routers to use cooler path to route the packets and reduces the peak chip temperature about 4 °C and omit thermal hotspots of middle tiles and moderate thermal distributing on each layer.

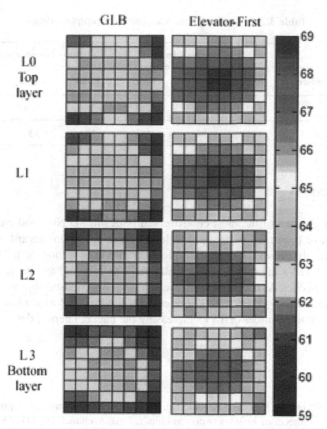

Fig. 3. Steady state temperature distribution in Random traffic patterns of 3D NoC.

4.3 Area and Power Evaluation

We use DSENT (Design Space Exploration of Networks Tool) [23] to estimate the area overhead and power consumption. DSENT is an architecture-level modeling tool designed for rapid design space exploration of both electronical and emerging opto-electrical NoC. We use 45nm SOI technology for baseline and GLB routers that its electrical parameters and network configuration. We also consider two virtual channels for baseline adaptive routers in estimation. The GLB router microarchitecture comprises some additional hardware components: congestion information, route computation module, and best output port table. Compared to the baseline adaptive router, additional hardware components need extra storage to store corresponding information. The layout area and power consumption of each platform are shown in Table 3. The GLB router imposes 4% area overhead and 2% power consumption compared to baseline adaptive routers.

Table 3. The area overhead and power consumption details.

Network platforms	Area Overhead(mm²)			Power Consumption (W)		
	5 port	6 port	7 port	5 port	6 port	7 port
Baseline adaptive routers	4.30	5.04	5.80	3.46	3.79	4.11
GLB routers	4.51	5.26	6.03	3.54	3.87	4.19

5 Conclusions

So far, routing is one of the most controversial issues in 3D NoC and currently many algorithms have presented in the field of load balancing. In this regard, we presented a new routing algorithm for exploiting global traffic information on a 3D chips with partially filled TSVs in order to dynamically pick the minimal and the least congested path for every packet. As the simulation result shows, our proposed algorithm reduces the packet average latency considerably in comparison with XYZ algorithm. Considering the reduction in the number of TSVs increasing the packet latency, the improvement is sizable.

References

1. Xu, T.C., Schley, G., Liljeberg, P., Radetzki, M., Plosila, J., Tenhunen, H.: Optimal placement of vertical connections in 3D network-on-chip. J. Syst. Architect. **59**, 441–454 (2013)
2. Tanaka, N., et al.: Through-silicon via interconnection for 3D integration using room-temperature bonding. IEEE Trans. Adv. Packag. **32**, 746–753 (2009)
3. Pavlidis, V.F., Friedman, E.G.: Three-Dimensional Integrated Circuit Design. Morgan Kaufmann, Burlington, MA (2009)
4. Rahmani, A.-M., Vaddina, K.R., Liljeberg, P., Plosila, J., Tenhunen, H.: Power and area optimization of 3D networks-on-chip using smart and efficient vertical channels. Integrated circuit and system design. In: Power and Timing Modeling, Optimization, and Simulation, pp. 278–287. Springer, Heidelberg (2011). https://doi.org/10.1007/978-3-642-11802-9
5. Liljeberg, P., Plosila, J., Tenhunen, H., Feero, B.S., Pande, P.P.: Networks-on-chip in a three-dimensional environment: a performance evaluation, IEEE Transactions on Computers, 2009, Integrated Circuit and System Design. Power and Timing Modeling, Optimization, and Simulation, pp. 278–287 (2011)
6. Pavlidis, V., Friedman, E.: 3-D topologies for networks-on-chip. In: 2006 IEEE International SOC Conference (2006)
7. Velenis, D., Stucchi, M., Marinissen, E.J., Swinnen, B., Beyne, E.: Impact of 3D design choices on manufacturing cost. In: 2009 IEEE International Conference on 3D System Integration (2009)
8. Shang, L., Peh, L., Kumar, A., Jha, N.K.: Thermal modeling, characterization and management of on-chip networks. In: 37th International Symposium on Microarchitecture (MICRO-37'04)
9. Zhu, C., Gu, Z., Shang, L., Dick, R.P., Joseph, R.: Three-dimensional chip-multiprocessor run-time thermal management. IEEE Trans. Comput.-Aid. Design Integr. Circ. Syst. **27**, 1479–1492 (2008)

10. Ebrahimi, M., Daneshtalab, M.: Learning-based routing algorithms for on-chip networks. In: Palesi, M., Daneshtalab, M. (eds.) Routing Algorithms in Networks-on-Chip. Springer, New York, pp. 105–125 (2014). https://doi.org/10.1007/978-1-4614-8274-1_5

11. Ramanujam, R.S., Lin, B.: Near-optimal oblivious routing on three-dimensional mesh networks. In: 2008 IEEE International Conference on Computer Design. (2008)

12. Tyagi, S .: Extended balanced dimension ordered routing algorithm for 3D-networks. In: India International Conference on Parallel processing Workshops, pp. 499–506. Centre for Development of Advance Computing, Noida, (U.P.) (2009)

13. Zhu, M., Lee, J., Choi, K.: An adaptive routing algorithm for 3D mesh NOC with limited vertical bandwidth. In: 2012 IEEE/IFIP 20th International Conference on VLSI and System-on-Chip (VLSI-SoC). (2012)

14. Dubois, F., Sheibanyrad, A., Petrot, F., Bahmani, M.: Elevator-first: A deadlock-free distributed routing algorithm for vertically partially connected 3D-nocs. IEEE Trans. Comput. **62**, 609–615 (2013)

15. Dally, S.: Deadlock-free message routing in multiprocessor interconnection networks. IEEE Trans. Comput. **C-36**, 547–553 (1987)

16. Rosen, K.H.: Discrete Mathematics and Its Applications. Braille Jymico Inc., Charlesbourg (1993)

17. Glass, C.J., Ni, L.M.: The turn model for adaptive routing. In: Proceedings the 19th Annual International Symposium on Computer Architecture (1992)

18. Kim, J., Park, D., Theocharides, T., Vijaykrishnan, N., Das, C.R.: A low latency router supporting adaptivity for on-chip interconnects. In: Proceedings of 42nd Design Automation Conference, 2005 (2005)

19. Jheng, K.Y., Chao, C.H., Wang, H.Y., Wu, A.Y.: Traffic-thermal mutual-coupling co-simulation platform for three-dimensional network-on-chip. In: Proceedings of 2010 International Symposium on VLSI Design, Automation and Test (2010)

20. Puttaswamy, K., Loh, G.H.: Thermal herding: Microarchitecture techniques for controlling hotspots in high-performance 3D-integrated processors. In: 2007 IEEE 13th International Symposium on High Performance Computer Architecture (2007)

21. Link, G.M., Vijaykrishnan, N.: Hotspot prevention through runtime reconfiguration in Network-on-chip. In: Proceedings of the conference on Design, Automation and Test in Europe (2005)

22. Sun, C., et al.: DSENT - a tool connecting emerging photonics with electronics for opto-electronic networks-on-chip modeling. In: 2012 IEEE/ACM Sixth International Symposium on Networks-on-Chip (2012)

Enhancing Dynamism of IoT Service Composition

Ruben Gomes[✉] [iD] and Noélia Correia[iD]

Center for Electronics, Optoelectronics, and Telecommunications (CEOT), University of
Algarve, Faro, Portugal
`{rdgomes,ncorreia}@ualg.pt`

Abstract. As IoT systems become more complex and interconnected, their ability to adapt to changes becomes essential. However, this dynamism needs to be addressed from early on and at different levels. Failure to recognize this will hinder the resulting system's flexibility. This article presents an analysis of composition approaches and technologies based on several criteria, in an attempt to identify common patterns or constructs that enhance specific dynamic traits which should be considered during development. Then, the identified elements within those criteria's methods and tools are mapped against the desired dynamic traits. By using cross classification, it is possible to recognize the most adequate alignment of dynamic traits among approaches. A comparative analysis is produced containing our findings. These outcomes are expected to contribute to the research community in developing more flexible distributed dynamic systems.

Keywords: Internet of Things · IoT Service Development · IoT Dynamic Composition

1 Introduction

With the number of internet of things (IoT) connections expected to reach close to 25 billion by 2025 [1], there is a unique opportunity to find ways to interconnect services and generate innovative solutions that bring value to businesses and users alike. Additionally, composing services into more abstract services is necessary for global systems to be able to manage the growing complexity.

By being a ubiquitous network of heterogeneous and pervasive devices, the IoT is capable of generating extensive information about the physical world [2], capturing a massive amount of data through embedded sensors in everyday objects, also known as things, and interacting with the environment via actuators. This enables the development of applications that interconnect physical and virtual things.

IoT areas of application include industrial, healthcare, retail, smart grid (energy), smart cities (public utilities and traffic management), agriculture, home automation, and potentially others still to be discovered. Typically, data that is collected by sensors in IoT applications is unstructured, and large in volume. This makes IoT an ideal candidate for

L. M. Camarinha-Matos and F. Ferrada (Eds.): DoCEIS 2023, IFIP AICT 678, pp. 268–278, 2023.
https://doi.org/10.1007/978-3-031-36007-7_20

taking advantage of big data tools and techniques for storage, processing, and analytics. The web of things (WoT) will be an added value in this context as it aims to work against IoT fragmentation through the use of web technologies. This layer abstracts and hides both the complexity and heterogeneity of the lower-level device specifications [3], enabling the integration across IoT platforms and application domains.

The present article aims to advance the understanding of how the dynamic composition of services in the IoT can be attained at different levels of the systems' composition process in order to maximize the flexibility of the final solution. By considering dynamic aspects at an early stage of design, the problem of restricting the dynamic potential of the following composition levels can be mitigated. It is worth noting that service components will benefit from WoT Security and Privacy Guidelines, stated in [4]. These recommendations are independent of architectural perspectives, so that the behavior of systems is not constrained, and can be applied to any operating service composition.

This work is guided by the following research question:

RQ. Which constructs and specific characteristics in currently available IoT composition approaches, used at different levels of system development, enable dynamic traits in those compositions? How can these be aligned in order to best ensure a flexible solution?

This awareness and comparative analysis between counterpart approaches provides guidance for the development of dynamic distributed IoT systems by the research community.

The remainder of this paper is organized as follows. Section 2 relates this research to the theme of connected cyber physical spaces. In Sect. 3 the taxonomy and techniques of service composition are examined, while Sect. 4 introduces the concept of dynamic composition and its key features, along with the mapping and discussion of composition approaches versus constructs. Finally, the conclusions and future work are detailed in Sect. 5.

2 Contribution to Connected Cyber Physical Spaces

Cyber physical systems (CPSs) integrate both virtual objects and physical devices, focusing on the efficient monitoring and controlling of the latter. The physical connection from digital processes to the factories' production processes is achieved through sensors and actuators.

While a CPS has a local focus, IoT introduces a wider approach at the networking level, allowing for the interconnection of many and varied CPS systems. This interconnection brings an enormous potential for composing applications in order to provide innovative services. However, it also introduces the challenge of providing reliable service interaction independently of the underlying technologies. In cyber physical spaces, where there is an interconnected environment composed of CPSs, which can be spread across different ownership domains [5], this challenge is even greater.

This work aims to understand the composition approaches and constructs that may impact on the overall dynamic composition, in order to improve the alignment between the system's software design aspects like interfaces specification, maintainability, or modularity, with such dynamic composition constructs. Such alignment facilitates the process of instantiating a system's conceptual behavior specification (e.g., finite state machine (FSM)), into the concrete physical execution plan implemented by specific service operations (e.g., application code). Furthermore, it enables the dynamic modeling of interactions at execution time.

According to [5], among the main requirements of a cyber physical space is adaptability. This characteristic is dependent on the dynamic capability of the systems that compose that space, and thus stands to gain from an alignment between software development processes and dynamic composition constructs. This alignment is particularly relevant in environments where different systems, with particular processing, storage, and communication capabilities, interact with production processes, as such alignment can help to streamline processes and make them more agile.

3 IoT Service Composition Taxonomy

Over the years, various forms of classification have been used to organize approaches and technologies linked to the composition of services.

3.1 Function Criteria

One point of view is that service composition may be classified according to functional and non-functional aspects [6].

Functional. Focused on validating a system's model against a specification, these approaches use formal-based techniques like model checking that evaluate composition factors such as correctness, reachability, deadlock, safety, and liveness. An example of a model checking technique is an FSM. In an FSM, the system is abstracted into a set of states and transitions between them. Distributed applications can be composed by assembling a chain of valid state transitions among services, thus representing the application's behavior. By being a state-based model, FSM approaches can easily be applied to model the behavior of representational state transfer (REST)-based web services. This is because in REST, any endpoint can be observed for some state evaluation, and subsequent action to be taken. Hierarchical finite state machines (HFSMs) are an extension of FSMs which add depth (superstates), orthogonality (concurrency), and broadcast communication [7].

Non-functional. Cover approaches that are based on quality metrics of the composite services, usually regarding IP-based network protocols, infrastructure, and applications. According to [8], there is a broad consensus on the definition of functional requirements, which refers to what a system must do to perform its function, and what inputs and outputs it can work with. On the other hand, while there are several definitions for non-functional requirements, there is not yet a thorough list that defines them. So, the definition by negation emerges, meaning non-functional requirements are mainly those that are not concerned with the functionality of a system. Other works, such as [9], take a more definite approach by simply defining non-functional attributes as those that relate to a web service (WS)' properties (what it is), instead of its function (what is does). These non-functional aspects define restrictions or properties that must be taken into account when developing the system, such as performance, reliability, appearance, failure and recovery, and other quality of service (QoS) metrics. The QoS-driven service composition is an example of a non-functional approach [10].

3.2 Conception Criteria

IoT service composition can also be classified in terms of the approaches used to build service composition structures. According to [11, 12], these can be framework, agent, heuristic, and service-oriented architecture (SOA)/REST-based.

Framework-Based. Grounded in a collection of assumptions, values, concepts, and practices that form a domain, which is used for organizing, searching, selecting, and composing IoT services in innovative ways [12]. Semantics-based and Rule-based approaches are examples of framework-based composition methods [13].

Agent-Based. Each service is a software component capable of autonomous decision-making and communication. In this approach, agents can have capabilities for discovering other services, composing, binding, executing, and monitoring. A downside, however, is that agent-based architectures present reliability and security issues [12].

Heuristic-Based. For discrete or combinatorial optimization problems such as service composition, doing an exhaustive search for the optimal perfect solution is not possible due to computational limitations and exponential time requirements. As an alternative to finding sufficiently good solutions, heuristics-based (problem-specific) and meta-heuristics (problem-independent) methods can be used [14]. The most commonly used algorithms for service composition, which typically have been inspired by natural phenomena, are ant colony optimization, greedy algorithms, genetic algorithms, and particle swarm optimization [15, 16].

SOA and REST-Based. Discovery and composition are strongly facilitated by SOA and REST-based architecting. On one hand SOA exposes the functionality of services via descriptive interfaces using simple object access protocol (SOAP) and web services description language (WSDL) and allows the integration of heterogeneous devices seamlessly. On the other hand, REST describes the guiding architectural principles of the interactions among those services or other resources, in a highly scalable and flexible way [17].

3.3 Coordination Criteria

The rapid growth in the number of IoT services means that compositions also grow in quantity and complexity. This places a concern in the scalability and control capacity of the composition approaches used. According to these criteria, methods can be separated into data flow, orchestration, and choreography [18].

Data Flow. Currently is the most popular mechanism, especially since the emergence of mashup applications. In a data flow, the workflow is defined implicitly by the data processing tasks that occur at each node and trigger the next step with the output of transformed data [19]. Workflow operations are data-focused such as filtering, splitting, sorting, or merging operations [20]. This method provides separation between data and control, allowing service developers to focus on data operations, while system developers work on connecting the nodes [21]. Node-RED and IBM's COMPOSE are two examples of data flow design tools.

Orchestration. The control flow of service invocations is explicitly and externally defined by one or more coordinator nodes, also known as orchestrators. This means that the workflow can be defined independently of the implementation details of the services used. Data are moved around as a consequence of this control flow and is not a driver of the flow.

Orchestration can be either centralized, under total command of a coordinator node, or be decentralized, where control is divided collaboratively among several coordinator nodes, according to control flow operators including sequence, branch, parallel, and loop [22].

Languages such as business process execution language (BPEL) originally developed by IBM and Microsoft and maintained by Oasis Open [23], or business process model and notation (BPMN) [24] initially published by the business process management initiative (BPMI) and maintained by the object management group (OMG), can be used to define orchestration workflows between services.

Since services have no information about the control flow, only the coordinator does, a separation is obtained between node computation and flow control. However, the centralized flow of all data going through the coordinator node can easily become a bottleneck in the system [25]. Another downside of orchestration in an IoT environment is that its workflows are based on synchronous invocations of other services, which may make this approach less suitable for designing flexible applications where loose-coupling is a guiding principle.

Camunda BPMN engine, AWS Step Functions and Kubernetes are examples of orchestration development platforms.

Choreography. Can describe the obligations and constraints of the interactions between two or more components, where each can be in separate responsibility domains [26]. In comparison with orchestration, this method gives more control flow autonomy to the services in the system.

The flow logic is not under the control of any external entity. Instead, it works with a public protocol that governs the messaging interactions, i.e., the global behavior, among services in a system where each node is self-contained and self-controlled [27, 28]. The distributed nature of the microservices' architectural style is well aligned with choreography [29]. Each microservice, or component in a choreographed application, is a self-contained building block of software, developed and maintained in isolation, that is scalable and language-agnostic. Microservices also take advantage of containerization, also known as servitization, as a form of lightweight virtualization.

Choreography enables application scaling and cohesiveness due to keeping the control logic in the execution nodes and out of the middleware links. Since data usually follows control, and control is distributed, this approach prevents data bottlenecks and makes choreography the most suitable approach for distributed workflows such as microservices [30]. Furthermore, IoT architecture is aligned with the distributed control flow of the choreography mechanism. By using message broadcasting and pattern matching, choreographed systems can communicate via events while keeping location independence among the nodes. The distributed nature of choreography composition can also, however, represent a downside as the application flow logic is implicit and divided among services without a centralized point of control, thus making it more difficult to understand and maintain the application [24].

Message exchanges defined in the protocol, which can be either the direct calling of REST application programming interfaces (APIs) or the sending of events, can be modeled using languages such as WS-CDL [31], BPEL4Chor [32], and BPMN [24]. Apache Kafka is an example of a software that works as a message bus, the public protocol, where services can subscribe channels and publish events. Other examples of composition platforms for choreographing IoT services include CHOReVOLUTION [33] and ChorSystem [34].

4 Dynamic Compositional Traits

In this section, several composition approaches and technologies are analyzed according to their composition dynamism, and the constructs that enable dynamic composition in these approaches are highlighted and compared.

4.1 Key Features

According to [35], dynamic composition is the process of searching and selecting concrete services to create additional composite services on demand at runtime. The dynamic composition of services has several advantages, such as responding to user requests by composing custom applications on-demand, being able to provide new services based on combinations of existing services, avoiding the need to maintain a catalog of available services in the system, and improving fault-tolerance [36, 37]. Additionally, upgrading and extending a service's functionality can be performed during runtime, enabling the service to adapt to changing conditions in the environment. This means that the following aspects can impact the success of a dynamic composition:

Scope. The range of applicability the composition covers.

Encapsulation. How wrapped up and independent are components in the composition.

Scalability/Adaptability. How well does the composition manage complexity and how does it adapt to a change in workload or environment conditions.

Interoperability. How do components in the composite service interact with each other and what is the degree of decoupling.

Observability/Maintainability. How easy it is to understand the composition structure and behavior, monitor the system and make changes to the original design.

Table 1 shows our mapping of these traits for different composition approaches, highlighting the constructs that enable their dynamism.

5 Discussion and Implications

The ongoing research around service composition in IoT focuses mainly on the data/outcome generated by things, i.e., it is data-focused. This results from having thing descriptions announcing how consumers can interact with things, and such information being used for the selection or rejection of things during the service composition process. Then, different coordination styles can be used depending on the required flow control level; either more directed in orchestration or less directed in choreography. Currently, performance optimization is accomplished through a suitable allocation of services to hosts, for achieving an adequate use of resources and the reduction of communication delay. Edge/Fog technologies are now available to tackle many of these concerns, holding the potential for more focused and efficient data processing, and consequently lower power consumption.

However, an ultimate optimization of IoT applications can only be achieved when the services themselves are able to adapt to dynamic environments and exceptional situations. In this case, each service in the composition must be aware of the behavior of its component sub-services. This is particularly relevant in IoT/WoT where resources are constrained and contingency plans for exceptional situations are a must. For instance, a service or thing may need to change how or where it fetches data from, if the current source (service/device) announces a low battery level. This does not happen in the traditional web, where resources are abundant and exceptional situations are less attached to the physical world. In short, behavioral and data-focused service composition types can be identified. Both can be used in parts of an IoT application, but these benefit from different dynamic traits.

Please note that some composition approaches share a common set of traits that make their comparison easier, while others, like the functional approach, are an umbrella term that covers substantially different approaches. This realization caused the following analysis to select the HFSM approach in particular as an example of a functional approach, since its focus on state seems useful for representing behavioral composition.

From analyzing Table 1, one can state that the REST architectural principles are more flexible, lightweight, and more aligned with the observe-evaluate-actuate pattern of IoT when compared to SOA. W3C WoT standardization is also moving towards REST. Based on this, the REST architectural style is preferable over SOA for any kind of service composition in IoT/WoT.

In general, the successful development of a dynamic IoT service composition depends on finding an equilibrium between generalization and specialization.

Applications that are less specialized exhibit more dynamic traits and consequently are more flexible and reusable in different scenarios than the ones they were initially designed for. On the other hand, more specialization means less adaptability, but a stricter following of the design rules and constraints, which is useful for mission-critical systems. Reusability is tied to the concept of encapsulation, which according to Table 1 varies considerably among approaches. While HFSM encapsulates the states' information under a superstate, agent-based and other approaches do so for control logic and data. As for the data flow approach, the nodes encapsulate data transformation rules, which is different from control logic, since the flow depends on the inputs and outputs of nodes, and not on a preset sequence of node executions. In data flow, any node can execute a data transformation as long as it handles the output format of a previous node.

Some approaches emerge as the most flexible (i.e., more generalized), such as agent-based and choreography compositions. Both of these share common properties that allow

Table 1. Mapping of composition approaches (*rows*) to dynamic traits (*columns*) and the constructs that enable them.[1]

	Scope	Encapsulation	Scalability/Adaptability	Interoperability	Observability/Maintainability
HFSM (Functional)	Any	Superstate encapsulates states	Parallel execution (concurrency) Hierarchy hides complexity Generalized transitions between superstates hide implementation	Synchronous generalized transitions	Explicit model (system states)
Non-Functional	Any	N/A	Scalability can be used as QoS metric for composition	N/A	Explicit model (QoS metrics)
Framework-based	Knowledge domain	N/A	Conceptual model abstracts implementation details	N/A	Explicit model (concepts)
Agent-based	Any	Agent encapsulates data and control logic	Loosely-coupled agents	Asynchronous broadcast message between agents	Implicit model (agents' interaction)
Heuristic-based	Any	N/A	Efficient algorithms allow complex compositions with less resources	N/A	Explicit model (algorithms)
SOA-based	Enterprise application	Self-contained services	Loosely-coupled services	Synchronous request-response	Explicit model (services)
REST-based	Distributed application	Self-contained resources	Uniform interfaces Resource caching Stateless server Loosely-coupled services	Synchronous request-response	Explicit model (resources)
Data flow	Distributed application	Modules encapsulate data transformations	Independent data transformations allow workflow partitioning	Synchronous messaging	Explicit model (data transformations)
Orchestration	Distributed application	Self-contained services	Central control increases coupling Limited by orchestrator resources	Synchronous messaging	Explicit model (coordination)
Choreography	Distributed application	Self-contained services	Distributed control decreases coupling Limited by interactions' complexity	Asynchronous messaging	Implicit model (coordination)

their components to be decoupled in control and data (implicit model and self-contained entities), and also in time (asynchronous communication). It should be noted that by using an implicit model, these approaches are harder to trace and to understand when debugging or making changes. On the other hand, there are approaches that can remain dynamic while using an explicit model. This is the case for HFSM with its superstates and generalized transitions, and for SOA and REST with their decoupled interfaces.

---

[1] An N/A value means the attribute is not a concern of the approach.

A functional approach is more behavior-focused, and orchestration can be as well since control is an important concern. On the other hand, the agent-based approach and choreography are more data-focused, along with other approaches like non-functional, SOA-based, REST-based, and data flow. Framework and heuristic-based approaches are general and applicable to any kind of service composition.

As previously stated, an ultimate optimization of IoT application can only be achieved when the services themselves are able to adapt to dynamic environments and exceptional situations. As web applications are ever more integrated with physical systems, behavioral service composition seems to have a key role, as a first composition layer in some web application component (more tied to the physical world). However, any behavioral service composition requires a validation step. This means that particularly in mission-critical IoT environments, additional validation steps should be applied to these behavior-focused compositions, according to concrete physical systems guidelines and constraints.

6 Conclusions and Future Work

In this work a survey was conducted in order to understand the most appropriate set of dynamic approaches and tools for use in specific types of service composition. While it is expected that the main dynamic traits have been identified and analyzed, it cannot be ruled out that others may be relevant and could be considered in the future.

After having identified two types of service composition, i.e., behavior-focused, and data-focused, it becomes apparent that the former can be useful for enabling each entity in a composition to become dynamic itself. Such flexibility allows the service to adapt to changing conditions, which is particularly relevant in environments where IoT devices are prone to failures or unavailability, caused by constrained environments or limited device resources. Data-focused approaches, on the other hand, are suitable where behavior adaptation is not needed. These approaches are expected to be useful for validating the robustness of composite services created with behavior-focused approaches and are an area where further research is needed. These context specific validation steps would, crucially, need to be kept as add-ons that are external to the service, in order to protect its congruence and ensure its compatibility and reusability by other potential applications.

Acknowledgements. This research was funded by Fundação para a Ciência e Tecnologia (FCT) through CEOT's (Center for Electronics, Optoelectronics, and Telecommunications) UIDB/00631/2020 CEOT BASE and UIDP/00631/2020 CEOT PROGRAMÁTICO projects, and the grant UI/BD/152864/2022.

References

1. GSMA: IoT connections forecast: The rise of enterprise. https://gsma.com/iot/resources/iot-connections-forecast-the-rise-of-enterprise/
2. Nitti, M., Atzori, L., Cvijikj, I.P.: Friendship selection in the social Internet of Things: challenges and possible strategies. IEEE Internet Things J. 2(3), 240–247 (Jun2015). https://doi.org/10.1109/JIOT.2014.2384734

3. Angulo, P., Guzmán, C.C., Jiménez, G., Romero, D.: A service-oriented architecture and its ICT-infrastructure to support eco-efficiency performance monitoring in manufacturing enterprises. Int. J. Comput. Integr. Manuf. **30**(1), 202–214 (2017). https://doi.org/10.1080/0951192X.2016.1145810

4. Web of Things (WoT) Security and Privacy Guidelines, https://www.w3.org/TR/wot-security/

5. Torres, C.E.: Cyber-Physical Spaces (December 2018). https://power-mi.com/content/cyber-physical-spaces

6. Asghari, P., Rahmani, A.M., Javadi, H.H.S.: Service composition approaches in IoT: a systematic review. J. Netw. Comput. Appl. **120**, 61–77 (2018). https://doi.org/10.1016/j.jnca.2018.07.013

7. Harel, D.: Statecharts: a visual formalism for complex systems. Sci. Comput. Program. **8**(3), 231–274 (1987). https://doi.org/10.1016/0167-6423(87)90035-9

8. Glinz, M.: On non-functional requirements. In: 15th IEEE International Requirements Engineering Conference (RE 2007), pp. 21–26 (October 2007). https://doi.org/10.1109/RE.2007.45

9. Vesyropoulos, N., Georgiadis, C.K., Ilioudis, C.: Analyzing the selection and dynamic composition of web services in e-commerce transactions. In: Proceedings of the Fifth Balkan Conference in Informatics. pp. 130–135. BCI'12, Association for Computing Machinery, New York, NY, USA (September 2012). https://doi.org/10.1145/2371316.2371341

10. Ma, H., Bastani, F., Yen, I.L., Mei, H.: QoS-driven service composition with reconfigurable services. IEEE Trans. Serv. Comput. **6**(1), 20–34 (2013). https://doi.org/10.1109/TSC.2011.21

11. Hamzei, M., Navimipour, N.J.: Toward efficient service composition techniques in the Internet of Things. Internet of Things J. **5**(5), 3774–3787 (2018). https://doi.org/10.1109/JIOT.2018.2861742

12. Vakili, A., Navimipour, N.J.: Comprehensive and systematic review of the service composition mechanisms in the cloud environments. J. Netw. Comput. Appl. **81**, 24–36 (2017). https://doi.org/10.1016/j.jnca.2017.01.005

13. Yao, Y., Chen, H.: A rule-based web service composition approach. In: 2010 Sixth International Conference on Autonomic and Autonomous Systems, pp. 150–155 (March 2010). https://doi.org/10.1109/ICAS.2010.29

14. Eusuff, M., Lansey, K., Pasha, F.: Shuffled frog-leaping algorithm: a memetic meta-heuristic for discrete optimization. Eng. Optim. **38**(2), 129–154 (2006). https://doi.org/10.1080/03052150500384759

15. Lopez-Garcia, P., Onieva, E., Osaba, E., Masegosa, A.D., Perallos, A.: GACE: a meta-heuristic based in the hybridization of Genetic Algorithms and Cross Entropy methods for continuous optimization. Expert Syst. Appl. (Elsevier) **55**, 508–519 (2016). https://doi.org/10.1016/j.eswa.2016.02.034

16. Asghari, S., Navimipour, N.J.: Review and comparison of meta-heuristic algorithms for service composition in cloud computing. Majlesi J. Multim. Process. **44**(4) (2015)

17. Zhang, L., Yu, S., Ding, X., Wang, X.: Research on IoT RESTful web service asynchronous composition based on BPEL. In: 2014 Sixth International Conference on Intelligent Human-Machine Systems and Cybernetics. vol. 1, pp. 62–65 (August 2014). https://doi.org/10.1109/IHMSC.2014.23

18. Arellanes, D., Lau, K.K.: Algebraic service composition for user-centric IoT applications. In: Internet of Things - ICIOT 2018: Third International Conference. vol. 10972 LNCS, pp. 56–69. Springer, Cham (2018). https://doi.org/10.1007/978-3-319-94370-1_5

19. Morrison, J.P.: Flow-Based Programming: A New Approach to Application Development. CreateSpace (2010)

20. Johnston, W., Hanna, J., Millar, R.: Advances in dataflow programming languages. ACM Comput. Surv. **36**(1), 1–34 (2004). https://doi.org/10.1145/1013208.1013209

21. Giang, N., Blackstock, M., Lea, R., Leung, V.: Developing IoT applications in the Fog: a distributed dataflow approach. In: Proceedings - 2015 5th International Conference on the Internet of Things, IoT 2015. pp. 155–162 (2015). https://doi.org/10.1109/IOT.2015.7356560
22. Hens, P., Snoeck, M., Poels, G., De Backer, M.: Process fragmentation, distribution and execution using an event-based interaction scheme. J. Syst. Softw. **89**, 170–192 (2014). https://doi.org/10.1016/j.jss.2013.11.1111
23. Open, O.: Web Services Business Process Execution Language (WS-BPEL) version 2.0 (2007). http://docs.oasis-open.org/wsbpel/2.0/OS/wsbpel-v2.0-OS.html
24. Valderas, P., Torres, V., Pelechano, V.: A microservice composition approach based on the choreography of BPMN fragments. Inf. Softw. Technol. (Elsevier) **127**, 106370 (2020). https://doi.org/10.1016/j.infsof.2020.106370
25. Chafle, G., Chandra, S., Mann, V., Nanda, M.: Decentralized orchestration of composite web services. In: Proceedings of the 13th International World Wide Web Conference on Alternate Track, Papers and Posters, WWW Alt. 2004. pp. 134–143 (2004). https://doi.org/10.1145/1013367.1013390
26. Decker, G., Kopp, O., Barros, A.: An introduction to service choreographies. Inf. Technol. (De Gruyter) **50**(2), 122 (2008). https://doi.org/10.1524/itit.2008.0473
27. Cherrier, S., Langar, R.: Services organisation in IoT: mixing orchestration and choreography. In: 2018 Global Information Infrastructure and Networking Symposium (GIIS). pp. 1–4 (October 2018). https://doi.org/10.1109/GIIS.2018.8635748
28. Peltz, C.: Web services orchestration and choreography. IEEE Comput. J. **36**(10), 46–52 (2003). https://doi.org/10.1109/MC.2003.1236471
29. Butzin, B., Golatowski, F., Timmermann, D.: Microservices approach for the internet of things. In: 2016 IEEE 21st International Conference on Emerging Technologies and Factory Automation (ETFA). pp. 1–6 (September 2016). https://doi.org/10.1109/ETFA.2016.7733707
30. Newman, S.: Building Microservices, 1st edn. O'Reilly Media, Sebastopol (2015)
31. W3C: Web Services Choreography Description Language (WS-CDL) version 1.0 (2005). https://www.w3.org/TR/ws-cdl-10/
32. Decker, G., Kopp, O., Leymann, F., Weske, M.: BPEL4Chor: extending BPEL for modeling choreographies. In: IEEE International Conference on Web Services (ICWS 2007), pp. 296–303 (July 2007). https://doi.org/10.1109/ICWS.2007.59
33. Autili, M., Di Salle, A., Gallo, F., Pompilio, C., Tivoli, M.: CHOReVOLUTION: service choreography in practice. Sci. Comput. Program. (Elsevier) **197**, 102498 (2020). https://doi.org/10.1016/j.scico.2020.102498
34. Weiß, A., Andrikopoulos, V., Sáez, S.G., Hahn, M., Karastoyanova, D.: ChorSystem: a message-based system for the life cycle management of choreographies. In: Debruyne, C., et al. (eds.) On the Move to Meaningful Internet Systems: OTM 2016 Conferences, LNCS, pp. 503–521. Springer, Cham (2016). https://doi.org/10.1007/978-3-319-48472-330
35. Lemos, A.L., Daniel, F., Benatallah, B.: Web service composition: a survey of techniques and tools. ACM Comput. Surv. **48**(3), 33:1–33:41 (2015). https://doi.org/10.1145/2831270
36. Alamri, A., Eid, M., El Saddik, A.: Classification of the state-of-the-art dynamic web services composition techniques. Int. J. Web Grid Serv. (InderScience) **2**(2), 148–166 (2006)
37. Fujii, K., Suda, T.: Semantics-based dynamic service composition. J. Select. Areas Commun. **23**(12), 2361–2372 (2005). https://doi.org/10.1109/JSAC.2005.857202

Systematic Design Methodology for Optimization of Voltage Comparators in CMOS Technology

João Xavier[1,2]($\boxtimes$), Pedro Barquinha[2], and João Goes[1]

[1] Nova University of Lisbon, School of Science and Technology, UNINOVA – CTS and LASI, Lisbon, Caparica, Portugal
jpg.xavier@campus.fct.unl.pt, goes@fct.unl.pt
[2] I3N/CENIMAT, Department of Materials Science, NOVA School of Science and Technology, Lisbon, Caparica, Portugal
pmcb@fct.unl.pt

Abstract. The increasing rate of digitalization and the growing use of the Internet-of-Things translate into a rise in demand for sensor-to-digital interface circuits and electronics for processing information. This demand increases the need for a standard workflow, which allows a straightforward comparison between active building-blocks (both amplifiers and comparators) with different architectures. Although comparators are essential building-blocks in many circuit architectures, there is no standard workflow to simulate and compare different circuit topologies. This paper proposes a systematic design workflow to simulate dynamic voltage comparators. The workflow consists of the "testbenches" and a simulation setup for extracting key parameters of comparator performance, such as static-offset, random-offset, worst-case comparison-time for both hard and soft decisions, power dissipation, and input-referred noise. As an example, this paper implements the methodology in Virtuoso environment and presents results for different dynamic comparators in a 28-nm standard bulk-CMOS technology.

Keywords: Dynamic Comparators · Comparator Testbench · Simulation Workflow

1 Introduction

The increasing rate of digitalization and the growing use of the Internet-of-Things (IoT) have led to a significant increase in the demand for sensors and sensor-to-digital interfaces. IoT relies on a vast network of sensors that are capable of collecting data from various sources, communicating with each other and other systems. These sensors are used in a wide range of applications, such as environmental monitoring, smart homes, industrial automation, and healthcare. To process and make sense of the data collected by these sensors, sensor-to-digital interfaces are required. These interfaces convert the analog signals generated by the sensors into digital signals, that can be processed by

© IFIP International Federation for Information Processing 2023
Published by Springer Nature Switzerland AG 2023
L. M. Camarinha-Matos and F. Ferrada (Eds.): DoCEIS 2023, IFIP AICT 678, pp. 279–289, 2023.
https://doi.org/10.1007/978-3-031-36007-7_21

digital circuits and systems. This conversion process is crucial to ensure accurate and reliable data analysis. Voltage comparators, as a key building block of these interfaces, play a critical role in meeting these requirements. By accurately comparing two input voltages, voltage comparators enable the detection and conversion of analog signals to digital signals with high precision and speed [1, 2].

The performance of a voltage comparator, which is critical for the overall performance of the integrated circuit, is determined by the following design parameters: input offset, speed, power consumption, metastability, and input-referred electronic noise [3, 4]. These parameters are affected by various factors, including transistor size, process variations, and temperature changes. Therefore, designing and optimizing a voltage comparator requires a thorough understanding of its operation and performance characteristics [5].

This paper describes a characterization under simulation environment of dynamic comparators, focusing mainly on key parameters such as the offset and comparation time. The comparator's operation will be briefly explained in Sect. 3, as well as the influence of its key parameters. In Sect. 4, it will be described the simulation methodology used to evaluate the performance of the comparator and extracted its key parameters. In Sect. 5, it will be presented the simulation results and discussed the impact of key design parameters on the comparator's performance. Finally, in Sect. 6, it will be summarized the findings and provided conclusions.

2 Connected Cyber Physical Spaces

Connected cyber physical spaces are the result of combining the digital and physical worlds. They can be found in a variety of applications, including smart homes, smart cities, and smart factories. In a smart home, for example, sensors and devices can be used to monitor and control temperature, lighting, security, and other systems. Similarly, in a smart city, data from sensors and other sources can be used to optimize traffic flow, manage energy usage, and enhance public safety. In a smart factory, cyber-physical systems can be used to optimize production processes, reduce downtime, and increase efficiency. Overall, cyber-physical spaces have the potential to transform how we live, work, and interact with the world around us.

Integrated electronics play a crucial role in the development and operation of cyberphysical spaces, making it possible to collect, process, and exchange data in real-time. As the interface between the physical and digital worlds, analog-to-digital converters (ADCs) are an essential component of these integrated electronics. To meet the increasing requirements of ADCs, it is crucial to improve and optimize the performance of building blocks, such as comparators. This work describes a characterization of dynamic comparators under simulation environment, making it possible to create a standard workflow to design these essential components.

3 Operation and Key Parameters

A comparator senses a differential input and generates a logical output according to the polarity of the input difference [3, 4]. Most of today's applications use dynamic, or clocked, comparators, since it allows for low power dissipation, as they do not have static consumption [6]. Most dynamic voltage comparators consist of a pre-amplifier and a latch. For example, strongarm latch combines both in a single stage [7]. In [8] is presented a dynamic comparator, however, in this case, a sense amplifier is used as a pre-amplifier. More complex topologies are also implemented, as in [9], where it is presented a triple tail comparator, using cascaded latches and feed-forward paths. Despite these differences in architecture, dynamic comparators present the same working principle. In short, when the clock signal goes high, the comparator makes a decision. Some operation parameters can be defined, such as the time that the comparator needs to make a decision, the minimum input voltage that the comparator is able to distinguish, and power consumption. These key parameters will be analyzed in this chapter.

3.1 Comparison Time

The time required for the comparator to make a decision is labeled comparison time. It it consists of the time delay between the clock signal going high and the comparator making the decision. It is one of the most important parameters in a comparator, since it can limit its application.

It can be measured in different ways. One of the ways is to measure the time duration from the beginning of the comparison phase (reset is released when the appropriate clock edge reaches typically 50% of V_{DD}) until a valid logical voltage level is available at the output. A more faithful way to measure it is to wait until the appropriate clock edge and the logical level output both reach 90% of V_{DD}. It will present a higher value, however, it guarantees that the following circuit reads it as a high value [4, 6].

The comparator must compare the signal during one clock cycle and provide a stable output before the next cycle. The speed of the comparator depends on its input voltage difference, as the difference between input voltages gets smaller, the slower the comparison will be, ultimately requiring a metastability analysis [6].

3.2 Offset Voltage

The offset voltage can be seen as the sensitivity of the comparator, it defines the minimum voltage for which the comparator makes a reliable decision. This is the input voltage difference required to make the output change from low to high or vice versa [4]. If the input voltages have a voltage difference smaller than that of the offset voltage, it will not be able to make a trustworthy decision. This offset voltage is caused due to mismatch in the manufacturing process of the transistors. Due to this non-ideality, the input pairs are not entirely identical and will therefore have slightly different threshold voltages. This will mean that their behavior is not exactly the same, which will result in an offset in the input pairs. When the voltage is exactly the same on the gates of the input transistors, one will draw a somewhat larger current and the corresponding drain node will move faster and give an output that might not be correct. Other transistors than the input pairs will also contribute to the offset, but in general, the input pairs are the most dominant source to offset due to a large gain from the input pairs before other transistors activate [6].

The offset voltage can be divided into two values: the systematic offset and the random offset. The systematic offset is the offset that is always present in the comparator. The random offset is caused by mismatch in transistor sizes, deviation from ideal symmetrical circuit structure, and other non-idealities.

3.3 Power Dissipation

A further important parameter to characterize a clocked regenerative comparator is its power dissipation. It is the amount of power consumed by the comparator during operation. It is an important parameter in low-power applications and can be minimized by optimizing the circuit design. Typically, it consists of a static and a dynamic part, which depends on the clock frequency and the capacitances, which have to be charged and discharged [4]. As in almost every electronic design, low power consumption is desired. One significant advantage of the dynamic latched comparator compared to the pre-amplified based comparator is that it does not consume any static power, if leakage currents are neglected [6].

3.4 Trade-Offs Between Performance Parameters

Before starting an optimization, it is important to set the specifications for the comparator, especially the critical ones that absolutely need to be reached. In general, there are trade-offs between the key parameters of a voltage comparator. For example, a high gain comparator may have a longer comparison time due to the need for multiple amplification stages. Similarly, increasing the gain of the comparator may lead to an increase in power consumption. Another trade-off is between speed and accuracy, where increasing the speed of the comparator may result in a decrease in the accuracy of the output. There are also trade-offs between power consumption and noise performance, where increasing the power may result in lower noise levels but higher power dissipation. In addition, there can be trade-offs between noise and speed, where increasing the speed of the comparator may result in higher noise levels. So, it is important to carefully consider these trade-offs and select the parameters that are most important for the specific application to optimize the overall performance of the comparator.

4 Testbench Setup

The testbench can be represented by the following figure, Fig. 1. It consists of a dynamic comparator which requires a clock signal, Clk. In the comparator's input there is a reference voltage, V_{ref}, and a stimulus voltage, V_{in}. Depending on the analysis, the waveform of the stimulus voltage can be different. Regarding the reference voltage, in this case, a DC value was applied. However, instead of using a DC reference voltage, a differential input signal can be used, which will not affect the comparator's operation, since it only relies on the voltage difference between both inputs.

The comparator separates the analog signals, at the input, from the digital signals, at the output. Depending on the logic structure, it might be necessary for the output to be connected to several logic gates. This action might overload the comparator's output stage, making it slower and power hungry. In order to avoid this, it is recommended to employ a digital buffer. This digital buffer consists of a cascade of two inverters. The first inverter must be a minimum size inverter, as it will relieve the load of the comparator's output stage. The smaller the size, the faster the output stage will be and less current will be consumed. If a high fanout is necessary, the size of the second inverter can be increased. In Fig. 1, the load consists of a minimum size inverter followed by a two-time minimum size inverter.

Values such as the clock frequency and the reference voltage depend on the comparator's characteristics, application, and technology used, among others. In this case, the reference voltage was defined as 450 mV, and the clock frequency is 1 GHz. In order to start the study, from this point on, it is necessary to set the above-mentioned comparator's desired specifications, such as the offset, comparison time, power consumption.

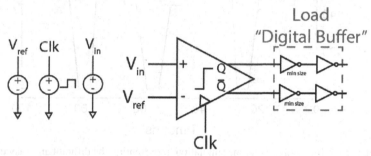

Fig. 1. Comparator Testbench. On the left of the comparator is presented the input signal. On the right is presented the digital buffer as the comparator's load.

4.1 Comparison Time

In order to measure the comparison time, Fig. 2 shows a sequence of the different decisions that the comparator will make. The input voltage, or stimulus voltage, will alternate between four levels, which will present "easy" and "difficult" decisions. These levels were defined as easy high, easy low, difficult high, difficult low. They are so called due to the voltage difference that they will force onto the comparator's input. For example, the easy high level is defined as a bigger voltage difference, when compared to the reference voltage, while the difficult high level is defined as a smaller voltage difference, when compared to the reference voltage. These values will depend on the comparator's application [3, 4].

The sequence presented in Fig. 2 was created in such a way to force the comparator to make decisions between all these levels. Alternating between these different levels has several advantages when it comes to the comparator's behavior analysis. All these different combinations of transaction between levels will allow us to infer if the comparator suffers from memory effects, that is, if the previous decision has influence on the next decision.

In order to properly evaluate the comparison time, it is necessary to simulate PVT corners and extract the longest time, in other words, the worst-case scenario comparison time.

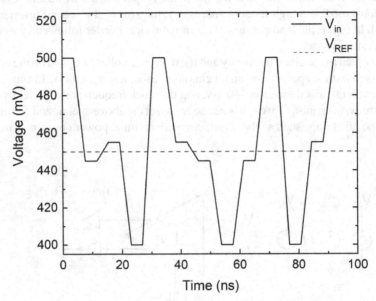

Fig. 2. Input wave for comparison time simulation, representing the difficult and easy decisions.

In Fig. 3 is represented a close-up of a clock signal when the comparator is making a decision. As explained before, this time will be better measured by subtracting the time when the clock signal reaches 90% of V_{DD} to the time when the comparator's output reaches 90% of V_{DD}.

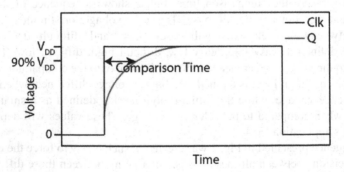

Fig. 3. Comparison time measured at 90% V_{DD}.

4.2 Offset

To analyze the comparator's offset it is necessary to have a static wave at the input, with a frequency much lower than the frequency of the clock. It is recommended to use a wave amplitude as small as possible, since it will reduce the measurement error. As presented in Fig. 4, a half-period triangular wave can be applied in one input, in such a way that it is possible to observe both transition moments, rise and fall, and the reference voltage in the other one.

In the start of the analysis is normal to have a high offset value or to don't know the offset value, so it is recommended to start with a higher amplitude value and reduce as you go along testing.

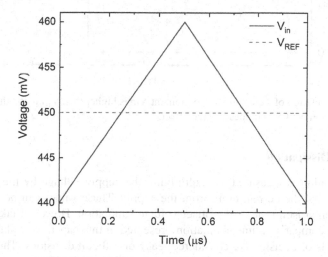

Fig. 4. Input wave for offset voltage simulation.

The offset can be separated into static offset and random offset. In simulation environment the static offset must be very close to zero, a value in the order of μV is acceptable. To measure the random offset, it is necessary to run Monte Carlo simulations, because it is this simulation that takes into consideration the mismatch of the devices.

Figure 5 shows how to extract the offset value. The first value to extract is the exact moment the output value is higher than VDD/2. This is the moment the comparator makes its decision; it is the time of the first clock cycle where the stimulus voltage is higher than the reference voltage. The offset value can then be obtained by subtracting the reference voltage value to the stimulus voltage value at that exact moment obtained. The described process should be performed using the simulator tools, such as the calculator.

In order to get a complete evaluation of the offset voltage, it is necessary to simulate Monte Carlo analysis across PVT corners. To have statistical importance a minimum of 200 samples is required.

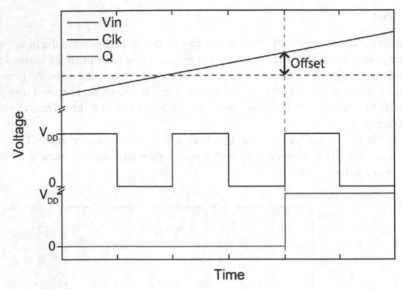

Fig. 5. Representation of a close-up of the moment Vin is higher than V_{REF} and the comparator makes its decision, and how to measure the offset.

4.3 Power Dissipation

Power dissipation is measured by multiplying the supply voltage by the Root Mean Square, RMS, of the current drain from the supply. These values can be obtained by either the comparison time or the offset voltage simulation. However, taking a closer look into the comparison time simulation presented in this paper, as explained before, different levels of decision are considered, easy or difficult decisions. These different decisions consume different amounts of current, which, as a consequence, will lead to different values of power dissipation: if a decision takes a longer time to be made, more power dissipation will occur, and vice versa. So, it is recommended to extract the power dissipation from these values presented in the comparison time simulation, as it will give a better idea of the range of power dissipation presented by the comparator.

To perform a complete power analysis may be important to separate the analog power consumption, associated to the pre-amplifier, and the digital power consumption, related to the latch. This gives an idea of which domain is more power hungry and can be important when designing the supply buffers.

5 Simulation Results

This section is going to put into practice the above-described simulation approach. To illustrate the analysis, two different topologies of dynamic comparators are going to be analyzed. Both double tail topologies, however, the difference is the latch used in each one of them: one is implemented with the latch presented in [8] and [10], we'll call it NMOS Latch, Fig. 6-(a); and the other is the latch presented in [11], we'll call it PMOS Latch, Fig. 6-(b). The way they work is essentially the same, however, the main difference is that one of the topologies has an NMOS transistor as the input device, and the other one has a PMOS transistor as the input device.

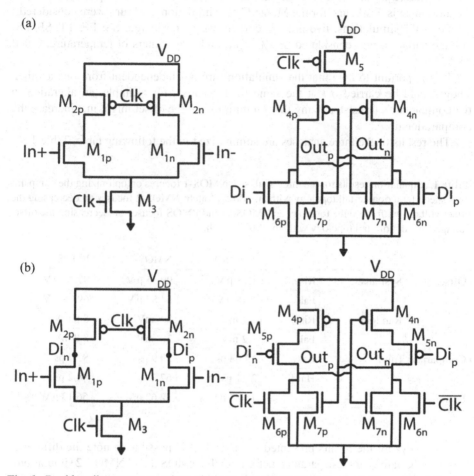

Fig. 6. Double-tail comparator schematic: (a) using NMOS Latch, adapted from [8]. (b) using PMOS Latch, adapted from [11].

Regarding NMOS Latch, two different analyses will be presented. One will focus on optimizing the comparator's speed (NMOS-1), while the other will focus on decreasing the offset voltage (NMOS-2). For PMOS Latch, only one analysis will be performed, identical to the second approach of NMOS Latch, where it will focus on decreasing the offset voltage (PMOS). These analyses will work as an example of the utility if this optimization approach, since it will be applied to two different topologies, and two different parameter optimizations, within the same topology.

All the simulations have been carried out in a 28 nm standard bulk CMOS process, a V_{DD} value of 0.9 V. and a clock frequency of 1 GHz, using Cadence Virtuoso environment. Regarding the comparison time simulation, as presented in Fig. 2, there should be between 3 and 4 clock signal periods in each level. For the difficult decisions the difference between V_{REF} and V_{in} is 5 mV, and for the easy decisions this difference is 50 mV. Regarding the offset voltage simulations, the input signal frequency is 1 MHz, the amplitude is 5 mV, and for the Monte Carlo simulation, 200 runs were considered.

For PVT simulations, five process corners were considered, SS, FF, TT, SF, FS; voltage variation was considered $\pm$ 5% V_{DD}; and two corners of temperature, 0 and 85 °C.

It is important to note that the simulations are not independent from one another. They should be carried out at the same time because, for example, an alteration in the comparator's transistor sizing that might improve the offset might just increase the comparation time.

The results of the three analyses are summarized in the following table, Table 1.

Table 1. Simulation results for the three analyses: NMOS-1 focuses on optimizing the comparator's speed for a double-tail topology with an NMOS Latch; NMOS-2 focuses on decreasing the offset voltage, with the same topology as NMOS-1; and PMOS focuses on decreasing the offset voltage for a double-tail topology with an PMOS Latch.

			NMOS-1	NMOS-2	PMOS
Offset	Systematic	Rise	1.78 μV	99.15 μV	97.41 μV
		Fall	1.48 μV	64.87 μV	69.29 μV
	Random	Rise	3.1 mV	2.8 mV	8.8 mV
		Fall	3.2 mV	2.8 mV	8.8 mV
Comparison Time		Easy	19.08 ps	59.9 ps	83.4 ps
		Hard	27.1 ps	67.2 ps	88.2 ps
Power			164.7 μW	32.62 μW	56.13 μW

By analyzing the results presented in Table 1, it is possible to note the difference between the values of these parameters for both the NMOS-1 and NMOS-2 simulations. For the first one, where speed was prioritized, it is presented an improvement of 60% when compared to NMOS-2. However, for the second simulation, where the offset was prioritized, a value of 2.8 mV was obtained. It doesn't show a great improvement when compared to NMOS-1, however, the power dissipation is five times lower, obtaining a value of 32.62 μW. Regarding PMOS, it shows worst results overall when compared to NMOS-2, since it presents a higher offset of 8.8 mV, a higher comparison time of 88.2 ps, and a power dissipation of 56.13 μW.

6 Conclusions

In this paper it was presented a testbench for standard comparison of dynamic voltage comparators, as well as an overview of dynamic comparators operation and key parameters, and a simulation setup for extracting key parameters of comparator performance, such as static-offset, random-offset, worst-case comparison-time for both hard and soft decisions, and power dissipation.

As an example, this paper implemented the methodology in Virtuoso environment and presents results for different dynamic comparators in a 28-nm standard bulk-CMOS technology.

Acknowledgments. The authors acknowledge the Portuguese FCT program UIDB/00066/2020 and UIDP/00066/2020 for providing partial financial support for this work.

References

1. Baker, R.J.: CMOS: Circuit Design, Layout, and Simulation: Third Edition (2011)
2. Razavi, B.: Design of Analog CMOS Integrated Circuits. McGraw-Hill, New York (2017)
3. Razavi, B.: The design of a comparator [The Analog Mind]. IEEE Solid-State Circuits Mag. **12**(4), 8–14 (2020). https://doi.org/10.1109/MSSC.2020.3021865
4. Goll, B.: Comparators in Nanometer CMOS. Springer, Cham (2015)
5. Razavi, B., Wooley, B.A.: Design techniques for high-speed, high-resolution comparators. J Solid State Circuits **27**(12) (1992)
6. Lund, P., Backenius, E., Vesterbacka, M.: Comparator design for high-speed ADCs. Linkoping University (2022)
7. Razavi, B.: The StrongARM latch [A Circuit for All Seasons]. IEEE Solid-State Circuits Mag. **7**(2), 12–17 (2015). https://doi.org/10.1109/MSSC.2015.2418155
8. Baghel, S.S., Mishra, D.K.: Design and analysis of double-tail dynamic comparator for flash ADCs. In: 2018 International Conference on Circuits and Systems in Digital Enterprise Technology ICCSDET 2018, pp. 1–5 (2018). https://doi.org/10.1109/ICCSDET.2018.8821129
9. Ramkaj, A.T., Pelgrom, M.J.M., Member, L.S., Steyaert, M.S.J., Tavernier, F., Member, S.: A 28 nm CMOS Triple-Latch Feed-Forward, vol. 69, no. 11, pp. 4404–4414 (2022)
10. Babayan-Mashhadi, S.: Analysis and design of a low-voltage low-power double-tail comparator **22**(2), 343–352 (2014)
11. van Elzakker, M., van Tujil, E., Geraedts, P., Schinkel, D., Klumperink, E., Nauta, B.: A 1.9μW 4.4fJ/Conversion-step 10b 1MS/s Charge-Redistribution ADC (2008)

Trans-Boolean Cyber Physical Systems

Francisco Neves[✉], Raul Rato, and Manuel Ortigueira

School of Science and Technology, UNINOVA – CTS and LASI, Nova University of Lisbon,
2829-516 Caparica, Portugal
fs.neves@campus.fct.unl.pt, {r.rato,mdo}@fct.unl.pt

Abstract. This paper discusses the interplay between discrete time signal processing and symbolic computation under a general Turing Machine approach in the Cyber Physical systems framework. Discrete signals and symbols are analyzed for their Turing computing capabilities using either Kolmogorov axioms or quantum probability amplitudes. It analyzes the discrete time Trans Boolean gate $\sqrt{}$NOT and its impact on conventional computational theories used for embedded systems and Internet of Things.

Keywords: Signal · Symbol · Qubit · Trans-Boolean · Turing · Computation · Cyber Physical Systems

1 Introduction

The integration of Cyber Physical (CP) systems into digital networks has played a crucial role in enabling embedded systems, where systems operate using a common digital computational framework that enables them to interact with peripheral devices. These embedded system applications rely both on software and hardware which is designed within the Turing Machine (TM) framework [1–3]. TMs are symbolic processors in the sense that operate and manipulate symbols belonging to a finite set Σ usually called Alphabet. It is a remarkable fact that the computational power of those TM devices does not depend on the Alphabet's cardinality [4–6]. As a result of this fact, practical reasons led to the generalized use of computational machines based on two symbol alphabets. The so called and now ubiquitous digital binary Boolean (BB) systems do fully embody any theoretical TM.

However, Feynman's quantum computational model proposed in [7] is capable of computing functions that cannot be effectively carried on by any BB or equivalently by any alphabet-based computing device. This paper uses the expression Trans-Boolean function (TB) for non-BB computable functions. Mind that Deutsch [8] showed that any classic Boolean computation can be performed by a quantum computer. This expresses the fact that any BB computation can be performed by a TB system.

In this paper we show that there is at least one trans-Boolean computation, the so called $\sqrt{}$ NOT, that no BB system is able to compute, either effectively or with an exponential slowdown. A word of caution is in order. Anyone acquainted with the real

© IFIP International Federation for Information Processing 2023
Published by Springer Nature Switzerland AG 2023
L. M. Camarinha-Matos and F. Ferrada (Eds.): DoCEIS 2023, IFIP AICT 678, pp. 290–300, 2023.
https://doi.org/10.1007/978-3-031-36007-7_22

number system knows that π or $\sqrt{2}$ are irrationals that no fraction is able to represent. That does not diminish the practical importance of such irrational numbers, albeit all our practical computations are performed with rational numbers. The discovery of numbers like π, $\sqrt{2}$ showed concrete and specific differences between the rational number system and the real number system.

The presented perspective reveals that there is at least one concrete and specific difference between any BB system and at least one TB system where the later can compute the $\sqrt{}$ NOT function which the former is unable to do. Nevertheless, as in the rational vs real number case, a BB system can be used to compute $\sqrt{}$ NOT up to a desired precision. This is the basis for the practical proof of concept put forward by Filipe Velasques in [9]. That work was the driving force behind this theoretical endeavor.

This computational nonequivalence has major consequences for embedded systems. Not only it spawns deep theoretical reasons for researching computational devices beyond the current digital paradigm given quantum computing paradigm is a reversible one, it also enables the use of the Landauer computational limit [10, 11] as a design goal for the research of efficient and novel computational systems both for Cyber-Physical systems and general applications.

This paper explores the possibilities of Quantum Computation within the framework of Discrete Time Signal Processing (DSP) Theory. Since both theories make extensive use of Hilbert spaces [12, 13] our research questions whether it is possible to use the algebraic signal processing theory approach [14, 15] to implement reversible logic and quantum computations in order to achieve efficient and novel computational systems both for CP systems and general applications, unlocking the potential for faster computations and improved communication devices [16, 17].

The second section of this paper relates our research to Connected Cyber Physical Spaces and emphasizes the importance of a broader symbolic conceptualization for embedded systems. The third section reviews the interplay between of signals and symbols, while the fourth section showcases the trans-Boolean function $\sqrt{}$ NOT. The fifth section discusses the non-equivalence between the conceptual computational framework of Turing machines and trans-Boolean systems.

2 Signals and Symbols in Cyber Physical Systems

With the emergence of advances in CP systems, such as IOT and Artificial Intelligence (AI), human connection to digital spaces has become ubiquitous across all daily activities [18]. The increasingly complex and intelligent systems available today enabled the advent of elaborated and efficient collaborative networks empowered by a diversity of computing and communications technologies distributed through the physical world [19, 20].

2.1 Signals in Cyber Physical Systems

At the deepest level all CP systems interact by way of physical phenomena. These are formalized as band limited signals and regarded as inputs and outputs of the system

[21–23]. It is well known that any band limited signal can be described by a discrete time signal.

A discrete time signal is an ordered value sequence associated with a phenomenon deemed of interest [24]. The numerical value assigned to each element stands for a quantified assessment of the phenomenon. Order is set by at least one independent variable, typically time which assigns a common coordinate system to the phenomena under study [25].

Kindred physical facts generate sets of related signals. These can be detected as events or classified as states. In CP systems the detection or classification procedure starts with a discrete signal whose values can sometimes be called observations or measurements. This signal is assumed to consist of relevant components embedded in more or less noise. The CP system processes the aforementioned signal to decide whether or not either a particular event has occurred or a state is present. Many current DSP techniques and concepts, such as the matching filter, are intrinsic to the methods used to detect or classify signals in the presence of noise.

2.2 Symbols in Cyber Physical Systems

The concept of a symbol is a useful abstraction for developing CP systems and conceptualizing real-world events or states. It is extensively used in the design of CP systems. Each and every symbol is a physical fact, as expressed by Patee: "Even the most abstract symbols must have a physical embodiment" [26].

In the abstract mathematical communication theory realm it is assumed that there exists an information source that supplies symbols with meaning not related to its representation or physical embodiment but whose collection is limited by the number of available signals [27–29]. In CP systems information sources are physical process, where symbols emerge from signal detection procedures [30, 31].

2.3 Trans-Boolean Functions in Cyber Physical Systems

Among the main concerns in the design of embedded systems are the security and interference within the network, with artificial intelligence being the main source of leaked private information [32]. These systems need extensive raw data storage and their security is limited by encryption technology. Attacks over these networks can directly interfere with the communication path between sensors and actuators, potentially falsifying data, and altering the behavior of the network.

In the past few decades, quantum computing has been considered a possible solution or threat to secure communications due to the intrinsic properties of quantum measurements [33]. There are algorithms that can jeopardize our current encryption methods due to the computational speedup provided by quantum computing, enabling fast factorization without the exponential slowdown [34]. On the other hand, these algorithms can be used to speed up computations, thus significantly improving the performance of artificial intelligence and machine learning algorithms.

Quantum computing also offers new encryption methods such as the Quantum Key Distribution algorithm that relies on the physical properties of entanglement to ensure secure communications in digital networks with a focus on either computational speed or security levels [35]. However, the inherent quantum and classical information theory that encompasses both models are a symbolic abstraction from the physical phenomena [33].

The arithmetic properties of qubits follow axioms established in the Hilbert Space and require operators to be defined by reversible logic [36]. This conceptualization, which is shared by signal processing theory, allows for the implementation of functions with decreased power consumption enabled by reversible logic [37]. The design of signal processing units that allow for low power consumption can reduce the environmental impact and the cost of embedded systems. Low power dissipation is a major constraint in reducing the size of devices, such as the size of transistors and batteries. Thus, power management is significantly important in increasing the battery life of each device in digital networks, and the consequent dependency on traditional power sources [38]. Our research focuses on a comprehensive computations based on trans-Boolean functions for Cyber Physical Systems. Incorporating trans-Boolean function and reversible logic into computational theory is a promising field of research that may bring valuable contributions to embedded systems.

3 The Interplay Between Signals and Symbols

It is well known that CP systems interact with humans, the environment and in between themselves. These interactions must be properly addressed, not only to develop good applications both at the software and hardware level, but also to optimize resources and reduce waste.

It is possible to assume the perspective that CP systems interactions are symbol based. This is the TM perspective, where either digital hardware design or software development is BB based. It ignores all signal processing subtleties since the final abstraction detail is at the bit level. There is no need to care how bits are implemented. For CP systems this is good, practical and straightforward, specially when dealing with digital information.

It is also possible to assume the perspective that CP systems interactions are signal based. This is the DSP perspective, where signals must be processed and detectors must be used in order to symbols to emerge. There is the need to care how bits are implemented. This is also good, practical and straightforward, specially when translating information to and from the digital CP systems realm.

As signals and symbols are considered disparate and it is also assumed that the operations appropriate for one realm have the same computational power those ones in the other, either perspective is used according to the problem at hand practicalities, since all problems are deemed computationally equivalent in the two realms. Both conceptualizations are interdependent and commonly utilized in CP systems to establish a connection between the physical environment and the relevant digital framework.

Existing a difference in computational power between the realms then some operation can be performed in one that will have no counterpart in the other. This will have a practical impact for all CP project designs, since some problems can be solved only in one realm. Moreover, there can be instances where there will be solutions for problems that seem unsolvable with current technology and know-how.

Another word of caution is in order. We have already addressed the rational/real number issue. Now it is necessary to address the ink/write issue. We need ink for writing characters, digits, or other symbols, which we can use to write about ink. But we all know that the writing is not the ink, even if it is about ink. We cannot manipulate ink just by writing. But we can write just by manipulating ink. In the same way we need signals to produce symbols, which we can use to compute and process a signal. Those symbols are not the signals. We cannot change the signal just with symbol manipulation and processing. But we do change symbols with just and only signal processing and manipulation.

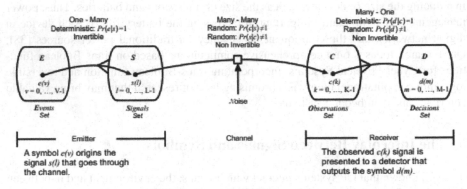

Fig. 1. Event to decision model.

DSP systems are formalized with theories and axioms emanant from vector spaces theory that differ from those in the symbolic computation formalization, emanant from the TM theory.

Communication: From Symbol to Signal to Symbol. An adequate approach to this problematic makes extensive use of sets. It is the event to decision model within a signals and symbols framework, as depicted in Fig. 1.

Computation and Signals. For most purposes, signals can be deemed as vectors [39]. Thus, vector space theory is a suitable tool for signal analysis. As an abstract entity, a vector is a descriptive tool that assigns arithmetic properties to the physical processes under study.

Computation and Symbols. A symbolic processor executes functions without the need to specify the physical operations underlying them. The communication channel established between the symbolic processor and the signal detector is considered to be an identity function with no additional noise in the system. In the TM conceptualization, the head scans for a symbol and either finds a corresponding symbol or discards the obtained value and imprints a new one on the tape. Boolean functions describe the possible transformations that occur at a symbolic level in the channel. Nevertheless, it's worth noting that trans-boolean transformations can also occur as signals are the physical embodiment of symbols.

4 Trans-Boolean Computations

The methods use for measurement and classification by a DSP system converts a discrete variable into a symbol. If the observable is deterministic, the estimator is simply a classifier which transforms a numerical input signal into a symbol. If the observable is probabilistic as in quantum computing theory, then the mapping realized in the transition from qubit to symbol converts a continuous variable randomly chosen into an estimation of the symbolic values. Since signal processing and quantum computing theory both give extensive use of Hilbert Spaces then both concepts can abstractly be used interchangeably though differing in meaning [40].

Although the measurements are probabilistic in nature, it is possible to define a composition of functions that is deterministic instead. Let us first consider the set of all possible Boolean transformations of one argument, as given in Table 1. The variables x and y represent the input and output of the table, respectively. This truth table corresponds to the Cartesian product between the symbol 1 and 0 with the possible symbolic transformations given by the relations $f_0(\,y = \ddot{F}), f_1(\,y = x), f_2(\,y = \bar{x})$ and $f_3\,(y = \ddot{V})$.

Table 1. Boolean Functions of One Argument.

x	y_0	y_1	y_2	y_3
0	0	0	1	1
1	0	1	0	1

Let us map the truth values $\ddot{V}$ and $\ddot{F}$ to a Euclidean vector space. These symbols are arbitrarily represented by the orthogonal vectors $[0\ 1]^T$ and $[1\ 0]^T$, respectively. The function has a one-to-one mapping if $p = 1 - q, \forall p, q \in \{0, 1\}$ for the generic vector $[p\ q]^T$. The matrix representation of each function f_i is given by the outer product between the input and output vector. Since the input and output vectors are orthogonal, each function f_i can be represented by M_i with $\langle x\,|\,y_i \rangle = x^T M_i\, y_i = 0$:

$$f_0 = \begin{bmatrix} 0 & 0 \\ 1 & 1 \end{bmatrix}, \quad f_1 = \begin{bmatrix} 1 & 0 \\ 0 & 1 \end{bmatrix}, \quad f_2 = \begin{bmatrix} 0 & 1 \\ 1 & 0 \end{bmatrix}, \quad f_3 = \begin{bmatrix} 1 & 1 \\ 0 & 0 \end{bmatrix}. \tag{1}$$

Let us consider that each function represents an independent event with a probability $p_o = P(f_i)$ of occurring. The possible transformations that can occur with given probability are represented in Fig. 1. Suppose $i = 1,2,3,4$ are chosen in order for f_i to generate the NOT function as a composition of two functions belonging to the set Y. Thus, the elements of the set F will be chosen from the set $\mathbb{R}$.

Let p and q belong to the set of real positive values, each representing the probability of obtaining a logic vector as a truth or false vector, respectively. While preserving the condition $p + q = 1, \forall\, p, q \in \mathbb{R}^+$, each function f_i sets the transition matrix as:

$$p_{00} = p_{01} = 0 \rightarrow f_0, \quad p_{01} = p_{10} = 0 \rightarrow f_1.$$
$$p_{00} = p_{11} = 0 \rightarrow f_2, \quad p_{10} = p_{11} = 0 \rightarrow f_3. \tag{2}$$

To achieve a deterministic output, it is necessary to force the probability of a given pair of transitions to be zero, which does not represent a random event. In the classical theory of transition probabilities, the probability of correctly reading a symbol is determined by the successive composition of functions. This composition yields:

$$\begin{bmatrix} p' \\ q' \end{bmatrix} = \begin{bmatrix} p_{00} & p_{01} \\ p_{01} & p_{11} \end{bmatrix} \cdot \begin{bmatrix} p_{00} & p_{01} \\ p_{01} & p_{11} \end{bmatrix} \cdot \begin{bmatrix} p \\ q \end{bmatrix} = \begin{bmatrix} p_{00}^2 + p_{01}p_{10} & p_{00}p_{10} + p_{10}p_{11} \\ p_{00}p_{10} + p_{10}p_{11} & p_{11}^2 + p_{01}p_{10} \end{bmatrix} \cdot \begin{bmatrix} p \\ q \end{bmatrix}$$

$$\begin{bmatrix} p' \\ q' \end{bmatrix} = \begin{bmatrix} P_{00} & P_{01} \\ P_{01} & P_{11} \end{bmatrix} \cdot \begin{bmatrix} p \\ q \end{bmatrix}.$$

(3)

with,

$$P_{00} = p_{00}^2 + p_{01}p_{10}, \quad P_{01} = p_{01}p_{11} + p_{01}p_{11}.$$
$$P_{11} = p_{11}^2 + p_{01}p_{10}, \quad P_{10} = p_{00}p_{10} + p_{10}p_{11}.$$

(4)

Since the possible values for each p_{ij} belong to the set of real numbers, the metric space L_1 is insufficient to define a transformation that when applied twice, it results in the *NOT* transformation. Let us assume the Hilbert vector space L_2 is sufficient to describe the $\sqrt{}$ NOT transformation. By setting $\alpha = |p|^2$ and $\beta = |q|^2$, with $\alpha, \beta \in \mathbb{C}$, there is a function $f = \sqrt{f_3}$.

$$C_{00} = c_{00}^2 + c_{01}c_{10} = 0, \quad C_{01} = c_{01}c_{11} + c_{01}c_{11} = 1.$$
$$C_{11} = c_{11}^2 + c_{01}c_{10} = 0, \quad C_{10} = c_{00}c_{10} + c_{10}c_{11} = 1.$$

(5)

By setting $c_{00} = c_{11}$, the possible solutions for the equation system are symmetric, with the square root of the function given by:

$$C_0 = \sqrt{-c_1^2} = ic_1, \quad c_1 = \pm \frac{1 \mp i}{2}.$$

(6)

The resulting matrix belongs to the $SU(2)$ group, in which any combination of possible roots results in $f'' = f_3$. The obtained amplitude of probabilities for both truth values is given by:

$$\begin{bmatrix} p' \\ q' \end{bmatrix} = \pm \frac{1}{2} \begin{bmatrix} (1 \pm i) & (1 \mp i) \\ (1 \mp i) & (1 \pm i) \end{bmatrix} \cdot \begin{bmatrix} p \\ q \end{bmatrix} = \pm \frac{1}{2} \begin{bmatrix} p \cdot (1 \pm i) + q \cdot (1 \mp i) \\ p \cdot (1 \mp i) + q \cdot (1 \pm i) \end{bmatrix}.$$

(7)

This function is a possible wave function Ψ and it is typically represented as:

$$\Psi = \pm \frac{1 \pm i}{2} |\ddot{V}\rangle \pm \frac{1 \mp i}{2} |\ddot{F}\rangle$$

(8)

where $|\ddot{V}\rangle$ and $|\ddot{F}\rangle$ represent the state vectors for the binary values of 1 and 0, respectively. The output vector of the $\sqrt{}$ NOT function becomes $\pm \frac{1}{2}[-i\ i]^T$, which has a many-to-one mapping from qubits to boolean bits.

The act of measurement becomes a decision problem in the vector space [41] with the probability of obtaining the truth symbol given by $|\alpha|^2$.

The quantum model highlights the possibility to implement trans-Boolean functions through reversible logic. A symbol is the result of a conceptual decision process that occurs at the instant of measurement. It is not a requirement to set a one-to-one mapping between the possible outcomes and the possible binary boolean values.

5 Discussion

The hierarchy of abstraction levels enables computational and communication theories to be developed without the need to define further the notion of symbol [42]. In [1], the Turing machine scans a symbol from a tape and executes an abstract process, also known as computation. The physical execution of the computational process is deemed irrelevant to the symbolic operations performed by the machine. However, it must be implemented as a physical event culminating in a result mapped into a symbol by a categorical decider.

The computational model of a classic Turing machine can only accept or compute a finite alphabet of symbols to represent the natural numbers field without errors. The real numbers that can be computed through a Turing machine are calculated by boolean functions. In [43], the quantum model is able to compute the set of all boolean functions and additional trans-Boolean functions. However, in the measurement act, the qubit value at the measurement instant is mapped into the same conceptualization as a regular TM. Thus, the computable numbers by a Quantum Turing Machine are equivalent to a classic Turing machine [44].

A trans-Boolean function is a relation that can not be represented by a truth table. The decision problem of trans-boolean operations in a quantum machine is said to invalidate the computation when a measurement takes place [34]. Since a one-to-one mapping between the two machines cannot be established, the decision procedure is capable of producing stochastic sequences of symbols [8]. If a "Gedanken-experiment" is applied to test for the equivalence between the two machines, nothing could be concluded from the measurements as there are no random procedures between two equivalent machines [45].

The approach taken in [46] proves that any numeration of sets of output symbols can be done either by a deterministic machine and a probabilistic machine, if and only if the probability of the transition between states is a computable real number. In Quantum computing theory, the $\sqrt{\text{NOT}}$ has complex amplitude of transition probabilities which has a many-to-one mapping to the real valued probabilistic machines.

Furthermore, the function $\sqrt{\text{NOT}}$ is not computable by a Turing machine as the law of excluded middle does not accept partial symbol [47]. The probabilistic approach is also insufficient to describe this trans-Boolean function as the probability for each output symbol is perpetually mixed in further computations. Thus, quantum mechanics provided us a trans-Boolean function that is not realizable with the axioms of Boolean operations of a vector space, yet it describes a physical event that takes place independently of the abstraction theory.

When dealing with amplitude probabilities, the act of measurement maps a L_2 space with an unknown choice procedure to a binary value that can become a deterministic process depending on the composition of applied functions. There is no binary boolean function that is able to compute the $\sqrt{\text{NOT}}$ function. Thus, the quantum machine is equipped with an extended set of trans-boolean functions that includes the Turing conceptualization of computable numbers.

6 Conclusion

This paper demonstrated that there exists at least one trans-Boolean computation that no binary Boolean system can compute. This concrete difference has significant implications for the design of Cyber-Physical Systems. The $\sqrt{}$ NOT is an example of a computations that is not accessible to embedded systems.

A TB system makes extensive use of reversible logic to implement functions in the Hilbert vector space conceptualization, resulting in greater energy efficiency compared to current BB systems. These systems are also capable of implementing new cryptography algorithms that can enhance security in communication channels.

Future research will focus on investigating the potential applications of TB functions in embedded systems under the algebraic signal processing framework.

Acknowledgments. The authors would like to thank professor Dr. Luís Camarinha-Matos for the useful instructions. This work was supported in part by the Portuguese FCT program UIDB/00066/2020.

References

1. Turing, A.M.: On computable numbers, with an application to the entscheidungsproblem. J. Math. **58**(345–363), 5 (1936)
2. Herken, R.: The Universal Turing Machine: A Half-century Survey. Springer, Heidelberg (1988)
3. Wegner, P., Goldin, D.: Computation beyond turing machines. Commun. ACM **46**(4), 100–102 (2003)
4. Cohen, D.I.A.: Introduction to Computer Theory, 2nd edn. Wiley, Hoboken (1996)
5. Yoeli, M., Rosenfeld, G.: Logical design of ternary switching circuits. IEEE Trans. Electron. Comput. **1**(1), 19–29 (1965)
6. Van Orman Quine, W.: Quiddities: An Intermittently Philosophical Dictionary. Harvard University Press, Cambridge (1987)
7. Feynman, R.P.: Feynman Lectures on Computation. CRC Press, Boca Raton (2018)
8. Deutsch, D.E.: Quantum computational networks. Proc. R. Soc. London A Math. Phys. Sci. **425**(1868), 73–90 (1989)
9. Velasques, F.J.F.: Aprimoramento de segurança a nível físico. Master's thesis, NOVA School of Science and Technology (2022)
10. Landauer, R.: Dissipation and noise immunity in computation and communication. Nature **335**, 779–784 (1988)
11. Lambson, B., Carlton, D., Bokor, J.: Exploring the thermodynamic limits of computation in integrated systems: Magnetic memory, nanomagnetic logic, and the landauer limit. Phys. Rev. Lett. **107**(1), 010604 (2011)
12. Kennedy, R.A., Sadeghi, P.: Hilbert Space Methods in Signal Processing. Cambridge University Press, Cambridge (2013)
13. Celeghini, E., Gadella, M., Del Olmo, M.A.: Applications of rigged hilbert spaces in quantum mechanics and signal processing. J. Math. Phys. **57**(7), 072105 (2016)
14. Puschel, M., Moura, J.M.F.: Algebraic signal processing theory: foundation and 1-D time. IEEE Trans. Signal Process. **56**(8), 3572–3585 (2008)
15. Shi, J., Moura, J.M.F.: Graph signal processing: modulation, convolution, and sampling. arXiv preprint arXiv:1912.06762 (2019)

16. Marella, S.T., Parisa, H.S.K.: Introduction to quantum computing. In: Quantum Computing and Communications (2020)
17. Sigov, A., Ratkin, L., Ivanov, L.A.: Quantum information technology. J. Ind. Inf. Integr. **28**, 100365 (2022)
18. Lesch, V., Züfle, M., Bauer, A., Iffländer, L., Krupitzer, C., Kounev, S.: A literature review of IoT and CPS—what they are, and what they are not. J. Syst. Softw. **200**, 111631 (2023)
19. Aceto, G., Persico, V., Pescapé, A.: A survey on information and communication technologies for industry 4.0: state-of-the-art, taxonomies, perspectives, and challenges. IEEE Commun. Surv. Tutor. 21(4), 3467–3501 (2019)
20. Monostori, L.: Cyber-physical production systems: roots, expectations and R&D challenges. Procedia Cirp **17**, 9–13 (2014)
21. Siegelmann, H.T.: Computation beyond the turing limit. Science **268**(5210), 545–548 (1995)
22. Lee, E.A.: Constructive models of discrete and continuous physical phenomena. IEEE Access **2**, 797–821 (2014)
23. Menin, B.: Construction of a model as an information channel between the physical phenomenon and observer. J. Am. Soc. Inf. Sci. **72**(9), 1198–1210 (2021)
24. Rato, R.E.C.T.: Formalização da tolerância à ausência de dados no processamento de sinais discretos. Ph.D. thesis, Faculdade de Ciências e Tecnologia, October 2012
25. Ortigueira, M.: Processamento digital de sinais. Fundação Calouste Gulbenkian (2005)
26. Pattee, H.H.: Laws and constraints, symbols and languages. In: Biological Process in Living Systems, pp. 248–258. Routledge (2017)
27. Shannon, C.E.: A mathematical theory of communication. Bell Syst. Tech. J. **27**(3), 379–423 (1948)
28. Hamming, R.W.: Coding and Information Theory. Prentice-Hall Inc., Hoboken (1986)
29. Ortigueira, M.D., Valério, D.: Fractional Signals and Systems. De Gruyter, Berlin (2020)
30. Hippenstiel, R.D.: Detection Theory: Applications and Digital Signal Processing. CRC Press, Boca Raton (2017)
31. Barkat, M.: Signal Detection and Estimation, 2nd edn. Artech (2005)
32. Onik, M.M.H., Chul-Soo, K.I.M., Yang, J.: Personal Data Privacy Challenges of the Fourth Industrial Revolution, pp. 635–638 (2019). https://doi.org/10.23919/ICACT.2019.8701932
33. Rieffel, E., Polak, W.: Quantum Computing: A Gentle Introduction, 1st edn. The MIT Press, Cambridge (2011)
34. Shor, P.W.: Algorithms for quantum computation: discrete logarithms and factoring. In: Proceedings 35th Annual Symposium on Foundations of Computer Science, pp. 124–134 (1994). https://doi.org/10.1109/SFCS.1994.365700
35. Scarani, V., Kurtsiefer, C.: The black paper of quantum cryptography: real implementation problems. Theor. Comput. Sci. **560**, 27–32 (2014). https://doi.org/10.1016/j.tcs.2014.09.015
36. Hirvensalo, M.: Quantum Computing, 2nd edn. Springer, Cham (2010)
37. Shende, V.V., Prasad, A.K., Markov, I.L., Hayes, J.P.: Reversible Logic Circuit Synthesis (2003)
38. Piguet, C.: Low-Power Electronics Design (2004)
39. Franks, L.E.: Signal Theory, revised edition. Dowden & Culver (1981)
40. Grochenig, K.: Foundations of Time–Frequency Analysis (2001). https://doi.org/10.1007/978-1-4612-0003-1
41. Stern, A.: Matrix Logic. Elsevier (1988)
42. Allouche, J., Shallit, J.: Automatic Sequences: Theory, Applications, Generalizations. Cambridge University Press, Cambridge (2003). https://doi.org/10.1017/CBO9780511546563
43. Imre, S., Balazs, F.: Quantum Computing and Communications: An Engineering Approach. Wiley, Hoboken (2005)

44. Yao, A.C.-C.: Quantum circuit complexity. In: Proceedings of 1993 IEEE 34th Annual Foundations of Computer Science, pp. 352–361 (1993). https://doi.org/10.1109/SFCS.1993. 366852

45. Moore, E.: Gedanken-experiments on sequential machines. In: Shannon, C., McCarthy, J. (ed.) Automata Studies. (AM-34), vol. 34, pp. 129–154. Princeton University Press, Princeton (2016). https://doi.org/10.1515/9781400882618-006

46. Fischer, P.: de Leeuw K., Moore E. F., Shannon C. E., and Shapiro N.. Computability by probabilistic machines. Automata studies, edited by Shannon C. E. and McCarthy J., Annals of Mathematics studies no. 34, lithoprinted, Princeton University Press, Princeton 1956, pp. 183–212. J. Symb. Logic **35**. 481–482 (2014). https://doi.org/10.2307/2270759

47. Hayes, B.T.: The Square Root of NOT (2016)

Author Index

© IFIP International Federation for Information Processing 2023
Published by Springer Nature Switzerland AG 2023
L. M. Camarinha-Matos and F. Ferrada (Eds.): DoCEIS 2023, IFIP AICT 678, pp. 301–302, 2023.
https://doi.org/10.1007/978-3-031-36007-7

Printed in the United States
by Baker & Taylor Publisher Services